The Al-Qaeda Doctrine

NEW DIRECTIONS IN TERRORISM STUDIES

A series edited by

Max Taylor

Professor of International Relations, University of St Andrews.
Earlier appointments include Director of the Centre for the Study of Terrorism
and Political Violence (CSTPV) at the University of St Andrews, Scotland, and
Professor of Applied Psychology at University College Cork, Ireland.

P. M. Currie

Senior Visiting Fellow at the School of International Relations
at the University of St Andrews, Scotland.

John Horgan

John Horgan is Professor of Security Studies at the School of Criminology
and Justice Studies of the University of Massachusetts Lowell where he is
also Director of the Center for Terrorism & Security Studies.

New Directions in Terrorism Studies aims to introduce new and innovative
approaches to understanding terrorism and the terrorist. It does this by
bringing forward innovative ideas and concepts to assist the practitioner,
analyst and academic to better understand and respond to the threat
of terrorism, challenging existing assumptions and moving the debate
forward into new areas.

The approach is characterized by an emphasis on intellectual quality and
rigour, interdisciplinary perspectives and a drawing together of theory
and practice. The key qualities of the series are contemporary relevance,
accessibility and innovation.

The Al-Qaeda Doctrine

The framing and evolution
of the leadership's public discourse

DONALD HOLBROOK

Bloomsbury Academic
An imprint of Bloomsbury Publishing Inc

BLOOMSBURY
NEW YORK · LONDON · OXFORD · NEW DELHI · SYDNEY

Bloomsbury Academic

An imprint of Bloomsbury Publishing Inc

1385 Broadway
New York
NY 10018
USA

50 Bedford Square
London
WC1B 3DP
UK

www.bloomsbury.com

BLOOMSBURY and the Diana logo are trademarks of Bloomsbury Publishing Plc

First published 2014
Paperback edition first published 2016

Library of Congress Cataloging-in-Publication Data
Holbrook, Baldvin Donald.
The Al-Qaeda doctrine : the framing and evolution of the leadership's
public discourse / by Donald Holbrook
pages cm. – (New directions in terrorism studies)
Includes bibliographical references and index.
ISBN 978-1-62356-314-1 (hardback)
1. Qaida (Organization) 2. Bin Laden, Osama, 1957-2011. 3. Zawahiri, Ayman. 4. Jihad.
5. Terrorism–Religious aspects–Islam. 6. Rhetoric–Political aspects. 7. Discourse
analysis–Political aspects 8. Ideology–Political aspects. I. Title.
HV6432.5.Q2H65 2014
363.325 – dc23
2014004282

ISBN: HB: 978-1-6235-6314-1
PB: 978-1-5013-1730-9
ePub: 978-1-6235-6476-6
ePDF: 978-1-6235-6667-8

Series: New Directions in Terrorism Studies

Typeset by Integra Software Services Pvt. Ltd
Printed and bound in Great Britain

For Matilde

Contents

Acknowledgments

This book presents the culmination of my research into Al-Qaeda leadership statements that began in earnest in autumn 2007, when I was a PhD student at the Centre for the Study of Terrorism and Political Violence (CSTPV) at the University of St. Andrews. Throughout this process, I have been fortunate and privileged enough to enjoy the support and guidance of my supervisors, whose assistance has been vital. I am particularly grateful to Professor Alex P. Schmid and Professor Max Taylor for their help with structuring and formulating this research and conveying the analysis. I would like to thank the CSTPV Director and my colleagues for their helpful feedback and advice. I am indebted to Professor Taylor, Professor John Horgan, and Dr P. M. Currie—the series editors of Bloomsbury's "New Directions in Terrorism Studies" series—for their support and advice concerning my proposal and preparation for this volume. I would also like to thank Professor Marco Lombardi and his ITSTIME team for sharing some of the more obscure statements from the Al-Qaeda leadership. I am especially grateful to Charles for his invaluable advice concerning different facets of this research and the theoretical models applied and for his assistance in procuring relevant primary sources. Finally, I wish to dedicate this book to my love Matilde, whose support throughout this process has been indispensable. I could never have completed this book without her.

List of tables
and figures

Glossary

al-firqa al-najiya	The "saved sect"—refers to a puritanical interpretation of Islam
al-wala wa-l-bara	Allegiance to the Muslim believers and disassociation from the unbelievers
aqidah/aqeedah	The Islamic creed
as-salaf as-salih	The pious Islamic predecessors, normally the first three generations of the Islamic society. Salafism refers to this concept
bid'ah	Innovation altering Islamic doctrine
bilad al-mushrikin	Refers to the "land of idolaters"
dar al-harb	The abode of just conflict
dar al-Islam	The Islamic realm
Deobandi school	Islamic revivalist school founded in nineteenth-century India, prominent in South Asia
dhimmi	The situation of non-Muslims living in Islamic states, according to religious law
EIJ	Egyptian Islamic Jihad—Egyptian terrorist group also referred to as Al-Jihad. Previous leaders included Ayman Al-Zawahiri and Mohammed Salam Faraj
fardh al-ayn	An obligation for each individual Muslim—as opposed to the collective obligation of *fardh al-kifaya*
fasiq	Disobedience from shariah law
fatwa (pl. *fatawa*)	Islamic jurisprudential edict
Hadith	Accounts of the words, actions, deeds, and prescriptions of the Prophet Mohammed that provide legal precedent in Islamic jurisprudence

hakimyya	The Islamic society base on the sovereignty of God
hijra	Migration. Refers initially to the Prophet Mohammed's migration from Mecca to Medina in 622 CE, which forms the beginning of the Islamic calendar
hisba	Commanding good and forbidding wrong (*al-amr bil-marouf wan-nahee an al-munkar*). Islamic jurisprudential concept referring to the need to ensure respect for Islamic law
hudud	Punishment carried out in accordance with shariah law
ijtihad	Individual interpretation of Islamic doctrine along prescribed guidelines
irhab mahmud	A concept that Abu Mus'ab Al-Suri referred to as "terrorism by the righteous who have been unjustly treated"
jahiliyya	The envisaged state where people and societies are in ignorance of divine Islamic prescriptions
Jamaat al-Tawhid wal-Jihad	Terrorist group led by Abu Mus'ab Al-Zarqawi, before he joined Al-Qaeda in Iraq
jizya	A tax non-Muslims have to pay according to shariah law, in accordance with their *dhimmi* status
khawaarij	Extremist outcasts from the Islamic society
khilafah	The Muslim Caliphate
kuffar	Unbelievers
kufr	Infidelity, the act of unbelieving
majlis-ash-shura	Consultative council
Maktab al-Khidamat	"Services Bureau"—support network for foreign fighters during the Soviet-Afghan war, established by Abdullah Azzam
mas'alatut at-tatarrus	Islamic juristic concept alluding to the permissibility of causing death when subjects have been used as "human shields" by the enemy

murtaddun	Apostates who had infringed upon the core principles of Islam
mushrikun	The idolaters
riba	Usury
shariah	Islamic law
shirk	Idolatry or polytheism
shura	Advisory council—see *majlis-ash-shura*
Sunnah	Records of the Prophet Mohammed's practices and what he forbade or permitted
taghuti	Idol-worshipping (adjective)
taifat al-mansura	The "helped group"—refers to a puritanical interpretation of Islam
takfir	Excommunication—declaring a believer a non-Muslim
taqlid	Rejection of the reliance on the main Islamic juristic schools
tawhid/tawheed	Literally the "oneness of God" or the core principle of monotheism
ulema	Islamic legal scholars
ummah	The community of believers
zakat	Charitable donations to increase equality

Preface

The death of Usama bin Ladin in a raid by US Special Forces on the Al-Qaeda leader's compound in Abbottabad, just north of Islamabad, Pakistan, on May 2, 2011, dominated news coverage across the globe in the following days and weeks. Bin Ladin had been America's most wanted fugitive, and his organization was seen (and by some observers and in some manifestations still is seen) as the principal enemy of the world's premier superpower. Many hoped his death would signal the demise of Al-Qaeda. As members of the press, academia, and the security and intelligence community began to debate the impact of bin Ladin's death, *The Economist* commemorated his end on the front cover, featuring an image of the leader superimposed on a mosaic of scenes from Al-Qaeda's protracted campaign of violence and from the wars in Iraq and Afghanistan. The title under the mosaic read: "Now, kill his dream."[1] Although the images reflected scenes of physical involvement in violence at a group level, the caption referred to a different phenomenon: the set of ideas and beliefs communicated by the Al-Qaeda leadership, beyond direct participation in specific attacks.

Indeed, "Al-Qaeda," in the broader sense, encompasses not only a terrorist group *per se* but also a much wider, deeper, and more comprehensive set of ideals that form part of and contribute to the wider discourse of Islamist violent extremism. The beliefs and ideas that make up this discourse pose a risk in their own right, since they promote, glorify, and legitimize violent confrontation with identified enemies.[2] The focus of this book is on how the Al-Qaeda leadership has, over the years, sought to construct its own version of this violent Islamist discourse. The following chapters explore how the two main representatives of Al-Qaeda's central leadership—Usama bin Ladin and Ayman al-Zawahiri—tried to develop a violent revolutionary discourse to support the movement. The components of this discourse are elucidated in the public statements that the two leaders issued on behalf of Al-Qaeda since its inception. Their goal was to mobilize activists and garner support from key communities and constituents in order to strengthen and sustain the violent campaign beyond their lifetime. For example, in a short strategic treatise titled "General Guidelines for Jihad" and published in September 2013, Zawahiri emphasized the importance of "spreading awareness amongst the general public so as to mobilize it."[3] Zawahiri and bin Ladin always wished and intended for others to join their fight, spread their word, and implement their vision, long after they themselves were gone. This book scrutinizes the two leaders' efforts to produce such a public discourse and discusses the way in which this has been constituted since Al-Qaeda was first established.

The aims of this book

Rather than dissecting group dynamics or discussing past or existing threat patterns, therefore, this book addresses the ideational elements that have been communicated publically by the Al-Qaeda leadership and the ways in which these have evolved over the past two decades. The goal, in short, is to explore the formation and evolution of this body of content as a distinct, central, and expansive facet of Al-Qaeda. The aggregate of these statements constitutes what can be referred to as the ideological doctrine of Al-Qaeda: the set of beliefs conveyed by the leadership over the years through public messages. "Doctrine," in this book, therefore, does not refer to military strategy or opaque tactical principles that have been drafted behind the scenes. The approach to doctrine adopted in this book concerns the set of ideas and beliefs, grievances, and ambitions that the Al-Qaeda leaders have sought to communicate. This is a public discourse, representing the public face of Al-Qaeda. The authors of this discourse, moreover, are not qualified scholars or necessarily sophisticated ideologues, but they represent the central leadership of Al-Qaeda. They have tried to "sell" the idea of Al-Qaeda and rationalize its existence. This is key to sustaining a broader movement around the initial group that the Al-Qaeda leaders founded. As we will explore in the following pages, Ayman Al-Zawahiri and Usama bin Ladin sought over the years to embed their group in a discourse that legitimized their actions and communicated with target audiences.

The purpose of this discourse is not to provide detailed prescriptions of how and when to strike or how to develop particular revolutionary campaigns but to bind people together behind a common cause, to legitimize and glorify the violence used to propel that cause, and to promote the sociopolitical agenda of Al-Qaeda. This message is intended for the wider public, potential supporters of Al-Qaeda, as well as its adversaries. It is by definition open, public, and also often repetitive and simplistic. Although several core themes are frequently reiterated, however, this discourse has also evolved over the years. For this reason, the longitudinal dimensions of this study are central to the overall aims of this book. The intention is not to provide a mere snapshot of some of the central themes in the Al-Qaeda leadership discourse at a given moment, but rather to analyze how these themes evolved over time. The Al-Qaeda leadership's approach to violence and civilian targeting, as well as its overall geographic scope, for example, changed significantly over the years and evolved. The aim is to capture this dynamic and provide extensive and detailed evidence of this development. It is only through adopting such a longitudinal perspective, moreover, that inconsistencies in Al-Qaeda's leadership narrative begin to emerge.

Understanding this discourse is essential in order to appreciate the way in which the Al-Qaeda leadership has perceived and communicated with its wider environment since its establishment and provides points of comparison with which to contrast other emerging jihadi currents. All terrorist movement leaders seek to form some sort of linkage with their perceived constituents and wider communities. They see themselves as presiding over a vanguard, which they hope will inspire others to support or join their campaign. Terrorist leaders also crave a legacy, where they can be seen to have had a lasting impact, even long after they die. In this sense, the leaders hope that the movement will continue despite the death of pivotal individuals given that the principal ideals have been developed and the agendas have been identified. Analyses of terrorism, therefore, need to look beyond specific terrorist acts or specific terrorist actors and include this wider context. Although there is the individual terrorist as an object of analysis, there is also the group, movement, or network to which the terrorist belongs, the wider community represented by the terrorist, and a host of social, cultural, and other issues that impact on the individual terrorist.[4] All of these factors should affect our understanding of terrorism. Engagement in terrorism is not a mere top-down, intelligently designed progression informed by a few core strategic principles but a far more complex phenomenon informed by a host of different sources of influence. To be successful, terrorism necessarily combines conviction with the capacity to act. The most dangerous, deadly, and sustained campaigns of terrorism combine organizational and operational rigor with justificatory rhetoric that promotes activism and reduces the emotional costs of participation. This book focuses on the latter set of ingredients.

The Al-Qaeda leadership has sought to shape and affect their particular movement and these sociocultural, religio-political, and ideological issues through the dissemination of public statements. This book is based on an analysis of just over 260 of these public statements (see full list in Appendix), issued by Ayman Al-Zawahiri and Usama bin Ladin since the early 1990s. English translations of each statement[5] were manually viewed, processed, and coded in detail in order to gauge the justifications put forward for Al-Qaeda's activism, the proposed solutions, and the communicative strategies adopted.[6]

The emphasis here is thus on achieving a detailed, comprehensive, and evidence-based understanding of how Al-Qaeda's public discourse has evolved within an environment of competing ideas, unfolding events, and diffuse actors and audiences.

This book begins with a very brief exploration of Al-Qaeda, its history, and different conceptualizations to capture the phenomenon. This is far from an exhaustive or detailed account, but merely intended to provide context for what follows. This initial review is developed into an examination of how Al-Qaeda fits within the wider ideological context in which it operates, which, in turn, leads to the major preoccupation of this book: the composition and evolution of Al-Qaeda's public discourse. The development of the Al-Qaeda leaders' problem diagnosis, suggested solutions, and communicative approaches in public statements is scrutinized in detail. Our exploration of the Al-Qaeda leadership's discourse concludes with an analysis of potential contradictions, tension, and inconsistencies in the way Al-Qaeda's message is constructed and delivered and an assessment of how this body of content may impact and resonate with future generations of jihadi sympathizers.

1

Introduction

Terrorism is a complex phenomenon and an elusive topic. Debates surrounding the concept often become emotive and convoluted, and the analytical vocabulary that is applied to the study of terrorism continues to provoke debate. Terrorism is also approached from multiple levels of analysis and perspectives. Three very broad levels of analysis can be discerned. At the micro level, analysts explore issues such as engagement in terrorist activity and the processes that might lead an individual to enter—and indeed exit from—such endeavors. At the meso level, scholars might explore the dynamics of groups and collectives, focusing for instance on the interaction of individuals within the wider context of engagement in terrorism and political violence. This book adopts a macro perspective. The preoccupation here is on the fundamental ideas, grievances, motivations, and sources of identity that propel terrorist movements and form the undercurrents—the context and ideational components—that rationalize and frame participation in terrorist activity. These ideas and objectives define particular dispositions and provide the cues to identifying different types of terrorist movements.

The ideological element is thus central in this context. This refers to the set of beliefs and reformist agendas that guide and shape the activism concerned. These ideas set out an alternative vision to challenge the status quo and present solutions and alternatives to the problems identified. When presented in such a way to particular audiences with the aim of conveying a set of principles that adherents are urged to follow, these beliefs and ideas can be seen as the evolving ideological doctrine that defines the movement. Usama bin Ladin and Ayman Al-Zawahiri—the two principal leaders of Al-Qaeda—sought over the years to develop and convey such a body of content through their public statements to followers, potential sympathizers, and perceived constituents, as well as their adversaries.

Messages to the world

What is the value of studying this content? The journalist and Al-Qaeda expert Jason Burke published an article in early 2013 entitled "Why Al-Qaeda Is a Spent Force." The organization that had reached its high point in 2005, Burke argued, had since then suffered blow after blow. The senior leadership was dead or dying and there were few credible replacements. More importantly, the Al-Qaeda "brand" was tarnished, mostly due to excessive targeting of Muslims perpetrated in its name. Yet, according to Burke, this did not mean that Islamist militancy would simply die away. This phenomenon would evolve rather than disappear: "Wherever the various factors that allow the 'Salafi-Jihadi' ideology to get traction are united, there is likely to be violence," Burke argued.[1] It is to these ideological components, therefore, that we must shift our attention.

As far as terrorist movements are concerned, organizational entities and individual personalities come and go but their legacy depends on their deeds and the discourse they have created over the years. For instance, Abdullah Azzam's Maktab al-Khidamat (see Chapter 2), which was a support network for foreign fighters in Afghanistan, faded away or was morphed into other organizations such as Al-Qaeda after Azzam's murder in 1989, but his words live on in the numerous books he published during the Afghan-Soviet war. Many of these have since been translated and republished by contemporary jihadi networks such as Babar Ahmad's Azzam Publications or the Birmingham-based Maktabah Al-Ansaar. Indeed, the death of a principal leadership figure in this context can often enhance the prominence and impact of their ideological output. The works of Mohammad Salam Faraj, Zawahiri's former colleague in the Egyptian Al-Jihad group (later called Egyptian Islamic Jihad (EIJ)), gained prominence *after* his execution in 1982, and some of his publications continue to be translated and disseminated on Islamist extremist websites. The same applies to Sayyid Qutb, another executed Egyptian revolutionary. More recently, after his death in September 2011 in a US drone strike, Anwar Al-Awlaki's material continues to be published online and is often repackaged by fans via social media and sharing sites such as YouTube.

The ideological discourses that bin Ladin and Zawahiri have created through their public statements, therefore, will outlive the physical and tangible elements of the Al-Qaeda leadership in its current form. With a weakened central base, Al-Qaeda has become almost a euphemism for Islamist-inspired terrorism, attempted terrorism, and militancy where global or transnational links play at least some role. As far as organized violence goes, moreover, much of the initiative has transferred to affiliates and sympathizers rather than the core leadership itself.[2] Within this myriad of actors that are seen to constitute Al-Qaeda, therefore, clarity is needed in terms of what the Al-Qaeda central leadership advocated, how these sentiments evolved, and how these differed in relation to affiliates, associates, and sympathizers.

Bin Ladin and Zawahiri did not emerge on the global stage in the 1990s with a fully developed set of beliefs and ideas for a transnational Islamist extremist movement. Their ideas evolved and the publically stated objectives and proposed solutions were honed in response to ongoing events and new challenges.[3] One such event was the publication of caricatures depicting the Prophet Mohammed in Danish newspapers in 2005, which caused widespread demonstrations and to which the Al-Qaeda leaders had to respond in a manner that would befit their perceived "vanguard." This book focuses on how this public narrative was created through the aggregate of the leaders' public statements and how it has evolved. To this end, over 260 statements from bin Ladin and Zawahiri, which constitute the bulk of the Al-Qaeda leaders' public output, have been scrutinized in order to construct this account of the Al-Qaeda leadership's ideological doctrine. Statements are here defined relatively broadly and include books, press interviews, and announcements as well as indigenous media output from Al-Qaeda that presented communiqués from bin Ladin or Zawahiri. The focus is on material that was made publically available, rather than captured or seized material, because this output tells the story of Al-Qaeda's public agenda—the evolving discourse that the two leaders developed in order to convey the core messages of their movement. The period under review in this volume covers the earliest days of Al-Qaeda following the Soviet-Afghan war up until the aftermath of the Arab revolutions in the Middle East and North Africa and Zawahiri's first years as leader of Al-Qaeda, after the death of bin Ladin in May 2011.[4]

The account offered in the following chapters, therefore, does not concern the composition of any organizational components or the detection of particular threat patterns. The emphasis is not on the internal workings of networks, on strategic doctrines, on personalities, or on terrorist acts that can be related to Al-Qaeda. The focus is on ideas and the public face of Al-Qaeda that its two principal leaders sought to create over the years in order to sustain their movement and appeal to potential sympathizers. Al-Qaeda's *raison d'être* has been expressed through the leadership's statements.

The construction of public messaging in this context raises questions that are central to Al-Qaeda and the Islamist extremist milieu more broadly but nonetheless move beyond the explanatory power of organizational approaches. How does the Al-Qaeda leadership interact with its wider environment? How does it define and justify its actions? How does it build its public agenda and discourse, to whom is it directed, and how has it changed? Organizational perspectives offer limited long-term insights when we are trying to address questions such as these and grasp the nature of Al-Qaeda's evolving ideas.[5]

By highlighting the aggregate narrative of the Al-Qaeda leaders' public statements, we underscore the ideas, beliefs, grievances, and discourses that bind jihadi militants together. Jihadi terrorism, in this sense, is less about the intelligent design of sophisticated strategic treatises and learned ideologues and more of a diffuse movement, bound together by these nonmaterial ideational bonds that serve to create a common identity and sense of purpose. Numerous sub-currents and strands exist within this movement and levels of sophistication vary. A host of different factors, such as tribal fabrics and geographic localities, impact different forms of jihadism, but the fundamental common themes remain the same. These fundamental themes, in turn, have evolved and grown in scope over the years.

What metrics can be discerned to manage this body of content? Since we are looking at the public narrative, rather than specific strategic arguments, the most obvious way to understand how this message has evolved is to study the statements of bin Ladin and Zawahiri, who—it can be argued—constitute the most public face of Al-Qaeda. They also represent continuity within the movement, which allows us to adopt a longitudinal perspective that is sensitive to elements of constants and change in Al-Qaeda's public discourse over time.

It should be made clear, however, that, aside from a brief historical review of Al-Qaeda in the next chapter, in order to situate the objects of analysis, the following is not a biographical account of the main Al-Qaeda leaders or a conventional chronology of the movement. These issues have all been addressed in numerous books and other publications that have focused on describing the Al-Qaeda phenomenon. The following, by contrast, is a record of the Al-Qaeda core's public message and how it has evolved over the years as conveyed by the two main protagonists of this story: Usama bin Ladin and Ayman Al-Zawahiri.

Assessing the Al-Qaeda leaders' output

Terrorism is an expression of political violence, a "violent language,"[6] whereby specific acts are designed to impact wider audiences. Additionally, Al-Qaeda's campaign of violence has always coexisted alongside the leadership's communicative campaign that rests on the dissemination of public messages. Publishing statements was always a central preoccupation of the Al-Qaeda leadership. Before becoming engaged with Al-Qaeda for instance, Zawahiri had written and published numerous treatises in order to rationalize and publicize his participation in Islamist militancy. Bin Ladin too entered the public stage first through his open letters to the Saudi regime and other public communiqués. Later, he would grant numerous interviews to journalists, much to the consternation of his Taliban hosts. Both Zawahiri and bin Ladin, moreover, became particularly active in disseminating indigenous media productions that were produced by Al-Qaeda "media labels," such as As-Sahab, and distributed online. With greater bandwidth and more widespread access to the Internet, this latter method has become particularly important for Al-Qaeda and other jihadi movements to deliver their message.

There are three main reasons why the Al-Qaeda leaders emphasized this communicative work. First, they had to legitimize their movement and its violence. Second, they had to propagate the movement by spreading the message to potentially sympathetic audiences. Third, they sought to intimidate their opponents and exploit the ripple effects of attacks.[7] Just as we can trace the timeline of Al-Qaeda and affiliated attacks, we can trace and visualize this communicative timeline where each point represents a statement, interview, or other publication from Al-Qaeda's central leadership, as represented by bin Ladin and Zawahiri. This timeline is displayed in Figure 1.1, and a list of the statements reviewed can be found in the Appendix. This graph illustrates the mainstay of the two leaders' public output on behalf of Al-Qaeda, as well as Zawahiri's major publications that he authored in the early 1990s.

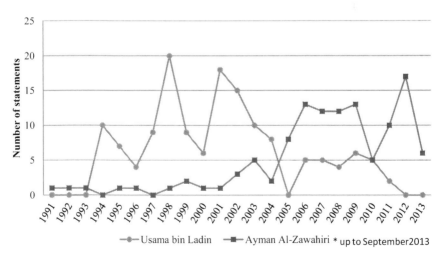

FIGURE 1.1 *Range of statements by bin Ladin and Al-Zawahiri analyzed (1991–2013)*

As well as illustrating the volume involved in terms of public communicative efforts on behalf of the Al-Qaeda leadership, the timeline reveals something of a transition around 2005, when Zawahiri's statements became more numerous than those of bin Ladin. The latter had always been prolific in disseminating statements and giving interviews during the 1990s, but in the years after 9/11, Zawahiri emerged as the more frequent voice of the Al-Qaeda leadership. Zawahiri's messages, moreover, were invariably longer and more substantive than those disseminated by bin Ladin. He would engage more with theological issues and historical contexts in relation to his particular focus each time and offered far more encompassing and wide-reaching messages than bin Ladin. Any analysis of the Al-Qaeda leadership statements and its aggregate message, therefore, necessarily needs to include Zawahiri's more voluminous output in addition to that of bin Ladin. This is particularly pertinent for the post-9/11 period.

"Terrorism research has tended to focus on the here and now," Weinberg observed in a paper published in 2008.[8] His observation seems especially relevant in the context of existing research on Al-Qaeda and Islamist-inspired militancy. The focus in this book, therefore, is on adopting a longitudinal perspective in order to describe the evolution of Al-Qaeda's public message through the years. The pronouncements of the Al-Qaeda leadership that were made prior to major attacks such as 9/11 are no less interesting or important than those that came after and offer important points of comparison with the rhetoric that surrounded periods of heightened activity. This book also seeks to address what many scholars have identified as an acute empirical deficit in our understanding of Al-Qaeda and its development.[9] This is particularly important in relation to understanding Al-Qaeda's evolving ideology, where a thorough analysis of primary sources, rather than secondary accounts, can shed light on the way in which Al-Qaeda's agenda and discourse has been shaped over the years.[10] Rather than relying on partial, limited, or selective sampling, moreover, the only way to appreciate the complexity of this discourse and the dynamics involved is to study the Al-Qaeda leadership's output thoroughly and systematically.[11] Zawahiri himself urged all those who "care about and are keen on knowing the reality of the *mujahideen* releases and words, whether from among the supporters or the enemies of the *mujahideen*, to depend only on the complete texts of the releases of the *mujahideen*, which they publish on the internet."[12]

This book adopts an in-depth and qualitative perspective where the analysis rests on the manual coding of Zawahiri's and bin Ladin's statements, with an emphasis on discerning long-term trends and changes over time to Al-Qaeda's public rhetoric.[13] To this end, each of these pronouncements was scrutinized using a bespoke checklist of themes intended to identify particular aspects of content.[14] These themes were arranged according to three broad categories.[15]

The first explored the problems, issues, and grievances that bin Ladin and Zawahiri identified and highlighted in their public statements over the years and the way in which these were presented and discussed. These references concern both historic and contemporary grievances as well as more fundamental societal aspects that the Al-Qaeda leaders identified in order to legitimize the existence of their movement and justify its activism.

The second set of themes explored the envisaged responses and alternatives to these identified problems. These relate to Al-Qaeda's escalating justificatory narrative for violence, as well as the leaders' attitudes toward tactics, different forms of violent and nonviolent activism, and areas of geographic concentration. Also contained within this perspective is Al-Qaeda's vision for societal reform, based on the religious and cultural objectives that bin Ladin and Zawahiri expressed in their communiqués.

The third thematic category involved the Al-Qaeda leaders' communicative efforts to convey these sentiments toward various audiences. The most important relationship concerns message dissemination toward different Muslim audiences. These can take the form of positive appeals, critical admonishment, and hostile condemnation, depending on the context and envisaged message recipients. Additionally, this perspective explored Al-Qaeda's discursive approach toward identified adversaries who, as noted above, are occasionally addressed directly in the Al-Qaeda leadership statements.

These three thematic categories correspond to theoretical constructs concerning message framing within the social movement literature. These constructs approach the communicative efforts of protest movements according to problem diagnosis, proposed solutions, and methods of message conveyance. These categories are interrelated, and a degree of overlap should be expected between the three core framing tasks. This theoretical approach, however, offers ways in which to dissect complex discourse and understand the rhetoric of a movement like Al-Qaeda. The way in which Al-Qaeda's message content can be divided according to these distinctions will be revisited below.

The issues captured in these three broad categories relate to the central features of Al-Qaeda's ideological doctrine and public discourse. In substantive terms, the focus of many of these preoccupations has evolved over the years and only a few fundamental components of the Al-Qaeda leadership's message have remained stable over time. The following chapters will explore the composition of this content in detail.

The perspective of this book moves our focus on Al-Qaeda away from functionalist, organizational, and descriptive accounts toward "culturalist" and ideational alternatives that emphasize the ideas, beliefs, ambitions, and grievances that are meant to bind members of the "jihadi" movement together and attract others to this cause.[16] The emphasis is on how the Al-Qaeda leaders have encased, shaped, interpreted, and contextualized events according to the ideological, cultural, religious, and political foundations of their group and its core agendas.[17]

These interpretive processes are central to the Al-Qaeda leadership's accumulated narrative and fundamental to understanding how the two leaders have approached their movement and seen their public statements as the way to channel their agenda to wider audiences in a message that was intended to have resonance long after they were gone.[18] Events and catalysts, in this sense, do not occur in an interpretive vacuum. Although individual or public anger and outrage, elation, or sympathy following watershed events do not depend on specific conduits, movements seek to translate these events (and the *emotions* they provoke) into action, support, or acquiescence—in a sense, different layers of mobilization—for their cause. This is a particularly important objective of Al-Qaeda and its affiliates as well as the wider militant Islamist milieu.

The plan of this book

The following chapters explore how the Al-Qaeda leaders have engaged in these acts of interpretation and mediation since the movement's inception. The next chapter traces the origins, evolution, and different conceptualizations of Al-Qaeda in order to situate the current object of analysis. This is not intended as a comprehensive review of Al-Qaeda's history or development, which has been explored in numerous dedicated volumes. Rather, the purpose is to provide background and context to the evolution of the Al-Qaeda leadership's public discourse, which is scrutinized in the following chapters. Chapter 3 locates this discourse in its wider ideational environment and describes how this content can be explored in terms of the problems bin Ladin and Zawahiri identified, the solutions and alternatives they offered, and the way in which these sentiments were communicated to different audiences. Chapter 4 dissects the evolution of Al-Qaeda's problem diagnosis in detail, while Chapter 5 explores the way in which the two Al-Qaeda leaders formulated their proposed response to these problems over the years. Chapter 6 discusses the way in which the Al-Qaeda leadership's communicative strategy was devised and the nature of these efforts as presented in the statements. Chapter 7 explores the contradictions, tensions, and inconsistencies that emerge when the Al-Qaeda leaders' public output is scrutinized in detail over such a long time frame. These observations, in turn, inform Chapter 8, the concluding chapter of this book, which assesses the composition and impact of the Al-Qaeda leadership discourse.

2

Understanding Al-Qaeda

The origins of "the Base"

What are the origins of Al-Qaeda, or "the Base"? Few social and political phenomena following the end of the Cold War have attracted as much scrutiny and shaped international relations and driven public debate to the same degree as the formation of the global "network of networks" that became known as Al-Qaeda.[1] Just as scholars and pundits struggled to come to terms with the factors that led to the collapse of the Soviet Union, a new and completely different set of conceptual challenges presented itself, as Al-Qaeda thrust its way onto the global stage. To this day, analysts continue to grapple with the Al-Qaeda enigma, studying the way it was first established and the factors that motivated those behind the group.

The formation of the group can, of course, be partly traced to the turmoil, upheaval, and vacuum of power—and resulting opportunities—presented by the decline and implosion of the Soviet Union. In August 1988, four months after the Red Army began withdrawing from Afghanistan,[2] Abdullah Azzam—the principal leader of the Arab Islamist militants fighting in Afghanistan—called a meeting in Peshawar, Pakistan. Based on the perceived success of the Afghan campaign, Azzam was eager to retain the momentum gained during the fighting against the Soviets and wished to establish a "pioneering vanguard" to continue the struggle.[3] To this end, Azzam resolved to consult Usama bin Ladin, his protégé, along with other major Arab figures involved in the war. Prominent among them was Ayman Al-Zawahiri, later leader of the Egyptian Islamic Jihad (EIJ)—a proscribed terrorist group—in Egypt, who had fled the country after being imprisoned for involvement with Islamist militancy in 1981. Having followed his mentor (and fellow medical doctor) Sayyid Imam Al-Sharif (aka Dr Fadl), another leader of EIJ, to Peshawar, Zawahiri established contacts with hardened veterans of the Egyptian militant scene, including Amin al-Rashidi (aka Abu Ubaydah al-Banshiri) and Mohammed Atef (aka Abu Hafs), who later became influential within Al-Qaeda.[4] According to

Cruickshank and Bergen, these meetings in Peshawar in August 1988 led to the establishment of Al-Qaeda, or what bin Ladin referred to as "Al-Qaeda al-Askariya" (the military base).[5]

However, united as the Arab-Afghan veterans were in their determination to establish a group that would continue the jihad beyond Afghanistan, in order to break secular regimes and sever links with foreign powers, these men could not agree on its scope. A memo discussing the future direction of jihad dating from this period and summarizing the position of all the major Arab veterans from Afghanistan illustrates this dilemma. Azzam, of Palestinian origin, wrote of the importance of "spreading the spirit of jihad among the Arabs, with the long-term goal being the waging of jihad against the Jews in Palestine."[6]

Zawahiri and other members of EIJ, by contrast, argued: "Egypt is the heart of the Islamic world and it is necessary to establish the Caliphate there first."[7] Azzam's affiliation with the Muslim Brotherhood (Azzam led the Jordanian Brothers at one time) also angered Zawahiri, who wrote in his book *Bitter Harvest*: "The [Muslim] Brothers have abandoned pursuing legitimate Muslim government in place of the current governments that rule Muslim lands. This deviation has made the Brothers idle from fulfilling their true calling, as Allah wills it."[8] With bin Ladin's backing, the new vanguard could become a powerful force undermining secular governance in Egypt. Bin Ladin's preoccupation, meanwhile, according to the memo, was the Arabian Peninsula and "the liberation ... of the south of Yemen from Communism."[9]

Three months after calling the Peshawar meeting, Azzam was assassinated,[10] leaving bin Ladin the undisputed leader of the group that became known as Al-Qaeda. Remarkably, however, more than 25 years after these events and despite the huge number of books and articles written on the topic, there is still no consensus on how or when Al-Qaeda was established. Cruickshank and Bergen, for instance, argue that by November 1989 Al-Qaeda existed as a formally established group that was "likely to have built up a sizeable force" of militants and a network of training camps in Afghanistan.[11] Gerges, meanwhile, dismisses such notions arguing that "as an operationally organized, independent, and centralized trans-national group, al-Qaeda did not exist until the second half of the 1990s—not the late 1980s, as received wisdom in the United States and the West would have it."[12] This latter claim, however, appears somewhat misleading. Some components of Al-Qaeda undoubtedly did emerge in the late 1980s while other components, such as a more ambitious global agenda, came later, as will be illustrated in the following chapters.

What is clear, however, is that bin Ladin's organizational prowess and financial largesse had already made him the pivotal figure within the organizational predecessor to Al-Qaeda, Maktab al-Khidamat or "services bureau" (formally led by Azzam), which coordinated the activities of the Arab fighters in Afghanistan and Pakistan.[13] Bin Ladin and his associates thus had the material means as well as the operational experience required to develop jihadi militancy beyond the confines of the Afghan-Soviet war.[14] For the time being, however, in terms of direction and scope, the elements that made up this nascent jihadi alliance of displaced militants remained remarkably focused on their respective native regions.

The process toward further globalization was initiated, at this stage, by a series of local events in the Arab world. In May 1990, South Yemen—following the loss of its major sponsor in Moscow, protracted conflict with the northern Yemen Arab Republic, and the discovery of oil in the disputed border territories—resolved to unite with the north, forming the Republic of Yemen.[15] This transformed Usama bin Ladin's chief preoccupation after Afghanistan.[16] Bin Ladin had been eager to focus the post-Afghanistan momentum on toppling the socialist regime in South Yemen and had provided crucial material support to this end, as well as sponsoring assassination campaigns in the region that continued well beyond unification. He had, however, failed in securing support from the Saudi authorities, which remained suspicious of his agenda and concerned about bin Ladin's perception of his apparent ability to operate freely in the region.[17] This tension marked the beginning of the Al-Qaeda leader's isolation and the severing of ties with his Saudi homeland. Events in Yemen, however, quickly became superseded by even greater cataclysms in the region affecting Saudi Arabia in particular. A few months after Yemeni unification, Iraqi president Saddam Hussein invaded Kuwait, prompting a UN-sanctioned international military response (again, made feasible by the collapse of the USSR).

Bin Ladin, by then almost an outcast in his native Saudi Arabia, was angered by the refusal of the Saudi ruling elite to form an Islamic response against the Iraqi secular regime and the threat it posed to the "Land of the Two Holy Places." He was even more outraged by Saudi acceptance of US military aid (placing "infidel" troops on hallow ground—where the Prophet himself embarked upon his *hijra*), which received backing from Grand Mufti Ibn Baz and the official Saudi religious establishment.[18] Speaking to his followers in 1992, bin Ladin is reported to have said: "we cannot let the American army stay in the Gulf area and take our oil, take our money. We have to fight them."[19]

Keen to invest in regions amicable toward various forms of Salafism and his own support network for puritanical Islamist militancy, bin Ladin had already started pursuing some of the opportunities presented by Hassan Al-Turabi's consolidation of power in Sudan through the National Islamic Front (NIF) in June 1989.[20] As events in Saudi Arabia forced bin Ladin to relocate, he found in Sudan—via a brief stint in Peshawar[21]—a haven to formulate his organization further, although the influence of Al-Turabi during this process was also considerable.[22] Here, he established an "Islamic Army Shurah," which included the advisory council (shurah) of his own group, for all the militant Islamist fringe groups that had been courted and invited to Sudan by the NIF.[23]

Zawahiri was one of bin Ladin's closest allies during his stay in Sudan and also relied on Al-Turabi and president Omar Al-Bashir for protection. He remained focused on his activities for EIJ, however, and orchestrated a plot from there to assassinate Egyptian president Hosni Mubarak in Ethiopia where he was due to visit in June 1995.[24] That same month, bin Ladin penned an open letter to the Saudi religious establishment entitled "Saudi Arabia Supports Communists in Yemen," where he warned that "all those who oppose the faith of the ummah" would face defeat through violent jihad.[25] During the Sudan years, moreover, bin Ladin began to form his plans to target America directly, in order to undermine the "head of unbelief."[26]

Following a series of such open denunciations of Saudi authorities and his ever-rising profile as significant financier of Islamist terrorist groups, bin Ladin had his passport revoked, thus rendering him stateless, and was formally disowned by his family. The need for him, and those who relied on his financial support, to secure a more permanent sanctuary was thus compounded.[27] Amid mounting pressure to expel bin Ladin and Zawahiri from Sudan, meanwhile, Khartoum resolved to direct them to leave. Continued involvement in their affairs was no longer worth the effort.

Al-Qaeda, as an organization, has always relied on some form of haven or base (after all, "haven" or "base" is one of the English translations of its name) to direct the operations of the vanguards. As the Taliban movement in Afghanistan was consolidating its power in the country, a new haven became available to bin Ladin, Zawahiri, and their followers, who were now free to settle again in the region that spawned the alliance in the first place.

The Afghan-Taliban period from 1996 up until the 11 September attacks, which prompted the downfall of the Afghan sanctuary in this form, became, in Sageman's words, Al-Qaeda's "golden age,"[28] at least as far as the central leadership was concerned. The group went from being "the most significant financial sponsor of Islamic extremist activities in the world," according to a 1996 State Department memo,[29] to being the most prominent and globally focused terrorist organization in the world. During this period, Al-Qaeda also reached its organizational zenith, establishing committees and sections with various responsibilities from oversight of "military affairs" to media relations. Indeed, engaging with the media in order to propagate Al-Qaeda's message was always a central aspect of its strategy.[30]

The isolation of the Afghan sanctuary was unprecedented. The Al-Qaeda leadership was protected not only by the virtually impassable terrain and geographical remoteness of the Taliban-ruled territories, but also by the Taliban's all-encompassing regime of terror, designed to stifle alternative voices and opposition and implement their extreme and puritanical vision of Pushtun Deobandism—what Esposito referred to as the "militant neo-Deobandi movement."[31] This provided the perfect platform from which to launch a public campaign against perceived treachery and corruption of local regimes, principally Saudi Arabia, the external entities that shored up these regimes, namely the United States and its allies, and the perceived impact of these alliances on the Muslim world.

While based in a camp near Khost called "Masada" or the "Lion's Den" (for which he fought a decade earlier),[32] bin Ladin published in August 1996 the "Declaration of Jihad against the Americans Occupying the Land of the Two Holy Places," where he called for Muslims (especially in the Arabian Peninsula) to mobilize against the "Israeli-American alliance occupying the land of the two holy mosques and the land of the ascension of the Prophet."[33] A year-and-a-half later, Zawahiri formally joined[34] bin Ladin in the "World Islamic Front against Jews and Crusaders"[35] with the now infamous declaration of war that announced that "the ruling to kill the Americans and their allies—civilians and military—is an individual duty for every Muslim who can do it in any country in which it is possible to do it."[36] The initiative served as a prelude to the first major attacks successfully orchestrated by the leadership against US embassies in East Africa six months later.

The transition from confined militancy and localized activism to an increasingly global campaign against major Western powers and their secular power networks and influences was neither straightforward nor immediate. Mohammad 'Abd-al-Salam Faraj, an Egyptian electrician and great admirer of Sayyid Qutb, who later became leader of the Egyptian Islamic Jihad group (thus exercising considerable influence over Zawahiri), is thought to be the first contemporary militant leader to have defined a distinction between near and far enemies, which subsequently became prominent in many analytical accounts of Al-Qaeda.[37]

In his attempts to rally support for militant implementation of Qutb's notions of a vanguard eliminating *jahiliyyah*—where people and societies are in ignorance of divine prescriptions—Faraj wrote a short book titled *Jihaad: The Absent Obligation*, which was first published during the early phases of the Soviet invasion into Afghanistan.[38] In his book, Faraj emphasized the need to channel the limited resources of Islamist militancy in the Middle East against the perceived inhibitors to the establishment of *hakimiyyah*—a society based on the sovereignty of God—namely the secular Arab rulers of Egypt and neighboring countries. Faraj wrote:

> the believer ... is aware of what is beneficial and what is harmful and gives priority to the definite and radical solutions. This point necessitates the illustration of the following: ... fighting the enemy that is near to us comes before that which is far ... Therefore to begin with destroying the Imperialists is not a useful action and is a waste of time. We have to concentrate on our Islamic issue, which is to establish the laws of Allaah in our land first and make the word of Allaah the highest. This is because there is no doubt that the prime field of Jihaad is to remove these leaderships and replace them with the complete Islamic system, and from here we start.[39]

Based on his interpretation of a fatwa issued by a prominent medieval scholar called Ibn Taymiyyah that classified thirteenth-century Mongol invaders who embraced Islam as legitimate targets outside the realm of Islam (*Dar al-Islam*), Faraj saw local secular leaders within the realm of just conflict (*Dar al-Harb*). This led to the crucial jurisprudential implication that rendered fighting these rulers not only legitimate, but an obligation for each individual Muslim (*fardh al-ayn*), invoked only when Islam is under direct attack from enemy forces and jihad has been declared by the leader of the Muslims.[40] This interpretation of violent jihad as an individual duty of all Muslims in order to defend their religion also constituted the mainstay of Abdullah Azzam's writings concerning the war in Afghanistan and later became prominent in the Al-Qaeda leadership's discourse.[41] The implication of this concept is crucial as the threshold for participation in violence is greatly reduced. Faraj's interpretation of the Mardin fatwa, as Ibn Taymiyyah's declaration became known, translated what was initially a religious ruling into a political manifesto relevant for contemporary events. His interpretation of the declaration thus amounted to what Michot terms a "fundamental misconstruction of its meaning" that ignored the "juridical-religious, ethical and person-orientated character" of the ruling, which Ibn Taymiyyah originally sought to convey.[42]

Zawahiri had joined Faraj, who was executed for his role in the assassination of Egyptian president Anwar Sadat in April 1982, down the path of local jihad against the near enemy. By 1998, however, he was frustrated with the lack of progress this strategy had brought, angered by the withdrawal from fellow Egyptian jihadists (who were increasingly isolated after the 1997 Luxor massacre), ever more reliant on bin Ladin's patronage and resolve, and attracted by the possibilities and attention that would no doubt be garnered by targeting the distant enemy.[43]

This transition, which kept local secular leaders within *Dar al-Harb*, initiated a re-prioritization of target sets as a result of shifting hierarchies of enmity. Violent jihad in the name of Allah, as an *individual* obligation of all Muslims, became a "cosmic war" between Al-Qaeda and the West, including its local interests and alliance structures.[44]

This ambitious agenda was well received by what Gerges terms "a new generation of freelance roaming jihadis": displaced (mostly Arab) militants and disillusioned sympathizers from Muslim diasporas in the West.[45] In Al-Qaeda they found a relatively structured group, which could provide seed money for operations, training and more direct involvement in the planning of terrorist attacks, as well as strategic guidance.[46]

As we have seen, however, Al-Qaeda was born not only out of the ambitions of its founders and their circumstances but also from the new political landscape that emerged after the Cold War. In the wake of the collapse of the Soviet Union, for instance, the United States had far greater scope to project power and force in the Middle East and elsewhere than had previously been possible, when greater strategic considerations were at stake and military interventions would be seen as provocation by the opposite side. This contributed to America's ability to commit troops to the Gulf War that followed Saddam Hussein's invasion of Kuwait and helped facilitate the UN sanctions regime, as well as the more permanent placing of US troops in Saudi Arabia, which infuriated bin Ladin. Other interventions, such as the short-lived campaign in Mogadishu, Somalia, in 1993—which convinced bin Ladin that America was a "paper tiger" that could be targeted—were also made possible in light of new strategic realities.[47] The unification of Yemen, which helped alter bin Ladin's immediate agenda, was also, in part, possible due to the fall of the USSR, a principal sponsor of the South Yemen regime. All these developments helped inform bin Ladin's thinking and affected his closest allies as well. Indeed, Al-Qaeda has never been immune to outside developments and has often been forced to react to ongoing events, as well as shaping them. This has been no less the case in the tumultuous period that followed the September 11 (9/11) attacks in the United States in 2001.

After 9/11

The loss of the Afghan sanctuary in the aftermath of the 9/11 attacks marked a new phase in the life of Al-Qaeda. There were remnants of an operational organization that relocated primarily to Pakistan. This core group continued to communicate with and inspire a number of dedicated allied and affiliated groups that formed part of the fabric in conflict zones and hot spots of Islamist militancy throughout the Muslim world.[48] A more diffuse set of disaffected fans and sympathizers of Al-Qaeda began to become more prominent in this post-9/11 period as well. This latter category concerns individuals who have come to agree with and support Al-Qaeda and its agenda and, in some cases, seek to carry out acts of violence in recognition of Al-Qaeda's aims and Islamist-inspired violent extremism. This wider milieu of fans and supporters often has scant operational experience or knowledge of religious or strategic treatises, but has become attracted to the rhetoric and worldview of Islamist militant figures, including bin Ladin and Zawahiri. Through public statements and other media efforts, the Al-Qaeda leadership has sought to nurture and expand this fan base. Here, prominent leadership figures and experienced militants rely less on direct lines of command and control to sustain militant activism and more on the generation of a compelling narrative that promotes and glorifies militancy as a solution to local and general grievances.

Aside from operational, organizational, and strategic preoccupations, therefore, the Al-Qaeda leadership has focused on developing a public narrative that binds diffuse elements together and offers the appearance of continuity, cohesion, and purpose, as well as "selling" the Al-Qaeda model and Islamist militancy as a solution to the challenges faced by potential sympathizers. The hope is that individuals act (orchestrate or support terrorism or join Islamist-inspired insurgents) on their own initiative, but are spurred on by a collective sense of purpose that is conveyed through this public discourse.[49]

As the Al-Qaeda leadership settled into its new home in Pakistan, allied, affiliated, and like-minded Islamist militant groups stepped up their campaign against anti-Taliban forces in Afghanistan and against the Pakistani state, which had pledged its support for the United States following 9/11.[50] This militancy grew into a full-blown Islamist insurgency in parts of the country and a bloody campaign of terrorist violence that has resulted in thousands of civilian deaths in Pakistan. An equally bloody Islamist insurgency spread in Iraq after the 2003 invasion, which Al-Qaeda managed to exploit, both as a physical space to support new affiliates and, through its rhetoric, enforcing the myth that Islam was under attack.[51]

Throughout this period, the Al-Qaeda leadership continued to grapple with two principal communicative tasks. First, it sought to coordinate and steer or impact the actions of different affiliate groups. Second, it continued to issue public pronouncements that added to an existing discourse designed to appeal to potential supporters and intimidate adversaries.[52] This study focuses on this latter set of initiatives.

After 9/11, therefore, Al-Qaeda ceased to be a holistic entity. It combined different elements and necessitated different layers of analysis.[53] Several typologies presented to capture the Al-Qaeda phenomenon, therefore, have adopted tiered approaches.

These typologies have grappled with the atomization of the concept of Al-Qaeda and the different actors and actor relationships at play. They have sought to capture the contrast between, on the one hand, a vulnerable sanctuary-dependent "conventional" group relying on a semblance of infrastructure and tangible networks and, on the other hand, a quasi deterritorialized (or globalized) corpus of followers and potential followers who could constitute a latent support base.

In the years after 9/11, for instance, Hoffman, developed his conceptualization of Al-Qaeda based on the premise that the "current al Qaeda ... exists more as an ideology that has become a vast enterprise—an international franchise with like-minded local representatives, loosely connected to a central ideological or motivational base but advancing the remaining center's goals at once simultaneously and independently of each other."[54]

Correspondingly, Hoffman discerned four layers of Al-Qaeda: (1) the central organization, comprised of the Afghan veterans and their direct associates who founded the group in the first place (or their replacements); (2) Al-Qaeda affiliates and associates, consisting of formal and established insurgent groups that followed the guidance of the central leadership; (3) Al-Qaeda locals, as individuals with militancy experience and some form of linkage with the other levels above; and (4) the Al-Qaeda network, the diffuse corpus of "homegrown" Islamist radicals and militants.[55]

Brachman similarly divided his analysis of Al-Qaeda into different layers, including:

[T]he Al-Qaeda high command (Bin Laden, Zawahiri); Al-Qaeda affiliate groups and individuals (Jemaah Islammiyyah, Lashkar-i-Taiba, Al-Qaeda in the [Arabian] peninsula, Al-Qaeda in the Islamic Maghreb) and those individuals and groups who are supported by Al-Qaeda (Istanbul bombers, London 7/7 bombers); and those individuals and groups who are inspired by Al-Qaeda but have no direct ties to it (Toronto cell).[56]

Likewise, when summarizing the ten years since the 9/11 attacks, Burke saw Al-Qaeda emerge in the aftermath of the attacks as "the best-known and most significant amid the hundreds of organizations involved in radical Sunni militancy" and comprising three main elements:

There was the hardcore leadership of the group, the network of other entities with formal affiliation to it and the ideology, the uniquely effective mix of modern and ancient historical references, filled out with selective quotations from scriptures and from other Muslim revivalist and reformist thinkers, that comprised the narrative, the language and the doctrines that underpinned the group's particular worldview.[57]

Sageman defined different "waves" of Islamist militancy. These involved, first, the "old guard" of Afghan veterans who established Al-Qaeda and, second, a corpus of younger, mostly middle-class, veterans of militancy in Bosnia, Kashmir, Chechnya, and elsewhere. Third, Sageman defined a wave of post-Iraq invasion mix of diasporas and privileged youngsters from the Middle East and North Africa who constituted the mainstay of the "leaderless jihad."[58]

Beyond academic deliberations, organizations engaged operationally in counterterrorism have also adopted tiered typologies for Al-Qaeda. The UK Joint Terrorism Analysis Centre, for example, introduced a three-tier model into its assessments in 2005 to "describe the varying degrees of connection between targets and the Al Qaida leadership: 'Tier 1' describing individuals or networks considered to have direct links with core Al Qaida; 'Tier 2', individuals or networks more loosely affiliated with Al Qaida; and 'Tier 3', those without any links to Al Qaida who might be inspired by their ideology." Although different from Hoffman's model, in terms of focusing on stages and variations in terms of linkages with Al-Qaeda central, the model nonetheless conveys similar notions in terms of a core leadership on the one hand and a more diffuse, autonomous base on the other. The majority of individuals of concern fell within the latter two tiers, subjects "who were only loosely affiliated to Al Qaida or entirely separate (albeit with shared ideological beliefs)."[59] FBI director Mueller's trichotomy for Al-Qaeda was virtually identical:

> I refer to it in three levels. The first is al Qaeda itself—bin Laden, the core, ... , and the second level is individuals who are not necessarily directed from the outset and the planning is not accomplished by core al Qaeda but have some ties to al Qaeda, whether it be financial or recruiting or otherwise. And the third level is self-radicalized without any ties whatsoever to al Qaeda.[60]

The *Economist* defined a journalistic ideal type with essentially the same components: "Al-Qaeda is a terrorist organization, a militant network and a subculture of rebellion all at the same time."[61]

The most interesting tiered conceptualizations, however, were those developed by the militant Islamist thinkers themselves, thus adding credence to those presented above. Wali al-Haq, for instance, a prominent member of militant Islamist forums, described Al-Qaeda after 9/11 as "not only an organization seeking to fight the Jews and Crusaders; rather it's an ideology and a mission calling on all Muslims to uphold God's religion and rescue the weak monotheists."[62] The resemblance with Al-Suri's tiered model for contemporary militant Islamist activism is more striking. The strategist found "three organizational circles in the units of the Global Islamic Resistance Call."[63]

The first circle consisted of a "militarily active...centralized unit," which spread "the literary production of the Call [to Global Islamic Resistance], its political-juridical, educational and organizational programs, among various segments of the Islamic nation, [oversaw] the issuance of media, and programmatic communiqués." The second circle comprised "de-centralized units," "elements...[that] can be subjected to ideological, programmatic, and educational qualification courses" that "upon request" could "spread throughout the world, each one according to [individual] circumstances and life situation, and operate completely freely and separately from the Centralized Unit." Al-Suri termed the third and final circle "the Da'wah circle or the General Units of the Global Islamic Resistance Call," "youth, who are determined to fight a jihad...and form their own Units entirely independently...without any organizational links with the Center."

Thus, numerous conceptualizations of Al-Qaeda and of Islamist militancy more generally sought to capture different layers that included the experienced leadership at the top and various types of affiliates, supporters, and potential supporters in the layers below. Rather than a tight-knit group, therefore, some approaches to Al-Qaeda have sought to present the actors involved as members of a movement—a nascent movement or a perceived movement—in order to capture the wider community of supporters and other elements with which the Al-Qaeda leadership has engaged, primarily through its public discourse. This is particularly important when we consider the emphasis the Al-Qaeda leaders have placed on disseminating statements—the focus of this book—in addition to operational matters. A West Point report on Al-Qaeda from 2007, for instance, argued that

> In what boils down to a struggle between branding and bureaucracy, Al-Qaeda has consistently put its ability to inspire a broader movement over the development of its organizational capacities to pursue strategic military goals. While its guerrilla strategists have fought for the resources to build an effective command-and-control military organization, its two supreme leaders—Usama bin Ladin and Ayman al-Zawahiri—have preferred press releases over battlefield preparedness.[64]

In order to understand Al-Qaeda, therefore, we need to go beyond operational and organizational models and look at the wider context of the movement that the Al-Qaeda leaders hoped to create.

Al-Qaeda and the wider movement

Conceptualizations of Al-Qaeda that focus on the more normative elements and particularly on its underlying ideology have often seemed simpler than the organizational models that have been posited. Looking beyond structures and "nodes," for example, Burke developed his concept of "Al-Qaedism" to capture the essence of what the leadership and its followers stood for, where a broadly common agenda and fundamental ideas would constitute the "glue" that bound activists together. Bale's "Bin Ladenism" highlighted similar notions.[65] This has become a particularly prominent form of Islamist-inspired violent extremism in the West, where local participants often retain the initiative to act but seek to conform to a more global justificatory and grievance narrative.[66] The Al-Qaeda leaders were always aware that any organizational components would have a limited shelf life, but hoped that their approach to Islamist militancy would be sustained via affiliates and, more broadly, through a more universal commitment to the jihadi agenda.

There appear, therefore, to be opportunities in approaching Al-Qaeda—and other associated jihadi groupings—as a social movement, or more accurately a *self-conceived* social movement, where Al-Qaeda sympathizers, associates, and affiliates, as well as the core leadership, perceive themselves to be members of a representative and pioneering vanguard leading efforts to change the overall status quo.[67]

Social movements can be understood as the organized and sustained efforts of a collectivity of interrelated groups or individuals to promote or resist social change with the use of different forms of activism.[68] In 1971, Professor Paul Wilkinson, in his first book, drafted a "working concept" to capture the core elements of social movements. These included a "conscious commitment to change," "minimal organization," and a scope for wider "normative commitment and participation."[69] Despite being identified 30 years earlier, these factors seem to be clearly relevant to the way in which Al-Qaeda emerged after the 9/11 attacks: as a loosely organized movement with a central leadership that sought to channel the frustrations of the broader community toward amending the status quo. Wilkinson went on to describe "millenarian social movements"—movements that exploited the mobilizing potential of perceptions of great imminent cataclysms, espousing a "revolutionary promise of the advent of an age of bliss, abundance and perfect justice."[70] In terms of understanding Al-Qaeda, this could refer to promises of divine social justice through introduction of (their interpretation of) shariah law, or ascent to paradise for those who died seeking to create such a society. Wilkinson also looked at religious social movements, defined as those laying claim "to a source of doctrinal authority," focusing on the need to "reorient radically individual personality and behaviour," using religion as a source for "primacy and ... authority on the basis of [a] monopoly of revelatory or rational ideological truth," and utilizing "religion's power of promoting social integration and solidarity."[71] Although defined decades before the emergence of Al-Qaeda, these conceptualizations of a social grouping seeking to mobilize others based on perceptions of common identity and duty seem applicable to the way Al-Qaeda developed. These precepts evoke notions such as abrogation of sins, cleansing, and rebirth from a life of depravity and guilt, which can form powerful emotions on the path toward participation in militancy.

More recently, other scholars have explored ways in which social movements, religious or otherwise, have adopted and promoted violence as the way to address grievances and achieve stated goals. Della Porta, for instance, saw violent social movements as having adopted "political violence as a particular repertoire of collective action that involved physical force, considered at that time as legitimate in the [respective] dominant culture."[72] Gusfield saw social movements as contributing to "the existence of a vocabulary and an opening of ideas and actions which in the past was either unknown or unthinkable."[73] The presentation of suicide bombings against non-combatants as the noble sacrifice of martyrs furthering the cause of Sunni Islam would be illustrative of this process.[74]

The extent to which Al-Qaeda morphs into a larger social movement that is, in part, informed by the leadership's public rhetoric may thus enhance its adaptability and durability.[75] The concept of social movements, it should be noted, does not necessarily imply that the subject is a mass movement.[76] Indeed, extremist fringe elements can and have been viewed through the prism of the social movement literature. This perspective can also be particularly helpful in underscoring the value of ideology and normative elements that are not always highlighted in organizational models. This includes the notion of individuals becoming attracted to (in this case) the Al-Qaeda "brand" and worldview that the central leadership has sought to create and nurture with its public statements and communiqués through the years. By adopting this perspective, the assumption is not being made that the sentiments expressed by activists are representative of their communities, but rather that there is a desire to create something beyond the immediate group, where mobilization is achieved on the basis of common principles, ideas, beliefs, identities, and objectives.

Indeed, some prominent Islamist ideologues have identified the creation and nurturing of (often revolutionary) social movements as essential features of a future uprising. Sayyid Qutb, for example, called for the creation of a vanguard to lead the *ummah* out of *jahiliyyah* (ignorance of religious duties), which would necessarily rely on the establishment of a "movement" (*haraka*) with popular support.[77] Qutb wrote: "we need to initiate the movement of Islamic revival in some Muslim country. Only such a revivalist movement will eventually attain to the status of world leadership, whether the distance is near or far."[78] Even in Qutb's earlier works, when the parameters for social change were less focused on religious purity, popular movements, nonetheless, constituted the essential vehicle for change in order to put Islam into practice in wider society.[79]

Similarly, it seems clear that the founders and leaders of Al-Qaeda have sought to create such a movement, a momentum for revolutionary change that goes beyond the capacity of the individual founding members. A year after the 1998 bombings of the US embassies in Kenya and Tanzania, for instance, bin Ladin remarked in an interview that the role of Al-Qaeda was to "instigate the nation to get up and liberate its land, to fight for the sake of God, and to make the Islamic law the highest law, and the word of God the highest word of all."[80] There was thus a clear desire for a violent uprising beyond the immediate capacity of Al-Qaeda itself.

To this end, the Al-Qaeda leadership has been particularly adept at utilizing new forms of media as "systems of amplification" to exploit particular events in their favor, in order to reach larger audiences rather than relying on formal and institutional lines of command and control.[81] The part of the social movement literature that looks at the attempts of movement leaders to influence and impact disparate audiences in their wider environment can thus be especially relevant for the study of Al-Qaeda and the wider context of Islamist militancy, including the way in which Al-Qaeda leadership statements are framed in order to convey the leaders' ideological doctrine as conveyed through public discourse.[82] This process consists of compiling and delivering this content to different types of audiences, as will be explored in more detail in the next chapter. In the context of Al-Qaeda, this refers to the attempts of the core leadership to sustain and nurture a broader movement—something akin to Burke's "Al-Qaedism"—that would outlive this core group itself. In this sense, therefore, the *idea* of Al-Qaeda would live on and continue to impact Islamist militant activists, long after the physical demise of "Al-Qaeda Central."

Beyond the Arab Spring

The resonance of Al-Qaeda's "idea" appeared rather weak as Arab publics— some of the Al-Qaeda leadership's core target audiences—took to the streets in the Middle East and North Africa, challenging their authoritarian rulers after mass protests that started in Tunisia in December 2010 spread throughout the region. Popular revolt led to the downfall of the Tunisian president Zine El Abidine Ben Ali on January 14, 2011, and president Hosni Mubarak of Egypt on February 11, 2011. Meanwhile, a NATO-supported insurgency in Libya resulted in the overthrow of the Gaddafi regime in August 2011. These methods for regime change could not be more different from what Al-Qaeda had prescribed. To make matters worse for Al-Qaeda, the events of the "Arab Spring"—as these seminal revolutions, protests, and antigovernment activities became known—coincided with the death of the Al-Qaeda's founder and inspirational leader Usama bin Ladin, leaving the far less charismatic Ayman Al-Zawahiri at the helm.

Even before these events, the obituary of Al-Qaeda (or at least the central organization) was again being written. At an operational level, the central group had lost many key leaders. Some of the franchises had also been weakened and the reputation of the "brand" had suffered due to excessive targeting of Muslims in acts of violence perpetrated by Al-Qaeda affiliates. In terms of Al-Qaeda's objectives, moreover, it had failed to force the United States out of the Middle East and faced an upsurge of Shia political influence in the region.[83] Even though the "grand objectives" remained elusive, however, jihadi groups in the Middle East were spurred on by precisely these developments and determined to continue the jihadi insurgency in Iraq and elsewhere. Regardless of how futile these efforts may seem to outside observers, therefore, Islamist militancy—including that which involves Al-Qaeda loyalists and affiliates, including rebel groups such as Jabhat al-Nusra—has become protracted, and sometimes flourished, in various regions of instability and conflict.

What about the Arab Spring? In many ways the initial impact appeared to be disastrous for Al-Qaeda. For some, these events even constituted the last nail in the coffin of its core leadership and added to existing organizational pressures affecting the Al-Qaeda command.[84] The immediate impact of the Arab Spring appears to have undermined Al-Qaeda in five significant ways. First, the authoritarian regimes did not fall according to Al-Qaeda's predictions or with its involvement, and the popular uprisings appeared to eclipse any jihadi groups in the region. Second, the methods used—such as sustained mass protest and NATO-sponsored insurgency—were contrary to what Al-Qaeda had prescribed and envisaged. Third, the removal of the Mubarak regime in Egypt and other authoritarian regimes in the region also weakened a prominent rallying cry of the Al-Qaeda leadership, namely to mobilize the masses to topple secular leaders in the Middle East and North Africa. Fourth, some argued that Al-Qaeda had been slow in responding to the evolving events of the Arab Spring and had been caught off guard. Fifth, the symbols and drivers of the revolutions appeared to contradict Al-Qaeda's core ideology. These emphasized national identity and mass participation and representation rather than Al-Qaeda's anti-democratic rhetoric and emphasis on pan-Islamism.[85]

Events linked to the Arab revolutions and their aftermath, however, could also present great opportunities that Al-Qaeda and the broader jihadi movement could exploit. The great political upheaval and euphoria of the Arab Spring was quickly followed by disappointment, disillusionment, and civil and ethnic strife in places like Egypt and elsewhere. Indeed, after the initial shock over the unfolding events of the Arab Spring abated, the Al-Qaeda leadership began to utilize this turmoil and disenchantment in its public messages. In early 2013, for instance, Zawahiri argued that the revolution in Egypt had already failed: corruption was still rife, police brutality widespread, America's influence remained strong, the rich were getting richer and the poor poorer. And the divine social justice of shariah law had yet to be realized.[86] The fact that the Muslim Brotherhood government was toppled in a military coup in June 2013 only served to reinforce Al-Qaeda's warnings, according to Zawahiri. There was thus every reason to continue the struggle as Al-Qaeda envisaged.

The wave of antigovernment protests that started in Tunisia then spread to Syria by spring 2011. Rather than resulting in the immediate overthrow of the regime, however, the unrest in Syria quickly developed into full-scale civil war with increasingly pronounced sectarian dimensions. Bashar Al-Assad's father and predecessor as president of Syria had previously dealt with Islamist insurgents in the country during the 1970s and 1980s and quelled the protests through ruthless use of force. His son now seemed determined to do the same. Al-Qaeda joined this fight by proxy, through affiliated and like-minded jihadist groups that shared Al-Qaeda's vision. These developments prompted concerns that Al-Qaeda was not necessarily dead, but still capable of exploiting new realities and gaining renewed momentum. In June 2012, for example, the director of the British Security Service warned that as a result of the disorder, parts of the Middle East and North Africa might "once more become a permissive environment for Al-Qaeda."[87] The aftermath of the Arab revolutions, of course, also produced mildly Islamist governments in Tunisia and, temporarily, in Egypt and witnessed a surge in the activity of Islamist groups that had been suppressed by the authoritarian state security apparatuses. These developments prompted some to suggest the Arab Spring had turned into an "Islamist Winter."[88] Mainstream Islamist parties such as the Tunisian Ennahda Movement and the Egyptian Muslim Brotherhood, of course, were still great adversaries of Al-Qaeda and Ayman Al-Zawahiri, and other leaders were quick to condemn them for watering down religious doctrine. After all, the relationship between Islamist militants like Al-Qaeda and democratic Islamists is in some ways comparable to the relationship between communist revolutionaries and social democrats: there are some vague similarities in terms of worldviews and perceptions but stark differences in terms of methods and direction, which often have led to vehement animosity.

Islamist militant insurgents also became embedded in Mali, before being dislodged by French forces in the summer of 2013. The Sahel and Maghreb regions, meanwhile, continued to see regular outbursts of jihadi activity that threatened local populations and foreign workers alike. Beyond these tangible examples of Islamist militancy, moreover, Islamist extremist sentiments and sympathies continue to surface in the wake of specific events, as they did, for instance, in response to the publication of excerpts from the anti-Islamic film *Innocence of Muslims* on YouTube in autumn 2012. Such isolated events are added to Al-Qaeda's repertoire of grievances and presented as justifications for further violence.

Gerges warned in his book *The Rise and Fall of Al-Qaeda* that "a gulf has emerged between the perception of the threat posed by al-Qaeda and its actual capabilities, and this gulf continues to widen."[89] He went on to make the case that "Al-Qaeda's core ideology is incompatible with the universal aspirations of the Arabs"[90] and that "preaching of a transnational jihad centered on violence no longer resonates with ordinary Muslims."[91] But has this ever been the case? The fact that Al-Qaeda's methods and messages do not have mass appeal does not appear to be anything particularly new or surprising. Al-Qaeda has always been an extremist group, a cohort of violent fringe activists that did not represent mainstream society. Indeed, Al-Qaeda's self-description as a "fighting vanguard" appears to emphasize similar notions. The fact that, as Gerges notes, "most Muslims do not subscribe to [Al-Qaeda's] rhetoric and ideology and have not joined its ranks" is not necessarily indicative of Al-Qaeda's failure.[92] Although mass mobilization and unity were a prominent feature of the Al-Qaeda leadership discourse, as the following chapters will highlight, mass appeal of such a violent fringe operator was never a realistic prospect. Most terrorist groups have, at some point, laid claim to some sort of mass appeal or representation without ever establishing a truly popular base. If such a base is established, this is normally when the terrorist group has morphed into or spawned a more inclusive and less extreme political alternative that can operate in the mainstream. The distinction between Sinn Féin and the Provisional Irish Republican Army appears to be a case in point. Al-Qaeda never purported to create a "popular" political alternative along those lines. In many ways, however, it appears that inaccuracies in contemporary perceptions of Al-Qaeda have risen from inflated and exaggerated perceptions of the group: to begin with is the neglecting of the fact that Al-Qaeda has always been a terrorist group operating on the extremist fringe of the Islamist militant periphery.

There is a particular danger that our perceptions of how Al-Qaeda has fared in the aftermath of the Arab Spring have become skewed due to the exaggerated and inaccurate representations of Al-Qaeda that prevailed after 9/11. This stems from a lack of thorough empirical analysis of the phenomenon, muddled conceptualizations, and vague yardsticks to measure success and failure. Analyses of Al-Qaeda's impact and legacy need to move beyond a preoccupation with its immediate operational capacity or the physical ability of the original founders to organize, commission, or carry out violent attacks. A neglected component of our understanding of Al-Qaeda, its impact, and legacy concerns the evolution and resonance of its ideas. In this regard, there is no danger of a mass movement responding to Al-Qaeda's messages. As mentioned, Al-Qaeda has always been a terrorist and extremist group, and mass appeal or mobilization—just as with other terrorist and extremist groups—is not a real danger. The extent to which Al-Qaeda contributed to the rise in popularity of jihadi solutions for a proportionately small corpus of individuals, however, is a much more important question. After all, the Al-Qaeda leadership—originally a small cohort of marginalized extremists who gathered in some of the most remote and deprived areas of the world—managed to become seen as the greatest enemy of the United States—the world's premier superpower—and of its allies. As an adversary to the West, it was equated even with the giant of the Soviet imperium. This elevation in perceptions might well prove inspirational for others, provided the Al-Qaeda leaders have managed through the years to generate an ideological doctrine that would survive after they departed.

The public statements of the Al-Qaeda leaders form the building blocks of this ideological doctrine. These communiqués are supposed to highlight grievances and aspirations of the *ummat al-mu'minin* or the Islamic nation, present alternatives to the status quo, prescribe methods for change, and identify the adversaries that threaten the common values of the community. These messages, moreover, exist within a broader ideological environment that promotes and glorifies Islamist militancy. The next chapter focuses on the components of this environment and the ways in which Al-Qaeda's public discourse can be understood and its evolution appreciated.

3

Jihadi ideology

Al-Qaeda and the ideology of Islamist extremism

In the late 1990s a new jihadi newsletter was published in Egypt titled *Characteristics of Jihad*. Ayman Al-Zawahiri, as leader of the Egyptian Islamic Jihad group, wrote the introduction for the new publication. As he would do on so many subsequent occasions, Zawahiri used the opportunity to seek to convince Muslim publics of the Manichean worldview that he—and many other jihadists—had adopted. He asked his readers:

> Do you belong in the party of America, Israel, France, Russia and their allies among the apostate rulers of our countries, their assistants, their soldiers, their journalists, their judges, and their clerics who spread confusion, pledge allegiance to them, and call them the care takers of the Muslims' affairs? Or, do you belong in the party of the monotheistic, Salafi *Mujahideen*?[1]

The former group that Zawahiri referred to constituted identified adversaries (these have often been divided into "far" and "near" enemies, as will be discussed below). The latter group defined the righteous alternative. This would refer not only to Al-Qaeda and its affiliates and allies but also to a wider corpus of Sunni Islamist militancy and extremism and the ideological currents that can be found within that realm.

This chapter explores this ideological environment before discussing ways in which Al-Qaeda's contribution to this discourse can be analyzed. The purpose here is not to map all the various ideological strands and cohorts that constitute the Islamist extremist and jihadi milieu, but to situate the Al-Qaeda core within this context. Al-Qaeda's ideological output has existed within this wider ideational corpus, and its leaders have conveyed some aspects of this Islamist extremist narrative while developing their own ideological discourse to serve Al-Qaeda's purpose.[2]

It is well documented that Al-Qaeda—and other jihadi groups—became preoccupied not only with sponsoring or planning physical attacks but also with developing a justificatory narrative and ideological doctrine that promoted the attacks, legitimized them, urged others to facilitate further attacks, and warned adversaries of more violence to come. Indeed, Hoffman notes that "one of the original four al Qaeda operational committees was specifically charged with media and publicity."[3]

This ideological perspective thus needs to form a distinct part of our understanding of Al-Qaeda and its environment. We can define the concept of "ideology" for our purposes as a set of belief systems and principles that guide political behavior and determine the goals and rationales of individual and collective action.[4] For terrorist groups, therefore, ideological treatises and public messages are used to legitimize their existence and deeds, while appealing to a wider support base.[5] In particular, as Della Porta noted, the ideology of terrorist movements offers ways of "reducing the psychological costs of participation in terrorist organizations."[6] This relates to the extent to which the ideology of a militant movement instills feelings of righteousness, legitimate violence, and noble causes using language and terminology that are central to the core belief system.

Correspondingly, as analysts and observers debated the linkage between perpetrators behind Islamist-inspired terrorist plots (both successful and unsuccessful) in the post-9/11 period and the core leadership, the role that ideology played in inspiring "followers" to mobilize also became an increasingly prominent focus of analysis. Islamist ideology became central to terrorist "threat assessments," as observers feared the impact of this ideology on local admirers of Al-Qaeda, who in many cases were Western nationals and therefore constituted "homegrown" radicals. In July 2010, for instance, the Washington Institute published a report titled *Fighting the Ideological Battle* that warned of "how the transnational threat posed by global terrorist networks is increasingly bringing the front line of the struggle against terrorism to our shores. *Ideology*, in other words, is the common strand that binds these plots and individuals and is a driver for this global movement."[7] As organizational hierarchies dispersed, the authors warned, "the ideological tenets of al-Qaeda thrive, and other, arguably smarter, adversaries continue to exploit its 'ideological package'."[8] Indeed, the publication of the Washington Institute report coincided with the dissemination of a different publication that suggested this was precisely one of the objectives of Al-Qaeda and its affiliates and fans. Thus, in summer 2010, Al-Qaeda in the Arabian Peninsula (via its media wing Al-Malahem) published the first edition of *Inspire*, an Al-Qaeda online magazine. The publication was the creation of Samir Khan, an American of Pakistani descent, who was unequivocal in his introduction to the first issue that the purpose of *Inspire* was to attract more support for the Islamist extremist ideology propagated by Al-Qaeda:

> This Islāmic Magazine is geared towards making the Muslim a *mujāhid* in Allāh's path. Our intent is to give the most accurate presentation of Islām as followed by the *Ṣalaf as-Ṣālih* [referring to the earliest generations of Muslims]. Our concern for the *ummah* is worldwide and thus we try to touch upon all major issues while giving attention to the events unfolding in the Arabian Peninsula as we witness it on the ground.[9]

Khan went on to publish nine issues of *Inspire* (prior to that he published four issues of another magazine titled *Jihad Recollections*) before being killed alongside the prominent jihadi ideologue Anwar Al-Awlaki in a US drone attack in Yemen in September 2011. Other publications similar to *Inspire* in content and scope have subsequently appeared in its wake. Shortly after the publication of the first edition of *Inspire*, Michael Leiter, Director of the US National Counterterrorism Center, delivered a statement to the Senate Homeland Security and Government Affairs Committee, where he reported that "plots disrupted in New York, North Carolina, Arkansas, Alaska, Texas, and Illinois during the past year were unrelated operationally, but are indicative of a collective subculture and a common cause that rallies independent extremists to want to attack the Homeland." This subculture and common cause, Leiter argued, centered on the creation of a narrative that "motivates individuals to violence."[10] A few years earlier, the US Director of National Intelligence had warned of the danger of "homegrown extremists, inspired by militant Islamic ideology but without operational direction from al Qaeda."[11] Similarly, in his analysis of the ten years after 9/11, Burke observed that

> There was one area, however, where al-Qaeda had achieved undeniable success. What cases like that of Faisal Shahzad [May 2010 Times Square bomb plotter] and Roshonara Choudhry [who attempted to murder British MP Stephen Timms, again in May 2010] showed was that bin Laden and his associates had been able to attain at least one of their major strategic aims: to disseminate the al-Qaeda worldview—the ideology, the third element of the post-2001 analysis—to a huge new audience, even if their own role within global Islamic militancy was now diminished.[12]

Analyzing the evolution of this ideological element, therefore, might be more fruitful than seeking to scrutinize the composition of different organizational "nodes" that may or may not form the ambiguous entity that is referred to as "Al-Qaeda." As Ronfeldt argued, the threads of Islamist militancy often appear "held together not by command-and-control structures...but by a gripping sense of shared belonging, principles of fusion against an outside enemy, and a jihadist narrative so compelling that it amounts to both an ideology and a doctrine."[13] Within this milieu, in turn, specific organizational groupings can emerge in particular localities that also seek to adhere to these broader ideological goals. The ideas and beliefs of Al-Qaeda and of modern jihadism, therefore, serve to bind together these disparate elements, which can include different groups, suborganizations, and individuals. Regardless of the Al-Qaeda core leadership's involvement in individual plots, the success of the movement has always depended on wider mobilization and support and the development of an ideological doctrine as a public discourse that would sustain the movement beyond the life of its founders. This perspective draws attention to the ability of the Al-Qaeda leadership to generate such a narrative in order to create a wider support base and nurture a new generation of young jihadists.

Al-Qaeda, of course, did not invent this narrative. Although the Al-Qaeda leaders added their own unique input, they too had been influenced by—and had borrowed from—the wider ideological currents of the Sunni Islamist extremist fringe. Primarily, these concerned contemporary extremist and activist versions of a particular form of puritanical Islamic thought known as Salafism.

Salafism: The wider ideological context

Many aspects of Al-Qaeda's public discourse, therefore, are not new. It rests on contemporary notions of Islamist revivalism and revolutionary puritanism that were originally developed by a few prominent Islamist ideologues during the twentieth century.[14] This vision permeates much of the Al-Qaeda leadership's narrative and forms the foundations of its faith-based agenda that expresses core aspirations of modern extreme manifestations of Salafism.[15]

The term "Salafism" is developed from the Arabic concept of "*as-salaf as-salih*," the pious forefathers or the first three generations of Muslim leaders and the societies over which they presided.[16] This "golden age" witnessed the rise of Islam.[17] Salafism teaches a return to the core tenets of Islam, "stripped of local customs and cultures,"[18] as conveyed through the Quran, the Hadith (oral reports of the Prophet's teachings and choices), and the Sunnah (records of the Prophet's practices and what he forbade or permitted).[19] The aim would be to recreate the traditional society of the Prophet Mohammed, although, as Esposito notes, what this "tradition" exactly constitutes has been "redefined and standardized" over the centuries.[20] The main objective would be to achieve "uninterrupted" implementation of religious doctrine and reestablish the Islamic community of the pious forefathers that had achieved political, economic, and military eminence.[21] Ostensibly, therefore, Salafism rejects any form of *taqlid* or blind following of the four principal juridical schools of Islam, in favor of individual interpretation along prescribed guidelines (*ijtihad*).[22] Those who follow this path (according to their own interpretation) therefore belong to the "helped group" (*taifat al-mansura*) or "saved sect" (*al-firqa al-najiya*).[23] This is important because the theological foundations are laid for individuals who lack official religious schooling to become prominent religio-political personas, espousing a far more radical message that challenges and seeks to undermine the mainstream religious establishment, especially when this is seen as corrupted by semi-secular authoritarian rulers. Young Islamist activists who are attracted to this approach are thus particularly susceptible to radical preachers who purport to interpret current events in light of the core Islamic tenets from the dawn of Islam, without "interference" from any subsequent scholarly, juridical, or philosophical approaches.

For the militant activist fringe, moreover, this freedom to maneuver elevates violent attacks to the level of religious expression whereby violence is a manifestation of religion in practice. Bin Ladin, for example, insisted that the 9/11 attacks had been "more effective than a million books in clarifying the doctrine of allegiance to the believers and disassociation from the unbelievers" (a concept known as *al-wala wa-l-bara*).[24]

A central foundation of Salafism is *tawhid*, literally the "oneness of God" or the core principle of monotheism.[25] The importance of the concept and the extent to which it demands a response from believers depends largely on political issues. In the interpretation of the medieval scholar Taqi al-Din ibn Taymiyyah (whose works inspired many contemporary Islamist extremist writings) and much later of Sayyid Qutb, the activist and purist (and even militant) insistence on *tawhid* in practice and the removal of rulers who failed to live by the tenet and implement shariah was paramount.[26] This version has remained central for modern militant Islamists both as a fundamental religious concept but also as a rallying cry or banner (Abu Musab al-Zarqawi, for instance, called his jihadi group Jamaat al-Tawhid wal-Jihad, before he joined Al-Qaeda).

This pursuit of uninterrupted *tawhid* and exclusive relationship with God, free from any cultural innovations of doctrine (*bid'ah*) that had corrupted the Islamic creed (*aqidah*) and led to *shirk* (idolatry or polytheism), was the driving force behind Ibn 'Abd al-Wahhab's revivalist movement that swept the Arabian Peninsula in the eighteenth century. Building upon the activist foundations laid by some of Ibn Taymiyyah writings, the followers of Wahhab denounced those whom they perceived to be in breach of this doctrine as *kuffar*, unbelievers outside the realm of Islam, or *murtaddun*, apostates who had infringed upon the core principles of Islam. Excommunication (*takfir*) of Muslims places them outside the realm of *dar al-Islam*, as mentioned above, thus potentially justifying violence against them.[27] In Meijer's words, by associating *takfir* with politics, Wahhabists unleashed "a monster [that] mainstream Salafism desperately tries to keep in its cage while other currents within the movement have done their best to let it escape."[28]

The branch of Salafism that endorses militancy as a method to achieve the above goals and punish those who stand in the way, which some have termed "jihadi-Salafism," is the most modern manifestation of this approach (albeit with spurious links to its classical arguments). The endorsement of "jihad" in reference to legitimate defensive war to protect Islam against foreign threats is universally recognized among Salafis. Contemporary Salafi-jihadis, however, go much further and elevate religiously justified violence as a sign of religious devotion and a legitimate tool to see through societal change and undermine identified adversaries (within Muslim societies and beyond).[29] Jihadi-Salafism concentrates on political realities—that are interpreted according to puritanical value systems and sources of identity—and ways to affect them.[30]

Not all manifestations of Salafism, therefore, demand violent solutions. There are also violent manifestations that do not rely on excessive application of *takfir*. The concept of *takfir*, even within Islamist extremist circles, is highly contested, and many jihadi-Salafist ideologues have been cautious in its application—for fear of being labeled extremists or outcasts—while others use the concept more aggressively.[31] The Al-Qaeda leadership's approach to *takfir*, in its public discourse, evolved through the years and was particularly affected by ongoing conflict in Iraq and Pakistan. The particulars of this approach will be discussed in detail in Chapter 6.

Salafism, therefore, is not a holistic entity, and several scholarly works have sought to dissect Salafism and identify different strands. Wiktorowicz, for instance, defined three major components of Salafism, "purists, politicos and the jihadis:"

The purists emphasize a focus on nonviolent methods of propagation, purification, and education. They view politics as a diversion that encourages deviancy. Politicos, in contrast, emphasize application of the Salafi creed to the political arena, which they view as particularly important because it dramatically impacts social justice and the right of God alone to legislate. Jihadis take a more militant position and argue that the current context calls for violence and revolution. All three factions share a common creed but offer different explanations of the contemporary world and its concomitant problems and thus propose different solutions. The splits are about contextual analysis, not belief.[32]

In tracing principal facets of the contemporary jihadi-Salafi current, moreover, Paz identified three major branches. First was the Egyptian branch from "among the radical sections of the Egyptian Muslim Brotherhood" (mainly Sayyid and Mohammed Qutb, Sayyid Imam al-Sharif (aka Dr Fadl)). Second was "neo-Wahhabism" as developed primarily by Shaykh 'Abd al-'Aziz ibn Baz (even though he later softened his response, endorsing the placing of US troops in Saudi Arabia, prompting bin Ladin's public rebuttals) and other Saudi religious leaders. Third was the branch led by the "Palestinian trio" of Abdullah Azzam, Umar Abu Qatada, and Islam al-Burqawi (aka Abu Muhammad al-Maqdisi).[33] This is not to suggest that jihadi-Salafi branches are rich and expansive ideological schools. Rather, as Meijer notes, it seems that "Jihadists plunder the Salafi terminological toolkit of intolerance, xenophobia, sectarianism, war against apostate governmental and unbelieving forces of global oppression with which Islam is locked in an apocalyptic clash of civilizations."[34] The result is an extremist narrative that justifies and promotes violence.

Central themes of this narrative include overall victimization of Muslims; rejection of pluralism; "liberation" of the Muslim world consisting of emancipation from both foreign influence and occupation as well as from alien ideologies and religious ignorance; implementation of shariah; the use of violence as religiously sanctioned due to actions of the West and "apostates"; and Muslims seen as duty bound to assist the fighting vanguards in achieving victory and establishing the prescribed order.[35]

The ideological context that informed the creation of Al-Qaeda's own public discourse in this regard, therefore, combines political and religious values and imperatives with related motivations and grievances. There is an ongoing debate in the analytical literature on Al-Qaeda and the wider jihadi-Salafi or Islamist violent extremist realms regarding the role of religion and politics.[36] Decoupling one from the other, however, does not seem relevant when describing this ideological base.[37]

Al-Qaeda, therefore, exists in a wider ideological universe consisting of radical Sunni Islamist revivalist movements that prescribe varying degrees of violence and extremist solutions in order to amend the status quo and implement their doctrine. Aside from the basic principles, however, wide disagreements exist within this universe, particularly concerning the time frame, scope, focus, and method of activism. This radical fringe, upon which the ideological foundations of militant Islam and Al-Qaeda are perched, is far from a holistic concept. Differences of opinion persist, divergent strands are forged, and arguments flourish in an ideational *community*, which is essentially fluid and dynamic.

Behind the façade of unity: Tensions, debates, and disputes

Apart from the core traditionalist and puritanical Islamist tenets, the content, breadth, and scope of Islamist militant strands differ substantially. This milieu is a "postmodern hybridity," with sources in multiple geographical localities, both past and present.[38] Al-Qaeda and many other Sunni Islamist extremist groups have gone to great lengths to display a public front of unity. Many of their public appeals often emphasize this need for people to unite under a common banner and in pursuit of a common cause. A more careful analysis reveals, however, that many of these groups and key individuals within this Islamist extremist community have clashed due to doctrinal differences, disagreements on implementation, or personal rivalry. The point here is not to expand on these differences in any detail but merely to highlight the fact that the ideological context in which Al-Qaeda operates is both dynamic and often heterogeneous. These Islamist extremist debates evolve, particularly in relation to ongoing events. Al-Qaeda's message has, of course, also changed over the years, as will be discussed in detail below. Given that these ideological debates are not static and uniform, it is essential that our understanding of these strands is informed by thorough empirical analysis.

The antagonism between Zawahiri and Azzam over the viability and direction of the Muslim Brotherhood was mentioned in the previous chapter. The tension centered on the pragmatic approach that the Brotherhood had taken to politics, with allegations from detractors that the movement's engagement in mainstream politics diluted its emphasis on religious purity. Such accusations were initially prompted, in part, by Nasir al-Din al-Albani, a twentieth-century reformer who criticized the Brotherhood for prioritizing politics over religious knowledge.[39]

Al-Albani's criticism of some Salafist strands, including the way in which Wahhabism relied on the Hanbali juridical school (in contrast with overt and apparent Wahhabite rejection of *taqlid*), reiterates the importance of recognizing the conflicting elements that fall under the category of Salafism. One of the more significant developments within this milieu, meanwhile, has been the rise in prominence of Wahhabism, based in no small degree on the school being propelled by the largesse of the Saudi elite. Thus, Wahhabism has had an impact on elements of the Muslim Brotherhood,[40] as well as the Deobandi school, a Sunni Islamic revivalist strand established in Deoband, India, in the 1860s. The curriculum of some Pakistani religious academies, for example, became "Wahhabized" due to the influence of Saudi benefactors.[41] This and other developments contributed to the creation of a contemporary

Deobandi movement that in some manifestations has been key in spreading Islamist radicalism in Pakistan[42] (and Pakistani communities elsewhere) and undermined the school's traditional tolerance (and indeed incorporation) of Sufi thought.[43]

This fusion of neo-Wahhabism with other forms of puritanical Islamism should not disguise frictions that remain and even differences and dynamics that are present exclusively within the militant camp. Indeed, Sunni militant groups in Pakistan and elsewhere in South Asia include a host of divergent ideological strands and membership compositions. Intra-Sunni tensions also complicate matters, particularly in terms of tribal dynamics and ethnic cleavages.[44] Among the actors underpinning and sustaining militant Islam, moreover, Lia identified a "struggle between ideological purists and politico-military pragmatists."[45] The strategist Abu Mus'ab Al-Suri, according to Lia's analysis, belonged to the latter camp, warning against the disruptive impact of the exclusivist narrative he identified with the former group. According to his more inclusive and pragmatic approach, which bin Ladin also embraced, the narrow agenda of some extreme forms of Salafism could seriously undermine the ability of the jihadi movement to expand. Describing a prominent Islamist militant thinker, Al-Suri wrote: "Abu Qutada was extreme in his support for Salafism and the Ahl al-Sunnah school and the ideas of the Wahhabite Call. He was strongly opposed to other schools within the broader circle of Ahl al-Sunnah." Even the Taliban were criticized for doctrinal impurity and for their short-lived pursuit for UN recognition.[46] There are, therefore, different "degrees" of extremism, which come to the surface, for instance, in relation to debates about the nature and reach of excommunication in Islam (takfir), as noted above.[47] Disputes over doctrine, tactics, scope, access to funds, and other issues have also, of course, contributed to and been exacerbated by personality clashes between key figures within Al-Qaeda or other jihadi groups.[48]

Moving beyond the differences within Al-Qaeda's alliance structure to the group itself, closer inspection reveals how homogeneous stasis should not be assumed even at such a narrow level of analysis. The emergence of the "Zarqawi doctrine," following the Al-Qaeda representative's campaign of ethnic slaughter in Iraq, prompted fierce debate, which again pitched the more pragmatic proponents of militant Islam against Salafi puritans and their endorsement of "indiscriminate violence against everyone who does not support Jihadi-Salafism."[49] Al-Qaeda's record in Iraq provoked harsh criticism from within the Islamist milieu from former militants and scholars.[50] One Saudi Imam, for instance, released a fatwa asking the leadership: "do they think that by exploding a building or killing a tourist, they will defeat a state and establish a new regime?"[51]

At a discursive, structural, and strategic level, too, there has been change. Hegghammer, for instance, observed how "the distinction between near enemy and far enemy groups seems less and less relevant." "A process of ideological hybridization has occurred, with the result that the enemy hierarchies of many jihadist groups are becoming more unclear or heterogeneous than they used to be.[52] The authors of the *Terrorist Perspective Project* reached a similar conclusion: "AQAM's [Al-Qaeda and Associated Movements] strategic thought is evolving over time, this is bad news for those who would offer simplistic strategies for countering the Salafi jihadist threat."[53] Along the same lines, Ranstorp and Herd argued: "In many ways, it is clear that al Qaeda's ideology is a constant work in progress with many directions of influences by salafist-*jihadi* thinkers and clerics and that its multiple strands change character according to circumstances."[54]

In light of such shifts and dynamics, references to Al-Qaeda's "constant message"[55] or "single narrative"[56] appear problematic. For instance, in their analysis of "ideology, framing processes and Islamic terrorist movements," Snow and Byrd noted that the "homogenizing tendency," in terms of seeking to identify a single "ideology" of terrorism, was "counterproductive because it glosse[d] over diversity among one's adversaries, thereby limiting understanding of them and indirectly affecting one's strategies for effectively combating and coping with the threats they pose."[57] The point is that a host of different actors, ideational strands, and environmental imperatives shape different facets and manifestations of Salafi-jihadist thought and practice. There are constants in this discourse, but significant components, such as the approach toward violence, have evolved over time. As a result, any in-depth analysis of the statements that construct and communicate the belief system in question needs to rely on concrete points of departure and a clear delineation of the actor sets under review. To this end, this book focuses on the public statements of bin Ladin and Zawahiri exclusively as the aggregate of their voluminous output can be traced over time, allowing for a more evolutionary or longitudinal perspective to be adopted than is often possible in other darker and less prominent corners of the Salafi-jihadi universe.

This is particularly important in light of the proliferation of "user-generated" content glorifying Al-Qaeda and Islamist extremist narratives where the affiliation or identity of the author is often not known.[58] This sees "jihobbyists"[59] and "fans" of Al-Qaeda and other jihadi movements generating and spreading videos, images, and other material via YouTube or other online channels in order to celebrate and promote violent jihad.

Two conclusions can therefore be drawn from this overview of the jihadi ideological milieu. First, as mentioned, when looking at jihadi-Salafism we need to be clear on precisely which actors are the focus of our analysis, because different groups and leaders adopt divergent approaches and interpretations of doctrine. For this book, as emphasized above, the focus is not on sophisticated scholars or strategists and their intricate output but on the public face of Al-Qaeda—the evolving public narrative as developed by the group's principal leaders, bin Ladin and Zawahiri. This is the body of content designed to propagate and sustain Al-Qaeda as a jihadi movement. Second, these ideological debates and perceptions are not static, and researchers need to develop empirical tools that capture this dynamic. Ideology, as Snow and Byrd observed, is a "social production that evolves during the course of interactive or dialogic processes among activists, targets, and events in the world."[60] The next section discusses the way in which we can understand and approach the ideological doctrine that the Al-Qaeda leaders constructed and presented to the world.

Approaching Al-Qaeda's public discourse

As with other protracted conflicts of the past, the campaign against Al-Qaeda has prompted governments and the defense and security community to include ideological agendas and motivations in their assessments of their adversary. In June 2011, for instance, the British government approved an amended version of the previous government's "Prevent" strategy, designed to "prevent radicalisation and stop would-be terrorists from committing mass murder."[61] At the heart of the revamped program was a desire to "respond to the ideological challenge of terrorism and the threat from those who promote it."[62] These efforts would primarily target Al-Qaeda and its affiliates, viewed as the most potent terrorist threat to the UK. As noted above, several US policy papers and the wider counterterrorist community have adopted a similar emphasis on understanding and undermining the ideology of Al-Qaeda and related movements in order—in part—to weaken their potential support base.

Several academic studies, in turn, have highlighted the importance of this ideational element for policy-makers and practitioners seeking to develop counterterrorism strategies.[63] Some have even suggested that studying ideological output and public terrorist communiqués might offer predictive indicators in terms of future attacks and offer detailed insights as regards operational components of Al-Qaeda and related movements. This concerns, for example, Al-Qaeda-sponsored attacks targeting nations that participated in the 2003 Iraq invasion. These observations, however, are invariably made *after* specific attacks have occurred with analysts trawling through terrorist communicative output for clues regarding these attacks after they took place.[64]

It seems more probable, however, that these attacks were carried out in support of the broader Al-Qaeda agenda—which was indeed communicated through statements—rather than in response to specific messages. Even those commissioned and planned by Al-Qaeda affiliates would not have been announced publically in any specific terms prior to the plot being attempted. Indeed, Zawahiri and bin Ladin issued countless calls for attacks in their statements—often without particular detail—urging followers and supporters to attack identified adversaries. The purpose was to shore up support for the general campaign of violence and reiterate the surrounding justificatory narrative. Tracing specific attacks or plots back to certain statements *after* these events occurred seems to rely too much on the benefit of hindsight and ignore the many false positives—directives that were not necessarily heeded immediately after statements were issued.

Public messages are different from dedicated strategic, operational, or tactical deliberations that will, for obvious reasons, mostly take place behind the scenes. Martin, for instance, warned against using Al-Qaeda leadership statements to gauge the motives and intentions of leaders and Al-Qaeda operatives. "These sorts of public statements can serve different functions and be intended for different audiences," Martin argued. "They may be intended to recruit Muslims to bin Laden's cause. They may also be intended to terrorize the West as part of al-Qaeda's strategy to generate fear. Thus they are not necessarily an accurate statement about al-Qaeda's aims and strategies."[65] However, the Al-Qaeda statements—or more accurately a systematic analysis of their content—convey the *public image* that the Al-Qaeda leaders have sought to construct and thus form a crucial prerequisite to understanding Al-Qaeda and the way it has evolved. The Al-Qaeda leaders have exerted considerable effort in order to disseminate messages that are intended to inspire supporters, mobilize potential activists, intimidate adversaries, rationalize and contextualize their activism, and—at their most basic—illustrate that the leadership remains active and alive.[66]

Deconstructing the Al-Qaeda message

The messages that bin Ladin and Zawahiri have disseminated communicated Al-Qaeda's worldview and agenda to different audiences. As well as legitimizing their movement and intimidating adversaries, these leadership statements contain specific appeals for actions that conform to Al-Qaeda's public discourse. Adversaries are threatened with violence unless they see through stated demands and potential supporters are urged to embrace Al-Qaeda's prescribed tactics. Bin Ladin's and Zawahiri's statements can therefore be seen as a "source of a mobilizing ideology."[67] In particular, this concerns what Wiktorowicz called "the mobilization of contention to support Muslim causes."[68] The goal was to expand activism and create a momentum for Islamist extremist violence that could be sustained beyond the physical life of the Al-Qaeda leadership. This would entail creating a nascent movement that was inspired by Al-Qaeda's brand and message that could continue the fight and engage in operations without the direct involvement of anyone who was "officially" tied to the Al-Qaeda leadership. Regardless of whether or not this movement is real, or the extent to which this "mobilizing" message has had the desired effect (these issues will be revisited toward the end of this book), the fact that bin Ladin and Zawahiri sought to establish such a movement—that would encompass everything from lone actors to high-impact rebel and insurgent groups—is crucial for our current analysis. This perspective is also important when it comes to assessing the development of the Al-Qaeda phenomenon after the demise of its original leadership and centers on the question of their legacy and impact, discussed in Chapter 8.

As a result, these efforts to communicate an ideological "package" in order to sustain a wider "movement" highlight the contributions from the social movement literature that can aid us in comprehending the nature of Al-Qaeda's message. Specifically, research on the way in which messages are *framed* in order to achieve specific purposes is of particular importance.

Framing, according to Wiktorowicz, refers to the process whereby leaders of nascent movements seek to draft "interpretive schemata that offer a language and cognitive tools for making sense of experiences and events in the 'world out there'." In this sense, therefore, we can see the Al-Qaeda leadership statements as offering interpretations of events and contexts that are designed to encourage further support and mobilization for the causes they identify. "As signifying agents engaged in the social construction of meaning," Wiktorowicz notes, "movements must articulate and disseminate frameworks of understanding that resonate with potential participants and broader publics to elicit collective action."[69] Crucially, as the literature on social movements and framing has emphasized, there is no "automatic, magnetic-like linkage between intensely felt grievances and susceptibility to movement participation." There are essential "subjective/interpretive considerations"[70] that we need to comprehend when looking at bin Ladin's and Zawahiri's contribution to the jihadi narrative. In other words, no matter how universal or deeply resonant a particular grievance may be, the response from the affected public is by no means predetermined or uniform. In addition to the individual's own interpretation of grievances, movements filter and contextualize events, thus framing the grievance-based narrative for their intended audience. In this sense, therefore, we can understand bin Ladin's and Zawahiri's efforts to frame their message by looking at the way in which they interpreted events and communicated these interpretations to audiences in the wider environment with the aim of promoting their movement and elevating their causes. The framing perspective, therefore, highlights "the way in which meaning is produced, articulated and disseminated"[71] by the Al-Qaeda leadership.

According to Benford and Snow's understanding of framing and Goffman's and Wilson's earlier work on the concept,[72] social movements were not merely carriers or transmitters of mobilizing beliefs and ideas but could be seen as "actively engaged in the production of meaning for participants, antagonists, and observers."[73] Al-Qaeda is, in this sense, not to be understood merely by studying essential principles of Salafism but rather through dissecting the leaders' own production of meaning, as articulated through public statements aimed at adversaries, potential followers, and the wider community whose support Al-Qaeda has sought to secure. Movement leaders, according to Benford and Snow, "frame, or assign meaning to and interpret, relevant events and conditions in ways that are intended to mobilize potential adherents and constituents, to garner bystander support, and to demobilize antagonists."[74] These efforts are thus directly relevant to our understanding of Al-Qaeda.

The framing approach allows us to emphasize how the communication of values, grievances, and goals has been an integral part of the composition and operation of Al-Qaeda and highlights the way in which public statements have been central to its output over the years. Bin Ladin and Zawahiri have used their statements to interpret events, developments, and religious tenets to sustain and promote Al-Qaeda as a representative fighting vanguard.

This concept is also significant in terms of wider processes of counterterrorism. Violent extremists, according to this approach, do not respond directly or in isolation to grievances that can be "addressed" (minimized, contextualized, or eliminated) or individual/communal frustrations that can be "countered" (refocused, channeled). The reality is more complex. These frustrations, grievances, values, norms, aspirations, and related *emotions* form part of a wider culture and narrative that justify and encourage violence and promote activity (direct activism as well as support) in the interest of the wider cause. The militancy of Al-Qaeda, its resource acquisition efforts, and its temporal viability are therefore all strongly influenced by this interpretive work. "Accordingly," as Benford and Snow emphasized in their seminal paper on framing and social movements, published in 1988, "a thoroughgoing understanding of the participation process requires that closer attention be given to the interpretation of grievances and other ideational elements, such as values and supportive beliefs."[75] Although written before Al-Qaeda was established, these words seem relevant to understanding how the group has evolved since its formation.

The messages from bin Ladin and Zawahiri interpret the wider environment according to Al-Qaeda's central belief system and these messages are communicated to wider audiences either through mainstream or indigenous media networks. These efforts appear to conform to what the social movement literature sees as a major objective of movement leaders: "they seek to affect interpretations of reality among various audiences [and] engage in this framing work because they assume, rightly or wrongly, that meaning is prefatory to action."[76]

As the review of Salafist ideological currents revealed above, these interpretive efforts and ideological frameworks are not static. Leaders of groups and potential movements need to react to specific events and frame ongoing developments so as to match the existing narrative that they have started to create. The framing of statements is "an active, processual phenomenon that implies agency and contention at the level of reality construction," as Benford and Snow observed:

> [It] is active in the sense that something is being done, and processual in the sense of a dynamic, evolving process. It entails agency in the sense that what is evolving is the work of social movement organizations or movement activists. And it is contentious in the sense that it involves the generation of interpretive frames that not only differ from existing ones but that may also challenge them.[77]

In order to capture this dynamic process, the authors identified a concept they referred to as "collective action frames." Simply put, "collective action frames are action-oriented sets of beliefs and meanings that inspire and legitimate the activities and campaigns of a social movement organization."[78] A particular focus of these efforts is to encourage mobilization against perceived injustice.[79] This approach, therefore, provides an established process by which to understand the communicative efforts of nascent movement leaders. For any movement trying to mobilize support for a given set of goals, establish a presence within a wider sociopolitical environment with existing competitive movements, or sustain the momentum and publicity of past activities, collective action frames are fundamental.

For the Al-Qaeda leadership, this relates not only to contextualization and legitimization of past attacks or violent campaigns. Messages to the wider public must also demonstrate the continued relevancy of opinions and options presented by the leadership and its ability to address concerns of those for whom the appeals are generated. Additionally, through collective action frames, the leadership must, in order to remain relevant, incorporate emerging issues within the broader framework of Al-Qaeda's ideational positioning. Framing and contextualizing events in accordance with the core message that has been communicated in the past, therefore, is a constant effort. Hence the evident emphasis that the Al-Qaeda leaders placed on issuing statements since the early 1990s that touched upon a number of topics and addressed various audiences. The literature on collective action frames, therefore, highlights the importance of studies that adopt longitudinal perspectives and long-term empirical analysis. As Benford noted, "we need studies which examine *continuities and changes* in framing strategies, their forms, and the content of frames over the life of a movement, throughout a cycle of protest, or across an historical epoch."[80]

Two conclusions can thus be derived from the way in which the concept of collective action frames has been developed. First of all, a theoretically grounded method can be found to deconstruct the Al-Qaeda leadership statements and understand their purpose. Second, the approach allows us to appreciate the importance of adopting an evolutionary perspective that assesses the attempts of bin Ladin and Zawahiri to create an ideological doctrine over time, through the aggregate of their public messages.

Three components of the Al-Qaeda message

The literature on social movements and collective action frames has identified three core tasks that leaders seek to fulfill as they disseminate messages to a wider audience. First, they want to highlight the sociopolitical problems they feel need to be addressed. Second, they propose solutions to these problems and elucidate the methods that should be embraced. Third, they try to mobilize their target audiences and encourage the changes that their messages elaborate.[81] Taken together, these components can be seen, over time, as constituting the nascent ideological doctrine of the particular movement. This is especially relevant in terms of revolutionary and militant movements—that would when compared to other sociopolitical activity be termed "extremist"—since they advocate the adoption of radical solutions to transform the status quo. How might these three core framing tasks be applicable to jihadi ideological content?

The first category refers to identified problems with the status quo. Benford and Snow refer to this as the "diagnostic" element of framing. This preoccupation concerns the need to diagnose "an event or aspect of social life as problematic and in need of alteration." Diagnostic appeals thus ask "what is or went wrong?" and "who or what is to blame?"[82] For Salafi-jihadi activists, for instance, this would relate to religious ignorance, man-made laws, and the absence of a pious Caliphate, with more immediate concerns relating to the presence and influence of non-Islamist actors, forces, and ideas and derived grievances, such as foreign occupation. In his seminal book *Join the Caravan*, for example, Abdullah Azzam began by listing the reasons why Muslims had to go out and fight in jihad.[83]

The second category elucidates solutions and thus refers to the "prognostic" part of the message. This involves a "proposed solution to the diagnosed problem that specifies what needs to be done" in terms of "strategies, tactics, and targets."[84] For militant Islamists, this would involve universal support for "jihad by the sword."

The third category consists of conveying these elements to diverse audiences with the aim of provoking them to act. This relates to the "motivational" part of framing where the "rationale for engaging in ameliorative or corrective action" has to be produced. This concerns the "elaboration of a call to arms" that goes beyond diagnosis and prognosis, as agreement about causes and necessary solutions does not "automatically produce corrective action" or the type of activity that the given movement was trying to encourage. "Participation is thus contingent upon the development of motivational frames that function as prods to action."[85] As Snow and Byrd observed, "constituents have to be moved from the balcony to the barricades."[86] This does not happen automatically, and an awareness of problems and potential solutions is not sufficient. Those disseminating messages on behalf of a group try to drive these messages home so the desired outcome is achieved. Here, militant Islamists direct the content of the diagnostic and prognostic observations toward specific audiences in an emotive narrative in the hope of encouraging specific changes to take place, detailing the consequences for those who fail to respond, and the rewards for those who do.

It should be stressed that a degree of overlap should be expected between these three divisions and this is recognized in the theoretical literature on framing. After all, descriptions of existing problems are often woven into discussions concerning possible solutions, and discerning clear differences between the two types of discourse can sometimes be difficult. These three categories, however, provide a tested and theoretically grounded framework for the analysis of Al-Qaeda leadership statements, the aggregate message that these convey and the way in which these three parameters have evolved.

The first objective is to study Al-Qaeda's diagnosis. What issues and problems did bin Ladin and Zawahiri choose to emphasize over the years? This question will be addressed in the next chapter. The diagnostic component is broken down into social, cultural, and normative issues on the one hand (i.e., what fundamental elements of contemporary societies are seen as unpalatable?) and more specific grievances (such as infringement of territory, past and present) on the other. Once these diagnostic issues are elucidated, the focus can shift to the Al-Qaeda leadership's suggested solutions. The evolution of these prognostic issues is explored in Chapter 5. The elements that make up the prescribed prognostic response in Zawahiri's and bin Ladin's communiqués are divided into tactical issues relating to the use of violence, the envisaged scope of these militant solutions, and broader questions concerning Al-Qaeda's strategic and political vision. An understanding of the development of the Al-Qaeda leadership's problem diagnosis and proposed solutions leads to the third major component of bin Ladin's and Zawahiri's communication efforts: their attempts to deliver this message to specific audiences in order to provoke appropriate action. Most of these messages address different Muslim audiences (both those whom the Al-Qaeda leaders view as potential supporters or "constituents" and those who are seen to have erred and sinned). Several statements are also directed toward non-Muslims, usually adversaries or identified enemies. Chapter 6 focuses on these efforts to communicate the message through specific appeals that could be seen as the dedicated "prods to action" that the literature on collective action frames identifies as the central objective of "motivational framing."

As well as providing theoretically grounded context to understanding Al-Qaeda's messages and the beliefs and ideas that these convey over time, the literature on social movements and message framing provides further parameters that might help in understanding the impact and potential effect of Al-Qaeda's communicative efforts. Fundamentally, the Al-Qaeda leadership's message has to resonate with at least a significant proportion of its desired target audience, be seen as coherent, and reflect the experiences and wishes of potential supporters as well as the wider population. Crucially, these aspects do not relate to violent attacks *per se*. Although these, of course, form part of Al-Qaeda's overall repertoire and outward communication in a more abstract sense, the central leadership itself has increasingly lost control over some of the targeting emphases of affiliates, as will be discussed below. It has been widely documented that excessive targeting of Muslims in particular in Al-Qaeda-affiliated attacks has been very damaging for the group and exacerbated its isolation.[87] By focusing on the content of messages exclusively, however, and the way in which these have evolved, the emphasis is instead on discursive output from the two principal Al-Qaeda leaders and a process over which they exert full control. The Al-Qaeda leaders may have lost the ability to steer affiliates in a particular tactical or strategic direction. This is particularly true toward the end of the period under review in this book. The same cannot be said, however, about the content of their statements. These have been disseminated by the leaders themselves and thus present metrics with which to understand the way in which the leadership's own worldview has evolved and the problems the Al-Qaeda leaders may have created for themselves through these communicative efforts.

Benford and Snow defined three tools to measure the connection between the communicative efforts of movements and their potential supporters.[88] First is "empirical credibility"—are the statements believable and consistent and are those who articulate this message credible? Second, "experiential commensurability"—does the message match the experiences of potential supporters? Third, "narrative fidelity"—does the message reference the cultural myths that are inherent in the ideological context? These three paradigms offer helpful indicators with which to approach the question of the effectiveness of bin Ladin's and Zawahiri's statements. These issues will inform the discussion in Chapter 7 on the contradictions, tensions, and inconsistencies that can be identified in the ideological "package" that the Al-Qaeda leadership sought to develop and deliver over the past two decades. The matter will also be revisited in the final and concluding chapter of this book.

To summarize, this literature on message framing highlights how statements issued on behalf of a movement are not mere reflections of stated ambitions. They rationalize movement activities, communicate dissatisfaction with the status quo, identify causal actors and responsible factors, prescribe solutions, elucidate rewards, and, crucially, define the audience of potential participants whom leaders seek to mobilize. These statements, therefore, establish the basis for a relationship between movement leaders and potential participants beyond face-to-face contact or where physical interaction is impractical or impossible. Hence, engagement in these efforts for clandestine or illegal movements like Al-Qaeda is of paramount importance.

These messages, moreover, necessarily reflect the core aspects and apply the wider vocabulary of the movement's belief system and culture and draw upon this normative environment as a source of identity. For Al-Qaeda, this broader environment represents the approach of militant Salafism. The framing literature also highlights the need for movement leaders to address and be sensitive to—through their messages to followers, prospective supporters, and adversaries—watershed events that are relevant to the movement's goals and the concerns and experiences of potential participants. In this sense, these events and their repercussions need to be presented in a way that supports and conforms to the narrative thread, which aggregated statements have formed throughout the movement's life span.

This relates to the important framing notion of consistency. As mentioned above, the framing model provides valuable measurements with which to assess specific attempts to communicate with potential participants and the wider environment. Implicitly, in a methodological sense, this model also highlights the importance of long-term, systematic, and empirical analyses whereby message consistency can be assessed and (by extension) observations can be made concerning the credibility of disseminators and message resonance.

Approaching statements and messages designed to promote movement activities of groups like Al-Qaeda in this way, therefore, can yield important insights. Snow and Byrd, for instance, suggested that "the success of al Qaeda on the global scale may be partly attributable to the ability of its leaders to adapt the diagnostic and prognostic components of its master frame to local contexts."[89] In his study of Islamic activism, meanwhile, Wiktorowicz observed how "frequent disagreements and framing contests over meaning encourage competitive pressures as various groups produce and disseminate interpretive schemata." Such competition could also take place within movements, the author argued, and these "intramovement divisions (such as hardliner-softliner, conservative-liberal, young-old, ideologue-pragmatist) [could] create internal framing disputes as each faction attempts to assert its own frame for movement-wide adoption."[90]

In their analysis of *Sada al-Malahim*, a newsletter of Al-Qaeda in the Arabian Peninsula, Page et al. detected specific examples of diagnostic, prognostic, and motivational framing in the publication, designed to encourage collective action.[91] The authors found frame consistency to be strong and assessed the credibility of frame articulators as high, based on their knowledge, religious prowess, and experience. Additionally, frame articulators were seen to place extensive emphasis on retaining empirical credibility, whereby *Sada al-Malahim* editors strove to be "responsive to local, regional, and international events, highlighting themes that have temporal resonance."[92] By contrast, Hegghammer's analysis of the ideological "hybridization" of militant Islamist groups suggested that the increased variation in content emphases and scope in their message output could be construed as opportunism and perceived as inconsistent by potential participants. Interrupted frame consistency, including blurred enemy hierarchies, could thus jeopardize the ability of these groups to produce a message that resonated with and encouraged mobilization of potential participants.[93] Wagemakers, meanwhile, demonstrated how approaching framing as a "reciprocal relationship between ideas on the one hand and the political and socio-economic context in which they are spread on the other" offered an analytical structure to understand the writings and ideas of Muhammed Al-Maqdisi.[94]

These studies all underscore the importance of dynamics in the evolving discourse of Al-Qaeda and related groups and the shifting currents of the ideological environment in which they operate. The following chapters, therefore, place particular emphasis on exploring the way in which bin Ladin's and Zawahiri's efforts to create an open and public ideological doctrine for Al-Qaeda developed since the early 1990s, as the group was becoming established. What were the issues that the leaders identified that were used to rationalize the establishment of Al-Qaeda? What solutions did bin Ladin and Zawahiri offer, and how were these legitimized and contextualized in light of Al-Qaeda's campaign of violence? Finally, how did the two Al-Qaeda leaders attempt to communicate these messages to diverse audiences, and what do these appeals teach us about the way their group evolved? The next three chapters explore each of these core message components in sequence.

4

Al-Qaeda's problem diagnosis

Introduction: Values and grievances

Why was Al-Qaeda established and what is it fighting for? A fundamental goal for the Al-Qaeda leadership after the group was established was to make the case for continued militancy beyond the Afghan jihad that concluded in 1989. Bin Ladin's and Zawahiri's communiqués from this period, and their subsequent output since then, thus described grievances and ailments that they felt provoked and justified a violent response. Al-Qaeda's problem diagnosis has, of course, evolved over the years. Taken together, a review of the statements from bin Ladin and Zawahiri over the past 20 years reveals that the list of grievances cited was initially fairly limited, but began to expand by 1997. The post-9/11 period, moreover, saw a significant increase in the list of grievances addressed, before becoming more focused again when issues such as the 2003 Iraq invasion and rendition came to the fore. In part due to these shifting diagnostic emphases, related discussions concerning the geographic source of malice often resulted in unclear and inconsistent emphases in terms of culprits and target prioritization. During a brief period, for instance, followers would be urged to prioritize variously local sources of grievance over external threats or vice versa. These points will all be revisited in detail below.

Whilst most statements focused to some degree on perceived sources of corruption, hardship, and suffering that affected Muslims, the 260 statements that were studied for this book also revealed how values and normative issues formed an important part of Al-Qaeda's problem diagnosis. Some authors, in their analyses of Al-Qaeda's statements and communicative efforts, have emphasized the centrality of tangible grievances, primarily relating to foreign occupation and interference. Hellmich, for instance, wrote that "a closer reading of bin Ladin's message soon reveals—contrary to the popular image—that his war is less a response to what the West *is* (i.e. freedom and democracy, in itself a summary of 'the West' whose accuracy is questionable at best), and more about what it *does*."[1] Mann similarly argued that "despite the religious rhetoric and the bloody means, bin Laden is a rational man. There is a simple *reason* why he attacked the US: American imperialism."[2] Careful scrutiny of a large corpus of statements, however, reveals that the Al-Qaeda leaders presented both tangible grievances as well as normative or value-based issues as reasons for organizing, expanding, and sustaining violent resistance. When seeking to dissect Al-Qaeda's stated problem diagnosis, therefore, tangible grievances relating to suffering and humiliation—important and central components to Al-Qaeda's narrative—need to be considered alongside these value-based frustrations that rest on Al-Qaeda's Islamist extremist outlook. These normative issues become particularly prominent when the content of Zawahiri's statements is considered. Zawahiri invariably offered far more detailed and substantive statements than did bin Ladin. The latter normally presented the key points of Al-Qaeda's agenda while Zawahiri's messages were much longer and often touched upon a large number of issues. Any analysis of Al-Qaeda's thoughts and words, therefore, must—as mentioned above—focus on Zawahiri's output in addition to that of bin Ladin.

As the account below argues, these diagnostic elements involve a multifaceted outlook and worldview that is equally informed by political as well as religious-cultural imperatives. The chapter is divided into two sections, with the first exploring these value-based diagnostic features and the second setting out Al-Qaeda's grievance argument and how this has evolved from a localized set of ills to a far broader, more confusing, and sometimes conflicting list of grievances and identified culprits.

The undesirability of existing societies

Through the course of their efforts to communicate with their wider environment, the two Al-Qaeda leaders were consistent in their condemnation of specific normative features and societal facets of contemporary cultures that they felt prevailed. An important element of Al-Qaeda's problem diagnosis, therefore, relates to the perceived undesirability of existing societies. The statements processed for this book revealed numerous references to this effect. These included comments relating to perceptions of what made contemporary societies unpalatable and defunct in the eyes of the leadership (for instance as regards man-made legislation, the spread of capitalism, and democracy). Many communiqués made brief references to such perceived societal ills. Several statements, however, especially those authored by Al-Zawahiri, offered more detailed insights into the way in which these perceptions were formed. To illustrate how pervasive references to undesirable aspects of existing societies are in the Al-Qaeda leaders' output, Figure 4.1 identifies the 57 communiqués where these positions were expressed, with each point on the graph illustrating an individual communiqué located on a timeline for the period under review. The timeline pinpoints statements by Zawahiri or bin Ladin where either figure made the case that existing forms of governance or societal organization were defunct and needed replacing and that this formed part of the revolutionary struggle that Al-Qaeda was pioneering.

As shown in Figure 4.1, references to the undesirability of prevailing societal forms featured throughout the 1990s and up to the present. These references, however, appear to have become particularly prominent in the post-9/11 discourse emanating from the Al-Qaeda leadership.

It appears, therefore, that the Al-Qaeda leadership's focus of animosity and source of anger was not exclusively based on immediate concerns over self-determination or infringement of territory by unbelievers. In 1991, for instance, Al-Zawahiri wrote a book titled *The Bitter Harvest*, condemning the corruption in the organizational and methodological thinking of the Muslim Brotherhood in Egypt. The Brotherhood, Zawahiri argued, was taking part in "jahiliyya governing" (a concept made popular by Sayyid Qutb) through its acquiescence of democracy, elections, and parliaments. Democracy, in the form of the "rule of the people," was seen as a "new religion," which gave "the masses the right to legislate without being shackled down to any other [divine] authority."[3]

Zawahiri's denunciation of democracy is therefore directly tied to his notions of *tawhid*, the oneness of God, and the fundamental impermissibility of idol worship. His reasoning was as follows: "Democracy is a new religion. In Islam, legislation comes from God; in a democracy, this capacity is given to the people. Therefore, this is a new religion, based on making the people into gods and giving them God's rights and attributes. This is tantamount to associating idols with God and falling into unbelief."[4]

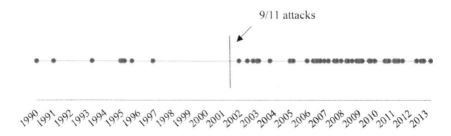

9/11 attacks

FIGURE 4.1 *Condemning existing societies: A timeline*

Anyone who embraced or participated in legislative councils or any form of majority rule and obeyed authorities selected through such assemblies thus committed sin.[5] In their statements both bin Ladin and Zawahiri insisted that any form of governance or jurisprudence where decisions were embedded in the will of the majority equaled subservience to the West,[6] was corrupted by capitalism and corporations,[7] and was one of the reasons a political culture of "surrender and concessions" had prevailed in Palestine.[8] In one communiqué, bin Ladin conceded it was no secret "that the selection of emirs or presidents is the right of the nation. However, this right is governed by conditions, whose absence makes participation in the selection of an emir prohibited."[9] The main condition was a leadership that would implement shariah, which no existing government, after the fall of the Taliban regime, had achieved or even contemplated, according to bin Ladin. Denunciation of democracy and elections featured intermittently throughout the communiqués analyzed, and the coding did not reveal substantial differences in this regard over time in terms of context and terminology. Nor was there a significant difference between messages from bin Ladin or Zawahiri, aside from their respective geographic bias in a large number of communiqués (the former often focusing on the Arabian Peninsula, while the latter on Egypt and neighboring regions).

When the overall trend in this regard since the 1990s was assessed, however, the period surrounding the Arab Spring emerged as the most strongly focused on issues relating to the fallacy of democratic governance or even un-Islamic forms of popular uprising. The revolutions that began in Tunisia and Egypt before spreading to other countries in the region appear to have caused anxiety within the Al-Qaeda leadership over the apparent appeal of democratic solutions to Arab masses and the *ummah*.

Zawahiri, for example, focused extensively on the matter in his multipart appeal to Arabs (primarily Egyptians) titled "A Message of Hope and Glad Tidings," intended to address and explain the significance of these watershed events. Arabs were warned that democracy was necessarily a *secular* form of governance[10] that "worships one idol, which is the wishes of the majority, without abiding by any religion, standards or ethics."[11] In an April 2013 statement titled "Unifying the Word toward the Word of Monotheism (*Tawhid*)," Zawahiri compared what he called "the national secular state" with the Islamic state. The former rested on the "whims of the majority," not God's law, he warned. Supremacy would be for the people, and such a state would permit women, Jews, Christians, and even atheists to hold senior political and juristic positions. For Egypt in particular, as it entered its postrevolutionary transitional phase, Zawahiri argued, emphasis had to be placed on implementing shariah and basing identity on Islam rather than the citizenship of states that were the products of colonial bargaining.[12]

Any concessions toward a democratic form of government or consultation in this regard are directly tied to the sacrificing of Islamic cultural prescriptions and proliferation of vice and degradation. When references to democracy were considered in their immediate narrative context, this revealed that democracy was not, therefore, only tied to specific grievances concerning perceived oppression by the democratic West. Its introduction or acquiescence involved a fundamental abrogation of the religious creed and abandonment of the *hisba*, commanding good and forbidding wrong (*al-amr bil-marouf wan-nahee an al-munkar*). "The truth about democracy," Zawahiri argued, is "it allows everything regardless of it being degrading or contradictory, as long as the majority agrees with it."[13] The triumph of the Tunisian Ennahda Movement, a moderate Islamist political party, in the wake of the revolution in the country, was thus a cause for great concern, according to Zawahiri. The party was not a "true" Islamist movement but a symptom of a "modern disease," Zawahiri insisted. "They are inventing an 'Islam' that pleases the American Department of State, the European Union and the Gulf scholars," he complained. This was Islam "according to demand," Zawahiri argued, which would allow "gambling, nude beaches, usurious banks, secular laws, and submission to international legitimacy."[14] Regardless of the fact that Ennahda's claim to power was far more legitimate than that of the previous government and far more representative than Al-Qaeda's extremist discourse, Zawahiri sought to tarnish its moderate Islamist manifesto by suggesting it promoted "un-Islamic" activities and represented a form of Islam that was designed to placate the West.

Handwritten margin note: "RAND Muslims" – Awlaki

The impious international order and its local implications

Al-Qaeda's Islamist extremist value system, in turn, informs much of the anger that the Al-Qaeda leaders express toward the international community, which, again, is not exclusively based on allegations of infringement of territory, sanctions, or other more immediate grievances (although this too is very important as will be discussed later in the chapter). America's legislative system whereby religion is separated from policy-making is seen as "contrary to the nature of mankind," for example.[15] This organizational principle, itself traceable to the secular French revolution, has produced a "false international legitimacy"[16] and a "secular international order" dominated by the ideals of "Anglo-Saxon protestant publics," according to Zawahiri.[17]

When references to the social, cultural, and normative undesirability of existing societies are aggregated in the leadership statements under review, two major manifestations of this "corruptive order" can be identified. First, the

Al-Qaeda leaders denounced what they saw as the chief pillar of this order, the United Nations. Second, the leaders, and particularly Zawahiri, denounced the impact of this "international order" on the drafting of written constitutions of Islamic countries.

Several specific reasons were cited for the perceived harmful impact of the UN. Examples included allegations that the organization prevented Muslims from defending themselves in Bosnia and elsewhere (through embargoing arms shipments) and the implementation of sanctions in Iraq and beyond, resulting in immense human suffering for the local population. In more fundamental ways, however, the extent to which the UN was seen to represent a system that was illegitimate through its elevation of ideals that contradicted the sovereignty of God remained a constant feature of the statements analyzed. Bin Ladin declared the UN "an organization of unbelief."[18] Its very charter, warned Zawahiri, "challenges the Shari'ah"[19] and membership to the UN renders governments illegitimate[20] and "forces" the recognition of Israel, Russian occupation of Chechnya, China's occupation of East Turkistan, and Spain's occupation of Ceuta and Melilla.[21] This animosity toward the main institution of, what Zawahiri called, the "post-war international order," therefore, combined anger over loss of territory and other such tangible grievances with denunciation of the values that were inherent in this order. In November 2012, for instance, Zawahiri issued a short statement titled "Document of the Support of Islam." The publication, which was essentially an open letter to the Muslim *ummah*, called on Muslims to unite behind seven principal goals that would, according Zawahiri, restore the primacy of Islam. One of these objectives was a complete rejection of the international order represented by the UN. Zawahiri cited four main reasons why this would be necessary: the UN promoted the "five oppressive parties" (the five veto-power nations); embraced rule by majority rather than God's law; legitimized non-Muslim control over Muslim territories, such as Russia's over the Muslim Caucasus; and issued resolutions harming Muslim interests, such as the partitioning of Palestine.[22]

The second manifestation of the corruptive power of international, secular, legal norms, according to the Al-Qaeda leaders, was the drafting of constitutions in Islamic lands. In this respect, detailed scrutiny of the statements under review reveals particular emphasis on the constitutions of Egypt, Somalia, Pakistan, and Saudi Arabia.[23] The fact that shariah law was not absolute in the judicial and legislative assemblies described in these written constitutions was blamed primarily on the West, mostly the United Kingdom, which was seen as instrumental in the creation of the Egyptian, Pakistani, and Saudi constitutions. Zawahiri in particular devoted substantial attention to the matter. In 2009 he even published a book dissecting the Pakistani constitution, assessing the way in which it departed from crucial tenets of Islamic law. The book admonished Pakistanis for tolerating majority rule as the benchmark for decision-making and warned that the Pakistani constitution legalized *fasiq*, disobedience from shariah, which was in itself an act of *kufr*, or infidelity, according to Zawahiri.[24]

In many of his older communiqués from the early to mid-1990s, bin Ladin too focused on the way in which the Saudi legal base failed to correspond with the Quran and how the *ulema* and political elite failed to rule according to the code sent down by God or the practices of His Prophet. When output from the two leaders was compared in this respect over time, subtle differences emerged. In particular, it seems that rather than dedicating extensive tracts exclusively to this aspect of contemporary societies, as Zawahiri has done, the more concise and apt bin Ladin mixed these constitutional concerns within more multifaceted criticisms of the established powers.

Thus, bin Ladin's early petitions and open letters to Saudi religio-political authorities, written on behalf of the Advice and Reform Committee, intertwined deviation from shariah governance with other socioeconomic and political issues that formed part of his problem diagnosis at the time.[25] The letters, written between 1994 and 1995, listed numerous "flaws" within contemporary Saudi society. These ranged from the corruption of man-made laws and usury (*riba*) to specific grievances, such as the acquiescence of non-Islamic political forces, impious alliance structures, economic stagnation and polarization, "blasphemous" regional cooperation platforms, and humiliating weakness of the armed forces. The culture of idleness, which saw the religious establishment ignoring and even endorsing these perceived ills, was very much tied to the initial and fundamental sin of selective application of shariah and elevation of un-divine authority.[26]

Zawahiri, in his "Message of Hope" to fellow Egyptians, similarly saw the dilution or "alienation" of shariah within society as a tipping point leading to the spreading of vice and sin throughout the populace, including "usury, adultery, insobriety, moral dissolution, familial schisms and forms of crimes, [of] which the man-made laws add to the increase and spread."[27]

Vices, sins, and "grotesque forms of depravity"

Aside from these perceived systemic iniquities and flaws, the Al-Qaeda leaders' output also reveals more specific condemnation of behavior regarded as offensive according to the puritanical norms that the Al-Qaeda leaders seek to elevate. As Zawahiri's concern over postrevolutionary order in Tunisia reveals, the proliferation of particular vices forms a distinct part of the diagnostic element of the Al-Qaeda leadership's communicative output. These vices include "illicit" behavior and novelties such as sex outside wedlock and the promotion of sex, usury, the consumption of alcohol, adherence to secularism/atheism, homosexuality, drug use, gambling, the sexual representation of women, adultery, disobeying parents, perjury, the desire for wealth and status, and "a family structure which is not necessarily composed of a father, mother and children, but rather grotesque forms of depravity," in Zawahiri's words.[28]

Bin Ladin and Zawahiri also accused the West of hiding behind the supposed values of free expression in order to legitimize their attacks on Islam. How, for instance, could "the West" slander the Prophet Mohammed (through cartoons and anti-Islamic films) and ban the glorification of terrorism and the *niqab* (in France), while tolerating homosexuality and banning any debate surrounding the Holocaust?[29] The physical presence of Westerners was thus polluting, due to the potency of their ideas. According to bin Ladin, US tourists were "spreading filth upon whoever comes into contact with [them]" and the United States, the world's greatest polluter, was also the "source of AIDS in the world," he insisted in a statement issued a year after the 9/11 attacks.[30] Characteristically more expansive in scope, Zawahiri similarly denounced the Western civilization of "degeneracy, adultery, freedom from ethics, morals and religion [and] the civilization of AIDS." According to Zawahiri:

> That is why, the female veiled Muslim brings out all of these provocations, and she uncovers their [Western] usage of women as a product to attract consumers and market supplies, and [she] uncovers the degeneracy of their capitalism that adopts the trade [in] obscenity in all its kinds and colors ... and she uncovers the fakery of their freedom as it is [acceptable] for them that a woman unveils her entire body, it is even [acceptable] for her to sell her body, but they cannot withstand a veiled Muslim woman.[31]

The spread of these ideas to the Islamic world is seen as catastrophic and no less an existential threat than that presented by Western interference and acts of aggression. Al-Qaeda's view of Western imperialism, therefore, does not only consider military intervention and direct political actions. Bin Ladin, for instance, warned of the "cunning, malevolent media and cultural invasion" orchestrated by Voice of America, the BBC (which Zawahiri called the "horn of the British intelligence"[32]), and other organizations at the forefront of an "ideological invasion" spreading "obscenity and depravity" in Muslim lands.[33]

The importance of values

At a conference about Al-Qaeda held a few years after 9/11, Rohan Gunaratna told his, primarily American, audience: "I want to tell you that al-Qaeda has no problem at all with your values. Al-Qaeda's problem is with your foreign policy."[34] This claim does not appear to stand up to scrutiny when Al-Qaeda's public statements are analyzed. Al-Qaeda's problem diagnosis is not based either on values or on more tangible and policy-related grievances but on *both*.

A strong normative theme, therefore, emerges when the diagnostic part of the Al-Qaeda leadership statements is analyzed. These value-based references, in turn, are often combined with references to some of the more specific grievances that form such an integral part of Al-Qaeda's message. Accusations of specific acts of aggression and hostility, therefore, are enveloped in these more profound and holistic denunciations of non-Islamic culture. Riedel's assumption that Zawahiri's ideology is "not rooted in a hatred for Western culture or values, nor the status of women there, nor the alleged decadence of the West"[35] does not correspond with long-term empirical analysis of bin Ladin's and Zawahiri's ideological output. Nor is there any evidence suggesting value-focused diagnosis is merely rhetorical. In Zawahiri's aforementioned book *The Morning and the Lamp*, for instance, one of the points cited supposedly exposing the infidelity of the Pakistani constitution concerned the fact that women were not prohibited from rising to the position of head of state.[36] At the same time Western values are seen as hostile to Muslim women as sisters wearing the hijab are being "persecuted"[37] through a ban on face covers "implemented in order to fight the values of Islam and to force our daughters to emulate the West and its immorality."[38] These values are a genuine concern for the Al-Qaeda leadership.

A thorough analysis of the leadership statements, therefore, highlights how Al-Qaeda's grievances are not merely "political" or specific to the actions of the West. They are to a very substantial degree based on *values* that are informed by the leaders' interpretation of the creed. This is important. The anger displayed in the actions and words of the Al-Qaeda leadership is not a mere reaction to actions of the West, local leaders, or other perceived belligerents. Nor do these diagnostic message elements rely on accounts of victimization and suffering exclusively. The anger displayed is based on a firm desire to implement specific normative criteria, opposing those that currently appear to prevail in the Islamic world and beyond. Fundamental issues relating to religiosity and cultural norms are mixed with more specific grievances, ongoing events, and the prevailing sense of violation and victimhood due to actions of powers outside the Islamic realm.

In one of the more unusual public relations initiatives undertaken by the Al-Qaeda leadership, Ayman Al-Zawahiri invited the public to send questions via an online forum regarding the role and operations of Al-Qaeda. Zawahiri answered many of the questions posted in this "open meeting" in extensive audio addresses, issued in two batches. The latter was posted on forums in April 2008. One of Zawahiri's answers typically demonstrates the way in which immediate concerns relating to territorial integrity and other developments that arouse anger within the potential support base are mixed with more long-term normative positioning:

> I reject and I am hostile to polytheism; scorn for religion; the establishment of relations based on profit, sensual delight, lies, deception, and treachery; usury, alcohol, gambling and vile deeds; seizing others' countries and inflicting justice on them based on arrogance and mischief; the plundering of their resources; double standards; and immunity to punishment for crimes for which others are punished; spreading killing, exploitation, and destruction; and the destruction of environment and climate in order to be elated with mighty arrogance and for the sake of plundering and looting.[39]

The spread of vice and sin, therefore, often seen as a by-product of past acts of aggression against the Islamic realm, is here intertwined with more immediate cases of suffering that are traced back to specific Western actors and their local stooges.

The problem diagnosis presented in Al-Qaeda's public messaging, therefore, serves as a reminder that Al-Qaeda is not just a militant revolutionary group targeting perceived oppressors. It is an extremist group, a militant organization perched on the peripheral fringe even within its immediate radical Salafi universe. Its leaders are angered not only by the suffering and hardships of fellow Muslims or the violation of territorial sovereignty, but also by what they perceive as acts of moral depravity and lack of Islamic purity. These elements combine to form the diagnostic element in the Al-Qaeda leadership's statements. Whereas value-based issues form a significant and consistent part of that discourse, however, references to hardships and tangible grievances are even more prominent.

The current study found that these references could be divided into two major categories. First, the leaders list and describe current issues and events that are presented to illustrate the suffering of the *ummah*, the hypocrisy and unfairness of the current state of affairs, and thus the need for defensive war. Second, numerous statements dwell more in the past or tie past events and historic legacies to more contemporary and ongoing developments. In the latter case, for instance, the colonial legacy of Western Europe and—going further back—the medieval Crusades are linked to the current situation in the Islamic world. Focus on events varies across the statements and is often dependent on the context of the communiqué (according to the prominence of a given set of issues each time), the scope of an individual statement, as well as the occasional geographic bias of bin Ladin and Zawahiri, as mentioned above.

Constructing a grievance narrative

Grievances and alleged historical crimes of the West and their treacherous "agents" in the Middle East, North Africa, and elsewhere set the political and event-specific context of Al-Qaeda's message. Almost all of the statements analyzed referred to grievances and developments (long and short term) in order to vilify the West and its allies and supporters, and appeal to Muslim audiences with the aim of mobilizing them to embrace militancy and justify violent methods. The leadership's take on current affairs is communicated, and specific reasons for the plight and victimization of Muslims are elucidated through an emotional narrative emphasizing the individual responsibility of Muslims to react against the perceived forces of evil in order to protect the sanctity, cohesion, dignity, and safety of the *ummah*.

The simplistic world vision of Al-Qaeda is Manichean at its core, pitching the United States, the West, Western culture and media, and local regimes and elites in one camp against the sacrosanct world of *dar al-Islam*. Aside from the normative clashes mentioned above, the content highlights the ways in which expansionism, conspiracy, hegemony, plunder, and subjugation are inherent characteristics of the former camp, thus rendering peaceful coexistence impossible for the time being, according to Al-Qaeda.

Various examples of penetration into and mistreatment of the Islamic world are presented to demonstrate this clash and the need to rise up against it. The oppression and hostility displayed by apparent forces of evil against Muslims illustrate not only their individual obligation to defend the *ummah* (by supporting Al-Qaeda—the *ummah*'s vanguard) but also the right of this vanguard to reciprocate in kind. For the Al-Qaeda leadership, these grievances have been used to develop some of the principal justifications presented for terrorist violence, within the context of reciprocity. Some of the most prominent events and grievances to feature in bin Ladin's and Zawahiri's statements since the early 1990s are listed in Table 4.1. Many of these events, of course, relate to genuine cases of suffering and hardship, which angered not only the Al-Qaeda leaders but millions of others across the world. The challenge for the Al-Qaeda leadership, however, was—and continues to be—framing these events so as to present a pattern of aggression and suffering that justified the existence and activism of Al-Qaeda.

Table 4.1 Principal grievances cited

Presence of occupying forces, corruption, creation of local "agent regimes" in Middle East, North Africa, Pakistan, Afghanistan, and elsewhere	2007 siege of Lal Masjid (Red Mosque) in Pakistan	Incarceration of Aafia Siddiqui, Omar Abdur Rahman, the wife of Abu Hamsa Muhajir, and bin Ladin's family
	2006 war in Lebanon	
	2008–2009 and 2012 war in Gaza	
Creation of Israel, aggression against Palestinians. Corruption of nationalist local rulers. Local, regional, and international peace initiatives (Madrid, Oslo, Camp David, Wey River, Sharm El Sheikh, Mecca accords, Annapolis, etc.) as way to annex/ "sell" Palestine. Plans to 'Judaize' Palestine	Gaza siege/blockade	Collusion between Iran and the US. Expansionist Iran and its alliance to the Assad regime
	UNSC Resolution 1701 on Lebanon ceasefire, disarming Hizbullah. Other resolutions which "cut off parts of the lands of Islam"	Alleged mistreatment of Muslim immigrants in West
		Protection of Salman Rushdie and knighthood
	Battle of Al-Falujah, Iraq	Perceived offensive remarks by Pope Benedict XVI regarding Islam
The "oppressive" and "hostile" campaigns by "Crusader-Zionist aggressors" and their allies in Afghanistan, Iraq, Algeria, Somalia, Sudan, Eritrea, Chechnya, Kashmir, Indonesia, East Turkistan (Xinjiang Uyghur in China), Philippines, Yemen, Nigeria, Mauritania. Attempts to "split" Muslim lands into manageable units	Support for Muqtada al-Sadr's army, Badr Brigades	
	Incarceration of Muslims in Guantanamo, Bagram, Abu Ghraib, and at other undisclosed facilities. Torture of Muslim inmates	Western support for "apostate" rulers of Muslim countries, leading to lack of development, poverty, unemployment, and proliferation of distracting "vices" in favor of Islam
	"Dishonoring" the Quran and slandering the Prophet Mohammed (Mohammed caricatures, allegations of Quran desecration, anti-Islamic films, etc.)	
Historical legacy of oppression, especially through colonialism, and the Sykes-Picot agreement, Balfour Declaration, and more modern equivalents—a Zionist and Christian Crusade. Usurping lands and stealing resources. The creation of un-Islamic "agent" regimes in the Islamic world		Spread of nationalism, particularly in Palestine
	People arrested for questioning Holocaust but not for "insulting" the Prophet	"Tyranny" of international law
	French ban on wearing veils in schools	"Cultural invasion" by Western media, "permitting disengaging moral behaviour" marginalizing the importance of Islam
Sabra and Shatila massacres	Hostile undemocratic regimes criticized by West but not friendly regimes, such as Saudi Arabia and Egypt (under Mubarak), despite the torture they inflict on Muslims	Global warming blamed on the West, US failure to sign Kyoto protocol
Massacre of Srebrenica and other atrocities of Bosnia war blamed on West and UN		Global capitalism and corporations causing world poverty

(Continued)

Table 4.1 Principal grievances cited (*Continued*)

Human cost of UN sanctions against Iraq and oil-for-food program	Muslim countries prohibited from acquiring nuclear weapons but not Israel	Al Yamamah arms deal between Britain and Saudi Arabia
Separating of East Timor from Indonesia and collusion of UN	Respect in the West for human rights alternates according to political agenda. Democracy celebrated only if outcome is in the interest of the United States/ West, not in, e.g., Algeria or Palestine	Pakistan collapsing from within due to reduced emphasis on Islam
Spanish control over Ceuta, Melilla, and Andalusia		Danger of democracy and secular rule in relation to "Arab Spring"
Russian control over Caucasus		Egyptian Military Council "protecting" Israel after fall of Mubarak regime
Darfur opened as another "Crusader front" against Muslims, under guise of protecting human rights	US pressure to hold Wafa'i Qustantin (an Egyptian Coptic woman who converted to Islam but was then forced to return to Christianity and moved to a Coptic monastery) in Egyptian "torture chambers"	False, "moderate" version of Islam being promoted, e.g., by the Tunisian Ennahda Movement
Pakistani security forces have become "hunting dogs" for the West through collusion of Pakistani government		
"Stealing Muslim wealth,": especially oil	Turkey cooperating with Israel and the West, watering down Islam	

As demonstrated, wars, sanctions, subjugation, and violent oppression feature prominently. However, the importance of events, which the Al-Qaeda leaders interpret as blasphemous and contemptuous of the Islamic creed, should not be underestimated. Military aggression, occupation, and economic colonialism are obviously fundamental to Al-Qaeda's grievance narrative, but so are cultural clashes and remarks or gestures that are seen as insulting, such as the publication of Mohammed caricatures in Danish and (later) European newspapers, Salman Rushdie's protection by British authorities, cases and alleged cases of Quran desecration, and the online distribution of anti-Islamic films. Such events are all tied together and presented as an all-encompassing conspiracy against Islam which is controlled by "the West" and demonstrative of "its" animosity toward Islam.

These perceived acts of aggression are equated with events resulting in bloodshed and suffering in the Al-Qaeda leaders' statements because the dignity and pride of the *ummah* and the legacy of the Prophet are seen to be at stake. Zawahiri, for instance, noted how the "latest decision by the French president to create a law preventing Muslim girls from covering their heads in schools is ... consistent with the burning of villages along with their people in Afghanistan, demolishing houses over their sleeping residents in Palestine, killing the children of Iraq."[40] Bin Ladin even suggested the publication of the Mohammed caricatures was a far worse atrocity for Muslims than bombings of innocent Muslim women and children.[41] The publication of anti-Islamic material, moreover, is not seen as being beyond the control of governments but linked directly to policies that are deemed hostile toward Muslims. Thus the Danish authorities, and even society as a whole, were found responsible for the publication of the newspaper cartoons. More recently, Zawahiri blamed the publication of an anti-Islamic film titled *The Innocence of Muslims*— which caused widespread protests in September 2012—on America as a whole, rather than the individual responsible. Despite the US administration's denunciation of the film, Zawahiri insisted that "America, in the name of personal freedom and freedom of expression *allowed* the production of a film hostile to the most honorable prophet."[42]

In his analysis of Al-Qaeda's future, Gerges argued that "plots against Western societies will persist as long as the United States is embroiled in wars in Muslim lands."[43] Although war fighting and suffering of Muslims are central points of grievance that could aid Al-Qaeda in its efforts to mobilize support for its campaign of violence, a careful analysis of its leadership statements suggests that Al-Qaeda's problem diagnosis does not focus on specific acts of aggression and physical hardship exclusively. Indeed, numerous terrorist plots have been directly linked to the publication of the Mohammed cartoons in Denmark—seen as a "cultural" act of aggression. The fact that these are beyond the direct control of governments appears to be of no consequence for the Al-Qaeda leadership.

Early localized emphasis

Bin Ladin's and Zawahiri's messages from the early 1990s focused primarily on local grievances in the Arab world before widening in geographic scope toward the end of the decade. Bin Ladin was at first largely preoccupied with the Arabian Peninsula and the perceived illegitimacy of Saudi authorities. In his early statements, bin Ladin spoke initially of the need to "expel" the "unbelievers from the Arabian Peninsula"[44] and for the United States to remove its forces and end material support for Jews in Palestine.[45] At this early stage the US presence in Saudi Arabia was seen as the "root of all problems" preventing (alongside the Al-Saud family) the establishment of a "pious Caliphate" on the peninsula. The struggle would continue until

Americans and their allies had been expelled from all the holy sites of Islam and shariah had been established in their wake.[46] When other regional or global issues were addressed, these were often traced back to the inability or unwillingness of the regime in Riyadh to protect the interests of Muslims, be that through supporting Yemeni communists or acquiescing UN "embargo" over shipment of arms to Bosnian Muslims.[47] A letter written by bin Ladin in June 1994 and sent in the name of the London-based Advice and Reform Committee, however, is an early example of a widening diagnostic scope in the messages. The letter discussed the "global Crusader conspiracy" and the dismal state of Muslim affairs in Sudan, Somalia, Lebanon, Kashmir, Algeria, Yemen, Bosnia, and—of course—the Arabian Peninsula and Palestine.[48] Just over a year later, bin Ladin penned another letter accusing the Saudi regime of seeking to deflect criticism over local issues through organizing debates concerning the plight of Muslims in Bosnia. Although the open letter was largely addressed to Muslims in "The Land of the Two Holy Places" (referring to Mecca and Medina), bin Ladin warned of the way in which the United Nations was being positioned to implement "the Crusaders' plan to kill the causes of the nation of Islam and its people."[49]

Nonetheless, most of the early messages concerned domestic issues relating to areas bordering the Red Sea. This is not to suggest that condemnation of the "distant" enemy was absent. Indeed, most of these local grievances were traced back to the domination of the United States and its defense of Israel. Zawahiri, for instance, wrote several articles on Abu Muhammed Al-Maqdisi's website "Minbar al-Tawhid wa'l-Jihad" criticizing the state of affairs in Egypt and the secular nature of the curriculum and constitution (much in the same way as he did in the wake of the 2011 Arab uprising), citing the close ties with America and Israel as a principal corrupting influence (as well as British colonial legacy).[50]

Similarly, issues of importance to Muslims in the Arabian Peninsula, from the price of wheat[51] and the inability of the regime to cater for pilgrims to Mecca,[52] to economic stagnation and unemployment, were traced to the influence and presence of the United States, which had coveted the region, according to bin Ladin, since Franklin Roosevelt became president.[53]

This implicit prioritization of diagnostic inferences characterized Al-Qaeda's first public "declaration of war" against the distant enemy and its local affiliates, which bin Ladin published in September 1996. A wide range of issues affecting Muslims from North Africa to the Far East were addressed, but the focus was on Saudi Arabia and the presence of US troops in the area, seen as "one of the worst catastrophes to befall the Muslims since the death of the Prophet."[54]

Thus, even though the distant enemy had been delineated, and the consequences for his presence in the Middle East elaborated, there was some degree of prioritization and limitation of diagnostic scope up until the mid-1990s. Gradually, however, the cluster of grievances identified in the statements proliferated exponentially, and bin Ladin, in particular, began to place more emphasis on the regional or even global implications of the issues that he highlighted.

Holistic, intertwined grievances

By August 1997, American presence in "all Muslim lands" was condemned, not just in the Arabian Peninsula.[55] Al-Qaeda's identified adversary also became more multifaceted, consisting of an "international Christian Crusade" with Zionist sympathies and agendas.[56] To counter this threat, a "World Islamic Front" was created, which declared war on Zionist Crusaders and Americans in February 1998. The declaration set out three major grievances: the occupation of the Arabian Peninsula, the suffering of the Iraqi people, and liberation of Muslims in Jerusalem and Palestine.[57] The World Islamic Front would operate as a vanguard for all Muslims in the region, according to bin Ladin, because all Arab land had "either been occupied or there [was] a conspiracy to occupy it." "For the first time since the Prophet's death, atheists [were] occupying [the] Mecca, Medina and al-Aqsa Mosques," the signatories lamented.[58]

The statements from this period illustrate the increasingly ambitious agenda of Al-Qaeda and attempts to garner broader appeal within and beyond the Arab world. Toward the end of the 1990s, for instance, bin Ladin made several references to the conflict in Kashmir, religiosity in Pakistan, and the perceived threat from India and highlighted the importance of supporting Chechen *mujahideen* as belligerents prepared for the Second Chechen War.[59] Ridding the Arabian Peninsula of American presence thus became merely the "first" objective, according to bin Ladin's interview with John Miller in February 1999.[60] In a joint statement issued with Zawahiri in September 2000, the two leaders pledged to "do all we can to support our religion, to establish the *shariah* of Islam in the land of Islam, to expel the Jews and the Christians from the sacred places, and to endeavor to release our ulema from the United States, from Egypt, from Riyadh, and from all Muslim lands."[61]

This broadening of diagnostic scope suggests that the Al-Qaeda leadership was seeking to mobilize a wider set of potential participants. In an interview that was released in January 1999, for example, bin Ladin congratulated himself on the "winds of change" his messages had brought to Muslims across the globe, through highlighting their common grievances.[62] The pressures following the 9/11 attacks compounded this necessity to mobilize as much support from as many regions as possible, and the messages from that period reflect this need. The US and NATO campaign in Afghanistan was presented as an attempt to destroy the only Islamic emirate in the world, rather than as a mission against Al-Qaeda, and thus part of a larger campaign against Muslims: "we are being attacked in Palestine, Iraq, Lebanon, Sudan, Somalia, Kashmir, the Philippines and everywhere else."[63] "This war is fundamentally religious," bin Ladin argued. "The people of the East are Muslims. They sympathize with Muslims against the people of the West, who are the Crusaders." Al-Qaeda was thus presented as the vanguard for the victims in Palestine, Iraq, Sudan, Chechnya, Somalia, Kashmir, Indonesia, the Philippines, and elsewhere amid the corruption and infidelity of local leaders and *ulema*, who had succumbed to the West.[64] The post-9/11 communiqués promised to revive the Caliphate, as it was at the height of its power, throughout the Middle East and North Africa (and into Europe) "as predicted by the Prophet, according to bin Ladin,"[65] even if it took "several generations to achieve," Zawahiri insisted.[66] "The banner of the Caliphate" would thus "flutter nobly after a long absence" from Al-Andalus (referring to southern Spain) to East Turkistan (referring to areas in western China) and beyond. Muslim lands would be liberated and God's way on earth implemented.[67]

Military operations against Taliban-ruled Afghanistan were thus not presented as a response to 9/11 (which Al-Qaeda presented as a just reaction to US aggression) but rather as something inevitable, a continuation of an existential struggle for Islam, and a symptom of the world order created by the West and its historic thirst for ever greater territorial expanse and riches. "It has become crystal clear that the West in general, and the US in particular, harbour an implacable, incredible Crusader hatred against Islam," bin Ladin announced shortly after the US and allied invasion of Afghanistan in the wake of 9/11.[68] "This war [in Afghanistan]," he argued, "is similar to the previous crusades, led by Richard the Lion-Heart, [King Frederick] Barbarossa of Germany and Louis [IX] of France. In the present age, they rally behind [president] Bush."[69]

The above examples show how holistic, intertwined grievances, representing a cosmic and zero-sum clash between Al-Qaeda and its enemies, replaced the more specific local and limited issues emphasized during the 1990s. The rather precarious assumption made was that the Al-Qaeda leaders could successfully appeal to a global sense of Muslim identity, tie together grievances, and channel sympathy for ostensibly common causes toward acquiescence and support for the *mujahideen* vanguard. A proliferation of topics addressed, however, risked the dilution of overall message potency and loss of consistency over time. Fortunately for the Al-Qaeda leadership, its physical flight from Afghanistan and the pressure of coalition efforts (now with partial Pakistani support) coincided with a set of events that proved to be invaluable rallying calls. For instance, rendition programs and prisoner abuse cases were presented as further evidence to support the movement, and the images that emerged of detainee abuse in places like Abu Ghraib appeared to strengthen Al-Qaeda's case that America applied human rights selectively.[70]

Furthermore, as has been widely reported in analyses of the Iraq war, the decision to invade provided the Al-Qaeda leaders with a propaganda victory, and this was clearly evident from the leadership's statements from this period. The invasion was presented as confirmation of wider hostility and animosity toward Islam, an argument that appeared weaker when related to Afghanistan, Chechnya, Kashmir, and other isolated conflicts alone, and aggressive determination to protect Israel. The invasion was portrayed, in bin Ladin's words, as a "scheme of fragmenting and ripping apart [the Muslim] nation, looting its resources and wealth, and preparing for the establishment of the greater State of Israel after expelling the Palestinians from it."[71] In this sense, the emotional appeal of the Palestinian cause as a rallying cry for further support was utilized to highlight the importance of completing these more limited objectives successfully. Iraq would thus become the "fortress of Islam,"[72] which could launch operations against Israel, once secured.[73] Message elements linking ongoing developments and preoccupations of Al-Qaeda in the region, especially in Iraq, with the plight of Palestinians also became prominent during outbursts of violence between Israel and its neighbors, for instance during the 2006 Lebanon War and, later, in the wake of Israel's "Operation Cast Lead" (December 2008–January 2009) in Gaza.

Muslims were urged to detect a pattern, rather than a set of isolated events whereby their homelands would inevitably be next in line in US and Western-Zionist efforts to colonize the Muslim world. The aim would be to divide and plunder the Arabian Peninsula, Egypt, Syria, Sudan, and even Iran.[74] The aim was to create and secure "a huge Jewish super state," bin Ladin argued at the time.[75] The Al-Qaeda leadership's grievance narrative, therefore, combines values and genuine cases of hardship and suffering with a more overarching conspiracy theory that binds these various elements together.

Al-Qaeda's counter-narrative

In addition to describing what they felt was wrong with the status quo, both Zawahiri and bin Ladin made a particular effort to undermine the credibility of Al-Qaeda's primary adversaries. This would also serve to weaken any efforts of the United States and the West to design "counter-narratives" aimed at discrediting and reducing the potential appeal of Al-Qaeda's message. The fact that counterterrorism policy-makers are searching for an attractive and effective counter-narrative, to be deployed as part of a wider set of policies, appears to reflect the perceived role that ideological material and arguments play in inspiring militant activists, potentially fomenting support for the prescribed violent extremist agenda.

In turn, the Al-Qaeda leadership has sought to undermine the credibility of the West and its allies by accusing these parties of dualism, double standards, and hypocrisy. According to Al-Qaeda, the United States and its allies apply legal codes and standards selectively, according to their interests, to serve the Zionist call and in order to harm Islam. As the case is presented in Al-Qaeda leadership statements, democracy is good if the results produce regimes that are favorable to the United States and friendly toward Israel, but not when they are Islamic, such as in Algeria or Palestine. According to the Al-Qaeda narrative, pressure is applied on some countries suspected of foul play during electoral campaigns, such as Zimbabwe, but not in relation to a series of shambolic Afghan elections, because focusing on the latter would not be in the interest of the West. America calls for democracy, the Al-Qaeda leaders observe, but yet it has a record of embracing tyrants in Egypt, Saudi Arabia, Yemen, and elsewhere. Force, coercion, and aggression should be used to stem the proliferation of nuclear weapons, the Al-Qaeda leaders note, but not against Israel or India. Nor should the powers that established the United Nations give up their weapons, especially not the United States, the only country that has ever used them, as the Al-Qaeda leaders are keen to remind their audience. America also has laws that, according to Zawahiri, "permit the attacking of the honourable prophet and the noble Koran with the claim of freedom of expression," but, he complains, these principles do not seem to apply when Jews are being criticized.[76]

According to the Al-Qaeda narrative, the United States and the West push for UN resolutions relating to Lebanon and elsewhere to be enforced, as Israel is threatened, but not when Israel itself is condemned. The United States pretends to be a vanguard of human rights, Al-Qaeda complains, yet takes part in such abuses against Muslims. America fights offensive wars in the name of capturing war criminals, while it protects and finances others, according to bin Ladin and Zawahiri. The UN and the international community cry over Darfur, the Al-Qaeda leaders lament, but these actors do nothing when Muslims are being massacred.[77] Finally, Al-Qaeda warns of lies and double standards when it comes to America's counterterrorism campaign against the group. America and its allies invaded Iraq to destroy Al-Qaeda, according to the leadership messages, but "since when has Iraq been the home of al-Qaeda? It is the land of all Muslims," as bin Ladin reminded his audiences toward the end of 2004.[78]

More recently, America has launched a campaign of targeted assassinations combined with efforts to "raise illusions that Al-Qaeda is getting weaker." But, Zawahiri warned, "Obama and the US leaders are deceiving themselves and their people by limiting the battle with Muslims to certain individuals, an organization, or several organizations and close their eyes to an apparent fact that they are facing the jihadist rising Islamic ummah."[79]

Efforts to undermine the character and discourse of the adversary, therefore, are not deployed by the United States and its allies alone. The Al-Qaeda leadership has also directed parts of its message to this end. Furthermore, in terms of its diagnostic focus, what constitutes the necessary fluidity of Realpolitik for one side, therefore, can be used to present the international order as inherently unjust, by others. In this sense, the Al-Qaeda leadership moves beyond specific grievances relating to perceived Muslim constituencies to a wider geopolitical repertoire to display the apparent falsehood and hypocrisy of the West.

Enemies far and near: Confused priorities

As mentioned, bin Ladin and Zawahiri generally offered more breadth in terms of problem diagnosis in the period after the 9/11 attacks than before, even though specific developments such as the Iraq War, Gaza wars and embargoes, and the 2006 Lebanon War would focus the narrative in geographic terms during particular events. However, matters relating to Saudi Arabia and Egypt—respectively bin Ladin's and Zawahiri's place of origin and focus of initial activism—continued to feature intermittently.[80] Many of Zawahiri's messages addressed the situation in Egypt at least to some degree. Additionally, Zawahiri placed increasing emphasis on matters relating to Pakistan from around 2005 onward, as local support from within the Al-Qaeda leadership's new haven was crucial.[81] Association with America and the distant enemy was ever present, however. After all, according to Zawahiri, Egypt's dictatorship was "imposed on the [Egyptian] people by America."[82]

In terms of diagnosing the source of grievance, however, Zawahiri's distant- and near-enemy distinctions have often been ambiguous, and his prioritization in this regard is nowhere near as clear as that of the late Egyptian jihadist Mohammed Faraj, for example, who made a sharp distinction between local and immediate adversaries versus more distant threats that were to be addressed only after the local enemies had been subdued. By joining bin Ladin in the World Islamic Front, Zawahiri signed up—publically at least—to a strategy that emphasized the distant enemy of the United States over impious local regimes and domestic sources of corruption.[83] However, Zawahiri's own messages in this respect were often unclear in their prioritization. Many of Zawahiri's communiqués would, as noted above, target America and the West directly and blame them for the situation in Pakistan, Egypt, and elsewhere, while in other messages, Zawahiri would trace the causal origins of many of the grievances highlighted to domestic developments, rather than external "oppression" or "corruptive influence."

Indeed, Zawahiri never fully abandoned local causes and domestic enemies that prompted him to embrace militant Islamism in the first place. Zawahiri's native Egypt, in particular, frequently reemerged in the statements even when the topic was ostensibly more global. In his written rebuttal of former EIJ leader "Dr Fadl's" denunciation of Al-Qaeda, for instance, Zawahiri emphasized the need to "establish a *mujahidin* Islamic state in Egypt that will seek to liberate Palestine and every Muslim land, eliminate corruption, establish justice and restore Egypt's historical role of defending Islam and the Muslim people," adding "this benefit is greater than the loss represented by the shedding of some innocent blood."[84] The primary objective was to consolidate the Islamic state in Egypt prior to launching operations in support of Palestinians.

In terms of communicating enemy targets to followers, much of Zawahiri's work, therefore, focused on *both* near and distant enemies. In what is arguably his clearest strategic treatise, *Knights under the Banner of the Prophet*, Zawahiri "reemphasized" and "reiterated" that focusing on the domestic enemy *alone* will not be feasible "at this stage." It was thus necessary, *at this stage*, as Zawahiri put it, to target the distant enemy too.[85] Jihad was to be waged against these "original infidels" in addition to apostate rulers in the lands of Islam, those who failed to rule according to shariah and befriended Christians and Jews.[86] Although not dismissing the distant enemy, therefore, Zawahiri refused to differentiate between foreign invaders and their "domestic agents" in terms of prioritization.[87] This contrasts much of bin Ladin's core argument when it comes to defining enemies, although this narrative too suffered a degree of "hybridization" toward the end. By contrast (and in an apparent contradiction with the remainder of that particular statement), Zawahiri's "glad tidings" to Egyptians, Tunisians, and Libyans during the Arab Spring called for the targeting of the distant enemy of the Zionist-American allies first and foremost. Only when this "invading enemy breaks, then, by Allah's permission, their agents and others, who seek their help and emboldening, will also break. So let us focus our efforts on this Zio-American invading enemy and its agents," Zawahiri insisted.[88] The political groupings that emerged during the Arab revolutions, Zawahiri argued, neglected to recall the fact that the dictatorships of Libya, Tunisia, Egypt, and Yemen had "all been appointed by America." Even the Islamist parties "talk only about the Zionist Entity and overlook or neglect the fact that America is the leader of the criminals that participated in the crime of establishing Israel," Zawahiri complained.[89] All efforts would thus have to be on targeting the American hegemon. The timing of this shift in emphasis toward the far enemy during the Arab Spring in particular, the pivotal event of resistance against local rulers in the region, seems baffling and far removed from the course of events as they transpired on the ground.

This ambiguity in enemy hierarchies and prioritization, or what Hegghammer termed "hybridization," [90] has been a feature of much of Zawahiri's output since he ventured beyond an exclusive focus on violent extremism in Egypt. Although a shifting focus over time is not surprising and not necessarily problematic in terms of overall consistency, the impact of the message appears more compromised when, as in the case of Zawahiri's collection of communiqués especially, the same dire state of affairs is traced back to a variety of potential causes—external and domestic—with shifting priorities in terms of the supposed primary causes. For instance, in December 2005, Zawahiri argued that there was no way to achieve reform "except by uprooting these corrupt and corrupting [local] regimes, and by establishing a Muslim government that will protect rights, defend sanctities, institute justice, spread consultation, raise the banner of jihad, and confront the invaders, the foes of Islam."[91] A video statement issued a year later emphasized similar priorities: "It is the duty of the Ummah's vanguard to strive for change, because getting rid of these puppets is the doorway to deliverance and *the beginning* of the serious Jihadi challenge to the Crusader invasion."[92] Much as Faraj would argue, therefore, the emphasis of activism was on local ills, prior to attacking the distant enemy. In one of his "interviews" with *As-Sahab* published three months later, however, Zawahiri appeared to swap these priorities, arguing:

> The road to reform, and Allah knows best, requires, in the Arabian Peninsula and the other Islamic lands, work on two plans. The first is in the near term, and seeks to strike Crusader and Zionist interests so that the ground erupts in flames under the feet of the Zionists and Crusaders in our countries and theirs and everywhere we are able to strike their interests until they leave our countries and stop their continuous and increasing interference in our affairs. And the second plan is for the longer term, and depends on two pillars: the first is preparation for the confrontation, by going forth to arenas of battle like Iraq, Afghanistan and Somalia, and the second pillar is diligent work to change the corrupt and corruptive regimes through invitation, incitement, mobilization and planning, and to persevere in that however much time it takes or sacrifice it requires.[93]

Periods where the leaders focused on global issues appeared to muddle these priorities even further. For instance, in a number of statements shortly before his death, bin Ladin became particularly preoccupied with environmental issues, climate change, natural disasters (which he claimed killed more people than wars), and relief work.[94] One of these statements even included tacit recognition of the efforts of the hated UN to address this threat and criticism of Arab elites for failing to realize their duty in this respect.[95]

Efforts to reach out to the "global oppressed"—including non-Muslims—also seemed to contradict the animosity toward non-Muslims expressed in some of the more belligerent statements as well as through Al-Qaeda's indiscriminate targeting. For instance, in his third "interview" with *As-Sahab*, published in May 2007, Zawahiri appealed to "blacks in America, people of color, American Indians, Hispanics, and all the weak and oppressed in North and South America, in Africa and Asia, and all over the world." Al-Qaeda, Zawahiri insisted, was "waging Jihad to lift oppression from all of mankind, because Allah has ordered us never to accept oppression, whatever it may be."[96] A year later, in his second reply to the Internet-based "open meeting" appeal, Zawahiri sought to develop this point further by stressing the way in which Al-Qaeda was providing a "great service to the human community" in protecting "mankind" from the oppressive West, its immoral desires, and treacherous allies. The mainstay of Al-Qaeda's discourse, however, elevates the leaders' version of an Islamist society above any other societal forms. In terms of Al-Qaeda's track record, moreover, the leadership's involvement in the 1998 East Africa embassy bombings—that killed over 200 mostly poor, nonwhite Africans and injured thousands—hardly seems to fit this image of fairness and sympathy for the poor and disenfranchised. Another contradiction is the Al-Qaeda leadership's approach to China. In an interview with a Pakistani newspaper in 1998, for instance, bin Ladin emphasized the extent to which China too was being manipulated and abused by the American hegemon and urged the People's Republic to "be more careful of the US and the West," adding: "China must use its force against the United States and Israel and should be friendly towards Muslims."[97] Yet numerous subsequent statements from Al-Qaeda called for armed insurrection against Chinese authorities in "East Turkestan," referring to the area of western China inhabited by the Sunni Islamic Uyghur people.[98]

A review of Al-Qaeda's leadership statements over time, therefore, reveals a comprehensive and somewhat confusing list of enemies. The most prominent alleged culprits are listed in Table 4.2.

Table 4.2 Al-Qaeda's grievance narrative: Enemies and targets identified

- The United States (in general, or more specifically, e.g., US media, corporations, US politicians)
- The West/"Zionist-Crusader alliance"
- Israel
- Jews
- Christians, Christian religious leaders
- Hindus
- India
- The United Nations
- Corrupt or "apostate" regimes in Muslim-majority countries, their supporters, the government bureaucracy, army, and support mechanism
- Palestinian Authority, Fatah
- Iraqi police, military, National Guard, government supporters, "Awakening Councils"—after invasion of 2003
- The United Kingdom (for fighting in Iraq and Afghanistan, closeness to United States, role in establishing Israel and colonial past, detaining radical preachers, protecting Salman Rushdie, and other issues)
- France (in relation to prevention of wearing veil, presence of troops in Afghanistan and Mali, publication of Mohammed cartoons, etc.)
- Spain (mainly for possession of Ceuta and Melilla; fighting in Iraq, Afghanistan)
- International media and news organizations (both for spreading "anti-Muslim propaganda" and "immoral" material)
- International relief agencies
- Russia (especially for fighting in Chechnya)
- Multinational corporations
- International communications companies
- Denmark, Norway (and to a lesser extent: Germany, France, and European and American publics)—for publication of Mohammed cartoons
- Australia (for taking part in operations in Afghanistan, and for its role in separation of East Timor from Indonesia)
- NATO
- Northern Alliance—and other militants fighting the Taliban
- Ethiopia and Kenya, as well as other members of the African Union
- Japan (for providing funds for Iraq War and other military operations)
- Iran (especially for supporting Shia militias in Iraq, working with coalition in Afghanistan, discrediting 9/11 attacks, and supporting Assad during the Syrian civil war)
- Serbia (early communications from bin Ladin)
- Yemeni Socialist Party (early communications from bin Ladin)

Some adversaries were referred to repeatedly throughout the period in question. "Key" enemies such as Israel and the United States were cited in practically all the statements analyzed. Some messages, however, discussed particular events or geographic locations, and the aggregate of these forms the "secondary" list of enemies and targets.

These long lists of grievances and identified perpetrators, as well as the shifting enemy hierarchies and competing trajectories of the messages, could impact upon the overall effectiveness and clarity of these appeals. The complexity of Al-Qaeda's problem diagnosis also calls for a particularly rich and well-articulated list of potential solutions and alternatives that address these problems. How have the Al-Qaeda leaders responded? The next chapter explores the solutions that the Al-Qaeda leaders have presented to address the various problems identified.

5

The solution

Long-term objectives and intermediate responses

Al-Qaeda was established as an activist movement. Presented as a vanguard, it seeks to guide the *ummah* through a revolutionary process that removes the shackles of the status quo. Presenting solutions to all the various problems identified therefore constitutes a vital part of Al-Qaeda's overall message. This concerns the delineation of alternatives, description of end goals, as well as the development of a framework for action, designed to incite participants to respond to diagnosed ailments and move toward recognition of end goals. The Al-Qaeda leadership communiqués are designed to inspire and mobilize support for the solutions offered. This chapter analyzes these solutions as presented in Zawahiri's and bin Ladin's statements. Some of these prescribed responses have remained unchanged throughout Al-Qaeda's lifetime. Other suggested solutions have evolved over the years, particularly as relates to the approach toward violence and targeting.

One part of Al-Qaeda's proposed solution to the identified problems that is clearly discernible in the leadership's statements is a description of the desired way forward and the sort of society and "end state" that would—according to this narrative—replace the status quo. These descriptions of the ultimate objective, however, are vague and probably serve the purpose to inspire potential followers rather than detailing particular societal aspects and other constructs that would replace the current order.

These references serve to underscore the supposedly pure and noble objectives that drive and inform the form of militancy and activism that the Al-Qaeda leaders also prescribe. Militants are reminded of what they are fighting for: something that goes beyond immediate tactical achievements and centers on a divine calling to implement a pious and just social order. That is the long-term goal.

In the short term, activists are urged to embrace violence as the principal tool with which to confront adversaries and sources of grievance. When bin Ladin's and Zawahiri's statements are studied in detail, however, it emerges that their approach toward violence (in terms of scope, direction, tactics, and targets) has evolved over the years. Caveats that were initially in place regarding the targeting of civilians, for instance, gradually disappeared, and the Al-Qaeda leaders had to grapple with the problematic issue of Muslim casualties in the violence they had sanctioned or endorsed. This chapter focuses on the responses and the alternatives to the problems identified that have been delineated in the Al-Qaeda leadership statements through the years. The chapter begins by discussing the ultimate objective that is presented in these communiqués before exploring Al-Qaeda's approach to activism and its justifications for violence.

The end goal

At their most fundamental, the solutions the Al-Qaeda leaders have presented in response to the current state of affairs consist of alternative societal and cultural constructions. According to the Salafi narrative, these are based on a shift in the balance of power from secular or impious forces to righteous communities that would operate in accordance with religious doctrine and law.

At its most basic, Al-Qaeda's "solution" to the problems identified consists of (1) ridding the Islamic world of alien, "occupying, robbing" non-Islamic influences, separating the pious and non-pious; and (2) ensuring Muslims have freedom to rule their lands according to the shariah, control their own resources, and promote virtue and prevent vice.[1] This process would ultimately culminate in the creation of a new and pious society. Although substantively consistent, these references often lack detail or any meaningful descriptions in terms of how this is to be implemented. The answer to all administrative and judicial conundrums would be "Islam" in its purest form. In 2004, for instance, bin Ladin remarked:

> The religion of Islam encompasses all the affairs of life, including the religious and the worldly, such as economic, military, and political affairs, as well as the scales by which we weigh the actions of men—rulers, ulema, and others—and how to deal with the ruler in line with the rules set by God for him and which the ruler should not violate. Therefore, it becomes clear to us that the solution lies in adhering to the religion of God, by which God granted us pride in the past centuries, and installing a strong and faithful leadership that applies the Koran among us and raises the true banner of jihad.[2]

Thus, full and unhindered implementation of religious law in its purest form would be the organizing principle of all facets of society. "Islam is one unit that cannot be divided … If someone believes in a part of it and rejects another part, then he becomes an infidel and his prayers and fasting will be to no avail," bin Ladin warned.[3] The Islamic government would, therefore, abide by the "heavenly" creed, relying on *shura* (consultation), whereby the *ummah* refers to the shariah to judge the rulers, who are also selected and held to account by them.[4] The role of the scholar would thus be central. A just scholar, according to bin Ladin, would be a "role model" for his *ummah*, ensure *fatawa* (juristic rulings) were sound, avoid temptations, have the courage to speak out against that which is offensive, and stay away from impious rulers.[5]

Responding to common criticisms that this vision called for the establishment of an authoritarian theocracy, Zawahiri insisted: "we are not calling for a dictatorship or despotism or tyranny in the name of religion. We are only calling the ummah to return to ruling by shura; justice; non-partisanship and elimination of discrimination between people except on the basis of *taqwa* [fear of Allah]." The Muslim *ummah*, according to Zawahiri, would be allowed to "elect its ruler and be able to hold him to account, just as was witnessed in the time of the *khilafah*."[6] Public participation in decision-making would thus not be prohibited, if conducted in the proper manner. "We Muslims," according to bin Ladin, "believe it is the nation's right to elect its president and we believe in *shura*, however we believe that the Western democracy [is] illegitimate heresy from the Islamic point of view."[7] Zawahiri similarly argued that elections under Islamic constitutions should be welcomed.[8] The "proper and just" government Al-Qaeda was seeking to install would allow "the Ummah to participate in the selection of its rulers and hold them to account," Zawahiri argued in 2011. The *ummah*'s representatives would be inclusive and "just in distributing the wealth of the Ummah, preventing its theft, prohibiting depravity and immorality."[9]

In a few statements, the leaders also suggested that under this form of governance, non-Muslims would be allowed to practice their faith under the protection of shariah, so long as they respected the Islamic authority (the *dhimmi* contract).[10] Indeed, had the Holocaust been planned closer to Muslim lands, Jews could have sought protection there, according to bin Ladin.[11] Although strict separation according to the principle of *al-wala wa-l-bara* would be in force, a small number of references can be found suggesting isolation would not be absolute. Oil could perhaps be sold abroad, as long as the price was determined by Muslims. After all, "we are not going to drink it," bin Ladin once remarked.[12]

Regardless of any partial pluralism of the described societal ideal types, all elaborations of the nature of this envisaged society, however, are exclusive, rigid, and tyrannical: "one must demand that it be the *shariah* that rules ... rather than it itself being ruled over by other systems. That its authority not be in need of any referendum and not open to cancellation, not have to compete with alternatives as an equal and not be subject to amendments and substitutions," Zawahiri insisted in 2009.[13] "Muslims must be aware of the facts, and the most important is the *aqeedah* of *tawheed* [the monotheistic creed], which must be the ruling authority in all systems."[14] The leader of the faithful will be the Imam of the caliphate state, which "every faithful Muslim seeks to establish," according to Zawahiri.[15] A Caliphate could be created once the "existing" emirates in Afghanistan and Iraq had been consolidated and others established. *Hudud* (shariah punishment) would, Zawahiri insisted, be implemented immediately,[16] but compliance would not be a problem as, according to bin Ladin, "a guilty man would only be happy if he was justly punished."[17]

As mentioned, these descriptions of the desired end state are, perhaps deliberately, ambiguous. When the objective is to inspire and mobilize, it seems, general descriptions of a better future with vague delineations of the ultimate system that will replace the status quo are thought to suffice. Thus, according to Al-Qaeda's vision, there would be holistic, legislative, political, and social reforms,[18] economic and social justice, with no taxes, apart from the 2.5 percent *zakat*.[19] More detailed accounts could expose this part of the argument to criticism from qualified Islamic scholars or prompt potential participants to doubt the attractiveness of the desired end goal.

Desperate to present an alternative to any pro-democratic voices that were greeted with so much enthusiasm in the Western media during the Arab Spring in Egypt and elsewhere, Zawahiri simply reiterated the basic features of an envisaged pious society that had been communicated before. He insisted that the path forged by Al-Qaeda promised

> to fulfill the hopes of the Muslim *ummah* of the establishment of a free Muslim nation in the Islamic world, which governs with the *shariah*, promotes justice, implements [the] *shura*... system in which the *ummah* chooses its rulers without domination, forgery or rigging, holds them to account, enjoining them with good and forbidding them from evil, and guards Muslim resources from domestic thieves and their international masters who loot the treasures of our lands.[20]

This societal vision and ideal type seems somewhat shattered, however, when we consider Al-Qaeda's endorsement of existing regimes that are presented as models for others to follow. The most obvious example is that of the Taliban and their "Islamic Emirate" in Afghanistan, although the Al-Qaeda leaders also sought to present the Islamic State of Iraq in similar terms, as examples to replicate and follow.[21]

Although infrequent and vague at first, numerous references to the Taliban underlined Al-Qaeda's public endorsement of the movement. Al-Qaeda was obviously dependent on its host after its exodus from Sudan, and its leadership had pledged allegiance to Mullah Mohammed Omar, the spiritual leader of the Taliban. Some early references to the Taliban appeared somewhat cautious. In a March 1997 interview, for instance, bin Ladin claimed that he believed the Taliban to be "sincere in their attempts to enforce Islamic religious law" and that there had been an "obvious improvement" in Afghanistan since they consolidated their power.[22] In another interview from this period, however, bin Ladin had to reject reports of Taliban authorities banning girls from receiving an education.[23] Public support for the Taliban became more prominent after the August 1998 bombings in East Africa. A few months after the attacks, bin Ladin praised the Taliban, who, he argued, had "established the system of God on God's land."[24] They were unquestionably a legitimate force that had secured "peace and restored the confidence in the public," bin Ladin insisted.[25]

Zawahiri dismissed suggestions that the Taliban were in any way an oppressive or tyrannical force. The people of Afghanistan "supported and accepted the Islamic Emirate," he insisted, as it replaced the "deterioration and damage" of the previous era. That Taliban rule was welcomed could be seen in the ways in which "citizens in the various provinces and districts have welcomed and incited the Taliban to come to them to purge their areas of those who spread mischief"; from the fact that "two thousand scholars at the Qandahar conference pledged allegiance to leader of the faithful, Mullah Mohammad Omar"; from that "the Islamic Emirate took control over large parts of Afghanistan"; and from the extent to which other jihadist groups had also stressed these factors.[26] In any case, their implementation of divine protocol rendered questioning their authority impermissible. For this reason it was "compulsory upon all the Muslims all over the world to help Afghanistan and to make *hijra* [emigrate] to this land, because it is from this land that we will dispatch our armies … to smash the *kuffar* all over the world," bin Ladin proclaimed.[27]

Taliban rule over Afghanistan (and to a far lesser extent, the Islamic State of Iraq's "reign" in several Iraqi districts) was thus endorsed as an intermediate, partial success in the establishment of a caliphate, even though some endorsements might have had as much to do with strategic expediency as with doctrinal recognition. The ultimate goal, as an inspirational target and consistent undercurrent throughout the material under review, was, however, more ambitious and expansive. Aside from Zawahiri's aspirational prescriptions in his messages of "Hope and Glad Tidings" in response to the Arab Spring and other similar communiqués emphasizing the "virtuous" alternative, one of the clearer elaborations of the ultimate end goal was presented in an open letter, "Calling for a Global Islamic State," written by bin Ladin in early 2001. Addressing the "sons and daughters of Islam," bin Ladin concluded:

> Today, every member of the Muslim world agrees that all the Muslim countries of the world having geographical boundaries on the basis of nationality, geography, religious discord, color and race, should be merged into one Muslim state, where men do not rule men. There should be one caliph for the whole state whose capital should be Mecca. There should be one currency and defense for this state and the Holy Koran should be its constitution. The name that has been proposed for this vast state is Global Muslim State. I want to congratulate you that by the grace of God, from today, we have begun the task of achieving a highly important and strong target of domination of Islam over all other religions.[28]

Although agreeing with these principles, Zawahiri, of course, had his own particular geographic focus, which shaped his vision of the end goal. Thus, in the same year that bin Ladin published his letter calling for a "Global Islamic State" with its capital in Mecca, for instance, Zawahiri's *Knights under the Banner of the Prophet* became available, predicting an "earth-shattering event" which would signal the "establishment of an Islamic caliphate [centered] in Egypt." "If God wills it, such a state in Egypt, with all its weight in the heart of the Islamic world, could lead the Islamic world in a jihad against the West."[29] In April 2013, Zawahiri issued a statement titled "Unifying the Word Toward the Word of Monotheism," with the specific aim of emphasizing the need for unity and disregarding national boundaries and borders. But even here, the Al-Qaeda leader emphasized that a primary objective of such a unified uprising would be to reestablish "Egypt's leading role in the Arab and Islamic worlds."[30] It seems hard to envisage that his predecessor as Al-Qaeda leader would have embraced such an emphasis. It would appear that geographic biases and parochialisms seep through even here, where the topic of discussion is Al-Qaeda's vision for a "global" Islamic state transcending traditional state borders.

Although essentially notional and abstract, these descriptions of the desired end goal play an important part in the communication of the Al-Qaeda leaders' message as they highlight the noble justifications behind mobilization and activism. These messages remind audiences of the promised ultimate reward and the collective benefits that the *ummah* will reap if the vanguard is adequately supported. They form the context for Al-Qaeda's glorification of violence, which is at the heart of the response advocated by its leadership.

Indiscriminate violence

Justifying violence

The Al-Qaeda leadership has strongly advocated a strategy of increasingly indiscriminate violence in pursuit of its long- and short-term goals. Al-Qaeda has implemented this strategy on several occasions through planning and executing dramatic mass-casualty terrorist attacks and through supporting and encouraging affiliates and followers to do the same. The Al-Qaeda leadership's approach toward violence has evolved over the years, particularly as relates to the forms of engagement and violent activism deemed acceptable, commendable, and effective. The essence of Al-Qaeda's argument in favor of violence is based on a fundamental belief in the utility of violent attacks, intertwined with evolving debates concerning the legitimacy of a given set of targets and methods. This campaign of violence, moreover, is invariably presented as defensive.[31] Violence is seen as a necessary response in the face of an existential threat, and, building upon Azzam's thesis of jihad as an individual duty (*fardh al-ayn*), it is seen as the responsibility of each true Muslim to ensure the *mujahideen* are successful, their ranks filled with new recruits, and the vanguard well funded and supplied.[32]

44 ways to support jihad

Tactical denials

Despite Al-Qaeda's unquestionable association with violence and its campaign to spread jihad beyond the Afghan war against the Soviets, bin Ladin was surprisingly cautious at first in claiming responsibility for specific attacks. Zawahiri, of course, brought a legacy of involvement in terrorism as he joined Al-Qaeda and was more unequivocal in his celebration of particular attacks. During the 1990s, bin Ladin would only endorse attacks attributed to Al-Qaeda and not claim responsibility. He insisted the principal role of the leadership was to instigate militant operations, not orchestrate attacks.[33] This included attacks for which Al-Qaeda would later proudly claim responsibility. It seems most likely that this initial reluctance to acknowledge responsibility for attacks was based on the relationship the Al-Qaeda leadership had with its Taliban hosts. Senior figures within the Taliban movement in Afghanistan had sought to rein in their guest by asking bin Ladin to avoid engaging in "political matters." This request—and bin Ladin's reluctance to adhere to these conditions—caused some friction between Al-Qaeda and the Taliban, and bin Ladin's frustration regarding the matter was palpable in some of the interviews he gave in the summer of 2001.[34] In this light, the Al-Qaeda leadership's initial reluctance to claim credit for the September 11, 2001, attacks can, in all likelihood, be traced back to this need to protect the Afghan sanctuary and the alliance with the Taliban. Bin Ladin reportedly claimed, in an interview with a Pakistani newspaper shortly after the 9/11 attacks:

> I have already said that I am not involved in the 11 September attacks in the United States. As a Muslim, I try my best to avoid telling a lie. Neither [have] I had any knowledge of these attacks nor [did] I consider the killing of innocent women, children, and other humans as an appreciable act. Islam strictly forbids causing harm to innocent women, children, and other people. Such a practice is forbidden even in the course of a battle... I have already said that we are against the American system, not against its people.[35]

Other interviews and announcements in the immediate aftermath of the attacks also aimed to distance Al-Qaeda from the 9/11 attacks, variously claiming no knowledge of the attacks or blaming a US-Jewish conspiracy.[36] Context would suggest that these were tactical denials, perhaps to buy time and facilitate preparations prior to inevitable US reprisals, rather than sincere doubts regarding the merits of mass-casualty attacks. Indeed, bin Ladin denied involvement in the 1998 East Africa embassy bombings in their immediate aftermath but began to at least endorse and welcome them when the limited impact of the lackluster US response became clear.[37]

By contrast, as soon as the extent of US and coalition efforts to target the Taliban and Al-Qaeda in Afghanistan became known, which resulted in the removal of the Taliban from power, the Al-Qaeda leadership began praising the 9/11 attacks and claiming responsibility for them. By that time they had nothing to lose and everything to gain by claiming credit for such spectacular attacks against the United States and its allies. The "martyrdom" of the hijackers was celebrated, their actions presented as examples for others to follow, and those who criticized the nature of the attacks were condemned as American stooges.[38] Later messages provided more detail of how the attacks were supposedly organized and what had inspired the specific tactics displayed.[39] Bin Ladin and Zawahiri also presented other attacks, generally attributed to sympathizers and affiliates as part of Al-Qaeda's grand strategy. The 2002 Bali bombings were tied to warnings against Australian involvement in East Timor and presented as a reciprocal response to "crusader aggression."[40] The Madrid bombings were discussed in a similar way,[41] and while investigators and analysts were still assessing the level of the Al-Qaeda core's involvement in the 2005 London bombings, Zawahiri declared that "the blessed London raid is one of the raids that the Qaedat al-Jihad organization had the honor of carrying out against the British Crusader arrogance."[42] A change in Al-Qaeda's physical situation thus appears to have prompted this shift in the way in which specific attacks were approached and acknowledged.

A detailed analysis of bin Ladin's and Zawahiri's media output, however, reveals a more subtle and significant change when it comes to assessing Al-Qaeda's approach to violence. When these messages are studied over time, a gradual escalation emerges in relation to Al-Qaeda's public justifications for violent methods. Limitations and caveats on the use of violence that were initially cited in the Al-Qaeda leaders' statements disappeared. New types of attacks and target sets were added to the list of "legitimate" forms of jihad and an evermore elaborate narrative justifying the use of violence was developed. Perhaps as a consequence of some of these media efforts, the Al-Qaeda leaders were soon confronted by the backlash caused by the excessive use and reach of violent attacks by the organization and its affiliates. Any analysis of Al-Qaeda's approach toward violence thus needs to include an examination of whatever limitations concerning the use of violence were initially cited or are still regarded as valid by the Al-Qaeda leadership and to what extent these differ from the physical reality of Al-Qaeda-associated terrorism.

Killing civilians

When we look at bin Ladin's early public messages, it emerges that he rarely alluded to the importance of violent attack as a valid activist method. Although his open letters to Saudi leaders would declare the need for regime change in Saudi Arabia, acts of violence—especially those targeting noncombatants or Muslims—were not discussed. Toward the later half of the 1990s, however, bin Ladin began publicly to endorse a violent uprising against US troops based in the Arabian Peninsula. Early communiqués called for the "expulsion" of civilian contractors from the area, rather than murder.[43] Nonetheless, bin Ladin celebrated the 1996 Al-Khobar bombings, noting that "only Americans were killed," rather than Saudi citizens,[44] adding "if liberating my land is called terrorism, this is a great honor for me."[45] The Khobar bombings, and similar attacks, constituted "praiseworthy terrorism" against "thieves": a defensive response to the "blameworthy terrorism" of America and its allies and the kind committed by "thieves against nations."[46] Terror, according to bin Ladin, could be a force for good, similar to when a police used force to contain a criminal. This was the terrorism of Al-Qaeda: "we practice the good terrorism which stops them [the Americans and Israelis] from killing our children in Palestine and elsewhere."[47] This seems similar to the arguments put forward by Abu Musab Al-Suri concerning *irhab mahmud*, "terrorism by the righteous who have been unjustly treated."[48] Bin Ladin's early justifications for violence, therefore, contained clear limitations on scope and targeting, including distinctions based on nationality and separation of combatants and noncombatants.

Distinctions between soldier and civilian, however vague, began to disappear with the 1998 declaration of war from the "World Islamic Front," where US and allied soldiers and civilians, "wherever they can be found," were equally legitimate targets.[49] Bin Ladin reiterated these calls in subsequent interviews and statements, although some variation persisted with messages issued a month after the declaration variously calling for the "expulsion" of the American "invaders"[50] or the total "annihilation" of America.[51] Corresponding with an expanded geographical scope, as mentioned above, bin Ladin's messages toward the end of the decade suggested more expansive fields of jihad against India and other identified enemies,[52] as well as jihad in "every street" of the US.[53] Bin Ladin claimed, in a 1999 interview with John Miller, that Al-Qaeda would not "differentiate between those dressed in military uniforms and civilians; they are all targets."[54] "All Americans are our enemies, not just the ones who fight us directly but also the ones who pay their taxes," bin Ladin argued in a statement issued in January 1999, practically incriminating vast swathes of the US population.[55] "The man is a fighter," bin Ladin elaborated further in an interview later that year, "whether he carries arms or helps kill us by paying taxes and by gathering information." Furthermore, he pointed out, "almost three quarters of the US people support [President] Clinton's strikes against Iraq [Operation Desert Fox]. They are people who increase their support for their president when he commits cardinal sins. They are a lowly people who do not at all understand the meaning of values."[56] Voters, taxpayers, and others were not, therefore, simple noncombatants: they constituted a "support network" for US aggression and contributed to its military machine.

For Zawahiri and his Egyptian colleagues in jihad, the debate surrounding the possible targeting of civilians had been ongoing for some time. In the wake of an attack on the Egyptian embassy in Islamabad in November 1995, orchestrated by the Egyptian Islamic Jihad (EIJ), Zawahiri penned an article in a local newspaper insisting that embassy workers had become legitimate targets since they perceived government loyalty as superior to divine loyalty.[57] Later, the EIJ *Majlis-ash-Shura* (consultative council) issued a lengthy treatise that justified civilian targeting. Noting how the Prophet's armies had used catapults in the seventh-century (CE) siege of Ta'if, it argued that indiscriminate attacks under contemporary circumstances could thus be legitimized. Although recognizing that reading of the Hadith offered no concrete justification of killing "protected people," the authors opined that killing noncombatants would be justifiable "as long as there [would be] a need or an obligation for Muslims to do so, or if not striking leads to a delay to jihad." Muslims would have to be warned not to be close to potential targets of "tyrants," the document's authors argued, and were they to be killed, apologies were in order and, funds permitting, there would be financial compensation for the families of casualties.[58]

In an interview with a sympathetic reporter of a Pakistani daily in October 2001, bin Ladin conceded that the Prophet had banned the killing of women and children but argued this was not absolute. Citing part of a verse from the An-Nahl (16th) surah on the right to retaliate in kind against disbelievers, bin Ladin sought to justify the stance which has been prominent in the Al-Qaeda rhetoric ever since: that killing of women and children is permissible since "infidels purposely kill [Muslim] women and children."[59] Bin Ladin, however, justified the 9/11 attacks as strikes against economic and military installations, rather than civilian targets. After all, the World Trade Center was not a "children's school," he argued.[60] Even so, "if a child is above thirteen and wields a weapon against Muslims," bin Ladin claimed in another interview two months after the attacks, "then it is permitted to kill him."[61] This applied to Americans in particular, who were all seen as "active members" in the "crimes" committed against Muslims.[62]

Reciprocity is, therefore, central to the Al-Qaeda leadership's justification for the killing of noncombatants. On few occasions the Al-Qaeda leaders have sought to add to these claims of counteraggression and defensive responses an aura of fairness with the aim of convincing Muslim audiences that such claims were religiously sound given the multiple warnings made and the alternatives offered to adversaries.[63] In his aforementioned interview with John Miller, for instance, bin Ladin warned: "the only way for us to fend off these [American] assaults is to use similar means."[64] Americans "only understand the language of attacks and killings. Just as they're killing us, we have to kill them so that there will be a balance of terror."[65] The 9/11 attacks were thus only a "reaction to the continuous injustice and oppression being practiced against our sons in Palestine and Iraq and in Somalia and Southern Sudan and in other places."[66] This was "equal treatment."[67] How could "defending oneself and punishing the aggressor in kind, [be] objectionable terrorism? If it is such, then it is unavoidable for us," bin Ladin insisted.[68] Al-Qaeda, according to this argument, would have every right to reply in kind. "As you kill, you will be killed, and as you capture, you will be captured, and as you ruin our security, we will ruin your security," bin Ladin warned, adding: "and the one who started it has done the greater injustice."[69]

Behind the scenes, the Al-Qaeda leaders continued to struggle with formulating jurisprudential justifications for the level and nature of the violence displayed on September 11. Ramzi bin al-Shibh, one of the attack's organizers, drafted an internal memo titled "The Truth about the New Crusade: A Ruling on the Killing of Women and Children of the Non-Believers" declaring "The sanctity of women, children, and the elderly, is not absolute." Four scenarios would render killing "infidel" civilians legal according to his interpretation: (1) if the enemy had targeted Muslim civilians; (2) if Muslim regions were being invaded; (3) if noncombatants were supporting attacks on Muslims, "whether in action, word, or any other type of assistance"; or (4) if the enemy attacked with indiscriminate weaponry which did not differentiate between combatants and noncombatants.[70]

A justificatory narrative was thus being developed where theological constraints on the killing of noncombatants were circumvented by expanding the categories of combatants to include normal citizens who voiced an opinion in favor of certain policies, paid taxes, or voted for particular parties. Americans and other people in the West were accused of acquiescing "Jewish takeover" of the banking system, permitting arms manufacturers to operate, joining or supporting the armed forces, and other alleged acts of hostility which made them legitimate targets.[71] People thus became complicit by association or through indirect acts that rendered them "combatants." As with the 9/11 attacks, the London bombings in July 2005 also prompted the Al-Qaeda leaders to engage in further public deliberations about the permissibility of civilian targeting. In communiqués following the attacks, ordinary civilians were classified as "combatants," simply for respecting British judicial norms and the legitimacy of democratic institutions, regardless of opinion on foreign or domestic policy: in December 2005 Zawahiri claimed that the fact Britons had failed to "depose" their government demonstrated that they had no qualms with its policy output.[72] A year later he stated: "even those who oppose the policies [of the West], still consider the governments legitimate. Also, all the political parties in the West supported the creation of Israel."[73] As for Jews, they can all be targeted since "all Jews support Israel" and thus are in fact Zionists, according to Zawahiri's interpretation.[74]

The implication is, of course, that virtually any member of society could thus be legitimately killed, according to this reasoning. This does not constitute a radical rethink of religious protocols, nor is the debate sophisticated or original in any doctrinal sense. As far as Zawahiri's and bin Ladin's interpretations are concerned, rudimentary jurisprudential guidelines from religious texts on the killing of certain groups of people still broadly apply. All the leadership has tried to do is to gradually widen this category, muddle the scenarios for which they apply, and include ever more people as legitimate targets for attack, citing increasingly vague and all-encompassing allegations of complicity.

Such a broad approach to complicity and legitimized murder, however, would not work to justify Muslim deaths in Al-Qaeda's attacks. The fact that Muslims—the people Al-Qaeda pretended to protect—were being killed in attacks endorsed and planned by the leadership risked alienating any supporters that the group might have. Indeed, the issue of Muslim casualties as a result of Al-Qaeda's violence has exposed the leadership to criticism, even within the radical Islamist community itself, which has severely undermined its position. Both bin Ladin and Zawahiri were conscious of the imperative need to limit the damage of this criticism and to come up with some sort of narrative that allowed for Muslim deaths as a consequence of Al-Qaeda's militancy.

Muslim deaths

Rather than engaging in difficult doctrinal debates about the permissibility of killing Muslims, for which the leadership lacked religious qualifications, Zawahiri and bin Ladin have instead sought to redefine the concept of "Muslim" through their messages.

Again, much of the groundwork had already been done by the Egyptian jihadists and Zawahiri's former colleagues, who needed to justify killing embassy employees and the targeting of government officials as mentioned above. Since the Quran strictly forbids the shedding of Muslim blood, the obvious way to do this was to try and convince followers and a wider audience of the discourse that the deceased had committed such grave sins that they were no longer Muslims. This is the essence of the *takfiri* narrative. Various sections of the Muslim population are in this way branded "apostates" and legitimate enemies and targets, since they have strayed away from the true creed. Although attitude toward violence varies slightly, the communiqués consistently identify "treacherous" Muslims who can be targeted. Initially, and more notably throughout, the subjects in question are secular leaders of Muslim countries and their closest associates in the military and intelligence services, who had allied with the West. Aside from the political elite, the Al-Qaeda leaders frequently adopted *takfiri* rhetoric to denounce Iraqis and Pakistanis who cooperated with the West, the local governments, or those who generally failed to embrace and support the Islamists in the country.

Bin Ladin warned his "brothers in Iraq" at the dawn of the conflict that those who supported the Crusaders, even just with words, were "apostates and outside the community of Muslims," rendering it "permissible to spill their blood and take their property."[75] The killing of members of the government, army, security agencies, and National Guard was sanctioned, as "they are infidels"[76] and they should be "killed, regardless of their sect or tribe."[77] Al-Qaeda loyalists in Iraq did not hesitate to implement this strategy, going to such excesses that the central leadership became concerned over the resulting damage to its image, as described below.

Zawahiri proudly announced in a 2006 video statement that "the group Qaida al-Jihad in the Land of Two Rivers alone has carried out 800 martyrdom operations in 3 years, besides the sacrifices of the other *Mujahideen*, and this is what has broken the back of America in Iraq."[78] Yet, according to Riedel, more than three-fourths of Al-Qaeda-affiliated attacks in Iraq targeted Muslims, mostly (but not exclusively) the Shia.[79] One of the questions posed to Zawahiri for his "open meeting" initiative addressed precisely this record of violence against Muslims:

> Who is it who is killing with Your Excellency's blessing the innocents in Baghdad, Morocco and Algeria? Do you consider the killing of women and children to be jihad? I challenge you and your organization to do that in Tel Aviv. Why have you—to this day—not carried out any strike in Israel? Or is it easier to kill Muslims in the markets? Maybe it is necessary [for you] to take some geography lessons, because your maps only show the Muslims' states.[80]

Even Hamas criticized the excessive use of violence displayed by Al-Qaeda-endorsed elements in Iraq and beyond that resulted in Muslim deaths, such as Zarqawi's Amman bombings in November 2005, arguing:

> The [Muslim] people loved Al-Qaeda because it declared war on the American enemy who supports the occupation of Palestine and is the occupier of Iraq and Afghanistan; however this love was taken out of people's chest when they hit the innocent. The victims of the Amman wedding and their families, of who we see and console them even today, are proof of the blind use of weapons which tainted al-Zawahiri and his group.[81]

Rather feebly, the Al-Qaeda leaders have responded by arguing that those stirring up ethnic hatred and fomenting civil war are forces loyal to the regime that want America to stay in Iraq.[82]

The most earnest attempt at engaging with more complex theological debates in order to justify killing of civilians and Muslims was put forward in Zawahiri's book *The Exoneration: A Letter Exonerating the Ummah of Pen and Sword from Unjust Allegations of Feebleness and Weakness*, which he completed in early spring 2008. The book was a response to a series of allegations made by his former associate 'Abd al-Qadir (more commonly known as Sayyid Imam al-Sharif or "Dr Fadl") and other criticism from former extremists and radicals in Egypt and elsewhere, who were uncomfortable with the level of violence displayed by Al-Qaeda and affiliates. Primarily based on reported deeds of the Prophet (*Ahadith*) and anecdotes and rulings of medieval jurists rather than the Quran, and weaved into assumptions concerning contemporary manifestations of religious protocols, *The Exoneration* set out a series of justifications for killing Muslims, children, women, the elderly, the infirm, and other people who were protected according to conventional interpretations of religious texts.

Three major justifications were cited for shedding Muslim blood: (1) Muslim deaths in and among other legitimate targets are justifiable since the Prophet allowed night raids, as they were necessary to achieve victory.[83] This means that attacks that do not distinguish between enemies within a confined space must also be allowed; (2) the seventh-century Muslim conquest used catapults—therefore indiscriminate weaponry and bombs must be justifiable even where Muslims live; (3) "captive" Muslims being held by enemy forces may be killed since this falls under the category of "persisting in combat," even if the enemy uses Muslims as "human shields" (a concept referred to as *Mas'alatut at-Tatarrus*). Zawahiri often cited interpretations by Ibn Taymiyyah, a thirteenth- and fourteenth-century Sunni traditionalist jurist, implying that such deaths would not be illegal, and attempted to apply these to current events in order to justify Al-Qaeda's tactics. These medieval jurisprudential justifications are applied, without question, to the contemporary scene and used to legitimize attacks where unarmed Muslim bystanders constitute most or all of the casualties. This justificatory narrative thus rests on a very weak theological and jurisprudential foundation. Extra-contextual interpretations are applied to modern-day scenarios and situations for which the medieval teachings were never intended, to make the increase in indiscriminate violence seem right and religiously justified. How, for instance, does the citing of century-old juristic opinion pieces designed for medieval hostage and siege situations apply to Al-Qaeda's continued desire for and endorsement of attacks in open spaces frequented by Muslim noncombatants? These arguments are then mixed with more "practical" excuses, such as complaints that regular leadership targets have become harder to strike—"forcing" jihadists to look elsewhere.

An old Islamist manual on guerrilla warfare, which US intelligence operatives found in Afghanistan after the fall of the Taliban regime, warned of the "negative effects" of attacks on civilians, pointing in particular to the way in which groups in Algeria and Egypt became isolated after excessive targeting of noncombatants. The manual cautioned there was a "lack of legal agreement" on action involving civilian deaths and that such a strategy could result in "political splits and disputes."[84] It seems the Al-Qaeda leaders had forgotten to heed this advice.

This does not mean, however, that the Al-Qaeda leadership has abandoned all limitations on the use of violence, even though its track record would certainly suggest otherwise. Furthermore, as noted above, there has been a gradual escalation in terms of the level and scope of violence that the Al-Qaeda leaders have come to justify. As a result, the *impermissibility* of certain types of targeting according to the Al-Qaeda discourse is worthy of particular scrutiny. This is particularly important as it shows how the Al-Qaeda leaders have not been consistent over time when it comes to justifying prescribed levels of violence and it provides opportunities to highlight contradictions between Al-Qaeda's rhetoric on the one hand and its physical participation in and support for violent acts on the other.

Constraints on the use of violence

The perceived moral superiority of the Al-Qaeda leadership, as opposed to that of the adversaries, is central to the leadership's argument. Through presenting itself as a pioneering vanguard of a righteous uprising against occupation and hardship, secularism, and infidelity and a defensive force fighting to retain the dignity and sanctity of the *ummah*, the Al-Qaeda leadership frames its violence as a noble and just form of activism. Regardless of the perceived right to "respond" through violent means, however, the Al-Qaeda leaders have occasionally made references to limitations and constraints on the use of jihadi violence. While most of Zawahiri's and bin Ladin's output referred to the need to use violence, therefore, approximately one out of every six statements also alluded to ways in which violent means should be constrained.

As with elaborations concerning the supposed permissibility of violent attacks, it is Zawahiri who has offered most detail concerning factors that limit the scope and focus of violence. These allusions add to the complexity of Al-Qaeda's rhetorical approach toward the use of violence and serve to highlight inconsistencies that have emerged in this respect over time.

In a few early publications, Zawahiri stressed the need to post warnings in advance when attacking areas that Muslims frequented in order to avoid harming them.[85] As regards non-Muslim deaths, Zawahiri also confirmed that women and children (boys under 13 years of age) ought to be spared. Non-Muslims in general could not be targeted if they had been awarded *dhimmi* status (pledge of protection for non-Muslims living in shariah states who pay tax, *jizya*, to the state), although he stressed that non-Muslims currently living in Egypt did not qualify.[86]

In *Knights under the Banner of the Prophet*, Zawahiri remembered the shock and remorse he felt when an attempted attack on the Egyptian Prime Minister's motorcade resulted in the death of Shayma Abdel Halim, an 11-year-old schoolgirl. The death resulted in public outcry against EIJ and served as an early reminder of the way in which Muslim deaths could result in rapid evaporation of public support. More than a decade later, Zawahiri would seek to remind his chief ally in Iraq, Abu Musab al-Zarqawi, of this danger in his letter made public by the US Director of National Intelligence. Ignoring this advice, Zarqawi went on to orchestrate coordinated attacks in Jordan resulting in 60 deaths, the majority of whom were Muslims. In the aftermath, popular support for Al-Qaeda in Jordan, which had until then been substantial, plummeted.[87]

Recognizing the death of Shayma as a "mistake," Zawahiri emphasized the need to pay blood money to relatives, funds permitting, when such "mistakes" were made. The death of Shayma and deaths of Muslims in general were revisited much later in Zawahiri's *Exoneration*. Here the author admitted that mistakes were unavoidable and that Muslims might sometimes be victims of *mujahideen* "operations," even though deliberate targeting of innocent Muslims remained strictly forbidden. "As in any other human activity," Zawahiri conceded, "mistakes have been and will be made in jihad. For every mistake, there is accountability according to *Shariah*." Ultimately, however, "jihad must continue."[88] The extent to which Al-Qaeda leaders intend to take responsibility was not explained and neither was the fact that many attacks endorsed by the leadership took place in crowded Muslim neighborhoods. Indeed, in an attempt to defend those who planned the 1993 attack that killed Shayma, Zawahiri stressed how Muslims needed to avoid being in areas where attacks against leadership targets may take place, regardless of the fact that that particular explosive device was placed next to a girls' school.

Although he largely stayed away from the issue, bin Ladin similarly expressed his regret over Muslim deaths in *mujahideen* "operations," and emphasized how those responsible must repent or face punishment.[89] Although killing innocents was sometimes unavoidable, the *mujahideen* must take care to fight "without going to excess," bin Ladin argued in a statement issued in December 2004.[90] In a more recent statement, bin Ladin argued that fighters "must be very cautious during operations targeting army garrisons, which are located near Muslims," implying Al-Qaeda and affiliates did indeed themselves limit their attacks to such military targets.[91]

A month after publishing *Exoneration*, *As-Sahab* announced the release of the first batch of responses to questions sent in for Zawahiri's consideration, in the aforementioned "open meeting." As noted above, many respondents questioned operations and tactics that had resulted in large numbers of Muslim deaths. In his retort, Zawahiri insisted: "we have not killed the innocents [Muslims], not in Baghdad, nor in Morocco, not in Algeria, nor anywhere else." As before, the killing of Muslims was said to be forbidden, but sometimes unavoidable in order to ensure that the battle against the infidels and apostates continued unabated. Muslim deaths were explained either as a "mistake," or "out of necessity in cases of at-Tatarrus" (the "human shield" argument). Zawahiri went on to defend the tactics of affiliates in North Africa, insisting that in Algeria, for example, they targeted only the UN and government security forces (regardless of the fact that the bombs kill mostly Muslim noncombatants or young conscripts). Finally, he tried to deflect some of the criticism on Al-Qaeda onto the Hamas Al-Qassam Brigades, since they employed indiscriminate rocket attacks against Israeli population centers.[92] Such arguments appear inherently weak and fly in the face of the actual target emphasis of Al-Qaeda and its affiliates. Along with excuses and deflections, another theme prominent in the Al-Qaeda leaders' response to accusations of indiscriminate killing is outright denial. In 2007, Zawahiri even claimed that Al-Qaeda's affiliate in Iraq—responsible for countless sectarian massacres— had "only killed spies and traitors" and declared "its innocence of any inviolable blood which one of its soldiers might spill." If there was any doubt concerning Al-Qaeda's track record in Iraq, Zawahiri insisted, the leader of its affiliate in the country could appear "before a judicial council" in order to respond to any complaints.[93] In the same statement Zawahiri argued that killing of Fatah members by Hamas militias must cause far greater jurisprudential controversy than actions of Al-Qaeda in Iraq, even though numerous prior communiqués from the leadership had made no distinction between Fatah and its leaders, on the one hand, and Israeli intelligence services or other "primary targets," on the other. Their blood could be spilled, according to Al-Qaeda. Part of these efforts to reject notions of excessive targeting involved weaving these denials together with the elaborate conspiracy theories that form such a significant element of Al-Qaeda's worldview. In one of his "interviews" with *As-Sahab*, for instance, Zawahiri argued that allegations of inflicting Muslim casualties in Al-Qaeda-sponsored operations were simply part of hostile "media campaigns" against the movement.[94] Such inability and unwillingness to address the issue of Muslim deaths indicates how flammable the issue is within militant Islamist circles and how damaging it is for Al-Qaeda.

"The property or life of a non-believer"

What about killing non-Muslims? As shown above, few limitations seem to remain in Al-Qaeda's discourse when it comes to discussing legitimate targets for violence. Some examples, however, have been cited in the Al-Qaeda leaders' statements offering some limitations, in order to reinforce the focus on more "significant" adversaries. Sweden, for instance, was once mentioned as a state that did not "harm Muslim interests," as were Vietnam and Switzerland.[95] There would be no need to target citizens of those countries at that particular time, according to Al-Qaeda. It would be wrong to think, however, that foreign policy neutrality or other features of government policy would in any way guarantee freedom from Al-Qaeda's wrath.

As noted above, the Al-Qaeda leadership has equated issues such as the "slandering of the Prophet" to more direct actions of hostility by states that have nonetheless "legitimized" the targeting of specific populations. The Danish cartoon publications, therefore, prompted a greater focus on Scandinavia as a legitimate target than before. Every indication is given, therefore, that states or communities singled out as "lesser enemies" might not remain immune from Al-Qaeda attacks for long.

Some very limited doctrinal limitations on the killing of "unbelievers" appear fairly constant. Invariably, this applies to their status within the desired Islamic shariah empire. In *Exoneration*, Zawahiri wrote: "as I said previously, the property or life of a non-believer are protected only by peace treaty [*al-sulh*], status as a protected alien [*al-dhimmah*], or safe-conduct [*al-aman*]."[96] Under these conditions, according to Zawahiri, the envisaged Muslim state would not be opposed to living in "coexistence with the nation's partners of Christians and non-Muslims."[97] But, "if none of these things is confirmed," Zawahiri warned, then "matters remain in their original state."[98] Zawahiri also recognized that some Christians might be true to their religion's prophet and would seek to amend relations with Muslims. Furthermore, he claimed not to desire open confrontation with Copts living in Egypt, even though he condemned their "alliance" with the Mubarak regime. Rather uncharacteristically, moreover, Zawahiri also noted, in a statement issued in October 2012, that "We must distinguish between the Christians who attacked us and our prophet, peace and blessings be upon him, and the Christians who are peaceful towards us and do not attack us."[99] Positive relations with non-Muslims, therefore, were not always excluded in this rhetoric, as long as these were established according to Al-Qaeda's terms.

Out-of-control affiliates

The Al-Qaeda leadership's attempts to reject accusations that the organization or its affiliates had been involved in indiscriminate mass murder and attacks that inflicted Muslim casualties have been particularly undermined by subsequent efforts of the leadership to rein in precisely these same affiliates, urging them to be more cautious in their violence. It seems inherently inconsistent that Zawahiri started by dismissing notions that Al-Qaeda's affiliates had anything to do with mass killings only to try publically to convince these groups to limit the scope of their violence a little later. The latter seems to constitute an inadvertent admission that Al-Qaeda's branches and affiliates had been responsible for such indiscriminate violence in Iraq and elsewhere all along.

Parts of Zawahiri's otherwise uncompromising messages of "glad tidings" during the Arab Spring, for instance, presented a clear and rather desperate message to those affiliates and followers of Al-Qaeda that had engaged in levels of violence that the leadership ultimately came to see as unproductive. "There are some operations which are ascribed to the *Mujahideen*," Zawahiri admitted, "some by due right and others otherwise, in which transgressions occur against Muslims in their mosques, their markets, and other gathering places. About this," Zawahiri continued, "I say the following: Regardless of whether the ascription of these acts to the *Mujahideen* are correct or incorrect, my brothers and I in Al-Qaedah declare to Allah that we are innocent from these attacks, and that we object to them, whether those who carry them are the *Mujahideen* or others." Al-Qaeda followers should "try their utmost," Zawahiri argued, to avoid killing those "whose blood is prohibited" when planning "operations." This included both Muslims and certain non-Muslims, although he insisted mistakes could still be made and that killing Muslims embedded within the ranks of the enemy would be inevitable (the *Mas'alatut at-Tatarrus* argument referred to above).[100] In his message confirming the death of bin Ladin, later during this period, Zawahiri urged the *mujahideen* to "stay away from any operation that exposes [Muslims] to danger in the markets, mosques, or crowded areas."[101] A similar cautionary note featured in Zawahiri's "Guidelines for Jihad," published in September 2013, where the Al-Qaeda leader urged his fellow *mujahideen* to

> avoid fighting the deviant sects ..., except if they fight the Ahl as Sunnah [Sunni Muslims]. If they fight the Ahl as Sunnah, even then the response must be restricted to those parties amongst them who are directly engaged in the fight ... Those from amongst them who do not participate in the fight against us and their families, should not be targeted in their homes, places of worship, their religious festivals and religious gatherings. However, this should not stop us from continuously revealing their falsehood and the deviation in their creed and conduct.[102]

Zawahiri, in turn, sought to make it clear that the jihadists ought to "avoid fighting or targeting those who [had] not raised arms against us or aided in any such hostile act." The fighters had to "refrain from killing ... non-combatant women and children," according to Zawahiri, "even if they are families of those who are fighting against us." Al-Qaeda's allies were also urged to "refrain from harming Muslims by explosions, killing, kidnapping or destroying their wealth or property" and to avoid "targeting enemies in mosques, markets and gatherings where they mix with Muslims or with those who do not fight us."[103] Great limits had thus been put in place on the level and nature of violence that could be used in Al-Qaeda's name, regardless of the fact that Zawahiri had spent considerable time and effort through some of his previous publications to present justifications for precisely this level of indiscriminate violence.

In February 2012, Zawahiri "accepted" the oath of allegiance from the leader of Al-Qaeda's ally in Somalia, the Shabaab Al-Mujahideen. In a joint declaration from the two leaders, however, Zawahiri did not place militant objectives at the top of the group's list of priorities. Rather, he urged Shabaab's leadership to be "humble with their Somali brothers, and to do as much as they can to meet their needs and solve their problems and help them in achieving their interests, especially for those in need like widows, orphans, the sick, the elderly, and poor people, through whom victory is laid down."[104] It would almost look as if Zawahiri was seeking to learn lessons from groups like Hezbollah and Hamas—which he had criticized, even denounced, on several occasions before—in combining social efforts within the broader campaign of jihad.

The fear of becoming an outcast—even within the jihadist community, perhaps something akin to the fate of the Algerian GIA (Groupe Islamique Armé)—due to excessive violence thus appears to have impacted on some of the Al-Qaeda central leadership's rhetoric and prompted efforts to "rebrand" the movement and seek wider appeal.

However, while excessive targeting became an ever greater problem for the Al-Qaeda leadership, these justificatory issues need to be contrasted with the tactical recommendations that have evolved as part of Al-Qaeda's narrative over the years. The leadership spent a lot of time seeking to justify the violence it advocated against identified adversaries. At the same time, as Hegghammer observes, it appears to have spent far less time elucidating in any detail the strategic and tactical guidelines that are seen as relevant.[105] Most of these deliberations, of course, would not take place so publically. But the Al-Qaeda leaders did use their statements to convey and hone some of the operational and strategic solutions that followers were urged to adopt in order to undermine the enemy. Principally, this concerns the use of suicide attacks—or martyrdom operations—which other terrorists, particularly Shia groups, had used to substantial effect in Lebanon and beyond. The next section explores the extent to which these tactical concerns form part of the solution as presented in the Al-Qaeda's leadership discourse.

Strategy and tactics in the public discourse

The Al-Qaeda leadership's strategic vision, as publically expressed through statements, can be summarized as follows: A vanguard has to be created, preferably in a region that provides the proper base to create a movement strong enough to tackle enemy forces—foreign and domestic.[106] The vanguard is made up of *mujahideen*, who attack the enemy, but should rely on the support of the *ummah* and on the *fatawa* of righteous, independent *ulema* who have not been corrupted by government institutions or "agents" of the Zionist-Crusader West. Young men from their mid-teens up to their mid-twenties provide the mainstay of the *mujahideen* vanguard,[107] while other members of the *ummah* should support them and supplement their operations through public protest, raising funds, working against "apostate" local regimes or Western governments, supporting radical Islamist publications, and so on. The vanguard's success is inevitable due to its closeness to God, dedication, and willingness to embrace martyrdom. Once a small region is secured, an Islamic emirate which implements the shariah will be created. This will be used as a base for further operations, which will not cease until all Muslim land has been freed of Zionist-Crusader-"apostate" influence and all its inhabitants start living under the strictest interpretations of shariah law.

The Al-Qaeda leaders' own experiences in Afghanistan informed much of their public strategic guidance. In Zawahiri's *Knights under the Banner of the Prophet*, one of Al-Qaeda's clearest discursive treatise, the Al-Qaeda leader emphasized how lessons from Afghanistan demonstrated to the leadership the importance of establishing a base, "an arena that would act like an incubator where its seeds would grow and where it can acquire practical experience in combat, politics, and organizational matters."[108] Other important ingredients of a successful violent resistance movement, according to Zawahiri, included perseverance, patience, and an "organization and leadership leading change."[109] A degree of structure and top-down guidance was thus essential, rather than the fluid, autonomous cells favored by Abu Musab Al-Suri. Nothing would be achieved, however, without the "mobilization of popular support."[110] "Striving to achieve popular sympathy for the Islamic Mujahid movement for change" was paramount, Zawahiri argued.[111] As a result, alienation of the general support base, due to excessive use of force, would be catastrophic, as would the failure to ensure the message resonated with identified constituents.

These general points on strategy were mixed with propaganda that depicted the enemy as inherently weak—a paper tiger. Afghanistan was, again, the source of inspiration. The withdrawal of Soviet forces and subsequent and rapid implosion of the Soviet Union itself "cleared from Muslim minds the myth of superpowers," bin Ladin insisted,[112] a point which Zawahiri reiterated in *Knights*.[113] This experience would inform the struggle against the United States. The abrupt withdrawal of US forces from Somalia, following the "Black Hawk Down" incident, convinced Al-Qaeda, at least according to public messages, that America was a "paper tiger."[114] It would not be able to suffer long-term casualties, military or civilian, due to the resulting political pressures domestically. In addition to provoking such a reaction in their own right, therefore, attacks could lure the United States into protracted wars of attrition that would cause immense political, psychological, and economic damage. In the first in a series of staged "interviews" for *As-Sahab*, Zawahiri noted (a year into the Afghan campaign and six months before the start of hostilities in Iraq) that "the continual attacks on the American system, [have] finally pulled the Biggest Satan to the arena of Jihad... Once in the arena of war, it will start feeling its own losses."[115] In a September 2013 publication titled "General Guidelines for Jihad," Zawahiri acknowledged that the "purpose of targeting America [was] to exhaust her and bleed her to death, so that it meets the fate of the former Soviet Union and collapses under its own weight as a result of its military, human, and financial losses." "Consequently," Zawahiri added, "its grip on our lands will weaken and its allies will begin to fall one after another."[116]

Bin Ladin also recognized the importance of provocation in undermining the enemy: "all that we have to do is send two *mujahideen* to the furthest point East to raise a piece of cloth on which is written al-Qaeda, in order to make the generals race there to cause America to suffer human, economic, and political losses."[117]

The utility of terrorism

Al-Qaeda's endorsement of terrorist tactics, therefore, is inherently linked to the perceived effectiveness of these methods in provoking the enemy to react in a certain way, particularly as relates to the redeployment of troops and withdrawal from territory.

In an extensive audio recording posted online in February 2003, bin Ladin detailed the impact of terrorist attacks against the United States through the years. The 1982 Beirut truck bombing against US marines—bin Ladin reminded his audience—resulted in the prompt withdrawal of US forces from Lebanon. Then the *mujahideen* confronted America and "rubbed her arrogance into the dust" in Somalia, after which "America and her allies fled into the darkness of the night." At the same time the United States was targeted in Aden and, again, "the cowardly Americans ran away and fled the country in less than 24 hours." US forces were struck in Riyadh and in Al-Khobar in 1996 prompting them "to move their bases from the cities to the desert." Refusing to heed the repeated warnings of the *mujahideen*, America was "smashed" twice in East Africa, and again in Aden with another martyrdom operation. "Denying reality and proclaiming that we (the *Mujahideen*) were striking them because we were jealous of them (the Americans), whereas the reality is that we

[were] striking them because of their evil and injustice in the whole of the Islamic World," Al-Qaeda struck the very "idols of America" on "the blessed Tuesday 11 September 2001," which destroyed the "Great American Dream and legend of Democracy," revealing the "true characteristics of the Crusade," according to bin Ladin.[118]

Predictably, the 9/11 attacks were presented as an unquestionable success in the statements, and others were urged to replicate the scale of the attacks in the future. In his first interview after the attacks, with a Karachi-based newspaper, bin Ladin argued that subsequent calls that were made by the US president and British prime minister, in the wake of the attacks, for the creation of a Palestinian state demonstrated their success.[119] The political impact of the attacks was compounded by the immense economic damage they caused, the collapse of shares in the stock exchange, the damage to the airline industry, as well as the wider "psychological shock."[120] Similarly, Zawahiri argued the British government set a date for withdrawal from Iraq a day after the London bombings in July 2005—a clear sign the attacks had had the desired effect.[121]

Unsurprisingly, having observed the impact of suicide bombings in Lebanon and elsewhere and having embraced the tactic for its own efforts, the Al-Qaeda leadership strongly endorses the use of "martyrdom operations." Force, according to Zawahiri, was the only language understood by the enemy, and in this regard inflicting "maximum causalities" was paramount. Martyrdom operations were the "most successful way" of inflicting such damage and the "least costly to the *mujahidin* in terms of casualties."[122] In this way a "small group in numbers and equipment" could inflict "immense slaughter" on the enemy.[123] Aside from these asymmetric qualities, the coding unveiled how psychological impact and differences that separated belligerents were seen as fundamental. The *mujahideen* possess what others cannot, Zawahiri proclaimed: "the love of death in the path of Allah."[124] As a result, a barrage of continuous suicide attacks would force even the strongest enemy to retreat.[125]

This was the advice communicated to affiliates in Somalia, Iraq, and elsewhere where suicide attacks could be a decisive weapon deployed by insurgents, in addition to ambushes and clandestine operations.[126] "Out of area" suicide operations would need to be well planned. Zawahiri complained that too many initiatives within the jihad movement were haphazard.[127] Well-orchestrated martyrdom operations against oil installations, supply lines, corporations, and other "economic targets" would be particularly useful in undermining the enemy, causing a ripple effect throughout the military, political, and economic infrastructure.[128] "Strike at the economic base that forms the foundation of the military establishment," bin Ladin advised in a video statement posted on Al Jazeera in the aftermath of the 9/11 attacks.[129]

One of the virtues of suicide bombings, as far as the Al-Qaeda leaders were concerned, lay in the simplicity of the attacks, whereby high-impact strikes could be based on relatively rudimentary planning, where perpetrators used simple devices that could often be assembled by nonexperts using household chemicals.[130] These types of attacks were toward one end of the spectrum in terms of technological sophistication. At the opposite end were attacks involving the use of weapons of mass destruction (WMD). The latter has received substantial attention in the analytical literature on Al-Qaeda. Apart from a few early and cursory references, however, the matter has been largely absent from Al-Qaeda's public discourse.

Weapons of mass destruction

Regardless of whatever interest the Al-Qaeda leadership may or may not have had in weapons of mass destruction behind the scenes,[131] the matter was nowhere near as prominent in the public domain as some of the commentary on Al-Qaeda would have suggested. Any references in the statements, moreover, were vague and often approached the matter geopolitically, rather than suggesting tactical applications. To highlight the infrequency of references to possession or usage of WMD, Figure 5.1 illustrates the handful

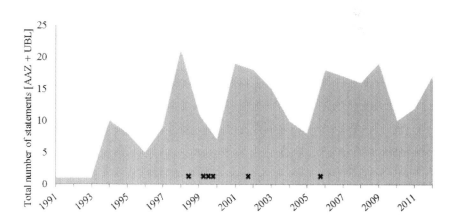

✖   Single statement referring to possession of WMD

FIGURE 5.1 *References to possession of WMD compared with total number of statements (1991–2012)*

of communiqués where these issues were discussed. The statements where these references were made are placed on a timeline that, in the background, illustrates the total aggregate of messages from bin Ladin and Zawahiri for comparative purposes.

As the figure shows, references to WMD were rare and insignificant when compared to the overall output.

Generally speaking, acquiring WMD was certainly seen as a right, even a duty, of Muslims and not beyond their means. In a letter to Mullah Omar, the leader of the Taliban "Islamic Emirate," which was later made public, bin Ladin noted that "It is a fact that the Islamic Republic's region is rich with significant scientific experiences in conventional and *non-conventional* military industries, which will have a great role in future Jihad against the enemies of Islam."[132] In an open interview, bin Ladin argued that Muslims "should not be lax in possessing nuclear, chemical, and biological weapons" and follow the example of Pakistan in this regard,[133] which Al-Qaeda urged to secure nuclear weapons of a "better quality" than those of India.[134]

What about the use of such weapons? When the Al-Qaeda leadership's few messages on the potential use of WMD are collated and analyzed, it emerges that the way in which such hypothetical deployments are discussed appears to bear far closer resemblance to Cold War rhetoric of deterrence and mutually assured destruction than it does to the discourse of a clandestine terrorist organization. It seems such references were intended, implicitly and explicitly, to elevate Al-Qaeda to superpower status, akin to the inflated image that was sometimes constructed of the group in the Western media following the 9/11 attacks. "If I seek to acquire these weapons," bin Ladin claimed in an interview with *Time Magazine*, "I am carrying out a duty. It would be a sin for Muslims not to try to possess the weapons that would prevent the infidels from inflicting harm on Muslims."[135] "Muslim" nuclear weapons would deter against Israeli and "Christian" nuclear weapons.[136] Thus, bin Ladin declared, "that if America used chemical or nuclear weapons against us, then we may retort with chemical and nuclear weapons. We have the weapons as deterrent."[137]

In practice, meanwhile, and for operational purposes, the focus would be on creating "light and agile" attack groups that could utilize the element of surprise and the benefits of asymmetric warfare.[138] Aside from violence, however, Al-Qaeda's activist prescriptions would occasionally refer to different tactics that could allow for more mass participation in efforts to undermine the ruling order and support the Islamist vanguard. More than anything else, these efforts would involve the boycotting of goods and other efforts to achieve mass mobilization of the *ummah* in order to deliver collective economic sanctions against the enemy.

Methods alternative to violence

Even as early as the mid-1980s, when the US-supported campaign against the Soviet Union in Afghanistan was still being fought, bin Ladin used his family mosque in Jeddah to distribute leaflets and give speeches protesting against US support for Israel and calling for boycott of US goods.[139] On several subsequent occasions, the Al-Qaeda leaders suggested economic boycott as a tool against enemy powers and urged a pan-Islamic embrace of such methods. The statements where these appeals were made are placed on a timeline in Figure 5.2.

Although initially presented as the main way to weaken the influence of the United States, these methods quickly became seen as supportive of a wider campaign of militancy and terrorism. The first declaration of war against the United States in 1996 asserted that "if the economic boycott is coupled with the *mujahidin's* military strikes, then the enemy's defeat is imminent" and added that women would be expected to take part in this as well.[140] Both Zawahiri and bin Ladin consistently reiterated such calls, stressing the need to boycott Western goods in tandem with planning and supporting acts of violence. Such calls were particularly prominent during the widespread Muslim outrage following the publication of Mohammed caricatures in Danish and Norwegian newspapers, although boycotts had already been widely planned by the time the Al-Qaeda leaders started urging their audiences to embrace such measures. In a June 2007 statement distributed by *As-Sahab*, moreover, Zawahiri called for universal boycott of British goods in response to British colonial "crimes."[141]

Even though Muslims may not all be able to partake in violent operations against the external or local enemy for physical or societal reasons, they are nonetheless expected to contribute to the fight through boycotting US, Israeli, and Western goods as well as preventing "Muslim resources," especially oil, from being sold to the West at a reduced price. In an interview with a Pakistani newspaper in the aftermath of the September 11 attacks, bin Ladin laid out the prerequisites, stressing that "Western products could only be boycotted when

FIGURE 5.2 *Calls for economic boycott: Statements on timeline*

the Muslim fraternity is fully awakened and organized" and when "economic self-sufficiency is attained and substitute products are brought out."[142]

When possible, therefore, these wider efforts of the grass roots could support jihadi activities, which remained the chief force for change. What about street protests and demonstrations? Although events such as the Palestinian *intifadas* were praised, the Al-Qaeda leaders generally dismissed the efficacy of public protest as a means for change, particularly regime change. This would be, Zawahiri argued, like "treating cancer with an aspirin."[143] In relation to Egypt, for example, Zawahiri argued in his 2008 book *Exoneration* that there would be no peaceful solution to the country's problems, especially after the authorities banned public protests after the Al-Azhar demonstrations in 2007.[144] Muslims had to focus on carefully planned attacks, seek funding and weapons in order to orchestrate coordinated strikes, and prepare martyrdom operations. Mere public protests were useless.[145] "Protests do no good in the face of bombs; Muslims must take 'effective steps'," Zawahiri argued, meaning the use of terrorist tactics.[146] Authoritarianism dictated jihad and terrorism was the only solution: "the system in Egypt and in most of the Arabic and Islamic countries cannot be removed except by force," Zawahiri insisted in a 2009 statement.[147] These words, of course, would come back to haunt Zawahiri after uprisings of the "Arab Spring" led to the toppling of dictatorships in the region, including the Egyptian Mubarak regime. Zawahiri's subsequent praise for the Egyptian revolutionaries and support for further protests appeared to contradict his earlier dismissal of the use of public protests to achieve such a result. Indeed, the issue served to illustrate how far Al-Qaeda's prescriptions were removed from the realities on the ground.

Both bin Ladin and Zawahiri always used their statements to express their desire to guide the *ummah* to what they envisaged to be the correct path and their confident determination that they could both represent the *ummah* and identify workable solutions addressing the major challenges it might face. Although occasional regional imperatives channeled the messages toward specific national or localized audiences, most statements were meant to appeal to the *ummah* as a whole and carry judgments for all Muslims, and occasionally non-Muslims too.

An essential common element in the construction and dissemination of these messages concerns the way in which the Al-Qaeda leadership communicates with its audience and shapes these appeals. The Al-Qaeda leaders have always done more than just describe problems and suggest solutions. They have used their statements to appeal to specific audiences: the global *ummah* as well as Muslims in specific localities; enemies, as well as potential supporters. The next chapter analyzes these communicative efforts, assessing the nature of the Al-Qaeda leadership's discursive approach toward Muslim and non-Muslim audiences.

6

Communicating the message

Loyalty and separation

The concept of *al-wala wa-l-bara*, or loyalty and separation, is ever present in Al-Qaeda's discourse. This refers to the distinction between the in-group and the out-group, whereby the former provides constituents and the latter constitutes immoral and hostile entities that threaten the cohesion and sanctity of the *ummah*. The Wahhabite interpretation of *al-wala wa-l-bara* perceives open enmity toward "idolaters," apostates, and nonbelievers as the clearest demonstration of true faith, loyalty, and dedication to Islam.[1]

This principle informs much of the communicative approach of the Al-Qaeda leadership. *Al-wala wa-l-bara* formed the basis of Al-Qaeda's Manichean worldview and highlighted the need for collective unity. Zawahiri even dedicated one of his books to the concept, where he warned the *ummah* that the enemy had "launched a campaign of intellectual and doctrinal deception in tandem with their militaristic, Crusading campaign."[2] In this context, deviating from the doctrine that prohibited befriending infidels was thus the greatest threat to Islam. Zawahiri, therefore, called on the *ummah*, in "all its factions, classes and groups," to join the caravan of jihad, adding that infidels and apostates "should not be shown affection, they should be hated and their love renounced."[3]

The concept of *al-wala wa-l-bara*, therefore, offers an initial cue to understanding the Al-Qaeda leadership's communicative strategy. The initial categorization that can be derived from this division is that which sets Muslims aside from non-Muslims. As this chapter will explore, however, these distinctions—although prominent in Al-Qaeda's discourse—become more ambiguous when bin Ladin's and Zawahiri's communicative efforts are scrutinized in detail. Although not without caveats, both leaders sought to "excommunicate" some Muslims, for instance, thus presenting them as "infidels" and legitimate targets. Furthermore, as discussed above, occasional appeals to supposedly disenfranchised non-Muslims appeared to undermine the strict notions of separation between believers and unbelievers that otherwise seemed to prevail.

An initial way to dissect Al-Qaeda's communicative approach, therefore, is to look at bin Ladin's and Zawahiri's appeals toward non-Muslims and Muslims separately. This dichotomy, in turn, which is readily embraced in the two leaders' communiqués, has a number of sub-layers where the complexities of the Al-Qaeda leadership's appeals and the diversity of their audiences become apparent. When the Al-Qaeda leaders addressed non-Muslim audiences directly, for instance, these messages sometimes contained threats of further violence but occasionally also conveyed more positive appeals. The far more comprehensive communicative approach toward Muslim audiences included positive appeals, negative criticism, as well as the rhetoric of excommunication. These layers and sub-layers of Al-Qaeda's communicative approach provide the structure for the discussions in this chapter. The first part focuses on approaches toward non-Muslims in the Al-Qaeda leadership's rhetoric, looking at threats and positive appeals. The second part of the chapter focuses on bin Ladin's and Zawahiri's intricate relationship with Muslim audiences that they identified in their communiqués. This relationship highlights their approach toward sectarianism and apostasy, as well as their rapport with the Muslim masses that Al-Qaeda has claimed to represent and protect.

Addressing non-Muslims

Bin Ladin and Zawahiri would occasionally speak directly to designated audiences within the "out-group" of non-Muslims. In messages to "the West," for instance, the Al-Qaeda leaders often presented warnings and ultimatums. These would often be communicated directly to leaders of major powers such as the United States. By addressing the United States, the US president, or British prime minister directly, of course, Zawahiri and bin Ladin elevated themselves and their Al-Qaeda vanguard to a position equal in power, authority, and legitimacy to the adversaries they targeted. Some observers have also argued that such threats and warnings were necessary due to doctrinal obligations to give adversaries the opportunity to mend their ways prior to attack.[4] In November 1997, for instance, bin Ladin issued a statement warning the United States to stop "international acts of terrorism" against the Muslims or else there would not be "any guarantee for the safety of American interests and its citizens in any part of the world."[5] Nine months later, Al-Qaeda targeted two US embassies in East Africa in simultaneous bombings, which killed 223 people.

A careful analysis of bin Ladin's and Zawahiri's statements, however, reveals that most of the direct warnings toward Americans from this period came *after* the August 1998 attacks took place and in the wake of the US reprisal operations code-named "Infinite Reach," which consisted of cruise missile attacks on targets in Afghanistan and Sudan. In a statement published shortly after the East Africa attacks, bin Ladin warned that the "battle" had "not yet started" and that the "answer" would be what the Americans could "see, not what [they could] hear."[6] Subsequent messages from this period reiterated these sentiments and warnings.[7] Most of the threats and warnings that were communicated directly toward US audiences, therefore, came after major attacks had been carried out, not before. With the exception of a brief reference in the spring of 2001, where bin Ladin promised to "make life miserable" for America,[8] most specific warnings and threats surrounding the 9/11 attacks were communicated after September 11, 2001. The same appears to apply as regards warnings to other identified adversaries. The Al-Qaeda leadership threatened Australians, for instance, just after the 2002 Bali bombings, which killed 202 people, including 88 Australians. Most of the clearest public warnings that were communicated toward the UK, moreover, came in the aftermath of the 2005 London bombings, not before. Figures 6.1a and 1b place these clear warnings of attacks on a timeline to illustrate this trend.[9]

As illustrated on the timeline, a flurry of public warnings were issued toward the United States in the months after the 9/11 attacks. In a statement

FIGURE 6.1a *Direct threats of attack issued toward the United States: statements and major attacks on timeline*

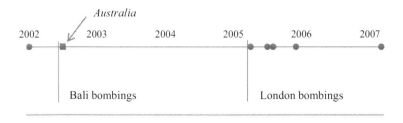

FIGURE 6.1b *Direct threats of attack issued toward the UK and Australia: statements and major attacks on timeline*

published on Al Jazeera in November 2001, bin Ladin warned that "neither the United States nor he who lives in the United States will enjoy security before we can see it as a reality in Palestine and before all the infidel armies leave the land of Muhammad."[10] These "conditions" for safety and stability in the United States and what became known as the "oath" of bin Ladin[11] were subsequently reiterated and referred to in numerous messages from both Zawahiri and bin Ladin and featured prominently in Zawahiri's eulogy of the latter in June 2011. "America will not be able to dream, not even in their sleep, of living in peace and security, as long as we don't live in real peace in Palestine, in the Land of the Two Holy Mosques, and throughout the Islamic world," bin Ladin declared in *As-Sahab*'s celebration of the 9/11 attacks, "The Wills of the Martyrs."[12] Such representations of just, even restrained, *quid pro quo* in the leadership messages portray Al-Qaeda as a heroic and righteous defender of the *ummah*: "just as you kill, you will be killed. And just like you bombarded, you will be bombarded. Be prepared to receive the glad tidings of what will be bad for you."[13] "The time has come for us to be equal."[14] The notion of reciprocity, which—as discussed above—is a central theme in Al-Qaeda's justificatory narrative for violence, thus features prominently in leadership communiqués toward identified adversaries.

The Al-Qaeda leaders' argument was that there was an imbalance in bloodletting that had to be rectified. The 9/11 attacks and other past attacks constituted mere "skirmishes" whereas the real battle had not yet begun, according to the Al-Qaeda leadership.[15] "Bush," Zawahiri warned, "fortify your targets, tighten your defense, intensify your security measures, because the fighting Islamic community—which sent you the New York and Washington battalions—has decided to send you one battalion after the other, carrying death and seeking heaven."[16] Al-Qaeda's most brazen attack, therefore, was followed by hyperbolic rhetoric where its leadership sought to exploit the impact of the attacks and convince followers of its capacity to take on its primary adversary.

The same message was directed toward the people of the UK: "Blair has brought destruction upon you, to the center of London, and he will have more of it, Allah willing."[17] "We address them [the British] in the only language they understand; and if they do not understand it this time around, we will repeat it until they understand it completely."[18] These specific warnings toward the UK, which again were issued *after* the London bombings, threatened the general population rather than specific leaders or elites.

Indeed, in several statements, the Al-Qaeda leaders placed particular emphasis on threatening general populations in line with allegations of complicity and collective responsibility for aggression against Muslims as detailed in the previous chapter. As long as the people of the Crusader nations failed to "interact with the Muslim Ummah on the basis of respect and mutual understanding," Zawahiri argued, they would "continue to move from one disaster to the next."[19] The people of the West had given the *mujahideen* "every legal justification for attacking them," Zawahiri argued.[20] All Americans, for instance, were on the side of "tyranny, criminality and failure" for voting for hostile regimes[21] and all had to "pay the price for their choice."[22] In an ironically twisted interpretation of democracy and inclusivity, therefore, and as a crucial justification for civilian targeting, the Al-Qaeda leaders directed their threats and warnings to "normal" members of the public. This not only implies that they are responsible and generally at fault but also suggests the general public can immediately alter any existing policies and the current state of affairs. "Most of you don't recognize the language of religion, morals and principles, and instead understand the language of running after pillage, and plunder," Zawahiri claimed, while addressing the general population in the West, adding: "you must honestly try to reach a mutual understanding with the Muslims for then, and only then, you might enjoy security."[23] Inclusive societies implied collective participation and thus joint responsibility, calling for a spontaneous and unified corrective response. "Normal Americans claim to be innocent," bin Ladin reflected, "and yet they failed to bring the leaders responsible for the Vietnam War to justice. And elected Bush twice and gave him continued mandate to wage war…This innocence of yours is like my innocence of the blood of your sons on [September] the 11th," he claimed.[24]

Normal citizens of the West, therefore, were seen as directly responsible for the suffering of Muslims and the "global oppressed," according to the Al-Qaeda rhetoric, and could thus be targeted.

Softer appeals

There have also, of course, been occasions where the Al-Qaeda leaders have sought to present a softer and more conciliatory image in their messages to the West. Although these appear, at first, to contradict the stark warnings and threats described above, it could be argued that the purpose is much the same. Notional offers of "truce" and de-escalation present the Al-Qaeda leadership as a fair operator while exaggerating the power and influence of the leaders. Furthermore, such appeals appear implicitly to underscore Al-Qaeda's justifications for targeting noncombatants, as the onus for implementing particular change is placed squarely on the public. Should the electorate or citizenry fail, therefore, they become complicit.

There are numerous examples of this more conciliatory stance toward Western publics. Bin Ladin, for instance, made several appeals to the "American people," urging them to select a "serious" government that looked out for their interests rather than their own material gain. After all, Americans had "risen against their government's war in Vietnam" and were thus urged to do the same today in order to "stop the massacre of Muslims by their government."[25] Bin Ladin recognized that both sides had suffered during this war, arguing that the US government's "hands are stained with the blood of all those killed from both sides, all for the sake of oil and keeping their private companies in business." The American public that voted for those in power thus held the key to ending hostilities: "your security is in your own hands."[26] In order to do this, all Americans had to free themselves from the "ideological terrorism" of the neoconservatives and the Israel lobby and were even urged to "work with" the Al-Qaeda leadership to amend US foreign policy.[27]

Any collective "failure" to recognize such initiatives implied common guilt. As mentioned above, moreover, both leaders extended several invitations to Islam, in order to underline the position of the leadership as a "true" vanguard. This ensured the people of the West had been presented with options and alternatives to insecurity and potential targeting by the Al-Qaeda leadership.[28] Further "options" were presented through offers of cease-fire and peace treaties, in response to "positive reactions" in the West where members of the public displayed their opposition toward war in opinion polls and through public protests.[29] Again, however, the responsibility of securing a pledge declaring that the West would not "attack Muslims or interfere in their business" and ensuring the "departure of its last soldier from our land" lay squarely with the ambiguously defined "people" to whom the messages were directed.[30]

Beyond the West, moreover, the Al-Qaeda leaders occasionally appealed to other non-Muslim publics, such as the Coptic minority in Egypt, with whom Zawahiri claimed "we would like to live with in peace and stability."[31] As mentioned in chapter 4, the Al-Qaeda leadership has also made some attempts to appeal to the "non-Muslim oppressed." In November 2012, for instance, in his "Document of the Support of Islam," Zawahiri claimed one of the goals of his organization was to support "every oppressed or unjustly treated person in the world against the unjust and oppressive."[32] However, these efforts to appeal to disenfranchised non-Muslims pale in comparison with Al-Qaeda's much more comprehensive and complex record of seeking to appeal to their perceived primary constituents, the Muslim masses.

Al-Qaeda and Muslim audiences

For the Al-Qaeda leaders, their statements have provided the essential vehicle for addressing supposed "constituents" and potential supporters. Most of their media output contains specific messages, advice, and appeals to the "Islamic nation" or individual Muslim communities, which are urged to see the world through Al-Qaeda's eyes. Al-Qaeda's narrative does not simply consist of a list of grievances and proposed solutions. There are concerted efforts to communicate these views to target audiences with the aim of fomenting support for Al-Qaeda's cause. The nature of the Al-Qaeda leadership's communicative approach toward Muslims, therefore, is worthy of particular analysis. As part of this analysis, moreover, we must consider Al-Qaeda's classifications of "true Muslims" and any efforts to rebuke and even excommunicate those who are seen to have betrayed their religion.

"On our path to reform," bin Ladin wrote in an open letter to the people of Saudi Arabia in 1995, "we are tasked with bringing the regime's dangers to the attention of the people."[33] Through their communicative efforts, therefore, the Al-Qaeda leaders hoped to prod at least a proportion of the wider Muslim population to act. The *ummah* must "wake up from their sleep"[34] and mobilize, bin Ladin argued. "The situation that Muslims are living in today requires the mobilization of everyone who belongs to this religion and the utilization of his resources."[35] By extension, Muslims had to recognize their individual obligation to respond to the situation that affected them all collectively: "It is obligatory upon the Ummah with all its groups and sections and its men and women, young and old, to provide themselves, their wealth, their expertise, and all types of moral and material support what suffices to carry on the Jihad in the fields of Jihad," bin Ladin declared in a 2006 statement titled "Oh People of Islam."[36]

The Al-Qaeda leadership has delivered this call to arms through repeated direct appeals to the Muslim *ummah* or more specific Muslim populations in particular localities. As part of this narrative, Al-Qaeda's harsher rhetoric toward perceived Muslim traitors emerges as a distinct *takfiri* element of this discourse. The notion of *takfir*, or excommunication, was discussed in Chapter 3. When the Al-Qaeda leadership's communicative approach toward Muslims is analyzed over time, however, its exasperation with Muslim publics begins to become apparent. The fact that repeated calls for mobilization and support for the jihadi cause failed to be heeded was inevitably going to affect the Al-Qaeda leaders' communicative approach toward their "constituents," and this will be the focus of particular scrutiny below. First, however, it is important to understand how bin Ladin and Zawahiri addressed Muslims through positive appeals that offered guidance and clarity in the hope that they would accept Al-Qaeda's vision.

Guiding the ummah

Through its direct appeals to Muslims, the Al-Qaeda leadership conveyed a sense of superiority and perceived experience and knowledge that would guide the masses on a path of reform. Zawahiri saw it as the duty of Al-Qaeda to "motivate the nation to support its *mujahideen* sons financially and morally" with "men, money, equipment and expertise."[37] The statements reminded Muslims of their duties, responsibilities, and obligations, reflecting the leadership's geographic ambition at the given moment and conveying Al-Qaeda's problem diagnosis and proposed solutions. The core theme was that wider mobilization of support for the *mujahideen* vanguard was seen as key to achieving success. These were emotive appeals resting on notions of common identity and responsibility.

"We seek to instigate the nation," bin Ladin remarked, "to get up and liberate its land, to fight for the sake of God, and to make the Islamic law the highest law, and the word of God the highest word of all...People must do all they can to rouse the nation with all the means in their power; with their tongues, pens, and persons."[38] "O nation of Islam," bin Ladin implored, "rise against injustice and tyranny, oppression and aggression, and humiliation and degradation. Bread is not more dear to us than our religion, nor is money more precious than our honor, or death more difficult than our sense of humiliation and degradation."[39]

The *ummah*'s greatest incentive, according to these appeals, was that victory would be imminent if Al-Qaeda's way was embraced.[40] This would be the only way for Muslims to achieve a genuine sense of purpose. The *ummah* is the "greatest human power on the face of the Earth [but] only if it establishes Islam properly," according to bin Ladin.[41] The alternative would be catastrophe. "If we sacrifice the rule of *sharia* and bestow legitimacy on those who sell nations and sign the surrender agreements," Zawahiri warned, "we will lose both religion and the present life and the land will remain occupied, injustice present, and sanctities violated."[42] By extension, such divisions between righteousness and infidelity eliminated the possibility for Muslims to be passive observers. They had only two choices: "[D]o you belong in the party of America, Israel, France, Russia and their allies among the apostate rulers of our countries, their assistants, their soldiers, their journalists, their judges, and their clerics who spread confusion, pledge allegiance to them, and call them the care takers of the Muslims' affairs?" Zawahiri asked, "or, do you belong in the party of the monotheistic, Salafi *Mujahideen*?"[43] The key purpose of this message, of course, is to achieve greater unity. "Have full trust in the victory of Allah," Zawahiri urged his audience, "and know that America has no power against you, if you unite as one body in its face."[44] "Unity is mercy and division is torture," bin Ladin warned.[45] This was not about allegiance to a particular group, but to the collective objective (as interpreted by Al-Qaeda) of the entire *ummah*. As Zawahiri remarked, the battle "is not of a group or organization, but is the battle of the entire Ummah."[46]

This message of unity became particularly acute after the fall of the Taliban regime toward the end of 2001. Just as Al-Qaeda faced losing its haven in Afghanistan, Zawahiri wrote a book imploring Muslims to realize their duty in uniting against the global front of infidelity and its secular "agents." "We call the Ummah—on all its factions, classes, and groups—to join the caravan of jihad," Zawahiri demanded. This would consist of: "staying clear of idolatrous tyrants, warfare against infidels, loyalty to the believers, and jihad in the path of Allah."[47] In order to fulfill this obligation, Muslims would have to abandon their attachment to earthly pleasures and ambitions. They had to "shun a life of play, amusement, extravagance and fun, and prepare [themselves] for the real life of killing, fighting, striking, and damaging."[48]

All conflicts where Muslim interests were at stake were interlinked, according to Al-Qaeda's message to the *ummah*. For that reason it was imperative that grievances would be perceived as collective rather than as a series of unrelated events. "If you leave Baghdad today," bin Ladin warned in a 2006 statement to the "Muslim nation," "then you will leave Damascus, Amman, the Gulf, and Riyadh tomorrow." Muslims were urged to "be cautious of the consequences of procrastination."[49] "It is a duty of Muslims to pledge allegiance to the 'most sincere' [i.e., Al-Qaeda and its affiliates] and follow them in the establishment of the Islamic state," bin Ladin argued. Having described the problem and presented the solution, the Al-Qaeda leadership thus had to inspire the *ummah* to go forth and support the jihad: "Stop playing around, listen, understand, wake up and pay attention…rush forward and do your duty…today Baghdad, and tomorrow Damascus, Amman, and Riyadh."[50]

To further instill a sense of collective identity, bin Ladin and Zawahiri both used their statements to relate events in one region to wider concerns of the *ummah*. Those who suffered man-made or natural disasters or long-term turmoil, for instance, were reassured that they would not be abandoned by the wider community of believers. In these statements, the *ummah* was also occasionally thanked for its support and praised for its resilience in the face of hostilities. Increasingly, however, criticism became a more common feature of the communiqués than gratitude, as will be discussed in detail below.

When the messages did not convey collective appeals, specific communities and regions were identified whose support and attention was perceived as particularly important. The groups identified included scholars and other members of the (righteous) religio-political elite; members of the security forces; traders, merchants, and wealthy Muslims; men of the (jihadi) media; Muslim women (whose role was seen as passive); writers; tribes and clans; and prisoners. One group was particularly prominent in these appeals: the Muslim youth.

Securing the support of young people was particularly significant for bin Ladin, who reminded his audience in one of his earlier public messages that "Mohammed's companions were young men."[51] Young people would provide the foot soldiers for the *mujahideen*. In an audio statement released in February 2003, bin Ladin argued that "although Jihad in person is obligatory upon the entire Ummah, then it is even more obligatory upon the youths in the prime of their lives than upon the old."[52] The youth must not "go astray," Zawahiri warned, and not aspire to become "a minister, an ambassador, a director, a wealthy person, a notable, a distinguished writer, a skillful physician, a successful engineer or a prosperous businessman, [in this case] we will lose the afterlife and we will be defeated in this world."[53] The only true call and worthy aspirations were those that would lead to or support the jihad.

Although Al-Qaeda has never abandoned these calls for unity and collective uprising, the leadership has also frequently targeted specific communities with their appeals. Several messages have thus been impressed on Kurds, Iraqis, Pakistanis, Lebanese, Somalis, Turks, and others to rise up against their secular and treacherous leaders and fight those who cooperated with coalition forces and their allies. Following the Arab Spring, dedicated appeals were directed toward the populations of Syria and the Levant, Tunisia, Libya, Yemen, and Egypt to struggle for the implementation of shariah rule, and for the population of Saudi Arabia to emulate the uprisings that had taken place in the region.[54] Concerned over the appeal of local groups in the West Bank and Gaza, moreover, bin Ladin and Zawahiri both addressed Palestinians directly, seeking to direct them from being deceived by "political solutions and regional deals"[55] and demanding instead that Palestinians declared that "they will take action to support the cause of establishing the Caliphate and fight until Allah's word reigns supreme."[56] The Palestinian needed to "carry the worries of his Muslim ummah at every place, the same way the Ummah carries the worries of Palestine," Zawahiri insisted.[57]

Those engaged in local conflicts had to realize that there was a wider struggle to be fought and that the crucial organizing principle was the implementation of God's law. Overthrow of tyrants or other more immediate goals did not suffice. Indeed, Zawahiri called on those who had successfully toppled the Tunisian and Egyptian regimes in the wake of the Arab uprisings to continue fighting until shariah was established.[58] The reason was that ruling classes and elites in the Arab and Islamic world, as well as the security establishment and intelligentsia, had become polluted by ideas and individuals who sought to undermine the establishment of God's law in favor of pursuing materialistic ambitions and secular principles. This is based on the assumption that some who claim to be Muslim have in fact committed such grave sins that they have "nullified" their creed and left the fold of Islam. This is the principle of *takfir*, which Meijer described as "a monster [that] mainstream Salafism desperately tries to keep in its cage while other currents within the movement have done their best to let it escape."[59] It would appear that in the case of the Al-Qaeda leadership, however, bin Ladin and Zawahiri both adopted a somewhat limited approach to the concept of *takfir*.

Accusations of apostasy

The notion of declaring Muslims apostates is a sensitive issue, even within Salafi circles, and several prominent Salafi-jihadi ideologues have cautioned against its excessive use. Muhammad Al-Maqdisi, a Palestinian Islamist ideologue, for example, sought to elaborate the process of excommunication along the following lines:

> We do not perform *Takfir* upon all who work for the governments of *Kufr* [infidelity] ... [W]e only perform *Takfir* upon the one who has in his work a type of *Kufr* or *Shirk* [idolatry] such as participating in the *Kufr* legislation, or the *Taghuti* [idol-worshipping] rule, or allegiance to the *Mushrikun* [idolaters] and *Kuffar* [the infidels], or aiding them against the people of *Tawhid* [the one God, i.e., Muslims].[60]

Takfirism, according to Maqdisi, therefore, would not be absolute, even with respect to those seen to have erred in their faith.

The Al-Qaeda leadership's approach toward *takfir* evolved over the years. Initially, allegations of apostasy were primarily made toward political elites in Muslim majority countries and their immediate support networks. Early references also relied more on context and "implicit excommunication," which stopped short of declaring individuals apostates in favor of describing behavior and supposed consequences of acts of apostasy. It was implied that these acts rendered a "notional Muslim" a non-Muslim, but the accusation was not spelled out in so many words. A degree of escalation, therefore, or at least elaboration, can be seen in the statements over time, for instance, in bin Ladin's criticism of Saudi authorities.

Early messages and "open letters" focused on the record of the Saudi leadership and the damage these inflicted, in terms of spreading disunity, harming the economy, and strengthening the enemy.[61] There was no doubt that this involved a betrayal of Islam, according to bin Ladin, as these actions would bring the Saudi authorities "shame in this world and torture in hell."[62] Rather than being a guardian of the holiest places, the royal family was driving people away from Islam, acted out of hatred of Islam and its "true" preachers, and strove to fight against it.[63] Although bin Ladin's early communiqués focused in some detail on economic plight, insecurity, and lack of social justice within the Arabian Peninsula, he was quick to emphasize that these were merely symptoms of far more profound crimes orchestrated by the Saudi regime. "Our differences with the Saudi Regime surpass important incidental matters like economic collapse, administrative corruption, oppressing the people and confiscating their legal rights," bin Ladin argued in July 1995. "These differences become more important, greater, and deep-rooted matters [when concerning] the basic matter of the requirements of monotheism." The Saudi regime had "abandoned these concepts, and thus...completely lost its legitimacy."[64] Rather than being just politically or economically inept, the regime had declared "war against Islam and those calling for an implementation of its teachings."[65] "Whoever permits himself or others to follow a positive or man-made law is transgressing God's Law and therefore is an infidel and an apostate who no longer belongs to our religious community," bin Ladin declared in another open letter to the Saudi regime in August 1995. It was clear that the Saudi king had "committed the forbidden things in Islam which [would] nullify [the Saudi regime's] validity before God," according to bin Ladin. "The devastating failure and the dishonorable corruption which have been proven against [the] regime," bin Ladin continued, "are enough reasons to overthrow it."[66] The regime had "deviated from Islam and...committed apostasy."[67] It is important to note, however, that the focus of these declarations and denunciations was on the regime as a whole and its track record rather than individual persons and leadership figures. Arguing its actions went against the core tenets of Islam was crucial in order to justify any action against it. Misdeeds and corruption alone did not suffice to justify the overthrow of a regime, however unrepresentative, or question its legitimacy. This could only be done when it had been demonstrated that the regime was hostile to the interests of Islam.[68]

Similar labels could thus be attached to other regimes in the region. Aside from the sidelining of Islamic jurisprudence and legal codes, according to the leadership's interpretation, domestic association and cooperation with the great infidel forces of the West would provide further evidence of the apostasy and illegitimacy of such regimes. Political elites in the Islamic world were presented as "agents" of the West, traitors, "rulers of debauchery," and "stooges," even governments that were created by the Americans to begin with so as to act as "treacherous puppet regimes," such as those in power in the Palestinian territories and in Afghanistan and Iraq after the post-9/11 invasions.[69] Secular and "treacherous" regimes were therefore declared non-Muslim in Al-Qaeda's discourse, but these references were perhaps more abstract and removed than the more direct excommunication of particular groups of people. In this context, the Al-Qaeda leadership's attempts to present those who worked for or supported these regimes as apostates appear more significant, not least in light of the violent targeting of such "collaborators" that became common in Iraq and elsewhere.

In an early statement, written on behalf of the EIJ, for instance, Zawahiri spoke of the "huge armies of traitors consisting of soldiers, writers, teachers, artists, judges, legislators, journalists and media people" that supported these regimes "against the Muslims and their Jihadist vanguard ... [selling] Islam in exchange for benefits and security."[70]

Then there were the *ulema*: members of the religious establishment qualified in Islamic teachings and law. The Al-Qaeda leadership was particularly dismayed by their support for secular regimes and, no doubt, concerned about their ability to undermine Al-Qaeda's religio-political rhetoric. These scholars were denounced as "religious scholars of beggary, the ulema of flattery and the philosophers of defeat," who legitimized the rule of secular regimes. These scholars "sold" their *fatawa* as "commodities" in exchange for power and influence in order to please the heretic ruling class, according to Zawahiri.[71] "The long beards, huge turbans, majestic titles, purported lineages and popular myths," Zawahiri complained, "are no substitute for the truth and cannot conceal the crimes of cooperation with the Crusaders, loyalty to the infidel invaders and killing of the Muslims in Iraq and Afghanistan."[72] Even after the revolution that toppled the Mubarak regime in Egypt, Zawahiri complained that the "Sheikhs of Al-Azhar are no longer the sheikhs of Al-Azhar, instead, they have turned into trumpets of the government and tools to issue rulings upon order."[73] The pro-government *ulema*, therefore, not only offered supposedly impious regimes important support, but it also threatened to undermine Al-Qaeda's position.

Another group that Al-Qaeda perceived in very similar terms was the military. Since the rank and file in the Middle East and elsewhere might enjoy popular support and given the fact that some soldiers had themselves become prominent jihadi figures, the Al-Qaeda leadership normally stopped short of declaring all members of the armed forces apostates. Indeed, Zawahiri warned in his first set of responses to the 2008 "open meeting" that he would not recommend the declaring of whole armies as apostate, as there were certain "particulars" involved.[74]

For instance, during the "Arab Spring" uprisings in Egypt, when the Egyptian Army became the most powerful (and popular) political organization in the country, Zawahiri noted that although the generals were "in the pockets of the Americans and Israel" there certainly were honorable people within its ranks.[75] In relation to the Pakistani military the immediate stakes have been higher, however, and there has been greater anxiety over ongoing operations against Taliban and Al-Qaeda loyalists along the Afghan border. As a result, the Al-Qaeda leaders used their statements to declare soldiers in the Pakistani army "enemies of Islam" and "hunting dogs" of the Zionist-Crusader alliance whose eternal abode in the hereafter would be hellfire, unless they mended their ways and recanted.[76]

The significance of such wide-reaching declarations of apostasy is clear in light of the high ratio of terrorist attacks in Pakistan targeting members and recruits of the army and security apparatus. Another watershed in the widening of *takfiri* rhetoric in the Al-Qaeda leadership statements was the Iraq insurgency and the perceived need to foment chaos and derail US- and coalition-sponsored attempts by the government in Baghdad to increase stability.

Within the context of the Iraq War, bin Ladin reminded Muslims that "supporting the infidels against Muslims is one of the ten things that nullify Islam, as stipulated by scholars."[77] Those who assisted the occupying forces or the government in Baghdad, or embraced any institution derived from these illegitimate entities had therefore committed major sin and left "the community of Muslims." As a result it would be permissible to "spill their blood and take their property," and their marriages would be annulled, according to bin Ladin.[78] Jihad had come to Iraq, and failing to support and participate in holy war against foreign invaders and their local "agents" would not be a "forgivable stumble"[79] but a "cardinal sin."[80] Furthermore, any Iraqis or other Muslims who expressed discomfort with the levels of violence displayed by jihadists, which often targeted normal Iraqi citizens, and acknowledged the legitimacy of the post-invasion ruling order "by hand, tongue or pen," had "no right to live."[81]

The Al-Qaeda leadership had therefore gone from relatively ambiguous denunciations of unpalatable regimes in the 1990s to far more holistic interpretations of *takfir* that applied equally to supporters of secular regimes and non-Islamist societies. This escalation is particularly discernible in bin Ladin's public output. Zawahiri, as mentioned above, had a longer history of involvement in domestic extremism and was involved in the development of a more wide-reaching *takfiri* discourse through the EIJ. A document issued on behalf of the group in 1993, for instance, which was authored or commissioned by Zawahiri, warned that "someone who claims to be a Muslim and cites a democratic or socialist thinker becomes an unbeliever and an apostate."[82] This issue of the alleged apostasy of nationalism, socialism and democracy, or secularism as an alternative belief system to (violent extremist) Islam featured prominently in Zawahiri's output later as he condemned supporters of Turkish secularism, the Palestinian Authority, Palestinian nationalist movements, and similar platforms. Even Hamas was accused of taking a "ride with the American devil and his Saudi representative,"[83] although Zawahiri later pledged solidarity with the movement *if* it corrected its "march."[84] Fundamentally, however, there would be no respite for those who claimed to be "democratic Muslims" or supported participation in democratic societies. This would be no different from saying "I am a 'Jewish Muslim', or I am a 'Christian Muslim': they are 'apostate infidel[s]'," Zawahiri argued in his book on the Muslim Brothers, *The Bitter Harvest*, which was published in 1991.[85] Any dilution of the creed, as interpreted by Al-Qaeda, was tantamount to abrogation of all of its tenets and the creation of a "new religion," a "fairy tale" that the Americans and apostates called "enlightened moderation."[86]

Sectarianism and Shia Muslims

When it comes to questioning and judging the sincerity of a Muslim's faith, conventional wisdom would suggest that Shia Muslims would be particular targets of angry condemnation in the Al-Qaeda leadership discourse for alleged deviation from the "true" path. Much of this narrative is based on puritanical interpretations of Islamist doctrine and a nostalgic aspiration to revive the spirit that prevailed during the time of the Prophet Mohammed and his companions. As Fradkin notes, Salafist glorification of the *Salaf as-Salih*— the pious forefathers—brings to the forefront "the historical circumstances that eventually led to the division of Sunnis and Shiites, and the original quarrels which energized the hostility between them." "Since Shiites detest and even publicly revile the first three caliphs," Fradkin argues, "as well as others of the Salaf, the general orientation of modern Sunni Islamism was bound to deepen the already potent divide between it and Shiism, including Shiite Islamism."[87]

Based on this logic and the policy of Al-Qaeda's affiliates in Iraq, Riedel argued that "the anti-Shia violence promoted by al Qaeda's leader in Iraq, Abu Musab Al-Zarqawi, was not an aberration but a reflection of fundamental jihadist and al Qaeda thinking." Fomenting sectarian war and violence, targeting Shia populations in particular, was part of the overall Al-Qaeda strategy, and any misgivings over the level of violence displayed by Zarqawi were not aired publically, according to Riedel.[88] Indeed, when asked about the Sunni-Shia hostilities in Iraq and how to stop them, Zawahiri seemed to suggest the Shia were the belligerents and that aggression was primarily aimed at Sunni districts: "[D]on't ask the one under attack not to defend himself," he demanded.[89] Kepel and Milelli, meanwhile, take an alternative view, arguing that anti-Shiism was not part of Zawahiri's "stock in trade."[90] Kepel suggests that, on the issue of Iraq especially, Zawahiri tried to find common ground between Sunni and Shia populations. He points out that Zawahiri did not deride Prime Minister Nuri Al-Maliki as a Shia, but rather for his collaborative stance with the Americans, and appeared to make respectful references to Imams Ali and Husayn.[91] A careful analysis of bin Ladin's and Zawahiri's public statements would indeed appear to support this latter observation, even though sectarian references became more prominent as the Syrian civil war unfolded.

A few of their communiqués directly decried the alleged doctrinal deviation of Shiites. An early statement attributed to Zawahiri, for example, condemned the "heresy" committed by (Twelver) Shiites in the way in which they "distort[ed] ... the Quran and the image of the Islamic Caliphate."[92] Much later, the Shia were publically warned against collaborating with the government in Baghdad and accused of double standards, since they fought in Lebanon but not in Iraq.[93] They were seen as being led by "unjust rulers" and "religion traders" who strove to collaborate with the invading forces. "We haven't heard even one Fatwa from one Shiite authority, whether in Iran or elsewhere, calling for Jihad against the Americans in Iraq and Afghanistan," Zawahiri complained in an "interview" with *As-Sahab*, published in December 2007.[94] Indeed, the Shiite religious authorities had issued *fatawa* prohibiting fighting against the Americans in Iraq.[95] The "Safavids" (referring to Persian Shia imperialists),[96] therefore, were "stabbing the Ummah in the back in Afghanistan and Iraq," just as they had done when the Ottoman Empire was about to conquer Austria.[97] The subject of Iran rose to prominence again during the Syrian civil war as Zawahiri lamented the support that Assad's Ba'athist regime received from both the Iranian government and Hezbollah. In two statements issued in the spring of 2013, for instance, Zawahiri spoke of Iran's three "mistakes" in a "single decade." The first was the decision to support the American invasion of Afghanistan to topple the Taliban regime. The second mistake "was when its agents entered Iraq closely following and holding onto the American tanks." With the outbreak of civil war in Syria, Zawahiri argued, Iran's third mistake was its decision to aid Assad in his campaign of secularism and oppression.[98] In these statements, Zawahiri also expressed more enthusiastic support for Zarqawi than he had done before. The civil war in Syria in the years after the Arab Spring revolutions, therefore, has added to the sectarian dimensions of Al-Qaeda's leadership discourse, even though the focus continues to be on individual actors such as Hezbollah and the Iranian authorities, as well as the Shiite religious elite. Some statements, however, would carry broader accusations relating to Shia populations in the region in the Middle East and beyond.

The Al-Qaeda leadership warned Shia Muslims in Iraq, for instance, against attempting to fulfill any territorial ambitions through "severing" southern Iraq and reminded them that any collaboration with Americans or other external forces amounted to apostasy.[99] Although he mostly avoided discussing sectarian issues in Iraq and the need to target Shiites, Zawahiri argued in the 2008 "open meeting" that Sunnis were in fact a majority in Iraq if the Kurdish and Turkomen populations were aggregated and added to the number of Sunni Muslims in Baghdad and elsewhere.[100] Animosity toward the Shia population in Iraq in these leadership statements, therefore, was directly tied to their concerns that the (Shia-dominated) government in Iraq might succeed in asserting its control over the country. Those who collaborated with the government were condemned, but the reason they were condemned appears to rest on the fact that they were aiding a secular regime and not on their particular forms of worship. Participants and supporters of the post-invasion regime in Iraq would be seen as traitors, regardless of whether they were Sunni or Shia. This message was far less sectarian than that of affiliated leaders, especially Abu Musab Al-Zarqawi, whose focus was less global than that of the Al-Qaeda central leadership.[101]

In a 2004 statement bin Ladin explained: "The Iraqi who joins the renegade government to fight against the *Mujahidin* ... is considered a renegade and one of the infidels, even if he were an Arab from the Rabi'ah or Mudar tribes."[102] The preferred targeting justifications of the Al-Qaeda central leadership, therefore, were based on deeds and loyalties rather than strictly on creed, as they were for Zarqawi. The message in bin Ladin's and Zawahiri's public statements was that targeting strategy in Iraq should be focused on coalition forces and on their domestic collaborators. Indeed, attempts by Zarqawi and others to alter this target emphasis by focusing more on Shiites was met with cautionary advice from the Al-Qaeda leadership, as mentioned above, for example, in Zawahiri's letter to Zarqawi. A statement issued by Zawahiri shortly before Zarqawi's death also appeared to contain veiled criticism of the latter's stance: "God knows better his [Zarqawi's] hidden intents, which I hope are better than his public ones. O Abu Musab: Be patient, stand fast, and rely only on God," Zawahiri implored.[103] Even bin Ladin's public "eulogy" of Zarqawi reemphasized that "whoever insisted on fighting along with the Crusaders against Muslims should be killed, *regardless of their sect or tribe."*[104]

The Al-Qaeda leaders recognized that the Shia population of Iraq would be tempted to accept the new post-Saddam order and used their statements to appeal to notions of Islamic solidarity and even the Shiite legacy itself and feelings of historical pride in order to appeal to the Iraqi Shiite population. Zawahiri, for example, issued the following appeal to Shia Muslims in a video message from December 2006:

And I call on [Shiites] to ask [themselves] a courageous and brave question: were Imam Ali ... or our chief Hasan ... or our chief Husayn [the first three

Imams] present today in Iraq or Afghanistan, would they have colluded with the Crusaders in the invasion of the lands of Islam, and then cooperate with them and fight the *Mujahideen* in defense of them? ... Or would they have declared Jihad against them and those who help them?[105]

Shiites were reminded that "the *Mujahideen* are the supporters of al-Husayn ... and are his allies and soldiers."[106] "You obey al-Husayn ... by obeying America?! And you raise the banner of al-Husayn ... under the cross of America?!," Zawahiri lamented in a video statement issued in July 2007.[107] The animosity expressed thus appeared to be linked to current affairs and alleged treachery of those who cooperated with the local government and coalition forces, rather than on doctrinal differences or foundational origins. In June 2011, Zawahiri even compared the "martyrdom" of bin Ladin to the assassination of Al-Husayn in Karbala.[108] When asked to explain his position regarding doctrinal issues vis-à-vis the Shia, Zawahiri retorted: "[M]y stance towards the Shii'ite laity is ... that they are excused through their ignorance." To those Shia Muslims who refrained from assisting the "Crusade," Zawahiri commented: "[O]ur way with them is invitation and displaying of facts, and clarifying the extent of the crimes committed by their leaders against Islam."[109]

The Al-Qaeda leadership's attitude toward Shia Muslims, therefore, is far from congenial, but still far less hostile than that expressed by the likes of Zarqawi. When Shiites are admonished in the statements, the focus is on "corrupt" leaders, and other actors, such as Iran, that shore up the "treacherous" regime in Baghdad, undermining Al-Qaeda's plans in the region. Animosity is therefore qualified in this way, and often linked to specific actors. Even with the case of Iran, some early statements suggested that ultimately any outstanding differences between the Sunni and Shia camps could be settled. In a 1997 interview, for instance, bin Ladin argued that "The United States is the common enemy of both Iran and the Taleban. One day, relations between Iran and Afghanistan will improve ... If Afghanistan, Pakistan, Iran and China get united, the United States and India will become ineffective."[110]

What is perhaps most striking from the Al-Qaeda leaders' aggregated statements is the extent to which the issue of Shia mobilization, that of the consolidation of Iranian influence in the region, and other issues relating to power balances and militant groups in the Middle East and beyond are largely absent. This lack of attention in the Al-Qaeda communiqués largely comes down to a question of emphasis. The Shia are certainly not potential allies or, necessarily, even sympathizers, but their targeting is not prioritized. Arguably, both leaders would have had plenty of opportunities to launch into elaborate juristic and theological attacks on Shiism but very rarely, if ever, chose to do so. Bin Ladin and Zawahiri instead decided to focus their statements and books on the alleged shortcomings of (those who claim to be) Sunni Muslims and the danger posed by foreign infidels.

Perhaps one of the most vivid examples of this is a video statement that *As-Sahab* published on behalf of Zawahiri in May 2012. Titled "Yemen: Between a Fugitive Puppet and His New Replacement," the focus of the publication was on the ongoing situation in Yemen following the departure of president Saleh. The video featured excerpts from Zawahiri's address as well as a message from Anwar Al-Awlaki. Both ideologues appealed directly to Muslim audiences urging them to fight for reform. While Zawahiri called for the end of corruption, the "purification" of society from secular rulers, and the establishment of shariah—all common themes in his rhetoric—Al-Awlaki struck a far more sectarian tone. "What is your program to resist the Shiite expansion that is taking over the region from Iran to Yemen?," Al-Awlaki asked local scholars. "The Iranian leadership," he warned, "does not work for the benefit of the Islamic program, but it is working for the sake of the Persian Shiite program, and the Sunni people of the Gulf will be Iran's first victim." [111] Other Sunni extremist figures have expressed far more vehement animosity toward the Shia than Al-Awlaki, but even he seemed to be more willing to engage in sectarian issues than the Al-Qaeda central leadership.

Takfirism, therefore, is certainly a feature of bin Ladin's and Zawahiri's discourse but its scope is not holistic, and allegations of apostasy are frequently linked to particular actions and actors rather than inherent qualities of specific communities. The justifications for such allegations, moreover, rest on the presumption that "apostates" and "traitors" have fundamentally harmed the core interests of the *ummah.*

The Sunni Muslim masses are Al-Qaeda's most significant target audience. Thus, if normal Muslim publics were alienated and their concerns ignored, the leadership would have failed to present Al-Qaeda as the pious vanguard dedicated to the physical and moral defense of the *ummah* that it purported to represent. When Zawahiri's and bin Ladin's direct appeals toward the *ummah* are analyzed in detail, however, it emerges that these aggregated messages reveal a sense of exasperation that undermines the image of unity and collective experiences that the leadership has sought so carefully to construct. Al-Qaeda's communicative strategy toward Muslims, therefore, does not simply consist of appeals toward those who are deemed "true" Muslims and denunciation of those seen as traitors. An increasingly prominent stance evolved in the leaders' public statements that falls between these two opposite positions—excommunication versus positive appeals—where Al-Qaeda's growing frustration with the *ummah* becomes tangible.

Giving up on the masses

In a statement published by *As-Sahab* in March 2008, bin Ladin defined three "factions" of Muslims. First were the *mujahideen* and their immediate supporters. These were the most heroic and righteous of all Muslims: the fighters who were prepared to sacrifice everything in order to replicate the spirit, practices, and achievements of the Prophet Mohammed and his companions. The second category referred to apathetic Muslims, those who had failed to support the *mujahideen* as they fought infidelity and injustice. Finally, the third faction of Muslims consisted of advocates of "Christian-Zionist" intervention in Islamic affairs, who were seen as apostates who had sinned and left the fold of Islam.[112] The preceding section described this third category that concerned the so-called apostates. Much of the Al-Qaeda leadership's communicative effort toward Muslims, however, has focused on bin Ladin's first two "categories" and the apparent need to reconcile both groups. The Al-Qaeda leadership's objective was to convince those deemed "apathetic" to support the glorious *mujahideen* and everything they represent. Positive appeals and expressions of unity formed part of this approach, as described at the beginning of this chapter. Given the length of time that the Al-Qaeda leadership had been engaged in militancy and its related public media campaign, however, it was also forced to respond to the fact that mass mobilization, as envisaged in its rhetoric, had failed to materialize.

Only very rarely did the Al-Qaeda leaders suggest that their organization might be responsible for the lack of popular support that they enjoyed. In his 2001 memoirs, for instance, Zawahiri wrote:

> The jihad movement must come closer to the masses, defend their honor, fend off injustice, and lead them to the path of guidance and victory...We must win the people's confidence, respect, and affection. The people will not love us unless they felt that we love them, care about them, and are ready to defend them...We must not blame the nation for not responding or not living up to the task. Instead, we must blame ourselves for failing to deliver the message, show compassion, and sacrifice.[113]

For most of Zawahiri's subsequent output, however, he appeared to contradict these words by blaming "the nation" for failing to respond. Criticism of Muslims, therefore, forms an important—and increasingly prominent—part of the Al-Qaeda leadership statements. This element of its communicative strategy, however, is more complex than its *takfiri* rhetoric.

Broadly speaking, Al-Qaeda's critical approach toward Muslim communities can be divided into two main categories, depending on the nature of the audience: approaches to confined groups of elites and activists on the one hand, and approaches to the wider public on the other. Figure 6.2 places these references on a timeline to illustrate the shifts in these attitudes that emerged over time.[114] The 9/11 attacks are placed on the timeline for illustrative purposes. As shown in the figure, criticism directed primarily against elites and specific groups has been fairly consistent throughout the period under review. Denunciation of Muslim publics, however, is a more recent phenomenon. Although these sentiments were expressed prior to the 9/11 attacks, they appear to have been a particular feature of the post-9/11 discourse, as shown in Figure 6.2.

Unsurprisingly, as the timeline in Figure 6.2 illustrates, the Al-Qaeda leadership expended considerable effort publically to criticize members of the religious, political, and activist elite, in order to highlight significant ways in which they had erred and where Al-Qaeda might thus present viable alternatives.

Indeed, in early communiqués, this was a chief preoccupation of the leadership, which was reflected in its output. Although mainstream politicians were quickly considered outside the realm of Islam, declaring *ulema*, or Islamic scholars, and leaders of Islamist groups as apostates would have been much more problematic and beyond the level of denunciation deemed appropriate at the time.

Bin Ladin's and Zawahiri's statements from the early 1990s focused their criticism on individual scholars or movement leaders who were accused of drifting away from the "true" interpretation of the faith. Such allegations,

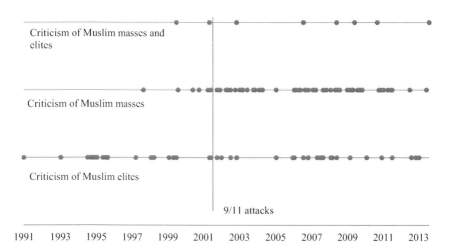

FIGURE 6.2 *Criticism of Muslim masses and Muslim elites: statements on timeline*

however, are distinct from those levied at "apostate" rulers or their collaborators and allies. Many of the figures in question were religiously ordained, or had considerable clout and experience, and could not be easily challenged. Even when responding to the scathing criticism of Sayyid Imam al-Sharif (or "Dr Fadl"), for example, Zawahiri attempted to separate the "words" from the person for whom he still claimed to have great respect,[115] even though he later implied "Dr Fadl" had always been a marginal figure within the EIJ.[116]

Nonetheless, any Islamist alternatives to the path prescribed by Al-Qaeda that undermined the use of violent jihad posed a considerable threat to the militant Islamist fringe. This anxiety contributed to Zawahiri's publication of *Bitter Harvest*, and many subsequent works,[117] and bin Ladin's letters to the Saudi grand mufti Ibn Baz. Other religious scholars in the Arab world were also warned that support for governments that failed to implement the shariah would be "viewed as a disgrace … on the day of judgment."[118] After the initial Arab Spring revolutions, the Al-Qaeda leaders sought to maneuver themselves into a position where they could celebrate the toppling of secular governments, but still criticize the "mildly" Islamist parties that emerged in the aftermath.[119]

Denunciations of members of the *ulema* and Islamist groups became increasingly irate over time. Initial communiqués talked of "errors" being made and expressed disbelief over some of the stances and declarations that were being disseminated, offering "polite advice" to those who had erred.[120] Later, in order to isolate those who issued *fatawa* that contradicted Al-Qaeda's public stance, bin Ladin sought to divide the *ulema* into "good" and "bad" scholars,[121] noting the immense gulf that separated "scholars who act and the scholars who compromise."[122] This avoided the more problematic stance of condemning all *ulema*. Scholars belonging to the latter category were chastised for their materialistic ambitions, closeness to secular leaders, acquiescence of foreign infiltration, and other ills. Support for secular regimes and failure to condemn the presence of foreign troops in Muslim countries provoked outrage within the Al-Qaeda leadership, which accused "the scholars of evil and hired writers [of changing] their attitude to best suit the ruler."[123] These "sellers of religion" and "scholars of beggary" needed to be isolated and challenged, as noted above.[124]

Aside from criticizing Islamist leaders and scholars, the Al-Qaeda leadership has also spent considerable effort admonishing leaders of other Islamist militant groups. Former colleagues—particularly in the case of Zawahiri—are obviously denounced for having abandoned jihad. In addition to Sayyid Imam's criticism, denunciations of militancy by other Egyptians, formerly prominent on the violent extremist scene, prompted angry responses from Zawahiri. One of the more embarrassing retractions involved members of Zawahiri's own EIJ, including Abu Yasir, who signed the February 1998 declaration in support of the establishment of the World Islamic Front against Jews and Crusaders. Less than a year later he and other members of his group had renounced violence. In response, Zawahiri wrote a private letter warning Yasir and others that they would lose "both in this world [and] in the thereafter" as a result of the decision.[125]

In relation to the Afghan jihad, moreover, the leadership was keen to emphasize that anything that detracted from the continuation and expansion of hostilities against infidels and their allies would put any military gains in jeopardy. This was no less important in relation to ongoing operations in Afghanistan against NATO and the government in Kabul. Militant leaders including Burhanuddin Rabbani, Ahmed Shah Masud (who was assassinated by Al-Qaeda operatives), and Gulbuddin Hekmatyar (who since became a potent adversary of coalition forces in Afghanistan) were thus accused of fomenting discord among the *mujahideen* following Soviet withdrawal in Afghanistan, failing to support the Taliban government and liaising with the United Nations.[126] Ironically, as already mentioned, bin Ladin also criticized his Taliban hosts for the restrictions they imposed upon him even when "the United States is free to do whatever it feels like."[127]

More recently, other militant groups operating locally in the Middle East, North Africa, South and Central Asia, and beyond have become the focus of criticism in the Al-Qaeda leadership communiqués. This relates, in particular, to Hamas and Hezbollah, both likely rivals for public support, sympathy, and attention in the Levant and beyond. Hamas, as mentioned, was accused of abandoning government by shariah, of betraying Muslims in the Caucasus, of sacrificing "four-fifths" of Palestine, and of other alleged shortcomings in increasingly angry outbursts from the Al-Qaeda leadership. Zawahiri was especially preoccupied with what he saw as a gradual abandonment of nonnegotiable red lines that Al-Qaeda was supposedly prepared to defend: "I took a gradual approach with HAMAS," Zawahiri insisted, "from support to repeated advice to warning to general criticism."[128] Hamas had thus been something of a last bastion of hope for indigenous Palestinian groups to respond correctly to the challenges presented, as other groups in the territories had, according to Zawahiri, "allied themselves with the devil, but lost Palestine."[129] Another reason for increased animosity toward the Hamas leadership of course, aside from ideological roots in the Muslim Brotherhood, was the group's success in purging Gaza of Al-Qaeda affiliates and loyalists.[130]

In terms of references to Hezbollah, substantive and doctrinal reasons were also prominent in bin Ladin's and Zawahiri's critique of the group and Hassan Nasrallah, its secretary-general, even though more immediate concerns over competition for public support no doubt played a prominent role. Indeed, both bin Ladin and Zawahiri became more vocal in their criticism of Hezbollah after the 2006 war with Israel when Hezbollah managed to generate widespread support and admiration in the region. The group was often presented in the statements as a largely secular organization that had diluted any religious elements in its charter through cooperating and compromising with apostates and infidels and taking part in the party political process. The Al-Qaeda leaders accused the group of failing to "liberate Palestine" when opportunities permitted, of being reluctant to attack Israel, and of ignoring the people of Gaza completely. Nasrallah was seen as a hypocrite who secretly liaised with the UN and other hostile entities in the region in order to maximize his power and influence. Zawahiri even compared Nasrallah to his former archenemy, Hosni Mubarak.[131] Bin Ladin drew parallels between Hezbollah and the hated regimes of Anwar Sadat and King Hussein of Jordan.[132] Interestingly, however, Hezbollah's Shia credentials were rarely the focus of this criticism until the group's involvement in the Syrian civil war, which broke out in spring 2011, became a more prominent topic, as noted above.

As the perceived pinnacle of a vanguard, it is hardly surprising that the Al-Qaeda leadership admonishes Islamic elites and activist networks that purport to provide alternative solutions and strategies, even when problem diagnosis is often similar and even when both compete for much the same grassroots support, in order to retain legitimacy and relevancy. What is much more significant, however, is the way in which the leadership approaches this grassroots support. In this respect, any evidence suggesting that the Al-Qaeda leaders present the general public as having failed their Islamist vanguard and, by extension as far as Al-Qaeda's narrative is concerned, the legacy of the Prophet, becomes particularly illustrative of the leadership's isolation.

"The nation has failed to support us"

Figure 6.2 shows how prior to the 9/11 attacks very few references were made in the Al-Qaeda leadership communiqués that were critical of the general Muslim population. The *ummah* was warned in the statements that "whoever denies even a minor tenet of our religion, commits the gravest sin in Islam." However, most of the content from the 1990s traced responsibility squarely back to elites and decision-makers.[133] The authorities and members of the *ulema* were accused of seeking to "anesthetize" the Muslim population with alternative versions of Islam that appeared to have had some impact on the youth and others who did not know better.[134] The general population in this sense was seen as gullible and susceptible to such impious forces unless led by a vanguard of righteous *mujahideen* to whom the *ummah* owes loyalty, according to Al-Qaeda.

In a statement issued together with bin Ladin and aired on Al Jazeera a year before the 9/11 attacks, the traditionally more scathing Zawahiri complained that Muslims had spoken much but done little to fight the "tyrannical" and infidel enemies that were damaging the interests of Muslims.[135] In his introduction to a new jihadi magazine published in Egypt during this period, Zawahiri warned that a new Islamic generation had grown up that had adopted Western-influenced norms and practices that were far removed from the traditional "Islamic manners and behaviors."[136] These criticisms were very similar to those put forward by other prominent Islamist ideologues, such as Sayyid Qutb. To address this deviation, according to Zawahiri, it was essential for the Al-Qaeda vanguard to guide the *ummah* to the correct path through the dissemination of statements directed toward the general public.

Rich Muslims were a particular focus of criticism in the leaders' statements, both before and after 9/11. In a statement published online in May 2005, bin Ladin condemned all Muslims who sought to secure worldly gains rather than live by the tenets of the faith.[137] "We live in a world where the majority of the people constantly worry about accumulating wealth," bin Ladin complained a year later, asking "how should I correct those who sell themselves for a few pennies?"[138] For Muslims, this was a particularly important moral question, given the extent of suffering that affected so many, especially in Palestine: "[H]ow can the wealthy hold on to their riches when the Palestinians are defending themselves without arms?"[139]

The aftermath of the 9/11 attacks brought unprecedented pressures on the Al-Qaeda leadership, which was forced to flee its haven in Afghanistan and abandon the support networks that had been established in the country. The impact of this pressure and the need to secure support from the wider Muslim population to compensate for the loss of Taliban protection was reflected in bin Ladin's and Zawahiri's statements. In one of his first messages after the attacks, bin Ladin warned Muslims that those who failed to support the new jihad in Afghanistan and Pakistan against America, its local allies, and coalition forces would face the wrath of God on the Day of Judgment.[140] Although hailed as a huge success for Al-Qaeda and for the interests that the leadership purported to represent, it appears—based on the nature of the evolving message directed toward Muslim audiences—that the attacks mark the beginning of a shift in this communicative approach. After the 9/11 attacks, the messages gradually became increasingly irate, and criticism— even condemnation—of the general population, the *ummah* that Al-Qaeda claims to represent, became a prominent feature of the discourse. A central theme was the perceived need for Muslims to realize that aid and support for Al-Qaeda and the *mujahideen* fighting in Afghanistan and Pakistan was the duty of all Muslims, irrespective of where they lived. A month after the commencement of hostilities in Afghanistan, bin Ladin released a statement to Al Jazeera warning that "anyone who lines up behind Bush in this campaign has committed one of the ten actions that sully one's Islam." Strikes against the Taliban in Afghanistan were merely part of a wider conspiracy against Muslims who all needed to unite under one banner.[141] Muslims were lying in slumber, failing to realize their duty and living in a world of "laziness and discontent," which was causing an acute crisis for defenders of the creed.[142] "For how long will real men be in short supply?," bin Ladin asked in a poem posted online in June 2002.[143] A year after the United States and its allies invaded Afghanistan in response to 9/11, bin Ladin reflected upon the developments over the past 12 months and the wider implications for the existing state of the Islamic nation, lamenting the absence of popular support:

> My *mujahidin* brothers and I were grieved when we saw our nation in the east and west watching the United States, the head of unbelief, afflicting the worst of torment on the oppressed men, women, and children while the nation watched the painful scene as if it was watching an entertainment movie … If every Muslim asks himself why has our nation reached this state of humiliation and defeat, then his obvious answer is because it rushed madly for the comforts of life and discarded the Book of Allah behind its back … Today, the nation has failed to support us and support the loyal ones from the students of religion who established the first Islamic state in Afghanistan that applied Allah's shari'ah.[144]

If Muslims continued to fail to rise up against these forces of infidelity, "then everybody will be sinful"[145] and remain sinful until the *ummah* "produces her sons, her wealth and her power to the extent of being able to wage Jihad and defend against the evil of the disbelievers," bin Ladin warned.[146] At a time of great volatility for the leadership, therefore, the onus was very much on the Muslim general public to come to its aid. Of the two leaders, criticism of Muslims seems even more vocal and hard-hitting in Zawahiri's output, who usually blamed normal Muslims, rather than himself or Al-Qaeda, for the lack of mobilization achieved in the face of ongoing hostilities in Afghanistan, Iraq, and elsewhere.

Indeed, bin Ladin's final communiqué was in many ways illustrative of his general approach to the *ummah* in the majority of his messages. The *ummah* was seen as numb and unresponsive despite the injustices it was facing, primarily because the rulers had "sabotaged the minds of the Ummah" through their control of the media and "religious governmental institutions."[147] The role of the Prophet Mohammed (and many other prophets before him), as a shepherd guiding and protecting his flock, provides a powerful metaphor that bin Ladin embraced. Muslims needed guidance and direction in order to respond to the challenges they faced, and the Al-Qaeda leaders were keen to put themselves forward for that role.

Alienating the grass roots

Like bin Ladin, Zawahiri's initial warnings toward the *ummah* also concerned the apparent "defeatism" that was preventing proper mobilization in support of Al-Qaeda and the Taliban in Afghanistan and beyond to materialize.[148] In his statements from 2005 onward, however, Zawahiri began to focus increasingly on the alleged failure of the general Muslim population to recognize and fulfill its religious and moral responsibility in the face of local and foreign adversaries and corrupting ideas. Local, secular regimes were thus "winning over the *mujahideen*," not because there was anything wrong with the tactics and ideology of Al-Qaeda but because Muslims were too afraid and protective about their safety and well-being. There were so many Muslims who had contracted this "malignant illness," leaving little hope for victory. The Muslim *ummah* had become paralyzed by "subjugation, ignorance, fear and resignation."[149]

As opposed to earlier messages in the 1990s, when bin Ladin blamed lackluster opposition against local "tyrants" on the smothering power of these elites themselves, Zawahiri saw the general public as responsible. "How? O Ummah, have you kept silent about this corruption in order for it to reach this degree of despotism?"—Zawahiri asked as he sought to rationalize the continued domination of Saudi politics and society by the House of Saud.[150] Even if the *ummah* did respond in some way to the oppression it witnessed, the force of its resolve paled in comparison to the strength of the opposition and extent of the crimes committed. Protests, screams, and shouts would lead nowhere, Zawahiri argued, except to defeat.[151] The repercussions of this lackluster response would be severe for the *ummah*. In his "open meeting" initiative, which was intended as a public relations exercise to mobilize popular support in favor of Al-Qaeda and to ensure that the movement did not become marginalized amid the turmoil, Zawahiri instead employed harsh rhetoric condemning the general Muslim population worldwide for its failings:

I call on the Islamic nation to fear the day when God will ask it why it failed to back its *mujahideen* brothers…The Islamic world has not only failed to support the Islamic Emirate in Afghanistan, but a propaganda campaign was launched against it by the rulers' scholars, Iran's agents, and groups affiliated with Islam in support of their colleagues who were in control of five per cent of Afghanistan … Muslims should repent to God for failing to support [the] Taliban, and they should know that God will ask them about their failure to support [the Taliban].[152]

In Zawahiri's view, therefore, Muslims were essentially cowards. They lacked the fighting spirit and resolve to tackle the domestic and external enemies that they faced, and their only possible salvation was to follow the example of Al-Qaeda and accept the worldview its leadership presented. The Muslims' most fundamental enemy, therefore, was "this defeatist spirit, hesitation, and attachment to safety which motivates us to backtrack whenever the tyrants attack us and to plead with them."[153] This "shame" could ultimately be the downfall of the *ummah*. Muslims had for too long favored safety and allowed Jews and America to become embedded in Palestine. Muslims had a "tendency to be enslaved," which explained why they had failed for so long to liberate Palestine and repel the threat posed by their enemies, far and near.[154] These general, often abstract and holistic references to the consequences of inaction and responsibility for failure shift the blame for the disappointing of stated objectives onto the general public and circumvent any reassessment of Al-Qaeda's arguments and its benchmarks of success.

Criticism and denunciation of Muslim publics in the Al-Qaeda leader's statements was even more pronounced when the focus was on particular geographic regions. This applied especially to those living in areas of ongoing conflict where there were opportunities for compromise, peacemaking, and reconciliation with external forces and domestic agitators. The criticism also reflects the anger of the Al-Qaeda leadership toward those who failed to embrace the belief system of Islamist violent extremism when they had the opportunity of doing so. This anger was directed primarily toward the people of Pakistan, Iraq, the Palestinian territories, and Egypt. Even though the publics involved often endured considerable hardships, the language used has often been stark and unforgiving.

Despite decades of conflict in the Palestinian territories, for example, Zawahiri expressed his disappointment with "people who have collapsed and are still collapsing" in Palestine and those who accepted UN resolutions and other peace initiatives. The only option available to the Palestinians, according to Zawahiri, was violent jihad. Indeed, as they were on the front line in the battle with infidelity, this was an individual obligation. It was imperative for Palestinians to multiply their rocket attacks, martyrdom operations, and ambushes against the Israelis regardless of the consequences. Anything else amounted to defeat, according to Zawahiri.[155] Even Palestinians who had been imprisoned were criticized in Al-Qaeda's rhetoric for not doing enough to liberate Palestine or for being members of nationalist and secular groups.[156]

The strongest criticism, however, has been reserved for Iraqis and Pakistanis—Muslims who have also suffered some of the most gruesome and sustained campaigns of violence by Al-Qaeda affiliates and associates. As mentioned above, Iraqis of all sects and tribes were warned not to cooperate with the government in Baghdad or participate in elections. Those who embraced the party political model were condemned as "charlatans" and blamed for the chaos the country had endured.[157] Perhaps the stakes became even higher in Pakistan, the adopted home of bin Ladin and Zawahiri, and numerous messages from both leaders addressed alleged hesitation, even betrayal, of the Pakistani population.

The people of Pakistan were asked how they could allow local and foreign security forces to "hurt" their "brothers," the Taliban, when it was an individual obligation to support them.[158] The only other option aside from jihad was idleness, which was the way of the disobedient ones.[159] "Rigged elections" and politics were not the way to salvation—only jihad was. As a result, the people of Pakistan were duty bound to "back the *Mujahideen* in Afghanistan with [their] persons, wealth, opinion and expertise."[160] If Pakistanis stood by passively without offering support to the *mujahideen* they would contribute to the destruction of both Pakistan and Afghanistan and would deserve the painful punishment that they would receive from Allah.[161] Indeed, the chaotic state of affairs in Pakistan was largely the fault of the general population itself, according to Al-Qaeda, and the fact that people had "abandoned the obligation of enjoining good and forbidding evil."[162] Their silence in the face of corruption and collusion with the enemy, moreover, had rendered the state incapable of responding to natural disasters and catastrophes that had befallen Pakistan. There were "deviations from Islam" among "many of the people of Pakistan," Zawahiri warned. Many were either secularists or would take part in Islamic traditions only as a ritual, which was meaningless beyond the walls of the mosques, and many would accept innovation.[163] "Aren't there any honorable ones in Pakistan?," Zawahiri asked in his "open meeting" appeal, "isn't there anyone who prefers the hereafter to the life of this world?"[164] The people of Pakistan had become a "people without honor, without sanctity, without pride [and] without any worth."[165] Their only hope was to repent and reenter Islam, warned Zawahiri.[166]

This alienation of large segments of Al-Qaeda's supposed target audience is distinct from the reputational problems it has incurred due to the excessive killing of noncombatants and Muslims by its affiliates. In terms of violent attacks perpetrated by affiliated groups, the role of the Al-Qaeda leadership has often been indirect. That is obviously not the case with its public media campaign. The way in which the Al-Qaeda leadership's public attitude toward normal Muslims has become more exacerbated in the years after 9/11 becomes very vivid when these leadership statements are reviewed over an extended period of time.

Isolation could be compounded by irrelevance. In terms of the latter, Zawahiri's criticism of the people of Egypt, to which he devoted the majority of his career in jihad, provides the best examples. Zawahiri traced the "primary cause of the humiliation and disgrace…reached in Egypt and the other countries of the Muslims" to the "Muslims' tardiness in resisting oppression, enjoining good and forbidding evil, fear, hesitation, clinging to life's crumbs, the culture of withdrawal, the methodology of defeatism." These were "the most important reasons for Egypt being transformed from a fortress for the defense of Islam into a helper, aide and partner in the American-Zionist Crusade assault." The only way out, again, was in the form of jihad, but specifically through a campaign led by a "believing vanguard" over which Zawahiri thought he presided.[167] For Zawahiri, the people of Egypt were largely apathetic and incapable or unwilling to topple the tyrannical system that prevailed in the country. They would be unable to change anything or organize any form of uprising without the stern, righteous leadership of an Islamist vanguard and unsuccessful so long as they thought protests and demonstrations would be a vehicle for change rather than violent jihad.[168] The events of the Arab Spring of course surprised many commentators and experts, and the fact that Zawahiri failed to predict how they unfolded is not necessarily a major challenge to his credibility in and of itself. More interesting is the way in which Zawahiri communicated, through his messages to the people of Egypt and the wider Muslim population, his lack of confidence in the strength of their resolve and bravery. It is almost as if Zawahiri in particular had dismissed the activist potential of precisely the people he was seeking to mobilize in support of his movement. This public exasperation appears to contradict the confidence that is otherwise implicit in Al-Qaeda's discourse that a substantial proportion of the masses can be mobilized in the interests of particular causes and stated objectives. This begs the question: How effective is Al-Qaeda's message and what might be its long-term impact?

Ideas expressed through public communiqués do not necessarily have a limited shelf life. Even if principal ideologues and advocates are deceased, the ideas conveyed can live on and often reach even more people and achieve greater prominence than before. Abdullah Azzam, for instance, who was killed when Al-Qaeda was being formed, still appears to be popular among Islamist extremists more than two decades after his death, at least judging by public tributes in his honor and the republication and distribution of his works.[169] The same, of course, applies to many medieval figures and scholars, including Ibn Taymiyyah.

There is little doubt that both Zawahiri and bin Ladin wished to secure such a legacy through the messages they published on behalf of their movement. The extent to which their words will live on, however, and the degree to which the model they created and sustained over the years will resonate with the wider community of potential supporters and sympathizers depend in part on the impact and permanence of their message. The next chapter offers reflections on the durability of the Al-Qaeda leadership's message, focusing on contradictions, tensions, and inconsistencies that have emerged over the years.

7

Contradictions, tensions, and inconsistencies

The impact of Al-Qaeda's message

Just over a month after bin Ladin was killed at his compound in Abbottabad, Pakistan, Ayman Al-Zawahiri, now the official leader of Al-Qaeda, issued a statement honoring the "noble knight." Zawahiri insisted that bin Ladin had achieved his objectives. Rather than any operational accomplishments, Zawahiri chose to focus on bin Ladin's desire to "incite the Ummah to jihad." Bin Ladin's message had "reached from East to West and all over the world. The Muslims answered it", Zawahiri argued, "as did all the oppressed on the face of the earth. And today, all praise be to Allah, America does not face an individual, group, or sect. No, it faces a rising Ummah that has awoken from its slumber in a Jihadi awakening that challenges it wherever it is."[1] Aside from Zawahiri's predictable celebration of bin Ladin's supposed accomplishments, his statement is revealing in the extent to which the dissemination of messages and mobilization of the *ummah* are presented as the leadership's main priority and hallmark of success, rather than any operational or activist achievements. In another eulogy of a fallen Al-Qaeda commander—Abu Yahya Al-Libi—Zawahiri again emphasized the extent to which "the martyrdom of our martyrs will make the message of jihad spread more and become more acceptable and more deeply-rooted." "Now that Shaykh Abu Yahya, God rest his soul, is martyred," Zawahiri argued, "people will take more interest in his writings and *dawah* [proselytizing]. The martyrdom brings the words alive as said by the two martyrs Sayyid Qutb and Abdullah Azzam." "The more our blood is shed for the sake of our faith, the more alive our words will become," Zawahiri insisted.[2] This was the legacy the Al-Qaeda leadership hoped for. Direct involvement in acts of violence was important and added to the credibility of the Al-Qaeda leadership within jihadi circles, but in the long term, the resonance of Al-Qaeda's message was what mattered.

This book has approached bin Ladin and Zawahiri as constants, a core within a wider array of actors, followers, and adversaries, throughout the fluid and tumultuous life span of Al-Qaeda from its inception in the aftermath of the Soviet-Afghan war and up until and beyond the death of bin Ladin and the revolutions of the Arab Spring. Looking beyond organizational models to focus on ideational components and the public discourse of the Al-Qaeda leadership, the evolution of Al-Qaeda has been studied through the systematic scrutiny of the leadership's statements. These, in turn, have been understood with reference to the literature on collective action frames that explain how movements and movement leaders seek to generate action-orientated messages that legitimize and inspire support for their particular stance and agenda. Based on this framework, the content of Al-Qaeda's message can be divided into problem diagnosis, offered solutions, and the efforts to communicate these elements to specific audiences. Zawahiri and bin Ladin have not acted as passive transmitters of stagnant or predetermined beliefs and ideas. They are, as Benford and Snow's framing concept assumes, "actively engaged in the production of meaning for participants, antagonists and observers." They interpret relevant events and conditions in an effort to "mobilize potential adherents and constituents, to garner bystander support and to demobilize antagonists."[3] Any assessment of the role and impact of Al-Qaeda, therefore, necessarily needs to include an evaluation of the messages disseminated. How could these messages and their impact be assessed?

Afghan war veteran Abu'l-Walid warned in 1993 that "a movement that is isolated from its masses, that is suspicious of its people, and whose people are suspicious of it, can achieve nothing but destroy itself."[4] Marginalization and isolation has become an increasingly acute danger for the Al-Qaeda leadership in recent years. The physical isolation of the leadership following the flight from Afghanistan after the Taliban regime collapsed raised questions about the leadership's ability to exert control over groups and individuals operating in Al-Qaeda's name. The sheer volume of the bloodshed inflicted by these affiliates and derivatives, moreover, presented new challenges as the Al-Qaeda leadership, or what was left of it, risked becoming so unpopular in the Muslim world and its pool of recruits and resources so diminished that it faced a similar demise to that of the ostracized Algerian GIA (Groupe Islamique Armé). At least to begin with, the Arab Spring revolutions also undermined the reach and credibility of the Al-Qaeda leadership as the hated Arab tyrants so despised in Al-Qaeda leadership statements were toppled by popular, largely secular, and, in some important cases, relatively peaceful revolts rather than a religiously fervent campaign of jihad, which was what the leadership had envisaged. The question that remained, therefore, was: What will be the legacy of Al-Qaeda and will its "brand" continue to resonate? For Zawahiri, this would rest primarily on the continued impact of Al-Qaeda's worldview, agenda, and message. This question does not concern the operational readiness or capacity of Al-Qaeda but relates to something less tangible, more abstract, but no less important. Questions concerning Al-Qaeda's continued ability to inspire and the continued resonance of its message are at the heart of the future development of Islamist militancy.

Numerous observers have sought to address this question through conducting or analyzing public opinion polls and surveys. Gerges, for instance, quoted a survey showing that "93 percent of respondents [in Muslim majority countries] condemned, on religious and humanitarian grounds, the killing of noncombatants."[5] The Pew Research Center conducted numerous surveys measuring the appeal of Al-Qaeda. On the surface, the results would appear to indicate that in recent years the leadership started to lose support from target audiences. According to Pew polls, by the time of his death, expressed confidence in bin Ladin had largely plummeted in Muslim majority countries from figures as high as 70 percent in the Palestinian Territories to less than 30 percent, with much less confidence expressed in the other Muslim countries surveyed. Around 20–30 percent of respondents claimed to view Al-Qaeda favorably in the Palestinian Territories, Jordan, Egypt, Indonesia, and Pakistan between 2010 and 2011, although far fewer expressed support in Lebanon and Turkey (with greater support, in turn, measured in Nigeria).[6]

However, opinion polls often give mixed, ambiguous, and sometimes contradictory results, and their outcome can be dependent on the way in which the question is phrased and the size and reliability of the sample. Surveys of Muslim public opinion, for example, have shown strong support for both the role of Islam in society, as well as greater democracy.[7] These of course are not mutually exclusive forces but, as discussed above, in the Al-Qaeda statements they could not be further apart. Furthermore, even though polls show Al-Qaeda's popularity is slipping, many of the points set forth in its public messages would appear to resonate with some of its target audiences, at least as far as sources of grievance are concerned. Vast majorities of Muslims for instance were angered by the Iraq invasion and actions of Israel.[8] More recently, the majority of Muslim publics polled in a survey conducted by Pew blamed US and Western policies for lack of prosperity in Muslim nations over other potential causes, and vast majorities in all Muslim countries surveyed, except Indonesia, viewed US and European policies in their regions as hostile toward Muslims.[9] Montasser Al-Zayyat, Zawahiri's former lawyer, noted that "almost all Muslims agree that the prophetic traditions clearly forbid attacks against civilians under any circumstances." However, there was, according to Al-Zayyat, broad consensus in the Muslim world with the issues Al-Qaeda frequently mentioned, including US hegemony, lack of freedom, and the Israeli occupation of Palestinian territories.[10] A 2013 survey by the British Council in Pakistan, moreover, found that the majority of Pakistani youth opposed democracy and favored either military rule or rule by shariah law.[11]

Opinion polls, therefore, give a mixed picture when it comes to assessing the potential impact of Al-Qaeda's message for some of its intended audiences. Another way of gauging the persistence of Al-Qaeda's message, which rests on an empirically stronger footing, consists of studying the content of this message and the way in which it has evolved. Any inconsistencies, tensions, or contradictions that may emerge when this aggregate message is assessed can add to our understanding of aspects that may weaken the cohesion and salience of terrorist organizations and leaderships. Hegghammer, for instance, observed that the "link between a lack of ideological clarity and group weakness, while yet to be firmly established, is a potentially important contribution to the nascent theoretical literature on militant group decline."[12] The literature on collective action frames, again, offers insights into ways in which such an assessment of aggregated statements can be constructed. Snow and Benford, for example, presented an "ideal type" for such a message intended to mobilize people. This would have to be substantively consistent and relevant to the life situations of potential participants and supporters and resonate with this key audience. Prescriptions about the way forward would have to be plausible and acceptable and proscriptions perceived as just. The core issues communicated would similarly need to be central to the concerns of the chief target audiences and the message disseminators would need to be perceived as credible actors.[13] From this ideal type, three central questions concerning the impact of Al-Qaeda's message can be generated. First: Is the message credible, are the message disseminators credible, and is the substance of this message consistent over time?[14] Second: Does the message reflect and address the realities and concerns of key target audiences?[15] Third: Does the message reference the central cultural myths and sources of identity that appeal to potential supporters?[16]

As regards cultural myths and sources of identity, the Al-Qaeda leadership of course represents skewed and extremist interpretations, but nonetheless utilizes references to Islamic pedigree and myths in a manner that is prominent and consistent over time. Al-Qaeda's overt traditionalist and literalist approach that forms such a prominent feature of its discourse conforms to the principal tenets of radical Islamist activism. Within this context, other revolutionary movements, much more influenced by Western ideas, such as nationalism, would face stronger opposition and accusations of innovation (*bidah*) than the Al-Qaeda leadership, which—as demonstrated in the previous chapter—has also been careful not to rely too much on excommunication (*takfir*), which could lead to the leaders being denounced as *khawaarij*, or extremist outsiders.

In terms of the credibility of bin Ladin and Zawahiri, moreover, both leaders could back up their rhetoric with their own experiences in jihad, their religious fervor, personal austerity, and life sacrifices in ways that might appeal to potential supporters. When Al-Qaeda's aggregated appeals to the wider community are assessed, however, obvious discrepancies emerge. Three points seem particularly important. First, although the Al-Qaeda leadership has managed to inspire some to support and participate in Islamist terrorism, there has been a broad rejection of its proposed responses, even though Al-Qaeda's problem diagnoses may often reflect wider concerns of its designated audiences. Second, an issue that has received much attention in the literature on Al-Qaeda is whether the publically expressed attitudes of the Al-Qaeda leadership concerning Palestine reflect those of their perceived constituents. The issue of Palestine is demonstrably central to the emotions provoking anger in the Arab world and beyond but something that the Al-Qaeda leadership has arguably failed to address convincingly, putting Zawahiri for instance on the defensive during his 2008 "open meeting" initiative. Third, the Al-Qaeda leadership has consistently dismissed Muslim diasporas and converts in Muslim minority countries even though some of its more prominent recruits and sympathizers have come from radicalized pockets of those communities. Looking beyond the extent to which Al-Qaeda's message reflects the realities of those to whom the leadership seeks to appeal, another point where tensions may emerge is the extent to which inconsistencies in terms of content and emphases appear over time in the Al-Qaeda leadership statements. Message consistency appears to be problematic for Zawahiri in particular, especially as relates to the use of violence and suggested targets of violent attacks.

The next subsections will explore each of these points in detail.

Rejection of proposed responses

The Al-Qaeda leadership's extensive and prolonged efforts to engage with target audiences through public statements beg the obvious question: To what extent have its recommended solutions been heeded? It goes without saying that participation in terrorism and militancy is always going to be relatively low given the thresholds and constraints that continue to inhibit involvement. The fact that Al-Qaeda's rhetoric has not produced the waves of fighters that bin Ladin's and Zawahiri's statements seemed to call for hardly appears surprising. Vagueness might also be an element that limits the practical impact of Al-Qaeda's publically communicated strategy of violence. As with many other militant revolutionary movements, the core leadership has offered scant details concerning the envisaged end goal or how such a society might function in practice, aside from reiterating core aspirations of Salafi jihadists. References to the desired end goal are nonetheless consistent over time and serve, to a degree, as a motivational frame to emphasize the need to address more immediate goals.

Although the statements sometimes appear contradictory over time in relation to justifications set forth for violence, careful analysis reveals that references in this regard appear to escalate in a relatively consistent manner, with communiqués, broadly speaking, becoming more indiscriminate, in terms of justifying civilian targeting, over time. A notable exception, however, was Zawahiri's more recent attempt to distance himself from Al-Qaeda affiliates that target Muslims in mosques and market squares in Iraq, Pakistan, and elsewhere, regardless of the fact that he had earlier sought to present justifications for precisely this form of targeting.

Al-Qaeda's definition of "participation" in jihad, however, goes beyond this sharper end of violent activism. Here the threshold for involvement is much lower. To begin with, involvement in the combined efforts of jihad includes simply vocal support from the masses in favor of the type of violent extremism that Al-Qaeda endorses. The Al-Qaeda leadership also repeatedly called for any forms of financial aid that could support the jihad and *mujahideen*. In terms of more direct activism, moreover, Muslims were urged to boycott goods of the West and other adversaries in the hope that this would weaken the economies of perceived enemies and, implicitly, send a message of unified resistance. These repeated calls for grassroots economic activism—made in the earliest days of Al-Qaeda and often reiterated since—have not had the desired effect. When popular boycott did become widespread, for instance in the wake of the Danish cartoon controversy, the role of Al-Qaeda in this uprising was widely perceived as marginal, belated, and ineffective.[17]

Public rejection of extremism is obviously not surprising but this serves to highlight how even the easiest forms of activism that the Al-Qaeda leaders prescribed have largely been ignored. The Al-Qaeda leadership has failed to see through the envisaged behavioral changes in the *ummah*, and this has resulted in targeted condemnation of precisely this audience and a gradual but significant alienation of those publics that would constitute potential supporters and sympathizers. As noted above, this is distinct from *takfiri* denunciations, which—in the case of bin Ladin and Zawahiri—are more specific and limited in reach. The lack of message appeal and, particularly, Zawahiri's insistence that the onus for change and reflection should be on the *ummah* rather than the Al-Qaeda leadership have presented a very public manifestation of both the physical and abstract isolation of the Al-Qaeda leadership. This detachment from the experiences and desires of the vast majority of the *ummah* is best demonstrated through understanding the leadership communiqués themselves.

This detachment became particularly obvious during the "Arab Spring" revolutions. A few years before the revolutions, Zawahiri had mocked and criticized those who took to the streets in protest against government oppression rather than joining the ranks of the *mujahideen*, bemoaning the "Muslims' tardiness in resisting oppression" through any meaningful ways.[18] The "Arab Spring," therefore, highlighted the irrelevance of Zawahiri's preferred method of regime change, during this period, and his prior accusations that Muslim publics would be unwilling to rise up against their leaders. Indeed, Zawahiri's frustration with the lack of mobilization of the Muslim populace, according to his own prescribed ways, became palpable in his statements at least six years before the 2011 uprising in Egypt. Another apparent manifestation of the detachment between Al-Qaeda's rhetoric and the concerns and aspirations of those it claims to represent is the issue of Palestine.

The question of Palestine

It has often been argued that one of the greatest sources of anger and grievance in the Middle East and among Muslims is the plight of Palestinians living under Israeli occupation and the relations between Israel and other countries in the region. The Palestinian situation has provoked outrage for decades. In his attempt to understand the "roots of Islamic militancy," Munson, for instance, found that, according to a series of opinion polls, "the issue that arouses the most hostility in the Middle East toward the United States is the Israeli-Palestinian conflict and what Muslims perceive as US responsibility for the suffering of the Palestinians."[19] The way in which the Al-Qaeda leadership has approached the issue is thus essential in terms of matching the narrative with the concerns of perceived constituents.

Crucial as the issue may be, analysts and observers do not appear to be in agreement when it comes to assessing the approach of Al-Qaeda leaders to the question of Israel and Palestinians. Randal, for instance, argued that "Osama was a latecomer to the Palestinian cause [but] came to appreciate it as the single most effective unifying force not just for Arabs, but for Muslims from Morocco to the Philippines."[20] Blanchard, Mendelsohn, and others have argued that Al-Qaeda's public support for the Palestinian cause is directly related to attempts by the leadership to increase public support and improve its image.[21] In this sense, the Al-Qaeda leadership has "used" the Palestinian issue for propaganda purposes. For Scheuer, by contrast, the Palestinian issue was central to Al-Qaeda, which supposedly was increasingly prominent operationally in the region through an ambiguous set of apparent affiliates.[22] Riedel, in turn, dismisses commentators who argued that the Al-Qaeda leadership was late in focusing on Palestine and maintains that "the Israeli-Palestinian conflict is the central all-consuming issue for al Qaeda" and the cause that "infuses every aspect of al Qaeda's thinking and activities and has become the rallying cry used to convince the ummah of the righteousness of al Qaeda's cause."[23] Hellmich similarly insisted that "Palestine is not incidental to the agenda—it is the agenda."[24]

These latter assertions, however, seem problematic. First, Islamist militant sympathizers themselves have accused the leadership of placing insufficient attention on the Palestinian issue. As discussed above, for example, the Al-Qaeda leadership was forced to defend its position on the Israeli question in Zawahiri's "open meeting" initiative after being accused of diverting attention away from the issue to focus on Iraq and other developments. The aforementioned "Dr Fadl," Zawahiri's former colleague, moreover, fumed that Al-Qaeda "did not offer Palestine anything except words."[25]

Second, a detailed analysis of the Al-Qaeda leadership's aggregated statements—particularly those from Zawahiri—reveals that matters relating to Israel and Palestinians have not always received top priority in this public discourse. Greater emphasis was clearly placed on other issues during the bulk of the 1990s in the public communiqués, prompting Gaza-born journalist Abdel Bari Atwan, for instance, to challenge bin Ladin to respond to criticism that he and his organization had sidelined the Palestinian cause in favor of other "Islamic issues." Bin Ladin responded, rather ambiguously, that "interest in issues is determined by their closeness to the people's life and their sequence."[26] According to bin Ladin's interpretation at this time, this meant that the primary emphasis would be on Afghanistan and the Arabian Peninsula for the time being, and not Palestine. This is not to suggest that the issue was ignored, or even that the Al-Qaeda leaders, bin Ladin especially, were not themselves concerned with developments in Palestine. Bin Ladin, for example, reportedly told a childhood friend, years before he became a renowned terrorist leader, that "unless, we, the new generation, change and become stronger and more educated and more dedicated we will never reclaim Palestine."[27] Indeed, the issue of alleged Israeli aggression was one of three core grievances mentioned for the establishment of the "World Islamic Front" in February 1998, following accusations relating to the perceived violation of the Arabian Peninsula and the suffering of the Iraqi people.[28] The point is that the prioritization of grievances presented in the Al-Qaeda leadership communiqués at this time did not place the question of Palestine at the top of the agenda, above other concerns.

The mobilizing potential of the Israeli question, however, was not lost on the leadership. In a remarkably frank clause in his book *Knights under the Banner of the Prophet*, Zawahiri explained how the conflict was of central importance to the Muslim community and key in their mobilization: "[T]he fact that must be acknowledged is that the issue of Palestine is the cause that has been firing up the feelings of the Muslim nation from Morocco to Indonesia for the past 50 years. In addition, it is a rallying point for all the Arabs, be they believers or non-believers, good or evil."[29] As the geographic scope of the grievance narrative expanded toward the end of the 1990s, therefore, the perceived role of Israel became more prominent. Bin Ladin was asked to explain this apparent shift in emphasis from the Arabian Peninsula to matters relating to Israel in a sympathetic interview conducted shortly after the 9/11 attacks. His response was that sometimes the Al-Qaeda leaders "find the right elements to push for one cause more than the other," with the second *intifada* providing the perfect opportunity to refocus on developments in the occupied territories.[30]

However, a close look at the public statements reveals how the Al-Qaeda leaders, in an attempt to rewrite their own history, engaged in several attempts to convince potential supporters that the Israeli question and the Palestinian population had indeed always been the main priority of the leadership and the chief inspiration behind its activities, contrary to what older messages had stated. In a communiqué issued in December 2001, bin Ladin decried the "deliberate murder of children" in Palestine—for instance that of Mohammad al-Durra, whose death was caught on camera—and noted how America, the target of the 9/11 attacks a few months earlier, was the principal backer of the "attackers of ours sons in Palestine."[31] In October 2004, again reflecting upon the 9/11 attacks, bin Ladin insisted that the inspiration behind these strikes was US support for Israel and the 1982 Israeli invasion of Lebanon, feasible only because "the US permitted the Israelis to invade." Bin Ladin reflected: "I still remember those moving scenes: blood, torn limbs, and dead women and children; ruined homes everywhere; and high-rises being demolished on top of their residents; bombs raining down mercilessly on our homes…As I was looking at those destroyed towers in Lebanon," bin Ladin continued, "I was struck by the idea of punishing the oppressor in the same manner and destroying towers in the U.S."[32]

As he commemorated the 60th anniversary of the Israeli occupation, bin Ladin emphasized how the question of Israel was a basic issue for the entire *ummah* and something that had motivated him to become an activist since childhood.[33] Bin Ladin's concern over the Palestinian issue was undoubtedly genuine, even if attempts to rearrange the hierarchy of grievances retrospectively may be due to the need to maximize the mobilizing appeal of the message. Zawahiri's approach to the Israeli question, however, seems murkier.

Zawahiri famously proclaimed in 1995, following the EIJ bombing of the Egyptian embassy in Islamabad, that "the way to Jerusalem passes through Cairo."[34] The way to serve the Palestinian cause, therefore, was to support militancy targeting the Egyptian regime. This way of highlighting the Israeli question by proxy, through emphasizing the need to address other more immediate concerns first as a means toward the ultimate goal of liberating Jerusalem when conceivable, again became a prominent feature of Zawahiri's communiqués almost a decade later. As Al-Qaeda became increasingly embroiled and desperate in a bloody and indiscriminate—and progressively unpopular—insurgency in Iraq, Zawahiri began to frame its efforts in the country as essential to the successful liberation of Palestine. As he paid tribute to the disastrous Al-Qaeda commander in Iraq, Abu Musab Al-Zarqawi, Zawahiri emphasized the need to focus on Iraq in order to establish an Islamic emirate that could subsequently launch operations against Israel, regardless of how long this would take to accomplish.[35] Iraq would become a "fortress of Islam" from where assaults on Israel could be conducted.[36] In his appeals for support for the Al-Qaeda operatives in Iraq who, despite Zawahiri's triumphant hyperbole, were engaged in an increasingly stagnant and sectarian struggle against Muslims in the country, the Al-Qaeda leader equated a solution to the Israeli dilemma with such lofty and ambiguous aims as the "reestablishment of the Caliphate state which the Crusaders and their helpers toppled."[37]

Thus, ten years down the line, the way to Jerusalem now passed through Baghdad. As with the Islamabad bombings, immediate objectives not only trumped potential secondary goals, but they formed the conduits through which the latter could be achieved.[38] This, interestingly, was precisely the argument put forward by Zawahiri's colleague Mohammed Salam Faraj on the need to target the near enemy and establish Islamic governance on a solid footing before engaging in other more ambitious activities, an argument that Zawahiri dismissed as misguided. It is as if, therefore, Zawahiri had come full circle. Judging by the "open meeting" venture (which has never been repeated since) and other factors, it would appear that Zawahiri's prioritization of Iraq and utilization of Palestinian suffering to rally support for Al-Qaeda in Iraq through his communiqués is far removed from the concerns of the vast majority of potential participants and Muslims in the region.

The same appears to apply to Zawahiri's insistence that the creation of a theocracy in post-Mubarak Egypt would somehow pave the way for

Palestinian liberation. The primary objectives would be to consolidate these forces in Egypt, before anything could be done for the Palestinians. Were this to be achieved, Zawahiri's road map for the liberation of Palestine leaves many questions unanswered. For instance, in a statement issued in autumn 2012, Zawahiri asked the rhetorical question: "[H]ow can the *ummah* liberate Palestine?" The first step toward this goal would be "spreading awareness among the Muslim *ummah*" (a task that appeared to be causing Zawahiri increasing frustration). Then the *ummah* would have to come to terms with the fact that victory comes only from God, that governments were incapable of freeing Palestine, and that collective mass participation in jihad was the prerequisite to any success on the ground.[39] Palestine, moreover, was only one facet of many in the ongoing jihad, and the Palestinians themselves would be expected to do their bit to aid the *mujahideen* fighting elsewhere. The notion of Palestine as the primary objective, therefore, seems rather remote in this context.

Another potential problem for the impact of Al-Qaeda's message concerns the way and extent to which the leadership has sought to address Muslims living "abroad," outside Muslim majority countries. Here again, the message fails to reflect the realities faced by many of those to whom the leaders have sought to appeal.

The wider diaspora

The Al-Qaeda leaders are often seen as presiding over a "global brand" that draws supporters from all corners of the globe, including an increasingly active, enthusiastic, and comparatively rich proportion of Islamist militant sympathizers living in the West. Several attacks and attempted attacks linked to or inspired by Al-Qaeda have been carried out by individuals who have lived in the West for years or were born there. Numerous individuals living in specific diaspora communities in Europe and North America and converts have also sought to become "foreign fighters" and join and support insurgency campaigns run by Al-Qaeda affiliates and allies in different parts of Africa, the Middle East, Central Asia, and elsewhere. Additionally, of course, the community identified in the Al-Qaeda communiqués does not recognize modern borders and purportedly represents Muslims globally, regardless of geographic concentration. Furthermore, the grievance narrative often refers to developments that are specific to Muslims living in the West, such as the French ban on religious symbols, that originate in the West, such as the cartoon controversy, or that are inherently global, such as bin Ladin's brief preoccupation with environmental issues.

Paradoxically, however, the Al-Qaeda leadership appears to have failed to relate to Muslims living outside predominantly Muslim regions, especially those living in the West. Remarkably, given the volume of statements and the length of the period involved, bin Ladin and Zawahiri hardly issued any appeals directed toward Muslims living in the West. Although the French *niqab* ban was alluded to in several communiqués, as noted, the point was to collate policies that supposedly exposed the overt hostility of Western regimes toward Muslims in general, and the legislation was portrayed as part of a wider campaign of aggression in the Middle East and elsewhere that started with the Crusades. In the very few cases where the Al-Qaeda leadership acknowledged the existence of Muslims in the West, this was usually prompted by a question. The answer given, in turn, was dismissive. Bin Ladin, for instance, reportedly told Abdel Bari Atwan (who has lived in London since 1979) that he "would rather die than live in any European state."[40] Later, in an interview with Pakistani English-language newspaper *The Dawn*, bin Ladin warned that "the Islamic Shariat says Muslims should not live in the land of the infidel for long."[41] Aside from these references, bin Ladin largely ignored Muslims in the West and never addressed the issue on his own initiative.·

Zawahiri also remained largely silent on the issue of Muslims living in the West, making a few limited references when, again, the issue was prompted by a question. Numerous participants in the "open meeting," for instance, wanted to know about their position as Muslims living in the West and some even claimed to be supporters of many of Al-Qaeda's causes. As with bin Ladin, Zawahiri's response was equally scornful, warning Muslims that "permanent residence in the countries of infidelity is only allowed when necessary…because this means that [a Muslim] accepts their laws to be applied to him."[42] In several other messages, Zawahiri condemned those who "take pride in their British citizenship, or 'beg for residency permits' outside Muslim lands."[43] At the same time, of course, those who had carried out attacks in the name of Al-Qaeda, such as the 2005 London bombers, were praised, regardless of the fact that they too had never emigrated, despite ample opportunities to do so.

The Al-Qaeda leadership's reluctance to recognize or even acknowledge the existence of the millions of Muslims living in the West is perhaps informed partly by, what Meijer terms, "xenophobic Wahhabism." This school of thought posits that a true believer could only express his belief and the sincerity of his faith by demonstrating open enmity toward "idolaters." This forbids the befriending of infidels and prohibits true Muslims from traveling to the land of idolaters (*bilad al-mushrikin*). Indeed, the Quranic verse that Zawahiri quotes in his communiqués more than any other is verse 51 of the fifth *surah*: "O you who have believed, do not take the Jews and the Christians as allies. They are [in fact] allies of one another. And whoever is an ally to them among you—then indeed, he is [one] of them. Indeed, Allah guides not the wrongdoing people."[44]

By occasionally admonishing, but largely ignoring, the millions of Muslims who live in the West (or even interact with non-Muslims), the Al-Qaeda leaders have set themselves apart from the experiences of vast proportions of those they claim to represent. Through this dismissive rhetoric, moreover, they have also failed to appeal directly to some who might otherwise be supportive of or attracted to Al-Qaeda's militant agenda and global vision. Here, bin Ladin's and Zawahiri's output differs from that of other prominent ideologues such as Anwar Al-Awlaki, who, of course, lived in the West for many years. Although Al-Awlaki's stance toward Muslims living in the West radicalized over time, he at least took the time to address the realities of these Muslim communities directly. Even in his last message, Al-Awlaki directed specific appeals toward Muslims in the West, urging them to either emigrate or support jihad at home, discussing in detail the realities and future that American Muslims, for instance, supposedly faced.[45] This failure of the Al-Qaeda central leadership to acknowledge Muslims in the West may affect the extent to which the content of its message resonates with extremist elements of these communities in the future.

Inconsistencies in the Al-Qaeda leadership narrative

Hellmich described Al-Qaeda's public statements as "an attempt to establish a certain status quo among a wider audience" whereby "the jihadis will attempt to appear as unified, competent and powerful as possible."[46] In this context, therefore, it becomes particularly important and valuable to highlight inconsistencies that emerge over time even when the focus is on only two (albeit principal) actors within this milieu. When a quantity of output over an extended period of time is analyzed in detail, a degree of variation is to be expected. The Al-Qaeda leadership public narrative is inherently dynamic and often reflects ongoing developments at any particular time.

Through their statements, bin Ladin and Zawahiri have confronted a wide set of challenges, reassessed the proposed solutions deemed appropriate, and reacted to watershed events that are framed within the existing dominating context of defensive jihad and collective identity based on common injustices. This variation is not necessarily problematic in terms of message consistency, so long as this fits within and enhances the overall discursive framework that the leadership has constructed over time. The preceding chapters have also shown, moreover, that there are a number of obvious differences when

Zawahiri's and bin Ladin's output is compared. In the early years of Al-Qaeda, for example, Zawahiri's output and efforts were not fully in line with those of bin Ladin. Both claimed to fight to reinstate the Caliphate, but for the former its heart would be in Cairo, whereas bin Ladin insisted upon the primacy of Mecca and the Land of the Two Holy Places.[47]

Following this transitional phase many argue that the scope of enmity and the focus of the communiqués became more coherent, with a clear delineation between far and near enemy for example, as discussed above, before becoming more fluid in recent years as the repertoire of issues expanded.[48] For Zawahiri in particular, however, the prioritization of different sets of enemies according to geographic proximity often seemed incoherent. For bin Ladin during the 1990s, moreover, his animosity toward the Saudi state was interwoven with his desire to strike at the United States and its allies as the principal source of grievance both as a "local" actor, via proxies, and as a more overarching external threat.[49]

Early threats to continuity and consistency in Al-Qaeda's leadership narrative, in the aftermath of the 9/11 attacks, were largely dispelled by the global outrage caused by the Iraq War, rendition programs, and accounts of detainee torture, which proved a comfortable fit with the core elements of the Al-Qaeda messages up to that point and helped to focus statements that were disseminated during that period. There exists, however, an underlying tension in terms of the scope and origins of grievance that appears to undermine message consistency over time. Chapter 4 discussed how Zawahiri, in particular, variously traced the root cause of the grievances described to the presence of America and the West in the Islamic world and to the overall corrupting influence of the ideas represented by these adversaries *or* to the traditional set of local tyrants and embedded elites. The result is a conflicting narrative with an ambiguous focus and set of targeting preferences that leaves many questions regarding the direction of activism and prioritization of mobilization unanswered. This apparent incongruity is no less acute in Zawahiri's more recent output. Nor does this change in scope appear to follow any logical or linear progressions as some statements emphasize the global, or US-focused, aspects of the struggle while other statements from the same period revert back to matters relating to Egypt and neighboring regions, which are prioritized over other developments. Rather than dismissing this haphazard prioritization as periodic nostalgia, the conflicting scope in Zawahiri's public messages, which have always been far more expansive than those of bin Ladin, should be seen as a clear weakness in the overall level of consistency in the Al-Qaeda leadership statements.

When the Al-Qaeda central leadership's proposed solutions are scrutinized, further inconsistencies emerge, especially in relation to justifications for violence and the reach of militant activism. Again, this is primarily a problem in

Zawahiri's output. Bin Ladin's shorter and simpler messages generally offer far less detail than those of Zawahiri, limiting justifications for violence to notions of reciprocity and concepts, which would be familiar in the West, such as the fundamentals of "just war" and "collateral damage."[50] Zawahiri's material is richer in content but, no doubt partly for this reason, also less consistent when it comes to deliberating the utility, prescribed form, and consequences of violence. An analysis of this material shows how early accounts insisted upon the necessity of informing Muslims prior to attacks being carried out in their immediate vicinity, advice which Al-Qaeda's affiliates appear not to have heeded. Later, the families of Muslims who were nonetheless killed were promised blood money, something which also appears to have failed to materialize. Zawahiri sometimes spoke of his profound regret for Muslim deaths in Al-Qaeda-linked attacks, promising to make those responsible accountable before the shariah courts. At the same time, Zawahiri developed a doctrine for Al-Qaeda that legitimized killing Muslims, not only collaborators (and thus as legitimate targets due to their alleged treachery) but also innocent bystanders who were unlucky enough to be close to an explosive device when it went off, equating such events to medieval sieges and night raids during the time of the Prophet's immediate successors.

As discussed in preceding chapters, Zawahiri initially claimed that Al-Qaeda's affiliates in North Africa, Iraq, and elsewhere simply had not targeted or killed innocent Muslims, contrary to accusations, but rather had targeted police or military assets only, while later seeking to rein in these very allies and affiliates that were targeting Muslims in markets and mosques. This belated appeal to affiliates contains an implicit admission of the fact that these groups had hitherto been endorsed and that their targeting followed a doctrine that the Al-Qaeda leaders helped to create. Zawahiri also tried to deflect some of the criticism aimed at Al-Qaeda onto Hamas (which he derided for alleged weaknesses) through questioning their targeting of Fatah activists in comparison with the targeting of Al-Qaeda affiliates of Iraq, regardless of the fact that numerous Zawahiri communiqués called for the killing of these very same Fatah activists and leaders.

In terms of the killing of non-Muslims, legitimization in this regard has also moved far beyond discriminate or selective targeting of military, police, or even financial and governmental targets to include all those who pay taxes, participate in society at large, and perceive the pillars of Western governance to be legitimate, regardless of whether or not the current politics and policies are supported. Although the principles of reciprocity still apply, in addition to those of asymmetry—rendering softer targets more attractive—any notions of moral superiority disappear when the scope and reach of permitted violence has expanded so demonstrably.

The importance of understanding
the Al-Qaeda narrative

As he responded to questions posted through online forums during his 2008 "open meeting," Zawahiri announced that "even if Usama bin Ladin doesn't become ill, he must die one day, whereas Allah's religion will remain until Allah inherits the earth and everything on it."[51] Three years later, in May 2011, Al-Qaeda announced the "martyrdom" of bin Ladin and that Zawahiri would take over as leader and principal spokesperson. Of all the tasks that then became his primary responsibility, maintaining and communicating Al-Qaeda's message in order to attract followers, inspire and mobilize existing supporters, and portray an image of cohesion is perhaps the most important, and the task that Zawahiri himself appears to have prioritized above all others. As he reflected on his experiences of working with bin Ladin in a media initiative titled "Days with the Imam," Zawahiri again emphasized the importance of nurturing the concept or idea of Al-Qaeda, rather than any particular organizational structure. In terms of bin Ladin's association with particular groups, Zawahiri claimed that bin Ladin's "organizational partisanship was among the least I have seen." "Bin Ladin was able to gather people behind a single project," Zawahiri argued, a project that would see Islamist activists attracted to the global jihadi call, regardless of particular group structures.[52] These organizational elements—particularly those of the Al-Qaeda leadership—would never last forever, but Al-Qaeda's message and agenda would, Zawahiri hoped, live on. The impact of this message, however, appears to have been undermined by the inability of the Al-Qaeda leadership to reflect core aspirations and experiences of perceived constituents and through generating a narrative that is, at times, incongruous and ambiguous.

It is particularly significant for the future of Al-Qaeda that these constraints are primarily to be found in Zawahiri's voluminous output, from the last "great emir" of Al-Qaeda's old command, responsible for shaping Al-Qaeda's public discourse after the death of bin Ladin and through the tumultuous period following the Arab Spring revolutions. Furthermore, the nature of this communication is characterized primarily by Zawahiri's bitter denunciation of vast proportions of the Muslim population, his dismissal of Muslims living in the West, and his frustration with the very same people Al-Qaeda claims to represent and protect. The manifestation and evolution of these elements in Al-Qaeda's leadership discourse only become apparent when large swathes of this material are analyzed, compared, and assessed over time. Selective sampling, in this sense, only gives a very partial—and often skewed—image of Al-Qaeda's public stance and the way in which this has developed over the years.

Once an empirically based and longitudinal understanding of the Al-Qaeda leadership public discourse has been established and the methodological tools have been honed, we, moreover, are in a far better position to comprehend and analyze the public agenda and worldview of groups affiliated with Al-Qaeda or, indeed, of other terrorist movements for comparative purposes. The extent to which justificatory narratives for violence differ between groups could be probed by applying such a comparative perspective. The Al-Qaeda leadership's dismissive attitude toward Muslims outside Muslim majority countries could also be contrasted with that of other personalities who have become associated with the Al-Qaeda brand, such as Anwar Al-Awlaki, who lived in the United States for an extended period of time. Other aspects of discourse, such as the presence, absence, and evolution of sectarian sentiments in public statements from different Islamist extremist groups and leaderships, could also be explored once the approach of one of the most prominent actors in this respect—the Al-Qaeda leadership as represented by bin Ladin and Zawahiri—has been established. Gaining a comprehensive understanding of the Al-Qaeda leadership's message and the way in which it has evolved is thus a necessary prerequisite to understanding the way in which other facets and affiliates within the Al-Qaeda franchise and the wider Islamist extremist milieu have developed. The impact of the Al-Qaeda leadership's discourse has reached beyond the immediate context of Islamist extremist militancy too. Some analysts have even suggested Al-Qaeda's agenda and message influenced that of Anders Breivik and the compilation of his "manifesto." All he did, Berntzen and Sandberg argue, was to exchange Islam for Christendom and Crusaders for multiculturalists, while keeping the rest of the jihadi frame.[53] This knowledge base of Al-Qaeda's public leadership discourse thus offers yardsticks against which other violent extremist groups and leaderships can be evaluated.

Sustaining the dream

For an organization that has become increasingly fractionated, dispersed, and diffuse since its inception in the wake of the Afghan-Soviet war, the ideational elements that underpin this movement represent the most concrete and testable measure of analysis. Indeed, the leadership statements—understood here as the building blocks that make up the narrative of Al-Qaeda—thus convey metrics that can be more tangible than organizational variables. When this output is studied in a systematic fashion that is sensitive to the dynamic and variable nature of this discourse, the Al-Qaeda leadership's evolving story and message emerges. This perspective shows how messages from the two Al-Qaeda leaders evolved from localized tracts to more expansive and ambitious media initiatives that coincided with the leadership's campaign of violence. These messages culminated in a narrative that at times appears confused, contradictory in terms of prioritization, struggling with the consequences of the violence it has presented as legitimate, and out of kilter with the desires and experiences of vast proportions of supposed constituents.

The abundance of grievances, which can be utilized to present and frame activist messages, bin Ladin's and Zawahiri's dedication to militant activism, and the two leaders' sophisticated grasp of key religio-cultural concepts and terminology constitute the ingredients of a poignant and potentially effective narrative. Aside from the impact of external developments, the impression of this narrative, however, appears to have been blunted by the leadership's own shortcomings in terms of presenting coherent or acceptable solutions and in terms of addressing the experiences and emotions of perceived constituents and potential sympathizers. The Al-Qaeda leadership certainly did not lose sight of, what Paul Wilkinson termed, "the revolutionary promise of the advent of an age of bliss, abundance and perfect justice," which features so prominently in the discourse of religious and millenarian social movements (see Chapter 1). At the same time, however, the leadership appears to have lost confidence in the ability of constituents to form a broad movement that will follow the example of the Al-Qaeda vanguard in fighting for this promised "age of bliss." As the preceding chapters explored, the leadership's message during Al-Qaeda's first two decades became inconsistent and ambiguous, its frustration with the publics it purports to protect and represent too vocal and prominent and its dismissal of realities faced by scores of Muslims living in diaspora communities in the West too stark. The *ummat al-mu'minin*—the Islamic nation—has rejected Al-Qaeda's set of prognostic solutions (from evermore indiscriminate forms of violence to economic boycott and other prescribed forms of uprising) and appears to have moved out of reach of Al-Qaeda's self-described vanguard.

This book opened with a description of press reaction to the death of Usama bin Ladin. At the time, *The Economist* implied that the battle with Al-Qaeda would not be over with the demise of its pivotal leader. It would still be necessary to "kill his dream."[54] The preceding chapters have illustrated that although constructing and communicating this dream was an essential preoccupation of the Al-Qaeda leadership, this vision has been blunted and weakened by the nature, direction, and scope that bin Ladin and (especially) Zawahiri chose to adopt in their own communicative efforts.

Al-Qaeda was formed as the result of a debate on the future directions of jihad in the wake of the perceived triumph of the *mujahideen* against

Soviet forces in Afghanistan. With the death of bin Ladin and other principal leadership figures just over a decade after 9/11 and amid the turmoil of the Arab Spring and its aftermath, a new generation of Islamist militants is again faced with the challenge of shaping the future directions of jihad. The strength of their effort and size of their movement will to some degree depend on the extent to which this new generation of Islamist activists will appreciate—and learn from—the shortcomings of the Al-Qaeda leadership. At the same time—despite these shortcomings—Al-Qaeda's affiliates and sympathizers continue to operate and pose a threat. Al-Qaeda entered the second decade of this century with far less central control than it had enjoyed during the ten years after 9/11. However, Islamist militants, including powerful insurgent groups, continue to operate in its name and jihadists across the globe continue to value their association with what is increasingly an intangible network. Al-Qaeda's presence after the demise of its central leadership and despite all the errors in terms of excessive targeting and dismissive and incongruent rhetoric thus presents something of a paradox. The concluding chapter of this book explores this apparent enigma, the importance of understanding Al-Qaeda's evolving public discourse and what this tells us about Al-Qaeda as a sociopolitical entity and a terrorist organization.

8

The Al-Qaeda doctrine: Understanding the public discourse

Evolving ideas

On the 11th anniversary of the 9/11 attacks Zawahiri released a statement titled "The Rising Sun of Victory on the Triumphant Ummah over the Vanquished Crusaders." The Al-Qaeda leader's aim was to dispel any notions that the movement over which he presided was in its death throes. "The group of Qaedat Al-Jihad was in Afghanistan before the outbreak of the Crusader war against it," Zawahiri reflected, whereas "now it has four branches outside Afghanistan and millions of supporters in every corner of the globe." "Obama and the US leaders are deceiving themselves and their people," Zawahiri insisted, "by limiting the battle with Muslims to certain individuals, an organization, or several organizations and close their eyes to an apparent fact that they are facing the jihadist rising Islamic ummah whose devout sons are involved in the US-Crusader-Zionist war in Afghanistan."[1]

It is revealing in and of itself that Zawahiri felt compelled to issue a public statement insisting that Al-Qaeda continued to pose a threat and that it could rely on "millions" of supporters. The emerging consensus that Al-Qaeda had become severely weakened appeared to have had some impact on its senior leadership. What is perhaps even more revealing, however, is Zawahiri's focus on sustaining the movement—the idea of Al-Qaeda—rather than any operational components. The leadership was fully aware of the fact that drone strikes and other accumulative counterterrorism efforts had severely reduced the material capacity of Al-Qaeda, but—partly for this reason—Zawahiri chose to focus on the less tangible, more abstract elements of Al-Qaeda. Al-Qaeda, according to this interpretation, cannot be killed just by killing key individuals, regardless of how prominent they are, since there will always be others to carry on from where they left off, shaping the existing doctrine to fit their specific agenda. Campaigns that are associated with or inspired by the broader concept of Al-Qaeda may well be more limited in scope and ambition, but the discourse developed by Zawahiri and bin Ladin over the years lives on.

This book has focused on the way in which this discourse has been developed and why it is important. Al-Qaeda did not emerge at the beginning of the 1990s with a fully formed ideological doctrine for a global Islamist militant movement. Its leadership borrowed from the existing discourse of Islamist militancy and established its own evolving discourse that rationalized Al-Qaeda's existence. This body of content consists of a set of evolving precepts that delineate problem diagnosis and proposed solutions in a discursive package that has been delivered to various audiences—supporters, potential supporters, and enemies—in multiple localities. It represents Al-Qaeda's public agenda as expressed through the leadership statements. It is not, of course, an accurate portrayal of the world. It mixes complex conspiracy theories with utopian visions for the future that are interwoven with more immediate value-based prescriptions, a wide-reaching grievance narrative, and a set of evolving justifications for (mostly) violent activism that became increasingly holistic and indiscriminate over the years. The core elements are the need to mobilize the masses (rhetorically and physically) in support of a righteous fighting vanguard that is engaged in a prolonged battle against status quo powers that sustain the suffering, impiety, and injustice of the current world order. The ultimate goal is to achieve divine social justice, while intermediate goals consist of impacting the policies of identified adversaries, achieving infamy within the right circles, and continuing the jihad. To this end, the Al-Qaeda leadership has developed a specific narrative justifying violence that rests on three main pillars. These consist of (1) reciprocity; (2) redefining the concept of combatant, making the general public complicit; and (3) stretching and twisting medieval religious justifications for specific tactics (such as night raids and catapult or siege warfare) in order to justify indiscriminate deaths and unintended casualties.

The purpose of the Al-Qaeda leadership's public discourse is to incite, inspire, and mobilize at least an element of the desired support base, to sustain Al-Qaeda as a movement. Even if the establishment of a society governed by Al-Qaeda's vision of shariah law is an obscure, long-term, and aspirational goal, references to such a desired end state add religious credence to the activism and foment a divine sense of purpose. The Al-Qaeda leaders have always emphasized the importance of issuing public statements through various conduits, and after their involvement in operational activities reduced, they placed ever greater emphasis on sustaining, developing, and disseminating their public message. This output thus forms a clear and important part of Al-Qaeda and constitutes a voluminous corpus that has grown considerably over the years. These communiqués present the metrics with which to understand Al-Qaeda's public discourse and help to place analyses of Al-Qaeda and Islamist militant movements more generally on a sound empirical and evidence-based footing.

Much of the debate concerning Al-Qaeda's discourse and the broader movement seems acutely polarized. Accounts range from explicit efforts to shore up counterterrorism initiatives, which draw parallels between Al-Qaeda and other security threats that have emerged over the past decades, to representations of Al-Qaeda as an inevitable, understandable, and almost just reaction to the policies of the West.

As an example of the former position, Bergen and Cruickshank, for instance, drew parallels between bin Ladin and Adolf Hitler and argued that "if Adolf Hitler's vehicle to keep the National Socialist Party together was anti-Semitism, then bin Laden's was, by 1993 *jihad* against the United States."[2] Moghadam and Fishman saw the United States as a "useful enemy" for Al-Qaeda as it could be tied to "proximate enemies around the globe."[3] Mann, by contrast, argued that "there is a simple *reason* why he [bin Ladin] attacked the US: American imperialism,"[4] and Hellmich described bin Ladin not as a terrorist but as a "radical anti-imperialist."[5] This polarization and (to some extent) politicization of the debate surrounding Al-Qaeda and its output stems partly from selective and insufficiently rigorous empirical analysis of the phenomenon. Mann, for instance, argued that "as long as America seeks to control the Middle East, [bin Ladin] and people like him will be its enemy."[6] Hellmich, meanwhile, argued that "with the force of history on his side, it is difficult to deny, in principle the legitimacy of his argument when bin Ladin recounts the impact of colonialism…and decries the betrayal of the Arabs, the West's unconditional support for Israel and American control of the entire region."[7]

Issues such as the Western colonial legacy, Israel, and the presence of US troops in Saudi Arabia and elsewhere in the Middle East are undoubtedly important, but Al-Qaeda's version of history is much less balanced than accounts that emphasize these factors would suggest. Al-Qaeda's historical grievances include, for instance, the loss of Al-Andalus to Spain and other loss of territory after the Ottoman invasion of Europe. The European powers were not the only imperialists to effect the acquisition of territory, and this seems to have been forgotten in Al-Qaeda's discourse—and in some of the descriptive accounts that are intended to shed light on this material. Al-Qaeda's defensive war called for the "liberation" of not only the Middle East but of all lands from the Caucasus to Zanzibar, from Afghanistan and Kashmir to East Timor and the

Philippines and from Xinjang in northwestern China to Al-Andalus in Spain.[8] All of these regions were to be governed by Al-Qaeda's interpretation of shariah law. America's war of aggression, moreover, was not limited to Palestine, the Arabian Peninsula, or Iraq but included, for instance, the apparent exploitation of, what bin Ladin called, "some differences between the tribes" in Western Sudan, in order to foment conflict in Darfur, a region where roaming jihadi bands had inflicted immense suffering.[9]

The notion of Al-Qaeda arising out of anger about Western foreign policy and military adventures (contemporary and historic) only tells half the story and presumably results from either deliberately selective or otherwise limited reading of the public discourse that the Al-Qaeda leaders themselves have created. Of course, Saudi-US collaboration and the presence of US troops in Saudi Arabia and any number of other grievances—including Palestine—that are shared with millions of other Muslims were crucial motivating factors for the Al-Qaeda leaders and these were prominent in their communiqués. More importantly, these issues (and subsequent developments such as the Iraq War) have served to increase support for violent responses, such as those promoted by Al-Qaeda, within a wider corpus of Islamist extremists.

No analysis of Al-Qaeda's public discourse would be complete, however, if the emphasis on values was overlooked. These are prominent in the Al-Qaeda leadership discourse and clearly motivated the leaders and indeed many of its supporters. Some of the most vehement expressions of anger in the Al-Qaeda leaders' statements related to incidents where the name and legacy of the Prophet Mohammed was "slandered" in cartoons or YouTube videos. These acts of individual stupidity and insensitivity—over which Western governments had no control—were, however, added to the existing list of grievances that were used to justify Al-Qaeda's campaign of violence.

The grievance narrative, therefore, goes beyond immediate and tangible acts such as infringement of sovereignty. For example, in a statement from October 2002 titled "Letter from Usama Bin Muhammad Bin Ladin to the American People," bin Ladin listed numerous grievances that supposedly justified the targeting of the United States and its allies. As well as allegations of oppression and imperialism, however, this list of grievances included accusations that America brought humanity "AIDS as a Satanic American invention" and complained that American tourists were "spreading filth upon whoever comes into contact with them."[10] This preoccupation with values and the perceived undesirability of the very "essence" of Al-Qaeda's adversaries forms part of Al-Qaeda's overall problem diagnosis and should not be overlooked. Particular countries are in this sense condemned not only for specific acts but also due to cultural, normative, and societal issues, which are presented as justifications for violence against them.[11]

There is a danger, if Al-Qaeda is depicted merely as a resistance group fighting oppression and occupation, that the references that show just how intolerant, bigoted, anti-Semitic, xenophobic, and extreme the group has always been become overlooked. This would be—more than anything—offensive to those Muslims who have indeed suffered from occupation, war, and other hardships. Studying Al-Qaeda—or any other violent extremists—is always an emotive issue, and debates surrounding political violence often become politicized themselves. It is particularly important, in this regard, therefore, to follow the evidence and base assumptions and observations on thorough empirical analysis rather than selective sampling of quotes or unsubstantiated anecdotes.

The end of Al-Qaeda?

The legacy of the two Al-Qaeda leaders and the resonance of their material will, to a substantial degree, depend on the way in which Al-Qaeda itself develops and on the nature of its eventual demise. Ten years after the 9/11 attacks, many observers saw Al-Qaeda as a movement in existential crisis.

Cronin, for instance, identified five principal developments contributing to the perceived demise and marginalization of the Al-Qaeda core leadership. First, the excessive targeting of Muslims had, as mentioned above, caused tremendous damage to the credibility of the leadership. Second, the end goals of the Al-Qaeda core leadership and those of its disparate affiliates had become increasingly separated. Third, and on a related point, events surrounding the Arab Spring underscored the historical irrelevance of Al-Qaeda. Fourth, and again related to the ongoing developments surrounding the Arab Spring and its aftermath, the leadership had failed to mobilize public opinion in ways that had initially been envisaged. Fifth, the core of the Al-Qaeda movement had been greatly weakened by the slaying of its principal leaders; foremost among them was bin Ladin himself.[12]

Gerges similarly drew the conclusion that the movement was in irrevocable decline from consulting denunciations of former (usually incarcerated) Islamist militants, opinion polls, and Al-Qaeda's legacy of excessive targeting. "Al-Qaeda's attacks on civilians," he argued, "have relegated it to the margins of Islamic society."[13]

Our perceptions of Al-Qaeda's existing strength and vitality, however, are inevitably tied to our perceptions of Al-Qaeda's position during its heyday. In many ways, therefore, it is hardly surprising to conclude that Al-Qaeda is on the "margins of Islamic society" because it has always been on the isolated fringes. Al-Qaeda was never a mainstream movement that became radicalized. Its involvement in violent activism evolved, but it has always been an extremist group. A tendency to exaggerate the real power of Al-Qaeda in the aftermath of 9/11 and during the beginning of the Iraq War, therefore, adds to skewed perceptions of its apparently precipitous decline.

This is related to notions of evaluating Al-Qaeda's supposed success or failure. This question, in other words, seems dependent on the nature of the yardsticks and measurements used. Judging by the Al-Qaeda leadership's own rhetoric, little appears to have been accomplished. After more than 20 years of militancy there were still no signs of some sort of pious emirate that could form the building blocks of the anticipated future Caliphate. However, these references to the desired end goal are, as mentioned above, aspirational and always vague. They serve to underscore the religious and supposedly noble sense of purpose. At the same time, these references were also intended to provoke some sort of popular uprising or mobilization—both tangible and intangible—in support of Al-Qaeda's cause. And this has clearly failed to materialize. One reason, no doubt, is the fact that Al-Qaeda's violence has increasingly become associated with the killing of Muslims—precisely the people the Al-Qaeda leadership has claimed to protect.[14] One manifestation of this problem is Zawahiri's belated set of appeals to Al-Qaeda affiliates and sympathizers to exercise greater care when selecting targets in order to avoid (excessive or unjustified) Muslim deaths. These appeals, of course, reveal deep inconsistencies in Al-Qaeda's narrative. First, the Al-Qaeda leaders justified and celebrated attacks of indiscriminate violence. Then they denied any responsibility for attacks that resulted in the killing of Muslims, before attempting to appeal to precisely those affiliates that had carried out these attacks in the hope that they would select more discriminate targets. The fact that Zawahiri started to appeal publically to these sympathizers and affiliates is proof not only of the fact that the targeting had gotten out of hand but also, implicitly, that the Al-Qaeda leadership recognized that these entities and affiliates had been responsible for this violence all along.

Furthermore, the failure to achieve the levels of mobilization and support that the Al-Qaeda leaders had hoped for clearly affected the nature and tone of their communicative output. As late as 2001, for instance, Zawahiri clearly stated that were the *ummah* to fail to respond to Al-Qaeda's mobilizing call, the leaders ought to blame only themselves and their failure to appeal to their constituents. A few years later, this rhetoric had changed completely, with Zawahiri in particular denouncing the "nation" that had "failed" to support its vanguard. This gradual alienation of target constituents undermines the image of a just and representative vanguard that the Al-Qaeda leaders have tried so hard to construct over the years. In this sense too, an attack of the scale of 9/11 could perhaps be seen as a huge strategic mistake. The obvious repercussions of the attacks—military intervention and much greater focus on counterterrorism—marked the beginning of a period when increasingly desperate and exasperated rhetoric emanated from the Al-Qaeda core.

As discussed in the previous chapter, moreover, the Al-Qaeda leaders were not always successful in communicating a consistent or apparently effective message that recognized the realities of perceived constituents. At the same time, however, it seems hard to justify Moghadam and Fishman's assertion that Al-Qaeda "failed to achieve even its partial goals."[15] After all, US troops did redeploy from Saudi Arabia (one of bin Ladin's early objectives), even though they did not go very far. More fundamentally, however, the Al-Qaeda leadership—which was never more than a network of dislodged militants operating out of some of the poorest and most deprived areas of the world—managed to dominate the foreign, defense, and security policy agenda of the globe's premier superpower and its allies. It provoked and engaged in protracted wars of attrition and spawned a host of affiliates and sympathizers—groups as well as isolated individuals—that continue to operate in its name or in recognition of its goals. If one of the objectives of terrorism is to utilize asymmetry in order to provoke conventional powers, dominate their political agendas, attract media attention, and achieve infamy, then some of Al-Qaeda's ventures can in many ways be seen as successful. More specifically, Western politicians have become very reluctant to commit substantial ground forces in conflict zones in the Middle East, particularly Syria, and beyond because of the carnage in Iraq. Al-Qaeda and its affiliates are responsible for much of the violence and sectarian turmoil that has become embedded in Iraq, and this protracted state has clearly affected policy-makers in the West, as well as their electorates. For a non-state actor to have such an impact on the policies of powerful states and their governments is in many ways remarkable.

Questions concerning Al-Qaeda's success or failure thus yield different—and often conflicting—answers. These depend on the yardsticks we choose to apply, our time frames, and perspectives each time. For example, the revolutions of the Arab Spring posed a clear challenge to Al-Qaeda and undermined core tenets of the leadership's message. These events thus serve to illustrate Al-Qaeda's isolation, but at the same time they might also present opportunities that Al-Qaeda, its affiliates, and like-minded jihadists could exploit.

The Arab Spring brought hope and emancipation but also, inevitably, discord, disillusionment, and turmoil. After the Muslim Brotherhood took over in Egypt in June 2012 and following continued unrest, violence, and lawlessness, fears grew that Islamist militants might be able to operate more freely in the country than before. After the Egyptian military ousted the Brotherhood from power in July 2013, moreover, equally grave concerns emerged over a violent Islamist backlash. The protracted civil war in Syria that broke out in spring 2011 saw jihadist elements becoming more prominent and the violence more sectarian. In April 2013, the leader of Jabhat an-Nusra, the principal jihadi group fighting in Syria, pledged allegiance to Ayman Al-Zawahiri, even though he dismissed earlier announcements from Al-Qaeda's discredited franchise in Iraq that the two entities had merged.[16] Regardless of an-Nusra's stance, Al-Qaeda's affiliate in Iraq continued to operate in Syria as the Islamic State of Iraq and As-Sham, as well as in Iraq.

This pledge of allegiance from Syria came a year after the leader of Al-Shabaab in Somalia also finally pledged formal allegiance to Zawahiri, as the new emir of Al-Qaeda, although this decision is reported to have caused considerable internal disputes.[17] Islamist insurgencies in Central and Western Africa, moreover, became emboldened by an influx of arms and recruits from Libya following the brief civil war in the country in 2011, thus providing material support for jihad (and other types of militancy), if not cohesive guidance.

Gerges wrote in 2011 that "Americans and Westerners should be told that the war [involving Al-Qaeda] is over."[18] Yet when armed groups continued to commit acts of violence in the name of Al-Qaeda and pledge allegiance to its senior leadership and while individuals responsible for terrorist plots continued to cite Al-Qaeda as a source of inspiration, it seems hard to justify such a claim. The concept of Al-Qaeda has certainly become broader and less tangible than before and attacks and attempted attacks inspired by Al-Qaeda in the West have become much less sophisticated and impactful, but it would be wrong to suggest that Al-Qaeda—and all that it has come to represent—is a spent force, despite the demise of its original leadership. How Al-Qaeda's fan base and various affiliates will evolve, moreover, depends on how a new generation of participants chooses to shape Al-Qaeda-inspired militancy. Shahzad, for instance, noted how the emergence of a new generation of Islamist combatants bolstered Al-Qaeda's position in Pakistan after its flight from Afghanistan.[19]

Despite its excessive targeting, self-inflicted marginalization, reduced material power, and loss of central leadership figures, therefore, Al-Qaeda continues to exist. The nature of this existence has evolved and mutated but still captures an element of the violent Islamist milieu. The fact that Al-Qaeda continues to resonate with some presents something of a paradox. Despite all the mistakes and drawbacks and in spite of the excessive violence, inconsistent messaging, and events that have discredited Al-Qaeda, the movement continues to have some presence and weight within Islamist militant circles. How could this be possible? One potential explanation is the fact that Al-Qaeda—partly due to the impact of its propaganda and violence—has achieved such notoriety and infamy that it will continue to inspire those who are attracted to such a legacy. The literature on the far-right and white supremacist milieus, for example, has identified the "counterculture" element as a crucial motivating factor that inspires some to support and join such movements.[20] This may be an equally strong motivation within the Islamist extremist milieu, and Al-Qaeda has certainly achieved great levels of notoriety that may add to the attraction for some. The fact that Al-Qaeda has publically been identified by so many governments and organizations as the central adversary only adds to its "name recognition" within those circles that are violently opposed to those same organizations and governments. Attaching the Al-Qaeda label or claiming Al-Qaeda links may well provoke a greater media reaction and attract more attention to the particular plots or activities in question than may otherwise have been the case. If part of the purpose of terrorism and other forms of political violence is to publicize a movement or a cause, then the Al-Qaeda label may indeed serve such a purpose.

What about Al-Qaeda's ideological doctrine? There is, of course, genuine collective grievance and anger with prevailing norms and values where Al-Qaeda provides an immediately recognizable brand and framework for activists. Furthermore, the extent to which the Al-Qaeda leadership pioneered contemporary Islamist terrorism with a true cross-border scope cannot be ignored. In this sense, therefore, Al-Qaeda may continue to provide an abstract or physical platform where local jihadi efforts are rationalized within the context of much wider religio-political goals. Indeed, much of Al-Qaeda's potency of late can be linked to the ambitions of local affiliates, while what is left of the central leadership has tried its best to ensure that these local affiliates continue to appreciate the broader objectives of the fighting. This has been far from an easy task with localized conflicts often becoming more sectarian than the Al-Qaeda leaders envisioned in their public statements.

Bin Ladin and Zawahiri both emerged from the Soviet-Afghan war with a determination to develop and foment the jihadi uprising that they saw as central in defeating the USSR. This fervor and determination, they hoped, could be channeled toward the creation of a new jihadi organization that was the most ambitious in the modern world. Alongside their operational concerns, the Al-Qaeda leaders gradually developed a set of precepts and an evolving discourse that defined their goals, ambitions, and justifications for their activism. This message has been divulged among multiple and diverse audiences since Al-Qaeda's earliest days in the wake of the breakup of the Soviet Union. Methods of delivery have changed over time, as has some of the content. Bin Ladin and Zawahiri strove to present ongoing events in light of the narrative that they had developed on behalf of Al-Qaeda, while reconciling the fact that the mass mobilization they envisaged had failed to materialize. Through these public statements, however, we can gauge how one of the most significant terrorist networks in modern history formulated its public vision and honed its core message. The aim of this book has been to shed light on this output and the evolution of the multifaceted discourse that the original leadership of Al-Qaeda left for a new generation of Al-Qaeda supporters, activists, and sympathizers.

Notes

Preface

1 *The Economist* (2011) (May 7).

2 In this context, and for the purposes of this book, Lahoud's approach to discourse as a "process that deploys ideas to instil certain inclinations in people's minds that would make them favourable to a political objective and dispose them to viewing those ideas as truth" is helpful and appropriate. See Lahoud, N. (2005) *Political Thought in Islam: A Study in Intellectual Boundaries*. Routledge, Abingdon: location 166 (e-book).

3 Zawahiri (2013) "General guidelines for jihad," published by *As-Sahab* (September 14) and distributed via Islamist Web forums and Archive.org: See, for example, http://ia801006.us.archive.org/8/items/tawakkalo-00/en.pdf [as of September 18, 2013]. [266]

The aims of this book

4 Horgan, J. (2009) *Walking Away from Terrorism: Accounts of Disengagement from Radical and Extremist Movements*. Routledge, London: page xx.

5 This study depends on transcripts of Al-Qaeda leadership statements in English as well as translated videos and other original output from Al-Qaeda itself. While most of this material was originally produced in Arabic, a number of interviews and other communiqués by bin Ladin during the 1990s featured in English or Urdu in Pakistani newspapers. The sources for this material were primarily government repositories, think tanks, and research centers, as well as Al-Qaeda-affiliated and Islamist extremist websites. These sources present the most reliable, comprehensive, and accessible gateways to the Al-Qaeda leadership statements over the time period of this study. Different sources were triangulated for each statement wherever possible. In terms of coding, it should be noted that the analysis was done in English but does not depend on specifics of language that may not have been picked up in the translation. The focus is on broader themes and longitudinal patterns rather than the use of specific words or phrases or other linguistic details. Therefore, although there are frequent references to discourse, this is not a study of discourse theory *per se*, which would often be more concerned with the use of language and particulars of syntax. The theoretical approach adopted in this study rests on the literature on collective action frames, as developed within social movement theory. See notes to Chapter 1 for more details concerning methodology, sources, translations, and coding.

6 This categorization is based on Benford and Snow's work on "collective action frames." See further in Chapter 3 in this volume and, for example, Snow, D. & Benford, R. (1988) "Ideology, frame resonance, and participant mobilization," in *International Social Movement Research* (vol. 1, pp. 197–217).

Chapter 1

1 Burke, J. (2013) "Why Al-Qaeda is a spent force," in *The Guardian Weekly* (February 1–7, vol. 188, iss. 8): pages 1 and 5.

2 Indeed, Zawahiri even had to admit that he had first heard of a suggested merger between Al-Qaeda in Iraq and the Al-Nusra Front in Syria via mainstream news channels. See Zawahiri transcript in Atassi, B. (2013) "Qaeda chief annuls Syrian-Iraqi jihad merger," in *Al-Jazeera* [online] (June 9) http://www.aljazeera.com/news/middleeast/2013/06/2013699425657882.html [as of June 2013].

3 As Ranstorp and Herd noted, Al-Qaeda's ideological battle grew increasingly complex in "an era of globalization where like the famous 'butterfly effect' one small local event translates in seconds into global consciousness." Ranstorp, M. & Herd, G. (2007) "Approaches to countering terrorism and CIST," in *The Ideological War on Terror: Worldwide Strategies for Counter-Terrorism*, ed. Aldis, A. & Herd, G. P. Routledge, London. See also on "collective identity" through propaganda Torres, M. R., Jordán, J., & Horsburgh, N. (2006) "Analysis and evolution of the global jihadist movement propaganda," in *Terrorism and Political Violence* (vol. 18, iss. 3, pp. 391–422) and the discussion about Al-Qaeda's media strategy in Lynch, M. (2006) "Al-Qaeda's media strategies," in *National Interest* (March, pp. 50–83).

4 The full list of statements analyzed is given in the Appendix. To ease the identification and cross-checking of individual communiqués, each statement has been given a unique identification number, which is displayed in the table in the Appendix as well as with each referenced statement in the text. The number is given in square brackets and follows the citation itself.

5 As the authors of the *Terrorist Perspectives Project* noted, Salafi jihadist leaders do not constitute a general staff that can promulgate binding strategic guidance to the movement's constituent organizations and to the masses. At best, leaders of individual organizations can exercise significant, though not total, control over their own people. Leaders of the movements often make their wishes known, however, through public statements and internal communications. Stout, M. E., Huckabey, J. M., Schindler, J. R., & Lacey, W. (2008) *The Terrorist Perspectives Project: Strategic and Operational Views of Al Qaida and Associated Movements*. Naval Institute Press, Annapolis: page 137.

6 McAllister, Bradley & Schmid, Alex P. (2011) "Theories of terrorism," in *The Routledge Handbook of Terrorism Research*, ed. Schmid, Alex P. Routledge, Abingdon: page 246.

7 Corman, S. R., & Schiefelbein, J. S. (2006) "Communication and media strategy in the jihadi war of ideas," in *Report #0601 Consortium for Strategic Communication* (April 20), Arizona State University, Phoenix: page 2.

8 Weinberg, L. (2008) "Two neglected areas of terrorism research: Careers after terrorism and how terrorists innovate," in *Perspectives on Terrorism* (vol. 2, iss. 9, June): page 13.

9 Hoffman, for instance, called for "sound empirical judgment" and a greater emphasis on establishing a "thorough, systematic understanding" of Al-Qaeda. Hoffman, B. (2007) "Challenges for the U.S. Special Operations Command posed by the global terrorist threat: Al Qaeda on the run or on the march?," Written Testimony Submitted to The House Armed Services Subcommittee on Terrorism, Unconventional Threats and Capabilities, Washington, DC.

10 "Press reports, organizational charts, and secondary material," Wiktorowicz noted, "are often insufficient for delineating and studying these [Islamic activist] networks and their relationship to contention." Wiktorowicz, Q. (2004) "Introduction," in *Islamic Activism: A Social Movement Theory Approach*, ed. Wiktorowicz. Indiana University Press, Bloomington, Ind: page 23.

11 The vast majority of statements analyzed for this book were secured and processed as entire pieces, rather than excerpts. For some of the oldest and more obscure communiqués, only excerpts could be found, however.

12 Zawahiri (2013) "Unifying the word toward the word of monotheism (*tawhid*)," in *As-Sahab* (April 7), distributed by Al-Fajr Media Center via jihadi websites. English transcript from the Open Source Center. [260]

13 Some have sought to approach this body of content through conducting automated and computerized studies that rely primarily on the detection of key words in relation to particular grammatical constructs. These studies can yield rapid and illustrative overviews that describe aspects of the Al-Qaeda leaders' narrative. Examples of automated studies into Al-Qaeda's narrative include Mendenhall, R. (2010) "Al-Qaeda: Who, what, why? Database applications for the Al-Qaeda statements index" (senior thesis, Haverford College, April 23, 2010); Pennebaker, James. W. & Chung, Cindy K. (2007) "Computerized text analysis of Al-Qaeda transcripts," in *The Content Analysis Reader*, ed. Krippendorff, Klaus & Bock, Mary. Sage, Thousand Oaks: pages 453–467. For problems involved in conducting such automated analyses, see, for example, the application of IntuView's "IntuScan" software as described in Ramsay, G. & Holbrook, D. (2013) "The violent part of violent extremism," (paper delivered at the Society for Terrorism Research, University of East London, June 27–28).

14 The coding was arranged according to the following categories: (1) Problem diagnosis—(a) references to undesirability of existing societies; (b) past grievances; (c) current grievances. (2) Proposed solutions—(a) references to the (i) use of violence, (ii) specific violent tactics, (iii) methods outside violence, (iv) constraints on use of violence, and (v) legitimacy of civilian targeting; (b) geographic focus of prognostic response and identified friends and enemies: (i) long-term vision and (ii) intermediate goals. (3) Motivational and communicative approaches—(a) messages directed toward Muslim audiences ((i) positive appeals, (ii) criticism, (iii) hostility and threats); (b) messages directed toward non-Muslim audiences: (i) threats and warnings, (ii) more conciliatory approaches. This process produced a database where each entry dissected individual statements from bin Ladin and Zawahiri according to the problem diagnosis, proposed solutions, and the communicative approaches employed. Each row of the database would thus capture the substance of one statement, as divided according to these categories, while each column captured the development of particular message components, such as references to the use of violence, in the Al-Qaeda leaders' statements over time. The reliability of the coding process was ensured by initiating a parallel procedure where another researcher coded the same material and comparing the results. Qualitative coding of this sort, however, is necessarily a somewhat subjective procedure, and the categories described above do contain some overlap.

15 English translations of the statements and communiqués were used for the coding, both for the material originally produced in Arabic, as well as for bin Ladin's numerous interviews with newspapers during the 1990s, although many of these were produced in English in Pakistani newspapers to begin with. A third of the 260 communiqués coded could be secured directly from the Islamist extremist websites and forums that now constitute the principal distribution network for propaganda material from Al-Qaeda and other militant groups. These were unedited productions disseminated by the Al-Qaeda affiliates themselves who provided original translations. Many of the more recent communiqués could be collected in this way, translated by jihadist "media sections" (such as "Ansar Al-Mujahideen English Forum" and the "Global Islamic Media Front," as well as As-Sahab). All this material could be triangulated, given that multiple links to different repositories were provided whenever announcements of new statements appeared on Al-Qaeda-affiliated forums.

Other translations were primarily sourced from The Combating Terrorism Centre (CTC), other Department of Defense/Defense Intelligence Agency sources, SITE, BBC Monitoring, The Nine Eleven Finding Answers (NEFA) Foundation (a nonprofit research foundation), The Foreign Broadcast Information Service (a service providing translations of articles for US government agencies) and its successor, the Open Source Centre, Chatham House, journalistic organizations (including Al-Jazeera, Pakistani newspaper *The Dawn*, *Al-Sharq Al-Awsat*, *Esquire* magazine, *The Observer*), Archive.org (via links from Islamist websites), YouTube (via links from Islamist websites), Italian Team for Security, Terroristic Issues & Managing Emergencies (ITSTIME) at the Catholic University of Milan, written compilation works with translations of Al-Qaeda primary documents (specifically: Ibrahim, R. (ed.) (2007) *Al Qaeda Reader*, Broadway Books, New York, NY; Kepel, G. & Milelli, J. P. (eds.) (2008) *Al Qaeda in Its Own Words*, Harvard University Press, Cambridge, MA; IntelCenter (2008) *Words of Osama bin Laden Vol. 1*, Tempest Publishing, Alexandria, VA; IntelCenter (2008) *Words of Ayman al-Zawahiri Vol. 1*, Tempest Publishing, Alexandria, VA), and the Norwegian Defence Research Establishment (Forsvarets forskningsinstitutt, FFI). These are reliable sources that provide transcripts which have appeared in multiple publications from journalists, policy-makers, and academics.

Furthermore, in order to ensure reliability of the data set, emphasis was placed on triangulating these sources and evaluating transcripts whenever possible. This consisted of securing translations and transcripts from as many sources as possible in order to compare the versions presented. Only minor discrepancies emerged, relating to basic transcribing errors rather than substantive issues of content. Finally, on the topic of source reliability, it should be noted that this book focuses on general themes that emerge over time, rather than specific linguistic elements of specific statements. The analysis, in short, does not depend on the accuracy of any single text, but rather on multiple statements that are secured from a large host of different sources and transcripts that have been triangulated and compared. David Aaron made a similar observation in his study of jihadi discourse: "The sheer volume and repetitiveness of jihadi statements help to ensure consistency and minimize misconstrual. Thus, while the translations may differ in quality and may even reflect particular agendas, they are more than adequate to capture the intent of the jihadi authors" (Aaron, D. (2008) *In Their Own Words: Voices of Jihad*, RAND Corporation, Santa Monica, CA.)

16 Here, the focus is on the "less apparent 'expressive' and 'existential' quality to al-Qaeda's character and its warfare that is not given due attention in the literature." Indeed, "the grand strategic level of warfare—whether that of a state or non-state actors—cannot be fully understood apart from the protagonist's culture, or the ideologies that express them." See Cozzens, J. B. (2007) "Approaching al-Qaeda's warfare: Function, culture and grand strategy," in *Mapping Terrorism Research: State of the Art, Gaps and Future Direction*, ed. Ranstorp, M. Routledge, Abingdon: pages 131–137.

17 In this context, Tololyan developed the concept of a *projective* narrative as one that "not only tells a story of the past, but also maps out future actions that can imbue the time of individual lives with transcendent collective values." These narratives "tell individuals how they would ideally have to live and die in order to contribute properly to their collectivity and its future." Tololyan, in this sense, identified and highlighted the notion *mediation*, where events are translated and interpreted in the interest of a particular cause. Tololyan, K. (2006) "Cultural narrative and the motivation of the terrorist," in *Critical Concepts in Political Science: Terrorism Volume IV: The Fourth or Religious Wave*, ed. Rapoport, D. Routledge, London: page 32.

18 The Al-Qaeda leadership statements thus offer essential metrics that illustrate how its wider agenda has evolved. Michael Scheuer, for example, noted in his study *Through Our Enemies' Eyes: Osama bin Laden, Radical Islam, and the Future of America*:

> The United States has never had an enemy who has more clearly, calmly, and articulately expressed his hatred for America and his intention to destroy our country by war or die trying. For five years in media interviews, public

statements, and letters to the press, bin Laden told us that he meant to defeat the United States and that he would attack—and urge others to attack. (page xi)

Anonymous (Scheuer, M.) (2002) *Through Our Enemies' Eyes: Osama bin Laden, Radical Islam, and the Future of America*. Brassey's Inc, Washington, DC.

Chapter 2

1 To borrow Wilkinson's conceptualization: see, for example, Wilkinson, P. (2005) "International terrorism: The changing threat and the EU's response," in *Chaillot Paper* (no. 84, October). Institute of Security Studies, European Union.

2 In April 1988 the Soviet Union signed the Geneva Accords, committing to full withdrawal from Afghanistan. Troops began redeploying shortly thereafter and withdrawal was completed by February 1989. See Reynolds, D. (2000) *One World Divisible: A Global History since 1945*. Penguin Books, London: page 552.

3 See Wright, L. (2006-A) *The Looming Tower: Al-Qaeda's Road to 9/11*. Penguin Books, London: page 130; Burke (2004-A) *Al-Qaeda: The True Story of Radical Islam* (2nd edition). Penguin Books, London: pages 2–3.

4 Wright (2006-A): pages 128–129; Bergen, P. & Cruickshank, P. (2008) "The unraveling: The jihadist revolt against bin Laden," in *New Republic* (Wednesday, June 11).

5 Bergen, P. & Cruickshank, P. (2012) "Revisiting the early Al Qaeda: Updated account of its formative years," in *Studies in Conflict and Terrorism* (vol. 35, iss. 1, pp. 1–36): page 4.

6 See Harmony Database (nd), document number AFGP-2002-600086; Combating Terrorism Center (2007) *Cracks in the Foundation: Leadership Schisms in Al-Qaeda from 1989–2006*, Harmony Project. West Point, NY: pages 8–9.

7 Harmony Database (n. d.), document number AFGP-2002-600086.

8 Zawahiri, A. Al (1991) *The Bitter Harvest: The Brotherhood in Sixty Years*, translation in Ibrahim, R. (2007) *Al Qaeda Reader*. Broadway Books, New York; and Kepel, G. & Milelli, J. P. (eds.) (2008) *Al Qaeda in Its Own Words*. Harvard University Press, Cambridge, MA.

Zawahiri was, however, a great admirer of Qutb and other more hardline elements of the Brotherhood. His criticism focused on the political processes prescribed by Hasan Hudaybi, who took over as Supreme Guide shortly after Qutb's execution, and those of similar disposition within the movement. See further on internal ideological tensions within different strands of the Brotherhood in Kepel, G. (2008-A) "The Brotherhood in the Salafist universe," *Current Trends in Islamist Ideology* (vol. 6, pp. 20–29),

Hudson Institute, Washington, DC. Many key figures in and around Al-Qaeda have, however, had close engagement with the Brotherhood, including bin Ladin and Mustafa Settmariam Nasar. See Filiu, J. P. (2009) "The Brotherhood vs. Al-Qaeda: A moment of truth?," in *Current Trends in Islamist Ideology* (vol. 9). See on bin Ladin Brotherhood links and resulting tensions with Zawahiri: Kepel, G. (2004) *The War for Muslim Minds: Islam and the West*, translated by Pascale Ghazaleh. The Belknap Press of Harvard University Press, Cambridge, MA: page 85.

9 Harmony Database, document no. AFGP-2002-600086. Combating Terrorism Center, West Point, NY. See: http://www.ctc.usma.edu/programs-resources/harmony-program [as of July 2013].

10 The death of Azzam remains a mystery, and numerous theories have emerged over the years about potential culprits. In their analysis of the formative years of Al-Qaeda, Cruickshank and Bergen suggested the most likely culprits were Egyptian jihadis, working together with Gulbuddin Hekmatyar, an Afghan militant commander, who coveted bin Ladin's wealth and were angered by Azzam's reluctance to embrace their strategic agenda and by his support for Ahmed Shah Massoud. See Bergen & Cruickshank (2012): page 9.

11 Bergen & Cruickshank (2012).

12 Gerges, F. (2011) *The Rise and Fall of Al-Qaeda*. Oxford University Press, Oxford: page 29.

13 See, for example, Gerges (2011): pages 49–50; Zelikow P. (as executive director of research team) & 9/11 Commission (2004) *Final Report of the National Commission on Terrorist Attacks upon the United States* ("The 9/11 Commission Report"). US Congress, Washington, DC: page 56.

14 There is disagreement over the extent to which bin Ladin relied on his Egyptian associates for strategic direction at this point. Wright and others have argued that bin Ladin during this period was predominantly reliant on Zawahiri's strategic guidance and the experience of his Egyptian colleagues, who retained their association with EIJ. The Zawahiri-bin Ladin alliance, at this stage, appears primarily to have been a marriage of convenience: "each man filled a need in the other," argues Wright. "Zawahiri wanted money and contacts, which bin Laden had in abundance. Bin Laden, an idealist given to causes, sought direction; Zawahiri, a seasoned propagandist, supplied it" (Wright 2006-A: page 127). Cruickshank and Hague appear to agree, arguing that Zawahiri was "attracted by bin Laden's financial resources and his reputation as a war hero [while] bin Laden admired the Egyptian for his long experience in the Islamist movement" (Bergen & Cruickshank (2012): page 7). Shahzad similarly emphasizes the centrality of Zawahiri's strategic guidance (Shahzad, S. S. (2011) *Inside Al-Qaeda and the Taliban: Beyond bin Laden and 9/11*. Pluto Press, London). Bergen argues that it was Zawahiri who "gradually won over bin Ladin to his more expansive view of Jihad" (Bergen, P. (2011) *The Longest War: The Enduring Conflict between America and al-Qaeda*. Free Press, New York: location 47 (e-book)). For Scheuer, however, it was bin Ladin who altered Zawahiri's agenda in the long term, much more than vice versa. Scheuer, M. (2011) *Osama bin Laden*. Oxford University Press, Oxford: pages 12–13.

15 Riedel, B. (2008) *The Search for Al Qaeda: Its Leadership, Ideology and Future* (2nd edition). Brookings Institution Press, Washington, DC: page 47.

16 Afghanistan, after Soviet withdrawal in February 1989, had reached a state of turmoil as local militant cadres fighting the Najibullah regime in Kabul had fractured and lost their focus due to internal tribal disputes, mutual distrust, and a lack of direction and coordination. These tensions would soon lead to open hostilities between rival factions. By the early 1990s, meanwhile, the Taliban began to consolidate their power in the south, which would later prove crucial for bin Ladin and his group.

17 Wright (2006-A): pages 153–154.

18 Wright (2006-A): pages 49–50; Zelikow, P. et al. (2004).

19 Bergen & Cruickshank (2012): page 19.

20 Zelikow et al. (2004); Randal, J. (2005) *Osama: Making of a Terrorist*. I.B. Tauris, London: page 115.

21 Bin Ladin spent a year in Pakistan, arriving in early 1991. Cruickshank and Bergen argue that during this period Al-Qaeda launched its first attempted attack overseas, plotting to kill the former king of Afghanistan in Rome. See Bergen & Cruickshank (2012): page 15.

22 See further in Taylor, M. & Elbushra, M. (2006) "Hassan al-Turabi, Osama bin Laden and al Qaeda in Sudan," in *Terrorism and Political Violence* (vol. 18, pp. 449–464).

23 Zelikow et al. (2004): section two.

24 Zelikow et al. (2004): section two.

25 See Harmony Database (nd) document AFGP-2002-003345. Combating Terrorism Center, West Point, NY. See: http://www.ctc.usma.edu/programs-resources/harmony-program [as of July 2013].

26 Bergen & Cruickshank (2012): pages 19–21.

27 Riedel (2008): Chapter 3; Kepel (2004): page 87.

28 Sageman, M. (2008) *Leaderless Jihad: Terror Networks in the Twenty-First Century*. University of Pennsylvania Press, Philadelphia: pages 49–50. "By early September 2001," Bergen (2011: location 34) notes, "al-Qaeda was at the height of its power the group and its Taliban allies were on the verge of taking over Afghanistan entirely."

29 Bergen, P. (2001) *Holy War Inc.: Inside the Secret World of Osama bin Laden*. Free Press, New York: page 2.

30 Bergen & Cruickshank (2012): pages 23–24.

31 Esposito, J. L. (2002) *Unholy War: Terror in the Name of Islam*. Oxford University Press, Oxford: page 16. The Deobandi movement is a strand of Sunni Islam established in nineteenth-century India, now prominent throughout South Asia, the UK, and elsewhere.

32 Zahab, M. & Roy, O. (2002) *Islamist Networks: The Afghan-Pakistan Connection*. Hurst, London: page 15.

33 Bin Ladin, U. (1996) "Message from Usama Bin-Muhammad Bin Ladin to his Muslim brothers in the whole world and especially in the Arabian Peninsula," in *Al-Islah* (London: September 2), translated in Foreign Broadcast Information Service (FBIS) (2004) *Compilation of Usama Bin Ladin Statements 1994–January 2004*: page 20. [5]

34 Although, as Bergen and Cruickshank note, Zawahiri's Egyptian Islamic Jihad (which had also gone by the name of Al-Jihad) had been closely tied to bin Ladin's group prior to the 1998 official alliance and later merger. Bergen, & Cruickshank (2012): page 24.

35 Cosignatories were Abu-Yasir Rifa'i Ahmad Taha of the Egyptian Islamic Group, Shaykh Mir Hamzah of the Jamiat-ul-Ulema-e-Pakistan, and Fazlul Rahman of the Jihad Movement in Bangladesh.

36 Bin Ladin, Zawahiri et al. (1998) "Text of World Islamic Front's statement urging jihad against Jews and Crusaders," in *Al-Quds Al-Arabi* (London, February 23), translated in *Compilation of Usama Bin Ladin Statements 1994–January 2004*. [161]

37 Sageman (2008): page 39; Hegghammer, T. (2009-A) "The ideological hybridization of jihadi groups," in *Current Trends in Islamist Ideology* (vol. 9, pp. 26–46) Hudson Institute, Washington, DC.

38 Kepel, G. (1984) *Muslim Extremism in Egypt: The Prophet and Pharaoh*. University of California Press, Berkeley: page 47; Qutb, S. (2006) *Milestones*, Islamic Book Service, New Delhi, India.

39 Faraj, M. S. (2000) *Jihaad: The Absent Obligation*, Maktabah al-Ansaar, Birmingham: pages 50–51. This version is still available from Muhammad al-Maqdisi's website tawhed.net (www.tawhed.net/dl.php?i=AbsntObl) [as of January 2011].

40 Faraj (2000): pages 60–61; Esposito (2002): page 46.

41 See, for example, *Defence of the Muslim Lands: The First Obligation after Iman* by Abdullah Azzam. Originally published in 1979. Published in English by Maktabah Al-Ansaar, Birmingham. No date.

42 Michot, Y. (2006) *Muslims under Non-Muslim Rule: Ibn Taymiyya on Fleeing from Sin; Kinds of Emigration; the Status of Mardin; Domain of Peace/ War, Domain Composite; the Conditions for Challenging Power*. Interface Publications, Oxford: pages 46, 49. Faraj's work, according to Michot, formed part of the "Mongolizing" of Islamism, where Ibn Taymiyyah's "anti-Mongol fatwas were being exploited to call to an armed rebellion against the rulers or governments of certain modern Muslim countries" (p. 49).

43 Kepel (2004): page 72; Gerges, F. (2005) *The Far Enemy: Why Jihad Went Global*. Cambridge University Press, Cambridge: chapters 1–2; Riedel (2008): chapter 2; Lacroix, S. (2008) "Notes to Part III: Ayman Al-Zawahiri," in ed. Kepel & Milelli: pages 316–341.

44 To borrow Jurgensmeyer's concept (see Jurgensmeyer, M. (2003) *Terror in the Mind of God: The Global Rise of Religious Violence* (3rd edition). University of California Press, Berkeley: page 145).

45 Gerges (2005): page 57.

46 See for instance Sageman (2008): pages 40–51. Although Gerges (2005) emphasized the importance of Al-Qaeda in developing a transnational agenda, as noted above, he also illustrated how the group was only one actor in a complex tapestry of Islamist militancy.

47 Bergen (2011).

48 Olivier Roy, for example, saw Al-Qaeda emerge from 9/11 as an "organization and a trademark [that could] operate directly, in a joint venture, or by franchising." According to Roy, Al-Qaeda embodied, but did not have the monopoly of, "a new kind of violence." Roy, O. (2004) *The Rise of Globalised Islam: The Search for a New Ummah*. Columbia University Press, New York: page 294.

49 9/11 thus brought about the conditions that ushered in a new form of Al-Qaeda-sponsored violence, where the organization relied less on direct operational control, especially in the West, but where individuals who acted on their own initiative in support of the broader Al-Qaeda and Salafi-jihadi agenda became more prominent. Although these developments were in many ways inevitable given the impossibility of retaining a cohesive organizational structure after 9/11, they also reflected the thinking of a prominent jihadi strategist called Abu Mus'ab Al-Suri (aka Mustafa Settmariam Nasar). See, for example, Cruickshank, P. & Hage, M. A. (2007) "Abu Musab Al Suri: Architect of the new Al Qaeda," in *Studies in Conflict and Terrorism* (vol. 30, iss. 1, pp. 1–14); Lia, B. (2008). "Dissidents in Al-Qaeda: Abu Mus'ab al-Suri's critique of bin Ladin and the Salafi-jihadi current." Lecture at Princeton University, December 3, 2007, Norwegian Defence Research Establishment (FFI); Lia, B. (2007) *Architect of Global Jihad: The Life of Al-Qaeda Strategist Abu Mus'ab al-Suri*. Hurst, London.

50 Islamist militants operated primarily out of the Federally Administered Tribal Areas, known in Pakistan as *ilaqa-e-ghair* or the "lawless land" (in particular North and South Waziristan Agencies), and Balochistan on the Afghan-Pakistani border. See Solomon, J. (2008) "The funding methods of FATA's terrorists and insurgents," in *Combating Terrorism Center Sentinel* (vol. 1, iss. 6, May, pp. 4–7). For detailed account of the fusion between Al-Qaeda and the Taliban, see, for example, Shahzad, Syed Saleem (2011) *Inside Al-Qaeda and the Taliban: Beyond bin Laden and 9/11*. Palgrave Macmillan, Melbourne.

51 For detailed descriptions of these conflicts, see Burke, J. (2011) *The 9/11 Wars*. Allen Lane/Penguin Books, London. These developments in Iraq and Pakistan allowed Al-Qaeda to become more deeply engaged in sustained Islamist militancy than ever before. Later on, the deteriorating security situation in Iraq (in no small part due to the groups endorsed by Al-Qaeda) and a truce between authorities in Islamabad and militants in Waziristan provided further breathing space for the group's central leadership to regroup and appeared to foster closer links with the Taliban. See, for example,

Gregory, S. (2007) "Al-Qaeda in Pakistan," in *Brief Number* (vol. 5, March 1, pp. 1–7), Pakistan Security Research Unit; Khan, I. (2005) "Waziristan Draft Accord approved," in *Dawn* (February 2, page 1); Gul, P. (2006) "Waziristan Accord signed," *Dawn* (September 6); Bergen, P. (2007-B), "Afghanistan 2007: Problems, Opportunities and Possible Solutions", *The House Committee on Foreign Affairs*, (February 15: 2007), http://foreignaffairs. house.gov/110/ber021507.htm [as of January 19, 2011]. At the same time, of course, the large numbers of Muslim casualties that were inflicted in Al-Qaeda-sponsored acts of violence in these conflicts caused outrage and widespread condemnation of the group, as will be discussed in more detail below.

52 Bruce Hoffman's February 2007 testimony submitted to the House Armed Services Subcommittee emphasized the continued resonance of two dimensions to Al-Qaeda, depending on the level of analysis and approach: "The al Qaeda of today combines, as it always has, both a 'bottom up' approach encouraging independent thought and action from low (or lower-) level operatives and a 'top down' one issuing orders and still coordinating a far-flung terrorist enterprise with both highly synchronized and autonomous moving parts" (Hoffman, B. (2007) "Challenges for the U.S. Special Operations Command posed by the global terrorist threat: Al Qaeda on the run or on the march?" Written Testimony Submitted to The House Armed Services Subcommittee on Terrorism, Unconventional Threats and Capabilities, Washington, DC).

53 Ronfeldt captured the ambiguity surrounding the organizational conceptualizations of Al-Qaeda in a 2007 paper written for the RAND Corporation: "For a while, the pressures put on the al-Qaeda network evidently reduced its structure from a hub-and-spoke design back to a scattered-cluster design. But now it is growing again, apparently into a multihub design. Which design is it? Do the pieces consist of chain, hub (i.e. star), or all-channel subnets? And where are the bridges and holes that may connect to outside actors? The answers matter, for each design has different strengths, weaknesses, and implications" (Ronfeldt, D. (2007) *Al-Qaeda and Its Affiliates: A Global Tribe Waging Segmental Warfare*. RAND Corporation, Santa Monica, CA. www.rand.org/pubs/reprints/2008/RAND_RP1371.pdf [as of January 20, 2011]).

Ronfeldt's own conceptual model for Al-Qaeda was based on a "tribal" paradigm in which the central leadership of Al-Qaeda operated through a network of kinship and bonds, projecting "ancient patterns of tribalism on a global scale" through "segmental warfare" (Ronfeldt 2007: pages 35–36). Constructing a broader spectrum, Mishal and Rosenthal argued that Al-Qaeda had moved from a relatively hierarchical structure, through a network phase in the run-up to 9/11, morphing into what the authors called a "dune organization," following a process of deterritorialization. In this condition, the authors argued, Al-Qaeda existed in an almost "geopolitical vertigo," whereby clusters of variously unrelated networks of groups represented Al-Qaeda in various regions of the world without being centered in a single location. There was no overreaching institutional presence, the activity was dynamic, command and communication chains were fluid and fragmented, and the structure and scope of the components was variable (Mishal, S. & Rosenthal, M. (2005) "Al Qaeda as a dune organization: Toward a typology of Islamic terrorist organizations," in *Studies in Conflict & Terrorism*, July, vol. 28, iss. 4, pp. 275–293).

According to this view, such networks embraced the Al-Qaeda agenda and operated as, what Sageman described as, a "collection of nodes connected through links" (Sageman, M. (2004) *Understanding Terror Networks*. University of Pennsylvania Press, Philadelphia: page 137). Arquilla, in turn, explored how these networks differed in composition according to type of activity, reach, and ability to preserve operability, according to what the authors described as the "netwar" paradigm (Arquilla, J., Ronfeldt, D., & Zanini, M. (2002) "Networks, netwar, and information-age terrorism," in *Terrorism and Counter-Terrorism—Understanding the New Security Environment*, ed. Howard, R. & Sawyer, R. McGraw-Hill, New York: page 91).

54 Hoffman, B. (2006) *Inside Terrorism* (revised edition). Columbia University Press, New York: page 282.

55 Hoffman (2006) *Inside Terrorism*: page 282.

56 Brachman, J. (2008) *Global Jihadism: Theory and Practice*. Routledge, London: page 15.

57 Burke, J. (2011) *The 9/11 Wars*. Allen Lane/Penguin Books, London: pages 469–470.

58 Sageman (2008).

59 Intelligence and Security Committee (2006) "Report into the London Terrorist Attacks in London on 7 July 2005": page 27.

60 Senate Select Committee on Intelligence (2008) *Annual Worldwide Threat Assessment* (February 5). Washington, DC: page 38. www.dni.gov/testimonies/20080205_transcript.pdf [as of January 21, 2011].

61 *Economist* (2008) "Special Report," (July 17).

62 Quoted in Bakier, A. H. (2008) "Jihadi website advises recruits on how to join al-Qaeda," in *Jamestown Terrorism Focus* (vol. v, iss. 18, May 6th).

63 This and subsequent references to Al-Suri's *Global Islamic Resistance Call* on this page are from Lia (2007): pages 443–445.

64 Combating Terrorism Center (2007): page 1.

65 See Burke, J. (2004-B). "Think again: Al Qaeda," in *Foreign Policy* (May/June, no. 142, pp. 18–26); Bale, J. M. (2009) "Jihadist ideology and strategy and the possible employment of WMD," in *Jihadists and Weapons of Mass Destruction*, ed. Ackerman, G. & Tamsett, J. CRC Press, Boca Raton: pages 3–59.

66 Some accounts have sought to reconcile these ideational approaches with the development of organizational and agency models. Soriano's study of Al-Qaeda messages relating to Islamist militant activism focused on Spain, for instance, defined a cluster of agents (with variously local or international ambitions) in a wider "global *jihadist* movement (GJM)" (Soriano, M. (2009)

"Spain as an object of jihadist propaganda," in *Studies in Conflict & Terrorism* (vol. 32, iss. 11, pp. 933–952): page 935, italics in original). Sageman also warned that while the organizational capacity of Al-Qaeda had diminished, "the al Qaeda social movement [had] flourished" (Sageman 2008: pages 133, 121). A similar approach was adopted in the US National Intelligence Estimate of July 2007 assessing the "threat to the US Homeland." This warned that the spreading of "radical—especially Salafi—Internet sites … and the growing number of radical, self-generating cells in Western countries indicate that the radical and violent segment of the West's Muslim population is expanding" (ODNI (2007) *National Intelligence Estimate: The Terrorist Threat to the US Homeland* (July)).

The UN also highlighted the impact of such fluidity, warning in a 2008 Security Council Committee report that "the Al-Qaeda and Taliban leadership continues to try to exert control over a movement that it inspires but does not direct" (Security Council Committee established pursuant to resolution 1267 (2008) *Report of the Analytical Support and Sanctions Monitoring Team Pursuant to Resolution 1735 (2006) Concerning Al-Qaeda and the Taliban and Associated Individuals and Entities* (2008/324): page 5).

Stepanova even talked of a "multiple-cell, transnational post-al-Qaeda movement"—as an autonomous, adaptable, and de-structured actor—in this context (Stepanova, E. (2008) *SIPRI Research Report No. 23 Terrorism in Asymmetrical Conflict: Ideological and Structural Aspects*. SIPRI, Stockholm: page 26).

67 The "Terrorist Perspectives Project" developed the concept of "Al-Qaeda and Associated Movements—AQAM." According to this model, "AQAM represents a large number of individuals united by a common theology, albeit with differing ethnic backgrounds, experiences, and perspectives on jihad," where ultimately, the "view of AQAM as a global movement with a revolutionary vanguard at its head is the dominant perspective" (Stout, M. E., Huckabey, J. M., Schindler, J. R., & Lacey, W. (2008) *The Terrorist Perspectives Project: Strategic and Operational views of Al Qaida and Associated Movements*. Naval Institute Press, Annapolis: page 55).

68 Neidhardt, F. & Rucht, D. (1991) "The analysis of social movements: The state of the art and some perspectives for further research," in *Research on Social Movements: The State of the Art in Western Europe and the USA*, ed. Rucht. Campus, Frankfurt: page 450.

69 Wilkinson, P. (1971) *Social Movement*. Pall Mall Press, London: page 46.

70 Wilkinson (1971): page 71.

71 Wilkinson (1971): page 47.

72 Della Porta, D. (1995) *Social Movements, Political Violence, and the State: A Comparative Analysis of Italy and Germany*, Cambridge University Press, Cambridge: pages 3–4.

73 Gusfield, J. (1981) "Social movements and social change: Perspectives of linearity and fluidity," in *Research in Social Movements, Conflict and Change* (vol. 4), ed. Kriesberg, L. JAI Press, Greenwich, CA: page 325.

74 Bowie and Schmid, meanwhile, underscored the contribution that this wider perspective could offer to the study of terrorism. Social and political movements, the authors argued, "produce both legal parties (and NGOs) and illegal underground organizations engaged in political violence and terrorism. A comprehensive understanding of terrorist campaigns and groups would require looking at this wider context as well," the authors argued (Bowie, N. G. & Schmid, A. P. (2011) "Databases on terrorism," in *The Routledge Handbook of Terrorism Research*, ed. Schmid. Routledge, Abingdon: page 339).

75 Several accounts of Al-Qaeda have, in turn, adopted social movement perspectives. For Riedel (2008: pages 135–136) and Brachman (2008: page 11), for instance, the extent to which Al-Qaeda had become an adaptable social movement was central to its strength and continued survival. Several authors, meanwhile, have emphasized the ability of the Al-Qaeda leaders to create a globalized social movement through inspiring followers to collective action. See, for example, Rabasa et al. (2006) (*Beyond al-Qaeda: The Global Jihadist Movement* (Part 1). RAND Corporation, Santa Monica) on "al-Qaeda and the universe of jihadist groups that are associated with or inspired by al-Qaeda": page 1; and Roy (2008) "Al-Qaeda: A true global movement," in *Jihadi Terrorism and the Radicalisation Challenge in Europe*, ed. Coolsaet, R. Ashgate, Aldershot: pages 109–115. See also Ranstorp: "the constantly mutating networks and cells that transformed al-Qaeda into a global 'salafist-jihadist' movement thrive in this globalization-affected media milieu" ("Introduction" to Ranstorp, M. (ed.) (2007) *Mapping Terrorism Research: State of the Art, Gaps and Future Direction*. Routledge, London: page 2).

76 This is an important caveat when we consider the application of the social movement literature to Al-Qaeda. Fawaz Gerges, for example, has argued against viewing Al-Qaeda as a social movement and dismissed notions that the broader network of Al-Qaeda followers could be referred to in such terms. "Far from being a social movement with deep historical roots in Muslim societies," Gerges (2011: page 29) argues, "al-Qaeda and transnational jihad in general, is an orphan within the militant Islamist family, an ambitious venture founded and led by a small vanguard." But this assumes that adopting the social movement approach to Al-Qaeda necessarily assumes the group has great pedigree and mass resonance, which is far from the case and irrelevant to the application of the social movement literature to this particular example. The leadership of Al-Qaeda can be seen as presiding over a diffuse set of groups loyal to their particular agenda and cause, as well as influencing and seeking to influence a broader set of constituents that nonetheless represent a tiny and peripheral proportion of their particular communities. The social movement literature offers valuable tools with which to understand these relationships and the importance of different communicative tasks in this regard.

77 Kepel (1984): page 55. This is not to suggest, however, that Qutb's thoughts did not evolve, or indeed that they were always radical in an Islamist sense. Shepard (1992), for instance, notes how "Sayyid Qutb appears to have moved from a Muslim secularist position in the 1930's to a moderate radical

Islamism (if I may use such an expression) in the late 1940's and then to an extreme radical Islamism during the last years of his life" ("The development of the thought of Sayyid Qutb as reflected in earlier and later editions of' social justice in Islam," in *Die Welt des Islams, New Series* (vol. 32, iss. 2, pp. 196–236)).

78　Qutb (2006): "Introduction."

79　Shepard (1992): pages 212–213.

80　Bin Ladin, U. (1999) Interview with bin Ladin titled "Usama Bin Ladin, the Destruction of the Base" aired on Al Jazeera (June 10), full-length version aired on Al Jazeera (September 20, 2001), transcript available from FBIS (2004). [184]

81　Cetina, L. (2005) "Complex global microstructures: The new terrorist societies," in *Theory, Culture & Society* (vol. 22, iss. 5, pp. 213–234): page 215.

82　See, for example, Benford, R. D. & Snow, D. A. (2000) "Framing processes and social movements; an overview and assessment," in *Annual Review of Sociology* (vol. 26, pp. 611–639): page 613. See also Kane A. E. (1997) "Theorizing meaning construction in social movements …," in *Sociological Theory* (November, vol. 15, iss. 3, pp. 249–276); Williams R. H. (1995) "Constructing the public good: Social movements and cultural resources," in *Social Problems* (February, vol. 42, iss. 1, pp. 124–144). Much of the work on framing and social movement is, of course, developed on Goffman's thesis on frame analysis: Goffman, E. (1974) *Frame Analysis: An Essay on the Organization of the Experience.* Harper Colophon, New York: especially page 247, and Gamson W. A., Fireman B., & Rytina S. (1982) *Encounters with Unjust Authority,* Dorsey Press, Homewood, IL.

83　Moghadam, A. & Fishman, B. (2010) "Chapter 1: Debates and divisions within and around Al-Qa'ida," in *Self-Inflicted Wounds: Debates and Divisions within Al-Qa'ida and Its Periphery,* ed. Moghadam, A. & Fishman, B. Harmony Project, Combating Terrorism Center, West Point, NY (December 16): page 2.

84　Burke (2011: page 473), for instance, wrote that "by late 2012, the least one could say was that the 'network of networks' was battered and disjointed. In many ways, it had simply ceased to exist." Partly for these reasons, bin Ladin appears to have been contemplating a "rebranding" exercise shortly before his death, in order to—as Hoffman argues—find a new name for the movement "that would more accurately reflect its ideological pretensions and self-appointed role as defender of Muslims everywhere" (Hoffman, B. (2013) "Al-Qaeda's uncertain future," in *Studies in Conflict and Terrorism* (vol. 36, iss. 8, pp. 635–653)).

85　Holbrook, D. (2012) "Al-Qaeda's response to the Arab Spring," in *Perspectives on Terrorism* (vol. 6, iss. 6, pp. 4–21).

86　Zawahiri (2013) "Unifying the word toward the word of monotheism (*tawhid*)," in *As-Sahab* (April 7), distributed by Al-Fajr Media Center via jihadi websites. English transcript from the Open Source Center. [260]

87　Hopkins, N. (2012) "MI5 warns Al-Qaeda regaining UK toehold after Arab Spring," in *Guardian* (June 25).

88 See, for example, Totten, M. J. (2012) "Arab Spring or Islamist Winter," in *World Affairs* (January/February), http://www.worldaffairsjournal.org/article/arab-spring-or-islamist-winter [as of December 2012].

89 Gerges (2011): page 3.

90 Gerges (2011): page 5.

91 Gerges (2011): page 16.

92 Gerges (2011): page 127.

Chapter 3

1 Zawahiri, A. (date unknown) "Introduction" to *Characteristics of Jihad*, magazine. From CTC Harmony Database, document no. AFGP-2002-600142.

2 This Islamist extremist milieu, it should be emphasized, exists as a peripheral phenomenon within a much broader framework of Islamic political thought referred to as Islamism. Islamism, as Lahoud notes, can be used to identify a host of different political currents, which present Islam as a political ideology. Islamism takes a selective and literal approach to the core religious texts. Quranic verses and Hadith reports are selected, according to Lahoud, without "due sensitivity to context or alternative traditional interpretations," but in a way that is conducive to faith-based political objectives. Lahoud, N. (2005) *Political Thought in Islam: A Study in Intellectual Boundaries*. Routledge, Abingdon: pages 180–181 (e-book).

3 Hoffman, B. (2006) *Inside Terrorism* (revised edition), Columbia University Press, New York: page 214.

4 Hegghammer, T. (2009-A) "The ideological hybridization of jihadi groups," in *Current Trends in Islamist Ideology* (vol. 9, pp. 26–46); Snow, D. & Byrd, S. (2007) "Ideology, framing processes, and Islamic terrorist movements," in *Mobilization* (vol. 12, iss. 2, June, pp. 119–136); Hegghammer, T. (2010) "The rise of Muslim foreign fighters: Islam and the globalization of jihad," in *International Security* (vol. 35, iss. 3, Winter 2010/2011, pp. 53–94); Quiggin, T. (2009) "Understanding al-Qaeda's ideology for counter-narrative work" in *Perspectives on Terrorism* (vol. 3, iss. 2, pp. 18–24, August): page 20.

5 Aldis, A. & Herd, G. P. (2007) "Introduction," in *The Ideological War on Terror: Worldwide Strategies for Counter-Terrorism*, ed. Aldis & Herd. Routledge, London, pp. 1–3.

6 Della Porta, D. (2001) "Left-wing terrorism in Italy," in *Terrorism in Context*, ed. Crenshaw, M. Pennsylvania State University Press: State College, PA: page 149. See also Rabasa, A., Chalk, P., Cragin, K., Daly, S. A., Gregg, H. S., Karasik, T. W., O'Brien, W. R., & Rosemau, W. (2006) *Beyond al-Qaeda: The Global Jihadist Movement* (Part 1). RAND Corporation, Santa Monica, CA: page 9.

7 Carpenter, J. S., Levitt, M., Simon, S., & Zarate, J. (2010) *Fighting the Ideological Battle*. The Washington Institute for Near East Policy, Washington, DC: page 2. Emphasis added.

8 Carpenter et al. (2010): page 6.

9 Khan, S. (2010) "Letter from the editor," in *Inspire* (iss. 1, Summer, p. 2), Al-Malahim publications of Al-Qaeda in the Arabian Peninsula.

10 Leiter, M. (2010) "Statement for Record: Senate Homeland Security and Government Affairs Committee: 'Nine Years after 9/11: Confronting the Terrorist Threat to the Homeland'" (September 22): page 6. http://www.dni. gov/files/documents/Newsroom/Testimonies/2010-09-22%20D-NCTC%20 Leiter%20Testimony%20for%20SHSGAC%20Hearing.pdf [as of December 5, 2012].

11 Senate Select Committee on Intelligence (2008) *Annual Worldwide Threat Assessment* (February 5), Washington, DC: page 9. www.dni.gov/ testimonies/20080205_transcript.pdf [as of January 21, 2011]. This is not to argue, of course, that the attacks themselves are less important. For terrorists, as Hoffman and McCormick note, "to hold their audience (and hold themselves together) they must continue to act." Association with attacks, moreover, adds credence to those who generate the extremist narrative. See Hoffman, B. & McCormick, G. (2004) "Terrorism, signaling and suicide attack," in *Studies in Conflict and Terrorism* (vol. 27, iss. 4, pp. 243–281): page 245.

12 Burke, J. (2011) *The 9/11 Wars*. Allen Lane/Penguin Books, London: pages 473–474.

13 Ronfeldt, D. (2007) *Al-Qaeda and Its Affiliates: A Global Tribe Waging Segmental Warfare*. RAND Corporation. www.rand.org/pubs/reprints/2008/ RAND_RP1371.pdf [as of January 20, 2011] (Originally published in: *Information Strategy and Warfare: A Guide to Theory and Practice*, chapter 2, pp. 34–55): page 44.

14 Gregg, H. (2010) "Fighting the jihad of the pen: Countering revolutionary Islam's ideology," in *Terrorism and Political Violence* (vol. 22, iss. 2, pp. 292–314): page 295.

15 Indeed, several analyses of the wider corpus of militant Islamists choose to apply the term "jihadi-Salafi," referring to puritanical Islamist revivalists who sanction the use of violence. See, for example, Senate Select Committee on Intelligence (2008); and Fradkin, H. (2008) "The history and unwritten future of Salafism," in *Current Trends in Islamist Ideology* (vol. 6, pp. 5–20).

16 This refers to the *al-Sahaabah*, or companions of the Prophet Mohammed, the second generation of followers, *al-tabi'un*, and the third generation, living according to the norms and practices of the first two generations (*atba' altabi'in*). This period thus spans the late seventh century up to the early ninth century CE. For some, however, the Rashidun or rightly guided Caliphs who ruled from the Prophet's death (632 CE) up to 661 CE, with the murder of Ali ibn Abi Taalib, are exclusively revered. Meijer, R. (ed.) (2009) "Introduction," in *Global Salafism: Islam's New Religious Movement*, Hurst, London: page 3.

17 Meijer (ed.) (2009): pages 3–4.

18 Zahab, M. & Roy, O. (2002) *Islamist Networks: The Afghan-Pakistan Connection*. Hurst, London.

19 Brachman, J. (2008) *Global Jihadism: Theory and Practice*. Routledge, London: page 23; Wagemakers, J. (2012) *A Quietist Jihadi: The Ideology and Influence of Abu Muhammad al-Maqdisi*. Cambridge University Press, Cambridge.

20 Esposito, J. L. (1984) *Islam and Politics*. Syracuse University Press, Syracuse, NY: page 214.

21 Lahoud (2005).

22 Meijer (ed.) (2009): page 4. But Salafis also argue with advocates of others strands of Islamic political thought as regards the interpretation of Quranic verses and, by extension, the way in which religious doctrine can be interpreted in contemporary societies. Lahoud, for example, defined three core strands of Islamic political thought: Islamists, Apologists, and Intellectuals. The first group has been referred to here as "Salafis." They advocate compliance with the teachings of the *salaf* by emulating their period, which they see as the template for contemporary societies. To this end, Salafis highlight verses that support the political measures that they see as essential prerequisites to achieving their objective. Apologists, meanwhile, draw on other Quranic verses to present their inclusive understanding of Islam as the only correct interpretation of the creed. The Intellectuals, Lahoud argues, emphasize philosophical currents in Islam that they see as underpinning liberalism and democracy in the contemporary Arab-Islamic world. Lahoud (2005).

23 Stemmann, J. J. E. (2006): "Middle East Salafism and the radicalization of Muslim communities in Europe," in *Middle East Review of International Affairs* (vol. 10, iss. 3, September): page 92.

24 Bin Ladin (2002) "The wills of the martyrs of the New York and Washington battles: The will of the Martyr Abdulaziz Alomari," in *As-Sahab*, published April 19, secured from Islamist Web forums.

25 More precisely, as Wagemakers notes, the concept of *tawhid* has three principal meanings for Salafis: *Tawhid al-rubbiyya* refers to the unity of Lordship, that is, the belief that there is only one creator. *Tawhid al-asm wa-l-ift* refers to the unity of the name and attributes of Allah that emphasize God's unique characteristics. *Tawhid al-ulhiyya* emphasizes how God alone is worthy of worship. Wagemakers (2012).

26 Mansfield, P. (2003) *A History of the Modern Middle East* (2nd edition). Penguin Books, London: pages 40–41; Meijer (ed.) (2009): page 4.

27 Meijer (ed.) (2009): pages 1–5.

28 Meijer (ed.) (2009): page 19. Wahhabism (including "neo-Wahhabism"), therefore, should not be grouped alongside the much broader strand of Salafism, but rather seen as a subcategory of the latter. Salafism concerns the general movement that seeks to recreate the society of the pious forefathers and includes multiple sub-strands and different approaches. (Neo-)Wahhabism, in turn, is a descriptive label attached to adherents of a particular form of Salafism developed by Mohammad Al-Wahhab, who came from Najd in modern-day Saudi Arabia. Wahhabism and its modern manifestation thus constitute distinct forms of Salafism. Wagemakers, for example, suggests Wahhabism could be referred to as the "Najdi branch of Salafism." Wagemakers (2012).

29 In this context, it should also be emphasized that the term "Salafism" is both used to refer to a contemporary movement of religious revivalism and a late-nineteenth-century movement led by Jamal al-Din al-Afghani, Muhammad Abduh, and others that coincided with the decline and fall of the Ottoman Empire. The purpose of this latter movement was to "purify" the creed in order to allow Islam to embrace modernity more effectively. Modern-day Salafism, by contrast, is obsessed with perceived "impurities" of the creed, particularly apparent forms of *shirk* and distractions that dilute the creed. See Wagemakers (2012).

30 Wagemakers (2012): page 24.

31 See, for example, Hafez, M. (2010) "Tactics, *takfir*, and anti-Muslim violence," in *Self-Inflicted Wounds: Debates and Divisions within Al-Qa'ida and Its Periphery*, ed. Moghadam, A. & Fishman, B. Harmony Project, Combating Terrorism Center (December 16), West Point, NY: pages 19–45.

32 Wiktorowicz, Q. (2006) "Anatomy of the Salafi movement" in *Studies in Conflict and Terrorism* (vol. 29, iss. 3, pp. 207–239): page 208. Wagemakers, in turn, suggested that these categories were more nuanced and argued that principal figures within this realm might transcend different categories of Salafism. The Salafi scholar Al-Maqdisi, for example, might thus, Wagemakers argued, be classified as a "quietist Jihadi-Salafi" given the nature of his arguments that combined quietist, puritanical, and activist jihadi elements of the Salafi milieu. See Wagemakers (2012).

33 Paz, R. (2009) "Debates within the family: Jihadi-Salafi debates on strategy, *takfir*, extremism, suicide bombings and the sense of the apocalypse," in ed. Meijer, R.: page 269. Al-Suri's assessment as to the origin of the jihadi ideology is remarkably similar; see Lia, B. (2009) "'Destructive doctrinarians': Abu Mus'ab al-Suri's critique of the Salafis in the jihadi current", in ed. Meijer (2009): page 286.

34 Meijer (ed.) (2009): page 26.

35 See, for example, Brachman (2008): page 11; McCants, W., Brachman J., & Felter, J. (2006) *Militant Ideology Atlas: Executive Report* (November). Combating Terrorism Center, West Point, NY: pages 9–10.

36 Hamid Mir, for instance, argued that bin Ladin (whom he met and interviewed) was "doing politics in the name of religion"(Mir, H. et al. (2005) "The real Twin Towers: Al-Qaeda's influence on Saudi Arabia and Pakistan," in *Al-Qaeda Now: Understanding Today's Terrorists*, ed. Greenberg, K. Cambridge University Press, Cambridge: page 138). Mohamedau too emphasized the "primacy of the political" in Al-Qaeda's agenda (Mohamedau, M. (2007) *Understanding Al-Qaeda: The Transformation of War*. Pluto Press, London, UK: page 67). Tibi, meanwhile, described Al-Qaeda as fighting "religionized" political causes (Tibi, B. (2008) "Religious extremism or religionization of politics? The ideological foundations of political Islam," in *The Ideological Foundations of Political Islam*, ed. Frisch, H. & Inbar,

E. Routledge, London: page 16). Some analysts have voiced concerns over the validity and accuracy of this apparent distinction between religion (and religious culture) and politics in the context of Al-Qaeda's campaign of violence and terrorism. Tololyan, for example, warns of the "disciplinary rush to the politicization of terrorism," whereby "the profession of political science seems powerfully impelled to turn enormously complex events into mere, or only, or just *political* facts that can be seen as motivating other political acts, including terrorism." He argues: "terrorism with an authentically popular base is never a purely political phenomenon"(Tololyan, K. (2006) "Cultural narrative and the motivation of the terrorist," in *Critical Concepts in Political Science: Terrorism Volume IV: The Fourth or Religious Wave*, ed. Rapoport, D. Routledge, London: pages 33–34, emphasis in original).

37 As Eickelman and Piscatori (1996) note, however, the separation of state and religion (*din wa-dawla*) in Islamic thought is not straightforward. Although the authors argue, "this view of indivisibility finds support in more than forty references in the Qur'an," in reality "politics and religion became separable not long after the death of the Prophet and the establishment of dynastic rule" (*Muslim Politics*. Princeton University Press, Princeton: page 46). Esposito (1984: page 26) similarly argues "The early extraordinary expansion and development of Islam as a state necessitated immediate decisions by caliphs and generals rather than reflective planning by scholars and policy makers." The indivisibility of state and religion (or what Eickelman and Piscatori prefer to call "sacred authority") in Al-Qaeda's discourse attests to its "postmodern hybridity" (Al-Rasheed, M. (2009) "The local and the global in Salafism," in Meijer, R. (ed.): page 305). In terms of the Al-Qaeda leadership's discourse, Hellmich argued that "an approach to bin Ladin's messages that focuses exclusively on the political leaves no room for the inherently religious dimension of his mission" (Hellmich, C. (2011) *Al-Qaeda: From Global Network to Local Franchise*. Zed Books, London: page 93). Mendenhall equally argued that "Al-Qaeda effectively intertwines its political and religious motivations, rendering the political *or* religious dichotomy false" (Mendenhall, R. (2010) "Al-Qaeda: Who, what, why? Database applications for the Al-Qaeda Statements Index" (Senior thesis submitted to Haverford College, April 23): page 17. http://thesis.haverford.edu/dspace/handle/10066/5064 [as of December 5, 2012]).

38 Al-Rasheed (2009): page 305.

39 Meijer (ed.) (2009): page 9.

40 See Filiu, J. P. (2009) "The Brotherhood vs. Al-Qaeda: A moment of truth?," in *Current Trends in Islamist Ideology* (vol. 9, pp. 18–26).

41 Zahab & Roy (2002): page 12.

42 Zahab & Roy (2002).

43 Meijer (ed.) (2009): pages 5–6.

44 Zahab & Roy (2002).

45 Lia (2009) in Meijer (ed.): page 283.

46 Lia (2009) in Meijer (ed.): pages 291, 297.

47 Hafez (2010).

48 Moghadam, A. & Fishman, B. (eds.) *Self-Inflicted Wounds: Debates and Divisions within Al-Qa'ida and Its Periphery*. Harmony Project, Combating Terrorism Center (December 16), West Point, NY: page 4.

49 Paz (2009): page 278.

50 See, for example, Bergen, P. & Cruickshank, P. (2008) "The unraveling: The jihadist revolt against bin Laden," in *New Republic* (Wednesday, June 11); Bale, J. M. (2009) "Jihadist ideology and strategy and the possible employment of WMD," in *Jihadists and Weapons of Mass Destruction, ed.* Ackerman, G. & Tamsett, J. (pp. 3–59) CRC Press, Boca Raton: page 41.

51 Paz (2009): page 275.

52 Hegghammer (2009-A): page 3. See also Brooke, S. (2010) "Strategic fissures: The near and far enemy debate," in ed. Moghadam & Fishman.

53 Stout, M. E., Huckabey, J. M., Schindler, J. R., & Lacey, W. (2008) *The Terrorist Perspectives Project: Strategic and Operational Views of Al Qaida and Associated Movements*. Naval Institute Press, Annapolis: page 155.

54 Ranstorp, M. & Herd, G. (2007) "Approaches to countering terrorism and CIST" in *The Ideological War on Terror: Worldwide Strategies for Counter-Terrorism*, ed. Aldis, A. & Herd, G. P. Routledge, London: page 3.

55 Ciovacco, C. J. (2009) "The contours of Al Qaeda's media strategy," in *Studies in Conflict & Terrorism* (vol. 32, iss. 10, pp. 853–875).

56 See Wright (2006-B) "The master plan: For the new theorists of jihad, Al Qaeda is just the beginning," in *New Yorker* (September 11): page 48. See also Bergen, P. (2011) *The Longest War: The Enduring Conflict between America and al-Qaeda*. Free Press, New York.

57 Snow & Byrd (2007): page 119.

58 Kimmage, for instance, underlined this factor in his analysis of "virtual media production and distribution entities" within the "Al-Qaeda media nexus" (Kimmage, D. (2008) "The Al-Qaeda media nexus: The virtual network behind the global message," in *RFE/RL Special Report* (March), Radio Free Europe: page 1). See also on Al-Qaeda's media strategy in Lynch, M. (2006) "Al-Qaeda's media strategies," in *National Interest* (March 1, pp. 50–83), republished in Cruickshank (ed.) (2012) *Al Qaeda*. Routledge: London, pp. 363–371).

59 To borrow Brachman's term. See, for example, Brachman (2008).

60 Snow & Byrd (2007): page 121.

61 HM Government (2011) *Prevent Strategy*. Presented to Parliament by the Secretary of State for the Home Department by Command of Her Majesty (June). Cm 8092: 1.

62 HM Government (2011).

63 Cigar, for instance, argued such insights would help "policymakers shape a more realistic profile of its leaders and of its strategy, which can be key in developing effective counterterrorism and counterinsurgency policies"

(Cigar, N. (2008) *Al-Qaeda's Doctrine for Insurgency: Abd al-Aziz al-Muqrin's "A Practical Course for Guerrilla War."* Potomac Books, Dulles, VA: page 4). Similarly, Riedel observed that "understanding al Qaeda's ideology is the first key to defeating the group" (Riedel, B. (2008) *The Search for Al Qaeda: Its Leadership, Ideology and Future* (2nd edition). Brookings Institution Press, Washington, DC: page 24). Or in the words of the Terrorist Perspectives Project, "understanding the culture and ideology of global salafi jihadism is the single most important component" in comprehending the nature of the threat (Stout et al. (2008): page 46). As a result, "ideology is … an essential component of any strategy designed to counter al-Qaeda" (Rabasa et al. (2006): page 7).

64 Ciovacco, for instance, concluded from his analysis of 64 bin Ladin and Zawahiri communiqués (post-9/11 material only) that "in this marketing-focused war of ideas, Al Qaeda's media strategy is the linchpin to unlocking its organizational DNA and deciphering its next moves" (Ciovacco (2009): page 854). Bergen, meanwhile, observed that some Al-Qaeda statements included specific instructions, such as in December 2003 when Zawahiri issued a call for an attack on president Musharraf, which was followed by two assassination attempts targeting the president. Then, after bin Ladin called for attacks on members of the Iraq invasion coalition, this statement too was followed by attacks targeting coalition partners (including Italian targets in Iraq, the November 2003 Istanbul bombings targeting a British bank and the British Consulate in March, and the 2004 Madrid bombings) (Bergen, P. (2005) in panel session titled "Al-Qaeda then and now," in *Al-Qaeda Now: Understanding Today's Terrorists*, ed. Greenberg, K. Cambridge University Press, Cambridge: pages 3–5). Mendenhall, meanwhile, described an IntelCenter study aiming to find "possible indicators" of the 2009 Christmas Day plot in Al-Qaeda's ideological output *after* the incident took place (Mendenhall (2010). http://thesis.haverford.edu/dspace/handle/10066/5064 [as of July 2013]. CQ Press: page 38).

65 Martin, S. (2009) "The threat is overblown," in *Debating Terrorism and Counterterrorism: Conflicting Perspectives on Causes, Contexts, and Responses*, ed. Gottlieb, S. (CQ Press, Washington DC, pp. 180–191): page 187. See also Mendenhall (2010).

66 See, for example, Corman, S. R. & Schiefelbein, J. S. (2006) "Communication and media strategy in the jihadi war of ideas," in *Report #0601 Consortium for Strategic Communication* (April 20), Arizona State University, Phoenix.

67 Snow, D. & Marshall, S. (1984) "Cultural imperialism, Social movements, and the Islamic revival", in *Research in Social Movements, Conflict, and Change*, ed. Kriesberg, L. (vol. 7, pp. 131–152), JAI Press, Greenwich, CT: page 136.

68 Wiktorowicz, Q. (2004) "Introduction," in *Islamic Activism: A Social Movement Theory Approach*, ed. Wiktorowicz. Indiana University Press, Bloomington, IN: page 4.

69 Wiktorowicz (2004): page 15; see also Snow, D. A. & Benford, R. D. (1992) "Master frames and cycles of protest," in *Frontiers in Social Movement Theory*, ed. Moms, A. D. & Mueller, C. M. Yale University Press, New Haven, CT: page 137.

70 Snow, D. A., Rochford, E. B., Worden, S. K., & Benford, R. D. (1986), "Frame alignment processes, micromobilization, and movement participation," in *American Sociological Review* (vol. 51, iss. 4, August, pp. 464–481). American Sociological Association: page 465.

71 Wiktorowicz (2004): page 15.

72 The authors' application of the "frame" term is based on Goffman's notions of frames as "schemata of interpretation" that enable individuals to "locate, perceive, identify, and label" occurrences within their life space and the world at large. See Goffman, E. (1974) *Frame Analysis: An Essay on the Organization of the Experience*. Harper Colophon, New York: page 21; and Snow et al. (1986). See also Wilson, J. (1973) *Introduction to Social Movements*. Basic Books, New York.

73 Snow, D. & Benford, R. (1988) "Ideology, frame resonance, and participant mobilization," in *International Social Movement Research* (vol. 1, pp. 197–217). JAI Press Inc., Greenwich, CT: page 198.

74 Snow & Benford (1988).

75 Snow & Benford (1988).

76 See, for example, Benford, R. D. & Snow, D. A. (2000) "Framing processes and social movements; an overview and assessment," in *Annual Review of Sociology* (vol. 26, pp. 611–639): page 613.

77 Benford & Snow (2000).

78 Benford & Snow (2000): page 614.

79 Benford, R. (1997), "An insider's critique of the social movement framing perspective," in *Sociological Inquiry* (vol. 67, iss. 4, November, pp. 409–430). See below on "injustice frames."

80 Benford (1997): page 417. Emphasis added.

81 Wiktorowicz (2004); Snow & Benford (1988); Gregg (2010); Tololyan (2006); Schmid, A. P. (1989) "Terrorism and the media: The ethics of publicity," in *Terrorism and Political Violence* (vol. 1, iss. 4, pp. 539–565); Schmid, A. P. (2005) "Terrorism as psychological warfare," in *Democracy and Security* (vol. 1, iss. 2, pp. 137–146); Hegghammer (2010); Seliger, M. (1976) *Ideology and Politics*. Allen and Unwin, London: page 11.

82 Snow & Byrd (2007): page 126.

83 See: Azzam, A. (2001) *Join the Caravan* (initially published in 1988). Azzam Publications, London & online: page 4.

84 Snow & Benford (1988): pages 199, 200–202.

85 Snow & Benford (1988): pages 200–202.

86 Snow & Byrd (2007): page 126.

87 This risk of "overkill" to the reputation of terrorist groups is not new, as Jacob Shapiro (2013) traces in his volume *The Terrorist's Dilemma: Managing Violent Covert Organizations* (Princeton University Press, Princeton, NJ).

88 Snow & Benford (1988): pages 207–208.

89 Snow & Byrd (2007): page 132.

90 Wiktorowicz (2004): page 17.

91 Page, M, Challita, L., & Harris, A. (2011) "Al Qaeda in the Arabian Peninsula: Framing narratives and prescriptions," in *Terrorism and Political Violence* (vol. 23, iss. 2, pp. 150–172).

92 Page et al. (2011): page 163.

93 Hegghammer (2009-A): page 39.

94 Wagemakers (2012): location 961 (e-book).

Chapter 4

1 Hellmich, C. (2011) *Al-Qaeda: From Global Network to Local Franchise.* Zed Books, London: page 87, emphasis in original.

2 Originally published in Mann, M. (2005) *Incoherent Empire.* Verso Books, : London, UK, page 169, emphasis in original. See also "Introduction" to Bruce Lawrence (ed.) (2005) *Messages to the World: the Statements of Osama bin Laden.* Verso Books, London.

3 Zawahiri (1991) *The Bitter Harvest: The Brotherhood in Sixty Years.* [46] See also Filiu, J. P. (2009) "The Brotherhood vs. Al-Qaeda: A moment of truth?," in *Current Trends in Islamist Ideology* (vol. 9): page 20. See Kepel, G. (1984) *Muslim Extremism in Egypt: The Prophet and Pharaoh.* University of California Press, Berkeley: page 47, for details regarding the Qutb's delineation of different types of *jahiliyya* societies.

4 Zawahiri (1993) "Advice to the community to reject the fatwa of Sheikh Bin Baz authorizing parliamentary representation: Published under the supervision of Ayman al-Zawahiri," in *Al Qaeda in Its Own Words* (2008) ed. Kepel, G. & Milelli, J. P. Harvard University Press, Cambridge, MA, pp. 182–193. [99] Bin Ladin also tied the concept of man-made law to alleged polytheistic practices of modern-day Jews and Christians who embraced such impious principles: (1995) "An open letter to King Fahd on the occasion of the recent cabinet reshuffle" (July 11), Harmony Database. [62]

5 Bin Ladin (2003) "Second letter to the Muslims of Iraq," in ed. Kepel & Milelli (2008), Cambridge, MA [98]; see also Zawahiri's denunciation of "accepting secularism and democracy and the spread of the majority's wishes and the social state" (Zawahiri (2010) "Al-Quds will not be converted to Judaism," in *As-Sahab*, secured from Islamist Web forums (July 19). [223])

6 Bin Ladin (2004) Audio statement (no title) published by *As-Sahab* (December 27), available in IntelCenter (2008-A) *Words of Osama bin Laden Vol. 1.* Tempest Publishing, Alexandria, VA. [86]

7 Bin Ladin (2007) "The solution: A message from Shaykh Osama bin Laden to the American people," in *As-Sahab* (September). Secured via links from Islamist Web forums. [10]

8 Zawahiri (2007) "Palestine is the concern of all Muslims," in *As-Sahab* (March 11), secured from Islamist Web forums (also available in IntelCenter (2008-B)

Words of Ayman al-Zawahiri Vol. 1 (2008). Tempest Publishing, Alexandria, VA). [18] See further references to democracy as a source or contributing factor to the plight of Palestinians, for example, Zawahiri (2009) "From Kabul to Mogadishu," in *As-Sahab* (February 22), secured from Islamist Web forums. [132]

9   Bin Ladin (2004). [86]

10 Zawahiri (2011) "A message of hope and glad tidings to our people in Egypt (1)," in *As-Sahab* (February 19), secured from Islamist Web forums. [232]

11 Zawahiri (2011) "A message of hope … (4)," in *As-Sahab* (March 4), secured from Islamist Web forums. [235]

12 Zawahiri (2013) "Unifying the word toward the word of monotheism (*tawhid*)," in *As-Sahab* (April 7), distributed by Al-Fajr Media Center via jihadi websites. English transcript from the Open Source Center. [260]

13 Zawahiri (2011) "A message of hope … (5)," in *As-Sahab* (April 14), secured from Islamist Web forums. [236]

14 Zawahiri (2012) "To the people of Tunisia: O' people of Tunisia, support your shariah," in *As-Sahab* (June 10), distributed by jihadist websites. English transcript available, for example, from globalterroralert.com [as of January 2013]. [249]

15 Bin Ladin (2002) "Letter from Usama Bin Muhammad Bin Ladin to the American people," in *Waaqiah* (October 26), available in FBIS (2004) *FBIS: Compilation of Usama Bin Ladin Statements 1994–January*. Foreign Broadcast Information Service, Reston, VA. [212]

16 Bin Ladin (2009) "Call for jihad to stop the Gaza assault," in *As-Sahab* (January 14), translated by Jihad Media Battalion. [122] See also bin Ladin (2008) "A message to the Muslim nation," in *As-Sahab* (May 18), secured via Islamist Web forums. [24]

17 Zawahiri (2010). [223]

18 Bin Ladin (2006) "Oh people of Islam," in *As-Sahab* (April 23), secured via Islamist Web forums. [90]

19 Zawahiri (2006) "Realities of the conflict between Islam and unbelief," in *As-Sahab* (December 22), available from IntelCenter (2008-B). [94]

20 Zawahiri (2007) "'A review of events'—As Sahab publishes fourth interview with Zawahiri," in *As-Sahab* (December 16), via Islamist Web forums (also available from IntelCenter (2008)). [13]

21 Zawahiri (2006) [94]; Zawahiri (2009) [132]; Zawahiri (2012) "The rising sun of victory on the triumphant ummah over the vanquished crusaders," in *As-Sahab* (September 13), available from jihadist websites. Transcript from BBC Monitoring. [254]

22 Zawahiri (2012) "Document of the support of Islam," in *As-Sahab* and made available on jihadist forums on November 13, transcripts from the SITE Institute. [257]

23 See, for example, bin Ladin (2004) Untitled audio statement (December 16), secured from Archive.org (January 12, 2009) via Islamist Web forums [84];

Zawahiri (2009) [132]; Zawahiri (2009) "The path of doom," in *As-Sahab* (August 26), secured from Islamist Web forums [142]; Zawahiri (2009) "Shaykh Dr. Ayman al-Zawahiri: Eulogy for the role model of the youth—The Commander and Shahid Baitullah [Mehsud]," in *As-Sahab* (September 28), secured from Islamist Web forums [147]; Zawahiri (2009) *The Morning and the Lamp to Be Extinguished: An Analysis of the Claim That the Constitution of Pakistan Is Islamic*, translated by Abu Musa Abdussalam, in *As-Sahab* (December 16), secured from Archive.org via Islamist Web forums. [141]

24 Zawahiri (2009). [141] Zawahiri, of course, was not alone in pointing to modern written constitutions and democracy as a major sign of corruption. In Muhammed al-Maqdisi's writings, for instance, the prevalence of these influences signaled the failure of separating truth from falsehood. Similar notions have been tabled by a host of contemporary Wahhabite scholars.

25 For example, bin Ladin (1994) "Our invitation to give advice and reform," open letter dated April 12, available from Harmony Database, document no. AFGP-2002-003345. Combating Training Center, West Point, NY. [36]

26 See especially: Bin Ladin (1994) "Open letter for Shaykh Bin Baz on the invalidity of his fatwa on peace with the Jews," open letter dated December 29, Harmony Archive, document no. AFGP-2002-003345 [63]; bin Ladin (1995) "Saudi Arabia continues its war against Islam and its scholars," open letter dated March 9, available from Harmony Archive, document no. AFGP-2002-003345 [66]; bin Ladin (1995). [62]

27 Zawahiri (2011). [236]

28 See on "grotesque forms of depravity" in Zawahiri (2011). [235] See for the listing of these "vices" in Zawahiri (1993) [99]; bin Ladin (2002) (purported), "Al-Qaeda's declaration in response to the Saudi ulema: It's best you prostrate yourselves in secret," in *Ibrahim* (2007) [43]; bin Ladin (2002) [212]; bin Ladin (2003) "A message to our brothers in Iraq," distributed by Al-Jazeera (February 11), transcript available from FBIS (2004); IntelCenter (2008-A); and Lawrence, B. (ed.) (2005) *Messages to the World: The Statements of Osama Bin Laden*. Verso Books, London [79]; bin Ladin (2004) [84]; Zawahiri (2005) "The freeing of humanity and homelands under the banner of the Quran," posted February 11, available from Jihadunspun. com [as of May 4, 2009] [109]; bin Ladin (2009) "Fight on, O' champions of Somalia," in *As-Sahab* (March 19), secured from Islamist Web forums [134]; Zawahiri (2009) "The realities of jihad and fallacy of hypocrisy," in *As-Sahab* (August 4), secured from Islamist Web forums [140]; Zawahiri (2010) "A victorious ummah, a broken crusade," in *As-Sahab* (September 15), secured via Islamist Web forums. [226]Despite all these examples many observers have been reluctant to acknowledge that Al-Qaeda's grievance narrative *combines* elements of foreign policy with value-based issues. Bergen, for example, wrote:

> In all the tens of thousands of words that bin Laden uttered on the public record, there were some significant omissions: he did not rail against the pernicious effects of Hollywood movies, or against the pornography protected by the U.S. Constitution. Nor did he inveigh against the drug

and alcohol culture of the West, or its tolerance for homosexuals. Judging by his silence, bin Laden cared little about such cultural issues. (Bergen, P. (2011) *The Longest War: The Enduring Conflict between America and al-Qaeda*. Free Press, New York: location 58 (e-book))

But bin Ladin *did* cover these "cultural" issues on several occasions and presented them as part of a wider discourse designed to undermine his adversaries. Furthermore, Zawahiri's public discourse, which is too often ignored or dismissed when Al-Qaeda's history is being written, focused extensively on these issues as we will see in this chapter.

29 Zawahiri (2006) "The alternative is da'wa and jihad," in *As-Sahab* (March 4), available from IntelCenter (2008). [73]

30 Bin Ladin (2002). [212]

31 Zawahiri (2009). [140]

32 Zawahiri (2012), "Yemen: Between a fugitive puppet and his new replacement," in *As-Sahab* (May 15), distributed by jihadi websites. Transcript available from jihadi websites and Flashpoint Partners. [248]

33 Bin Ladin (2006). [90]

34 Gunaratna, R. quoted in Greenberg, K. (ed.) (2005) *Al-Qaeda Now: Understanding Today's Terrorists*. Cambridge University Press, Cambridge, UK: page 42.

35 Riedel, B. (2008) *The Search for Al Qaeda: Its Leadership, Ideology and Future* (2nd ed.) Brookings Institution Press, Washington, DC: page 24.

36 Zawahiri (2009). [141]

37 Zawahiri (2011) "A message of hope … (3)," in *As-Sahab* (February 27), secured via Islamist Web forums. [234]

38 Zawahiri (2001) *Knights under the Banner of the Prophet*, initially published in *Al-Sharq al-Awsat* (December 2), available in translation from the Foreign Broadcast Information Service [119], even though Zawahiri did not feel women had a choice in wearing the veil, arguing "the duty of Muslim girls and women in the Islamic Maghreb is to face-off those who want to remove their Hijab"—Zawahiri (2009). [140]

39 Zawahiri (2008) "The open meeting with Sheikh Ayman al-Zawahiri, part two," the second part of responses to the "Open Meeting," in *As-Sahab* (April 21), IntelCenter (2008). [107]

40 Zawahiri (2004) Untitled statement aired on Al-Arabiya and Al Jazeera (February 24): See Hegghammer, T. (2005) "Al-Qaeda statements 2003–2004: A compilation of translated texts by Usama bin Ladin and Ayman Al-Zawahiri," in *FFI Rapport*, FFI, Kjeller. [58]

41 Bin Ladin (2008) "May our mothers be bereaved of us if we fail to help our Prophet. Peace be upon Him," in *As-Sahab* (March 19), transcript available in IntelCenter (2008-A). [11]

42 Zawahiri (2012) "In support of the Messenger, May the peace and blessings of God be upon Him," produced by *As-Sahab* and distributed on jihadi websites on October 12. BBC Monitoring transcript. [256] Emphasis added.

43 Gerges, F. (2011) *The Rise and Fall of Al-Qaeda*. Oxford University Press, Oxford, UK: page 200.

44 Bin Ladin (1994) "The banishment of communism from the Arabian Peninsula: The episode and the proof," open letter dated July 7, available from Harmony Archive, document no. AFGP-2002-003345. [38]

45 Bin Ladin (1996) Interview with 'Abd al-Bari Atwan, in *Al-Quds Al-Arabi* (as "Bin Ladin interviewed on jihad against US," November 27), available from FBIS (2004). [150]

46 Bin Ladin (1998) Interview published in *Jang* (Rawalpindi) (November 18), available from FBIS (2004). [175]

47 For example, bin Ladin (1994) "Saudi Arabia supports the communists in Yemen," open letter dated June 7, available from Harmony Archive, document no. AFGP-2002-003345. Combating Training Center, West Point, NY. [37]

48 Bin Ladin (1994). [37]

49 Bin Ladin (1995) "The Bosnia tragedy and the deception of the Servant of the Two Mosques," open letter dated August 11, from Harmony Archive, document no. AFGP-2002-003345. Combating Training Center, West Point, NY. [69]

50 See, for example, Zawahiri (1999) "Muslim Egypt between the whips of the torturers and the administration of traitors," posted in "Minbar al-Tawhid wa'l-Jihad" (January 14): See McCants, W., Brachman, J., & Felter, J. (2006) *Militant Ideology Atlas: Research Compendium*. Combating Terrorism Center, West Point, NY. [116]

51 Bin Ladin (1997) "Pakistan interviews Usama Bin Ladin," article/interview published in *Pakistan Daily* (March 18): see FBIS (2004). [154]

52 Bin Ladin (1997) "The Saudi regime and the reputed tragedies of the pilgrims," open letter dated April 16, from Harmony Archive, document no. AFGP-2002-003345. [70]

53 Bin Ladin (1998) "One of them bears witness," statement embedded within article published in *Al-Quds Al-Arabi* (March 23), available from FBIS (2004). [162]

54 Bin Ladin (1996) "Message from Usama Bin-Muhammad Bin Ladin to his Muslim brothers," in *Al-Islah* (September 2, pp. 1–12), published in FBIS (2004). [5]

55 Bin Ladin (1997) "Usama Bin Ladin urges 'befitting reply' to Horan," article with comments from bin Ladin, first published in *Pakistan Daily* (August 7), available in FBIS (2004). [157]

56 Bin Ladin (1998) "Bin Ladin condoles with Al-Bashir on Salih's death," statement embedded within article published in *Al-Quds al-Arabi* (February 16), see FBIS (2004). [160]

57 Bin Ladin, Zawahiri et al. (1998) "Text of World Islamic Front's statement urging jihad against Jews and Crusaders," in *Al-Quds Al-Arabi* (February 23), see FBIS (2004). [161]

58 Bin Ladin (1998) "United States admits that keeping its troops in the Gulf is causing dissatisfaction; Bin Ladin threatens to launch attack soon," in *Al-Quds Al-Arabi* featuring a statement from bin Ladin: See FBIS (2004). [169]

59 See, for example, bin Ladin (1998) "Bin Ladin congratulates Pakistan on its possession of nuclear weapons," article in *Al-Quds Al-Arabi* (June 1): See FBIS (2004) [170]; bin Ladin (1998) "In the way of Allah," statement in article published in *News* (June 15) (Islamabad), available in FBIS (2004) [171]; bin Ladin (1999) "Usama Bin Ladin pens letter in support of Kashmir jihad," report giving text of letter published in *Wahdat* (Peshawar) (June 8), available in FBIS (2004) [183]; bin Ladin (1999) "UBL orders mujahidin to shoot US commandos 'on sight'," in *Khabrain* (September 12): See FBIS (2004). [186]

60 Bin Ladin (1999) Interview with John Miller and *Esquire Magazine* (February), conducted in 1998, later aired on *ABC News* (September 18), available from *Esquire Magazine* and FBIS (2004). [179]

61 Bin Ladin & Zawahiri (2000) Statement regarding Muslim prisoners aired on Al Jazeera (September 21), available from FBIS (2004). [191]

62 Bin Ladin (1999) "Wrath of God: Osama Bin Laden lashes out against the West," *Time Magazine* (January 11, vol. 153, iss. 1, pp. 38–40). [178]

63 Bin Ladin (2001) "Tayseer Allouni interviews bin Ladin in Afghanistan," interview with *Al Jazeera* (October 10): See transcripts in FBIS (2004) and Hegghammer, T. (2003) *FFI Rapport 1990–2002*. FFI, Oslo. [130]

64 Bin Ladin (2001) Untitled statement aired on *Al Jazeera* (November 3), transcript available in Hegghammer (2003). [77]

65 For example, bin Ladin (2001). [130]

66 Zawahiri (2001). [119]

67 Zawahiri (2007) "The advice of one concerned," video statement published by *As-Sahab* on July 4, made available via Islamist websites. Transcript also available from IntelCenter (2008) [102]; Zawahiri (2007) [103]; Zawahiri (2007) "Annapolis: The betrayal," in *As-Sahab* (December 14), available in IntelCenter (2008). [12]

68 Bin Ladin (2001) "The facts of the conflict between us and America," video statement aired on *Al Jazeera* (December 13), secured from Islamist Web forums. [129]

69 Bin Ladin (2002) Untitled video release reported and quoted in *The Times* (as "Bin Ladin film vows revenge on the UK," May 19), available from FBIS (2004). [209]

70 See, for example, Zawahiri (2002) "The interview of Dr Ayman al-Zawahiri," available from IntelCenter (2008). [22] for early references.

71 Bin Ladin (2002) Untitled statement distributed by Al-Qal'ah (October 14), available from FBIS (2004). [211]

72 Zawahiri (2007) "Shaykh Ayman Al-Zawahiri: On the fifth anniversary of the invasion and torture of Iraq," in *As-Sahab* (April 17), secured from Islamist Web forums, also available from IntelCenter (2008). [7]

73 Zawahiri (2007) "Lessons, examples and great events in the year 1427," in *As-Sahab* (February 13), available from IntelCenter (2008). [97]

74 Zawahiri (2002) "Al walaa wa al baraa—Loyalty and separation: Changing an article of faith and losing sight of reality," available in ed. Kepel & Milelli (2008) [45]; bin Ladin (2003) Untitled audio statement, unknown distributor (February), available from IntelCenter (2008) [78]; bin Ladin (2003) "Usama Bin Ladin urges Muslims to launch suicide attacks against US," statement embedded within article published in *Ausaf* (Islamabad) (April 9), available from FBIS (2004). [217]

75 Bin Ladin (2003). [78]

76 Zawahiri (2012). [256]

77 Bin Ladin (2002) [212]; Zawahiri (2005) First in a series of interviews with Zawahiri, in *As-Sahab* (December 7), available in Ibrahim, R. (2007) *The Al Qaeda Reader.* Broadway Books, New York [49]; Zawahiri (2007). [18]

78 Bin Ladin (2004). [86]

79 Zawahiri (2012). [254]

80 One example was bin Ladin's message from December 2004, which he dedicated to developments in Saudi Arabia. See bin Ladin (2004). [84]

81 Zawahiri, for instance, sought to appeal to ubiquitous anxiety in Pakistan concerning Indian aggression and anger over Kashmir, in order to shore up support: "Musharraf's recognitions of Israel," he argued, was "to psychologically prepare the Pakistanis to recognize a Hindu state in Kashmir": Zawahiri (2006) "Letter to the people of Pakistan," in *As-Sahab* (April 28), available from IntelCenter (2008). [81]

82 Zawahiri (2006). [73]

83 See more on this element in Zawahiri's thinking in Al-Zayyat's biography on Zawahiri (Al-Zayyat, M. (2004) *The Road to Al-Qaeda: The Story of Bin Laden's Right-Hand Man.* Pluto Press, London)—with excerpts reproduced as "Changes in Zawahiri's ideology: The near and far enemies," in (2012) *Al Qaeda*, ed. Cruickshank. Routledge: London: pages 163–173.

84 Zawahiri (2008) *Exoneration: A Letter Exonerating the Ummah of the Pen and the Sword from the Unjust Allegation of Feebleness and Weakness*, advertised by As-Sahab early in 2008. Open Source Center. [20]

85 Zawahiri (2001). [119] Emphasis added.

86 Zawahiri (2002). [45]

87 Zawahiri (2006) "Congratulations on the Eid to the ummah of tawhid," in *As-Sahab* (December 30), IntelCenter (2008). [95]

88 Zawahiri (2011) "A message of hope and glad tidings to our people in Egypt (2)," in *As-Sahab* (February 24), secured via links from Islamist Web forums. [233]

89 Zawahiri (2013) "Sixty-five years since the establishment of the state of occupation: Israel," in *As-Sahab* (June 6), distributed by Al-Fajr Media Center via jihadi websites. English transcript from the Open Source Center. [259]

90 Hegghammer, T. (2009-A) "The ideological hybridization of jihadi groups," in *Current Trends in Islamist Ideology* (vol. 9, pp. 26–46).

91 Zawahiri (2005). [49]

92 Zawahiri (2006). [94] Emphasis added.

93 Zawahiri (2007) "The empire of evil is about to end, and a new dawn is about to break over mankind," in *As-Sahab* (May 5), available from IntelCenter (2008-B). [23]

94 Bin Ladin (2010) "The way to save the earth," in *As-Sahab* (February 19), secured from Islamist websites [149]; bin Ladin (2010) "Some points regarding the method of relief work," in *As-Sahab* (October), secured from Islamist Web forums [227]; bin Ladin (2010) "Help your brothers in Pakistan," in *As-Sahab* (October 13), secured from Islamist Web forums. [228]

95 Bin Ladin talked of how the UN Secretary General traveled to areas affected by vast floods in Pakistan in 2010 "as part of his job" whereas Arab leaders never ventured there despite being much closer. See bin Ladin (2010). [228]

96 Zawahiri (2007). [23]

97 Bin Ladin (1999) Interview published in Pakistani newspaper (February 20), available in FBIS (2004). [182]

98 See, for example, Zawahiri warning of the need to alleviate the pain of Muslims in East Turkistan and elsewhere in Zawahiri (2009) "My Muslim brothers and sisters in Pakistan," in *As-Sahab* (July 15), secured from Islamist Web forums [139]; Zawahiri (2010). [226]

Chapter 5

1 See, for example, Zawahiri (2005) Unknown title, video statement published by *As-Sahab* (June 17), available from IntelCenter (2008-B), *Words of Ayman al-Zawahiri Vol. 1* [72]; Zawahiri (2009) "The realities of jihad and fallacy of hypocrisy," in *As-Sahab* (August 4), secured via links from Islamist Web forums. [140]

2 Bin Ladin (2004) "Resist the new Rome," audio statement aired on Al Jazeera (January 4), transcript also published in *The Observer* (January 4) and FBIS (2004) *FBIS: Compilation of Usama Bin Ladin Statements 1994–January 2004*, Foreign Broadcast Information Service, Reston, Virginia. [111]

3 Bin Ladin (2004) Audio statement (no title) published by *As-Sahab* (December 27), available in IntelCenter (2008-A) *Words of Osama bin Laden Vol. 1*. Tempest Publishing, Alexandria, VA. [86]

4 Zawahiri (2011) "A message of hope and glad tidings to our people in Egypt (1)," in *As-Sahab* (February 19), secured via links from Islamist Web forums. [232]

5 Bin Ladin (1995) "Scholars are the Prophet's successors," open letter dated May 6, available from Harmony Archive, document no. AFGP-2002-003345. [67]

6 Zawahiri (2009) *The Morning and the Lamp to Be Extinguished: An Analysis of the Claim That the Constitution of Pakistan Is Islamic*, translated by Abu

Musa Abdussalam, in *As-Sahab* (December 16), secured from Archive.org via link from Islamist Web forums. [141]

7 Bin Ladin (2009) "Call for jihad to stop the Gaza assault," in *As-Sahab* (January 14), translated by Jihad Media Battalion, secured via link from Islamist Web forums. [122]

8 Zawahiri (2007) "The empire of evil is about to end, and a new dawn is about to break over mankind," in *As-Sahab* (May 5), IntelCenter (2008-B). [23]

9 Zawahiri (2011) "A message of hope and glad tidings to our people in Egypt (4)," in *As-Sahab* (March 4), secured via links from Islamist Web forums. [235]

10 Zawahiri (unknown date) "The forbidden word," excerpts published in McCants, W., Brachman, J., Felter, J. (2006) *Militant Ideology Atlas: Research Compendium*. Combating Terrorism Center, West Point, NY. [113]

11 Bin Ladin (2007) "The solution: A message from Shaykh Osama bin Laden to the American people," in *As-Sahab* (September), secured via links from Islamist Web forums. [10]

12 Bin Ladin (1996) Interview with 'Abd al-Bari Atwan, in *Al-Quds Al-Arabi* (as "Bin Ladin interviewed on jihad against US," November 27), available from FBIS (2004). [150]

13 Zawahiri (2009). [141]

14 Zawahiri (2010) "A victorious ummah, A broken Crusade," in *As-Sahab* (September 15), secured via links from Islamist Web forums. [226]

15 Zawahiri (2008) "The open meeting with Sheikh Ayman al-Zawahiri, part two," the second part of responses to the "Open Meeting" public appeal, in *As-Sahab* (April 21), available from IntelCenter (2008-B) *Words of Ayman al-Zawahiri Vol. 1*. Tempest Publishing, Alexandria, VA. [107]

16 Zawahiri (nd). [113]

17 Bin Ladin (1996) Interview with Robert Fisk published in *The Independent* (June 10, page: 14), available from FBIS (2004). [4]

18 Zawahiri (2011) "A message of hope and glad tidings to our fellow Muslims in Egypt (5)," in *As-Sahab* (April 14), secured via links from Islamist Web forums. [236]

19 Bin Ladin (2007). [10]

20 Zawahiri (2011) "A message of hope and glad tidings to our people in Egypt (3) by Sheikh Ayman Al-Zawahiri H.A," in *As-Sahab* (February 27), translated by Global Islamic Media Front, secured via links from Islamist Web forums. [234]

21 A large number of communiqués refer to the Afghan or AQI "emirates": See, for example, Zawahiri (2007) "A review of events'—As Sahab publishes fourth interview with Zawahiri," in *As-Sahab* (December 16), secured via links from Islamist Web forums (also available from IntelCenter (2008-B) *Words of Ayman al-Zawahiri Vol. 1*. Tempest Publishing, Alexandria, VA [13]); Zawahiri (2008). [107]

22 Bin Ladin (1997) Report of interview published in *The Independent* (as "Interview with Usama bin Ladin," March 22), available from FBIS (2004); see full transcript: "Transcript of Osama Bin Laden interview," by Peter

Arnett (CNN, March 22). Available on news.findlaw.com/hdocs/docs/binladen/binladenintvw-cnn.pdf [accessed March 3, 2009]. [155]

23 Bin Ladin (1997) "Pakistan interviews Usama Bin Ladin," article/interview published in *Daily Pakistan* (March 18): See FBIS (2004). [154]

24 Bin Ladin (1998) Interview published in *Jang* (Rawalpindi) (November 18), available from FBIS (2004). [175]

25 Bin Ladin (1999) Interview published in Pakistani newspaper (February 20), available in FBIS (2004). [182]

26 Zawahiri (2008). [107]

27 Bin Ladin (2000) "Usama speaks on hijrah and the Islamic state?," statement published on ummah.net and elsewhere (May 22), made available in FBIS (2004). [189]

28 Bin Ladin (2001) Untitled open letter published in *Nawa-i-Waqt* (Rawalpindi) (January 7), available in FBIS (2004). [192]

29 Zawahiri (2001) "Knights under the Banner of the Prophet," initially in *Al-Sharq al-Awsat* (December 2), available in translation from the Foreign Broadcast Information Service. [119]

30 Zawahiri (2013) "Unifying the word toward the word of monotheism (*tawhid*)," in *As-Sahab* (April 7), distributed by Al-Fajr Media Center via jihadi websites. English transcript from the Open Source Center. [260]

31 See, for example, bin Ladin (2001) "Letter to the Pakistani people," aired on Al Jazeera (September 24), available from FBIS (2004) [201] on defensive jihad.

32 Azzam, A. (2003) *The Lofty Mountain*. Published and translated by Azzam Publications (first published in 1989). See references to jihad as an individual duty (Zawahiri (unknown date) "Response to a grave uncertainty from Shaykh al-Albani regarding silence in the face of apostate rulers," distributed online through "Minbar al-Tawhid wa'l-Jihad," excerpts in McCants et al. (2006) [117]) and the "sixth undeclared element of Islam" (bin Ladin (2001) "The US should search attackers within itself," interview with *Ummat* (Karachi) (September 28), available from FBIS (2004) [202]), a "priority over seeking knowledge or marriage because it is an individual duty" (Zawahiri (2008) [107]).

33 See, for example, bin Ladin (1999) Interview with bin Ladin titled "Usama Bin Ladin, the destruction of the Base," [184]; bin Ladin (1998) Interview with *The News* (Islamabad/Peshawar), reported in AFP (August 21) as "Bin Ladin calls for 'jihad' against Jews, Americans," available in FBIS (2004) [172]; bin Ladin (1998). [170]

34 See, for example, bin Ladin (2001) Letter from bin Ladin published in *The Dawn* (Karachi) (April 3) titled "Usama regrets curbs by Taliban," available in FBIS (2004) [195]; bin Ladin (2001) Statement published in Pakistani newspaper (May 17) in article titled "If Taleban allow, I can make US life miserable: Usama," available in FBIS (2004). [198]

35 Bin Ladin (2001). [202]

36 See, for example, bin Ladin (2001) Statement reported by the Afghan Press
Agency (September 16), available in FBIS (2004). [200]

37 Bin Ladin (1998). [172] In a statement reported in December 1998, bin
Ladin claimed not to be responsible for the bombings, even though he did
welcome them. Subsequent messages followed this trend: Bin Ladin (1998)
Statement distributed by Afghan Islamic Press, reported in AFP (December
24), titled "Bin Ladin denies role in bombings of US missions," available in
FBIS (2004). [176]

38 Countless examples of praise for the 9/11 attacks feature in the discourse.
Zawahiri and bin Ladin featured together in a sophisticated video production
six months after the attacks took place, titled *The Wills of the Martyrs of the
New York and Washington Battles*, which also featured excerpts from the
last testimonies of the hijackers themselves: *As-Sahab* (2002) "The Wills of
the Martyrs of the New York and Washington Battles: The will of the Martyr
Ibn ul Jarah Al-Ghamidee Ahmed al-Haznawi," published April 18, secured
from Islamist Web forums. [207] Early examples of denunciation of those
criticizing the attacks as "agents of America" featured in bin Ladin (2001)
"The facts of the conflict between us and America," video statement aired
on Al Jazeera (December 13), secured from Islamist Web forums. [129]

39 Bin Ladin discusses how he selected the hijackers, for example, in bin
Ladin (2006) "A testimony to the truth," in *As-Sahab* (May 23), secured from
Islamist Web forums [91], noting he had decided to "destroy towers in
America" in response to the pain and suffering inflicted in Lebanon during
the 1982 invasion: Bin Ladin (2004) Untitled statement distributed by *As-
Sahab* (October 30), available in IntelCenter (2008) [83]. Zawahiri, meanwhile,
claimed he had been present at a lecture in Kandahar a year prior to the
attacks where Al-Qaeda leaders and Mohammed Atta discussed how best
to respond to aggression in Palestine, with the conclusion being they should
plan the multiple hijackings displayed on September 11, 2001: Zawahiri
(2006) "The Zionist Crusader's aggression on Gaza and Lebanon," in *As-
Sahab* (June 27), available from IntelCenter (2008). [88]

40 Bin Ladin (2002) Untitled statement aired on Al Jazeera (November 12),
available from IntelCenter (2008) and FBIS (2004) [76]; Zawahiri (2005) First
in a series of interviews with Zawahiri, in *As-Sahab* (December 7), available
in Ibrahim, R. (2007) *The Al Qaeda Reader*. Broadway Books, New York. [49]

41 See, for example, bin Ladin (2004) Untitled audio statement aired on Al
Jazeera and Al-Arabiya (April 15), IntelCenter (2008). [80]

42 Zawahiri (2005). [49]

43 See, for example, bin Ladin (1997) Interview with *Dispatches* aired on
Channel Four Television (February 20), transcript in FBIS (2004), titled
"Correspondent meets with opposition leader Bin Ladin' [151]; Bin Ladin
(1997). [155]

44 Bin Ladin (1997). [154]

45 Bin Ladin (1997). [155]

46 Bin Ladin (1996). [150]

47 Bin Ladin (2001) "Tayseer Allouni interviews bin Ladin in Afghanistan," interview with Al Jazeera (October 10): See transcripts in FBIS (2004) and Hegghammer, T. (2003) *FFI Rapport 1990–2002*. FFI, Oslo. [130] See also on further notions of "praiseworthy terrorism" in bin Ladin (2001). [129]

48 In Al-Suri's Global Islamic Resistance Call, chapter 8 in Lia (2007): pages 383–386.

49 Bin Ladin, Zawahiri et al. (1998) "Text of World Islamic Front's statement urging jihad against Jews and Crusaders," in *Al-Quds Al-Arabi* (London, February 23), translated in FBIS (2004). [161]

50 Bin Ladin (1998) "One of them bears witness," statement embedded within article published in *Al-Quds Al-Arabi* (March 23), available from FBIS (2004). [162]

51 Bin Ladin (1998) Interview published in *Al-Akhbar* (Islamabad) (March 31), available in FBIS (2004). [163]

52 Bin Ladin (1998) [170]; Bin Ladin (1998) "In the way of Allah," statement in article published in *The News* (June 15) (Islamabad), available in FBIS (2004). [171]

53 Bin Ladin (2000) Statement published in *Daily Pakistan* (May 2), available in FBIS (2004). [188]

54 Bin Ladin (1999) Interview with John Miller and *Esquire Magazine* (February), interview conducted in 1998, later aired on *ABC News* (September 18), available from *Esquire Magazine* and FBIS (2004). [179]

55 Bin Ladin (1999) War declaration distributed by CBS (January 13), published in FBIS (2004). [180] Other jihadi ideologues have of course voiced similar sentiments.

56 Bin Ladin (1999). [184]

57 Zawahiri (1996) "Healing the hearts of believers: On some concepts of jihad in the Islamabad operation," distributed online through "Minbar al-Tawhid wa'l-Jihad," excerpts published in McCants et al. (2006). [118]

58 Zawahiri (purported) (unknown date) "Jihad, martyrdom, and the killing of innocents," available in Ibrahim (2007). [48]

59 Bin Ladin (2001). [130]

60 Bin Ladin (2001). [130]

61 Bin Ladin (2001) Interview with Hamid Mir published in *The Dawn* (November 10). http://archives.dawn.com/2001/11/10/top1.htm [accessed March 16, 2012]; see also Hegghammer (2003). [125]

62 Bin Ladin (2002) "Letter from Usama Bin Muhammad Bin Ladin to the American people," first published in *Waaqiah* (October 26), available in FBIS (2004). [212]

63 Scheuer (2006) notes how there are three actions that need to be undertaken before the Prophet's conditions on attacking an enemy are fulfilled—"clear warnings of an intention to attack; offers of a truce; and public calls on the foe to convert to Islam"—arguing the Al-Qaeda leadership has fulfilled all three. "The Western media's misreading of al-Qaeda's latest videotape," in *Terrorism Focus* (vol. 3, iss. 34), Jamestown Foundation.

64 Bin Ladin (1999). [179]

65 Bin Ladin (2001). [130]

66 Bin Ladin (2001). [129]

67 Bin Ladin (2002). [76]

68 Bin Ladin (2004). [83]

69 Bin Ladin (2010) "Message from Shaykh Usama bin Ladin to the people of France," in *As-Sahab* (November 7), translated and distributed by Ansar Al Mujahideen English Forum, secured from Islamist Web forums. [230]

70 Cullison, A. (2004) "Inside Al Qaeda's hard drive," in *Atlantic Monthly* (vol. 294, iss. 2, September): page 11.

71 Bin Ladin (2002). [212]

72 Zawahiri (2005). [49]

73 Zawahiri (2007) "Forty years since the fall of Jerusalem," audio statement published by *As-Sahab* on June 25, transcript available from IntelCenter (2008). [101]

74 Zawahiri (2008) *Exoneration: A Letter Exonerating the Ummah of the Pen and the Sword from the Unjust Allegation of Feebleness and Weakness*, advertised by *As-Sahab* early in 2008, Open Source Center [20]. See further on the development of Taymiyyah's thoughts, for example, in Esposito, J. L. (2002) *Unholy War: Terror in the Name of Islam*. Oxford University Press, Oxford, UK: pages 45–46.

75 Bin Ladin (2003) "A message to our brothers in Iraq," distributed by Al Jazeera (February 11), transcript available from FBIS (2004); IntelCenter (2008-A); and Lawrence, B. (ed.) (2005) *Messages to the World: The Statements of Osama Bin Laden*. Verso Books, London. [79]

76 Bin Ladin (2004). [86]

77 Bin Ladin (2006) "Elegizing the ummah's martyr and emir of the martyrs, Abu Musab al-Zarqawi," in *As-Sahab* (June 29), available in IntelCenter (2008). [92]

78 Zawahiri (2006) "Letter to the people of Pakistan," in *As-Sahab* (April 28), available from IntelCenter (2008-B). [81]

79 Riedel, B. (2008) *The Search for Al Qaeda: Its Leadership, Ideology and Future* (2nd edition). Brookings Institution Press, Washington, DC: page 101.

80 Page, M., Challita, L., & Harris, A. (2011) "Al Qaeda in the Arabian Peninsula: Framing narratives and prescriptions," in *Terrorism and Political Violence* (vol. 23, iss. 2, pp. 150–172): page 162.

81 Cragin (2009) "Al Qaeda confronts Hamas: Divisions in the Sunni jihadist movement and its implications for U.S. policy," *Studies in Conflict and Terrorism* (vol. 32, iss. 7, pp. 576–590).

82 Zawahiri (2007) [23]; bin Ladin (2007). [10]

83 Zawahiri bases this assumption mostly on the rulings of Ibn-Qudamah and Ibn Rajab al-Hanbali, influential medieval scholars.

84 Stout, M. E., Huckabey, J. M., Schindler, J. R., & Lacey, W. (2008) *The Terrorist Perspectives Project: Strategic and Operational views of Al Qaida and Associated Movements.* Naval Institute Press, Annapolis: page 54. See Harmony Archive (nd), document no. AFGP-2002-000026.

85 Zawahiri (unknown date) "The forbidden word," excerpts published in McCants et al. (2006) [113]; Zawahiri (1996) "Healing the hearts of believers: On some concepts of jihad in the Islamabad operation," distributed online through "Minbar al-Tawhid wa'l-Jihad," excerpts published in McCants et al. (2006). [118]

86 Zawahiri (nd) [113]; Zawahiri (purported) (nd). [48] See also separately on killing Western tourists in Zawahiri (2008). [20]

87 Brachman, J., Fishman, B., Felter, J. (2008) *The Power of Truth: Questions for Ayman Al-Zawahiri,* Combating Terrorism Center (April 21), West Point, New York.

88 Zawahiri (2008). [20]

89 Bin Ladin (2004) Untitled audio statement (December 16), secured from Archive.org (January 12, 2009) via link from Islamist Web forums. [84]

90 Bin Ladin (2004). [86]

91 Bin Ladin (2007) "The way to frustrate the conspiracies," in *As-Sahab Media* (December 29), IntelCenter (2008). [27]

92 Zawahiri (2008) "The open meeting with Sheikh Ayman al-Zawahiri, part one," answers published by *As-Sahab* (April 2), secured from Archive.org and Islamist Web forums, transcript also available in IntelCenter (2008-B). [105]

93 Zawahiri (2007) "The advice of one concerned," video statement published by *As-Sahab* on July 4, made available via Islamist websites. Transcript also available from IntelCenter (2008). [102]

94 Zawahiri (2008) "Al-Azhar: The lion's den: Interview with Shaykh Ayman al-Zawahiri," in *As-Sahab* (November 21), secured from Archive.org via link from Islamist Web forums. [237]

95 See, for example, for references to Sweden in bin Ladin (2004) Untitled statement published by *As-Sahab* (October 29), secured via link from Islamist Web forums. [31] And references to Switzerland and Vietnam in Zawahiri (2005). [49]

96 Zawahiri (2008). [20]

97 Zawahiri (2011). [236]

98 Zawahiri (2008). [20]

99 Zawahiri (2012) "In support of the Messenger, May the peace and blessings of God be upon Him," produced by *As-Sahab* and distributed on jihadi websites on October 12. BBC Monitoring transcript. [256]

100 Zawahiri (2011) "A message of hope and glad tidings to our people in Egypt (2)," in *As-Sahab* (February 24), secured via links from Islamist Web forums. [233]

101 Zawahiri (2011) "The noble knight dismounted," in *As-Sahab* and the Global Islamic Media Front (June 8), secured from Islamist Web forums. [239]

102 Zawahiri (2013) "General guidelines for jihad," in *As-Sahab* (September 14) and distributed via Islamist Web forums and Archive.org: See, for example, http://ia801006.us.archive.org/8/items/tawakkalo-00/en.pdf [as of September 18, 2013]. [266]

103 Zawahiri (2013) "General guidelines for jihad." [266]

104 Zawahiri (2012) "Glad tidings by the two sheikhs Abu al-Zubayr and Ayman al-Zawahiri," video statement published by *As-Sahab* (February 9), translated by the Global Islamic Media Front and distributed on jihadist forums. [258]

105 Hegghammer, T. (2006) "Global jihadism after the Iraq War," in *Middle East Journal* (vol. 60, iss. 1, Winter): page 15.

106 Such strategic preferences strongly resemble those of twentieth-century communist revolutionaries. *Cf.* Stout et al. (2008).

107 Over the years, however, the sense of urgency has served to enlarge the group deemed eligible for *mujahideen* operations. In 1998, for instance, bin Ladin explained that those doing most of the fighting would be between 15 and 25 years of age, since younger people would not fully comprehend the nature of the battle and older men would have family obligations. Ten years later, however, Zawahiri stressed that "Going to jihad is a priority over seeking knowledge or marriage because it is an individual duty." Women do not have an operational role. See bin Ladin (1999) [184]; Zawahiri (2008). [107]

108 Zawahiri (2001). [119] Zawahiri reiterated the importance of creating a secure base in Zawahiri (2008) "The open meeting ..., part one." [105]

109 Zawahiri (2002) "The interview of Dr Ayman al-Zawahiri," available from IntelCenter (2008-B) [22]; Zawahiri (2007). [102]

110 Zawahiri (2008). [105]

111 Zawahiri (2007). [102]

112 Bin Ladin (1999). [179]

113 See Zawahiri's fourth point on the "Lessons from Afghanistan" (Zawahiri (2001). [119])

114 Bin Ladin (1999). [179]

115 Zawahiri (2002). [22]

116 Zawahiri (2013). [266]

117 Bin Ladin (2004). [83]

118 Bin Ladin (2003) Untitled audio statement, unknown distributor (February), available from IntelCenter (2008-A). [78]

119 Bin Ladin (2001). [202]

120 Bin Ladin (2002) Statement aired on MBC Television (London) (April 17), transcript available in FBIS (2004) [206]; bin Ladin (2003) "Second letter to the Muslims of Iraq," statement released on October 18. Available in ed. Kepel & Milelli (2008) and FBIS (2004). [98]

121 Zawahiri (2005), "Obstacles to jihad," in *As-Sahab* (December 10), available in IntelCenter (2008). [25]

122 Zawahiri (2001). [119]

123 Zawahiri (2002). [22]

124 Zawahiri (2002). [22]

125 "The United States will retreat in the face of your [martyrdom] mission": Bin Ladin (2003) "Usama Bin Ladin urges Muslims to launch suicide attacks against US," statement embedded within article published in *Ausaf* (Islamabad) (April 9), available from FBIS (2004). [217]

126 Zawahiri (2007) "Rise and support our brothers in Somalia," statement published by *As-Sahab* (May), available in IntelCenter (2008) [96]; Bin Ladin (2003). [79]

127 Zawahiri (2001). [119]

128 Zawahiri (2006) "Bush, the Vatican's Pope, Darfur and the Crusaders," in *As-Sahab* (September 29), available in IntelCenter (2008-B) [89]; Zawahiri (2006) "Hot issues with Shaykh Ayman Al-Zawahiri," in *As-Sahab* (September 11), secured from Islamist Web forums, also available from IntelCenter (2008-B). [21]

129 Bin Ladin (2001). [129]

130 Al-Qaeda's affiliate in the Arabian Peninsula would later take this notion a step further with the publication of the *Inspire* magazine in summer 2010, which featured the—now infamous—article "Make a bomb in the kitchen of your mom."

131 See on early interest in acquiring, for example, enriched uranium in Bergen, P. & Cruickshank, P. (2012) "Revisiting the early Al Qaeda: Updated account of its formative years," in *Studies in Conflict and Terrorism* (vol. 35, iss. 1, pp. 1–36).

132 Bin Ladin (no date) Letter from bin Ladin to *"Amir al-Mu'mineen"* Mullah Omar, made available by Department of Defense (translated June 5, 2002), Harmony Archive, document no. AFGP-2002-600321. [61] Emphasis added.

133 Bin Ladin (1998). [170]

134 Bin Ladin. (1999) [182]

135 Bin Ladin (1999) "Wrath of God: Osama Bin Laden lashes out against the West," *Time Magazine* (January 11, vol. 153, iss. 1). [178]

136 Bin Ladin (1999). [184]

137 Bin Ladin (2001). [125]

138 Bin Ladin (1996) "Message from Usama Bin-Muhammad Bin Ladin to his Muslim brothers in the whole world and especially in the Arabian Peninsula: Declaration of jihad against the Americans occupying the Land of the Two

Holy Mosques; expel the heretics from the Arabian Peninsula," in *Al-Islah* (September 2, pp. 1–12), published in FBIS (2004). [5]

139 Bergen, P. (2006) *The Osama Bin Laden I Know: An Oral History of Al-Qaeda's Leader*. Free Press, New York; Riedel (2008); Wright, L. (2006-A) *The Looming Tower: Al-Qaeda's Road to 9/11*. Penguin Books, London.

140 Bin Ladin (1996). [5]

141 Zawahiri (2007) "Malicious Britain and its Indian slaves," in *As-Sahab* (July 10), available in IntelCenter (2008-B). [103]

142 Bin Ladin (2001). [202]

143 Zawahiri (2006) "Realities of the conflict between Islam and unbelief," in *As-Sahab* (December 22), available from IntelCenter (2008-B). [94]

144 Zawahiri (2008). [20] This is not to suggest the Arab Spring represented a purely peaceful revolt; indeed, the National Democratic Party (NDP) headquarters were burnt down and several instances involved violent clashes, but the force of the revolution was not of the kind that Zawahiri envisaged.

145 Zawahiri (2007) "Annapolis: The betrayal," in *As-Sahab* (December 14), available in IntelCenter (2008-B). [12]

146 Zawahiri (2009) "The massacre of Gaza and the siege of the traitors," in *As-Sahab* (January 6), translated by Global Islamic Media Front, secured from Archive.org. [121]

147 Zawahiri (2009). [140]

Chapter 6

1 Meijer, R. (ed.) (2009) "Introduction," to *Global Salafism: Islam's New Religious Movement*. Hurst, London: page 10. See also Kepel, G. & Milelli, J. P. (eds.) (2008) *Al Qaeda in Its Own Words*. Harvard University Press, Cambridge, MA: page 168.

2 Zawahiri (2002) *Al Walaa wa al Baraa—Loyalty and Separation: Changing an Article of Faith and Losing Sight of Reality*, in ed. Kepel & Milelli (2008). [45]

3 Zawahiri (2002). [45]

4 See, for example, Scheuer, M. (2006) "The Western media's misreading of al-Qaeda's latest videotape," in *Terrorism Focus* (vol. 3, iss. 34).

5 Bin Ladin (1997) Statement published in *Nawa-i-Waqt* (Rawalpindi) (November 27), available from FBIS (2004) *FBIS: Compilation of Usama Bin Ladin Statements 1994–January 2004*, Foreign Broadcast Information Service, Reston, Virginia. [158]

6 Bin Ladin (1998) Statement published in *Al-Quds Al-Arabi* (August 23), available in FBIS (2004). [173]

7 See, for example, bin Ladin (1999) Interview with Rahimullah Yusufzai, in *News* (Islamabad) (January 6), available in FBIS (2004) [177]; bin Ladin (1999) "Wrath of God: Osama Bin Laden lashes out against the West," *Time Magazine* (January 11, vol. 153, iss. 1) [178]; bin Ladin (1999) War declaration distributed by CBS (January 13), published in FBIS (2004). [180]

8 Bin Ladin (2001) Statement published in a Pakistani newspaper (May 17) in article titled "If Taleban allow, I can make US life miserable: Usama," available in FBIS (2004). [198]

9 Only major attacks are shown, for illustrative purposes. Less significant attacks and failed plots are not shown.

10 Bin Ladin (2001) Statement aired on Al Jazeera (November 7), transcript available from FBIS (2004). [203]

11 See, for example, Zawahiri (2009) "The massacre of Gaza and the siege of the traitors," in *As-Sahab* (January 6), translated and distributed by the Global Islamic Media Front, secured from Archive.org via link from Islamist Web forums. [121]

12 *As-Sahab* (2002) "The wills of the martyrs of the New York and Washington battles: The will of the Martyr Ibn ul Jarah Al-Ghamidee Ahmed al-Haznawi," published April 18, secured via link from Islamist Web forums. [207]

13 Bin Ladin (2002) Untitled statement aired on Al Jazeera (November 12), available from IntelCenter (2008-A) *Words of Osama bin Laden Vol. 1.* Tempest Publishing, Alexandria, VA, and FBIS (2004). [76]

14 Bin Ladin (2002) "Statement from Abdallah Usama Bin Ladin to the peoples of countries allied to tyrannical US government," distributed by Alneda (November 21), available in FBIS (2004). [214]

15 Zawahiri (2003) Untitled statement aired on Al-Arabiya (August 3), available in IntelCenter (2008-B) *Words of Ayman al-Zawahiri Vol. 1.* Tempest Publishing, Alexandria, VA, and Hegghammer, T. (2005) "Al-Qaida Statements 2003– 2004: A Compilation of Translated Texts by Usama bin Ladin and Ayman Al-Zawahiri" in *FFI Rapport* (2005/01428). Forsvarets Forskningsinstitutt (Norwegian Defence Research Establishment), Kjeller, Norway [55]; bin Ladin & Zawahiri (2003) Audio statement aired on Al Jazeera (September 10), available from FBIS (2004). [110]

16 Zawahiri (2004) Untitled statement aired on Al-Arabiya and Al Jazeera (February 24): See Hegghammer, T. (2005) "Al- Qaida statements 2003–2004". [58]

17 Zawahiri (2005) Interview with Al-Zawahiri aired on Al Jazeera (August 4): see MEMRI clips nos. 799 and 791. [128]

18 Zawahiri (2005) First in a series of interviews with Zawahiri, in *As-Sahab* (December 7), available in Ibrahim, R. (2007) *The Al Qaeda Reader.* Broadway Books, New York. [49]

19 Zawahiri (2005) "The victory of the Islamic religion in Iraq," in *As-Sahab* (December 6), available from IntelCenter (2008). [26]

20 Zawahiri (2006) "Hot issues with Shaykh Ayman Al-Zawahiri," in *As-Sahab* (September 11), secured from Islamist Web forums, also available from IntelCenter (2008-B). [21]

21 Zawahiri (2007) "Lessons, examples and great events in the year 1427," in *As-Sahab* (February 13), available from IntelCenter (2008-B). [97]

22 Zawahiri (2007) "The empire of evil is about to end, and a new dawn is about to break over mankind," in *As-Sahab* (May 5), available from IntelCenter (2008-B). [23]

23 Zawahiri (2008) "The correct equation," in *As-Sahab* (January 22), available from IntelCenter (2008), also available as a collection of clips posted on YouTube. [28]

24 Bin Ladin (2007) "The solution: A message from Shaykh Osama bin Laden to the American people," in *As-Sahab* (September). Secured via links from Islamist Web forums [10]. Similar tone and direction is applied to other non-Muslim audiences, addressed as holistic entities rather than multifaceted societies with a range of opinions, for example, toward the French in some of bin Ladin's last communiqués (see bin Ladin (2011) "From al-Sheikh Osama bin Mohammed bin laden to … the French people," in *As-Sahab* (January 22), secured via Islamist Web forums [231]).

25 Bin Ladin (2001) Interview with Hamid Mir published in *The Dawn* (November 10). http://www.dawn.com/2001/11/10/top1.htm [accessed July 2013]; see also Hegghammer, T. (2003) *FFI Rapport 1990–2002*. FFI, Oslo. [125]

26 Bin Ladin (2004) Untitled statement, distributed by *As-Sahab* (October 30), transcript available in IntelCenter (2008-A). [83]

27 Bin Ladin (2009) "A statement to the American people," in *As-Sahab* (September 13), translated and distributed by the Global Islamic Media Front, secured via Islamist Web forums. [144]

28 Numerous invitations to Islam were communicated through the messages, with Islam presented as an alternative to insecurity, capitalism, and immoral materialism. See bin Ladin (2002) "A message addressed to the American people," message aired on Al Jazeera (October 6), IntelCenter (2008) [75]; bin Ladin (2002) "Letter from Usama Bin Muhammad Bin Ladin to the American people," first published in *Waaqiah* (October 26), available in FBIS (2004) [212]; Zawahiri & Gadahn (2006) "An invitation to Islam," video message published by *As-Sahab* (September 2), distributed on Al-Boraq. com. [33] See further: Bin Ladin (2007) [10]; *As-Sahab* (2002) "The wills of the martyrs of the New York and Washington battles: The will of the Martyr Abdulaziz Alomari," published April 19, secured via link from Islamist Web forums. [108]

29 Bin Ladin (2004) Statement offering peace treaty to Europeans, audiotape distributed to media networks (April 14), transcript available in Ibrahim (2007) [52]; bin Ladin (2004) Untitled audio statement aired on Al Jazeera and Al-Arabiya (April 15), transcript available in IntelCenter (2008-A) [80]; bin Ladin (2006) Message to Americans, audiotape distributed to media networks (January 19), transcript available in Ibrahim (2007). [50]

30 Bin Ladin (2004). [52]

31 Zawahiri (2011) "Message of hope and glad tidings to our people in Egypt part 8: And what about the American hostage Warren Weinstein?," in *As-Sahab* and Al-Masadh Media in December, English transcript by *As-Sahab*. Distributed by Islamist Web forums, such as Ansar1.info. [244]

32 Zawahiri (2012) "Document of the support of Islam," produced by *As-Sahab* and made available on jihadist forums on November 13, transcripts from the SITE Institute. [257] See also on proselytizing and appeals to the oppressed in, for example, Zawahiri (2006) [21] and Zawahiri (2007) [23].

33 Bin Ladin (1995) "Prince Sultan and the Air Aviation Commissions," Committee for Advice and Reform (July 11), Harmony Archive, document no. AFGP-2002-003345. Department of Defense, Washington, DC. [68]

34 Bin Ladin (2001) "The facts of the conflict between us and America," video statement aired on Al Jazeera (December 13), secured from Islamist Web forums. [129]

35 Bin Ladin (2003) Statement reported and published in *Al-Sharq al-Awsat* (January 19), available in FBIS (2004). [216]

36 Bin Ladin (2006) "Oh people of Islam," in *As-Sahab* (April 23), secured via links from Islamist Web forums. [90]

37 Zawahiri (2006) "The alternative is da'wa and jihad," in *As-Sahab* (March 4), available from IntelCenter (2008-B). [73]

38 Bin Ladin (1999) Interview with bin Ladin titled "Usama Bin Ladin, the destruction of the Base," aired on Al Jazeera (June 10), full-length version aired on Al Jazeera (September 20, 2001), transcript available from FBIS (2004). [184]

39 Bin Ladin (2002) Statement published in *Al-Quds Al-Arabi* (March 28), also distributed through www.jihad.net, available from FBIS (2004). [205]

40 See, for example, bin Ladin (2004) Audio statement (no title) published by *As-Sahab* (December 27), available in IntelCenter (2008-A). [86]

41 Bin Ladin (2003) Untitled audio statement, unknown distributor (February), available from IntelCenter (2008-A). [78]

42 Zawahiri (2006). [73]

43 Zawahiri (unknown date) "Introduction" to *Characteristics of Jihad*, a magazine of Egyptian militant Islamist activists, available in Harmony Archive, document no. AFGP-2002-600321. Combating Terrorism Center, West Point, NY. [35]

44 Zawahiri (2002) "The interview of Dr Ayman al-Zawahiri," available from IntelCenter (2008-B). [22]

45 Bin Ladin (2004). [86]

46 Zawahiri (2006) "Realities of the conflict between Islam and unbelief," in *As-Sahab* (December 22), available from IntelCenter (2008-B). [94]

47 Zawahiri (2002). [45]

48 Bin Ladin (2003). [78] This point was reiterated in Zawahiri's "Obstacles to jihad"—see Zawahiri (2005) "Obstacles to jihad," in *As-Sahab* (December 10), available in IntelCenter (2008-B). [25]

49 Bin Ladin (2006) "To the ummah in general and to the mujahideen in Iraq and Somalia in particular," statement published by *As-Sahab* in July. Transcript available, for example, from IntelCenter (2008). [93]

50 Bin Ladin (2007) "The way to frustrate the conspiracies," in *As-Sahab Media* (December 29), transcript available in IntelCenter (2008-A). [27]

51 Bin Ladin (1996) "Message from Usama Bin-Muhammad Bin Ladin to his Muslim brothers in the whole world and especially in the Arabian Peninsula: Declaration of jihad against the Americans occupying the Land of the Two Holy Mosques; expel the heretics from the Arabian Peninsula," in *Al-Islah* (September 2, pp. 1–12), published in FBIS (2004). [5]

52 Bin Ladin (2003). [78]

53 Zawahiri (2007) "Forty years since the fall of Jerusalem," audio statement published by *As-Sahab* on June 25, transcript available from IntelCenter (2008). [101]

54 See Zawahiri (2012) "To our people in the place of Revelation and cradle of Islaam," video statement published by *As-Sahab* (May 18) and translated by Fursan Al-Balagh Media, distributed via jihadi websites. [246]

55 Zawahiri (2007) "The aggression against Lal Masjid," in *As-Sahab Media* (July 11), available in IntelCenter (2008-B). [104]

56 Zawahiri (2007) "Annapolis: The betrayal," in *As-Sahab* (December 14), available in IntelCenter (2008-B). [12]

57 Zawahiri (2011). [244]

58 Zawahiri (2011) "A message of hope and glad tidings to our people in Egypt (4)," in *As-Sahab* (March 4), secured via links from Islamist Web forums. [235]

59 Meijer (ed.) (2009): page 19.

60 Al-Maqdisi, Muhammad (nd) *This Is Our Aqidah.* http://www.kalamullah. com [as of November 21, 2012]. For a detailed analysis of Al-Maqdisi's approach to *takfir*, see Wagemakers, J. (2012) *A Quietist Jihadi: The Ideology and Influence of Abu Muhammad al-Maqdisi.* Cambridge University Press, Cambridge.

61 Bin Ladin (1994) "Saudi Arabi supports the communists in Yemen," open letter dated June 7, available from Harmony Database, document no. AFGP-2002-003345. Combating Terrorism Center, West Point, NY. [37]

62 Bin Ladin (1994) "The banishment of communism from the Arabian Peninsula: The episode and the proof," open letter dated July 7, available from Harmony Database, document no. AFGP-2002-003345. [38]

63 Bin Ladin (1994) "Saudi Arabia unveils its war against Islam and its scholars," open letter dated September 12, Harmony Archive, document no. AFGP-2002-003345. Combating Terrorism Center, West Point, NY [40]; bin Ladin (1994) "Higher committee for harm!!," open letter dated October 15, Harmony Archive, document no. AFGP-2002-003345. Combating Terrorism Center, West Point, NY. [47]

64 Bin Ladin (1995). [68]

65 Bin Ladin (1995) "Saudi Arabia continues its war against Islam and its scholars," open letter dated March 9, Harmony Database, document no. AFGP-2002-003345. Combating Terrorism Center, West Point, NY. [66]

66 Bin Ladin (1995) "An open letter to King Fahd on the occasion of the recent cabinet reshuffle" (July 11), Harmony Database, document no. AFGP-2002-000103-HT-NVTC. http://www.ctc.usma.edu/wp-content/uploads/2010/08/AFGP-2002-000103-Trans.pdf. Combating Terrorism Center, West Point, NY. [62]

67 Bin Ladin (1995) "The Bosnia tragedy and the deception of the Servant of the Two Mosques," open letter dated August 11, Harmony Database, document no. AFGP-2002-003345. Combating Terrorism Center, West Point, NY. [69]

68 It was only much later when bin Ladin began to state more unequivocally that the Saudi leadership should suffer physically for its betrayal of Islam. In May 2003, for instance, he issued a statement promising Al-Qaeda's next messages to Saudi authorities would be "dripping in blood": Bin Ladin (2003) Statement distributed by Movement for Islamic Reform (London) (May 29), available from FBIS (2004). [219] Over a year later, bin Ladin issued a statement online expressing similar sentiments, arguing Saudis needed to "unseat the ruler," and "if he declines, then arms would be taken up to unseat him." Bin Ladin (2004) Untitled audio statement (December 16), secured from Archive.org [January 12, 2009] via link from Islamist Web forums. [84]

69 Bin Ladin (1999) [184]; bin Ladin (2002) [205]; bin Ladin (2003) "Second letter to the Muslims of Iraq," statement released on October 18. Available in ed. Kepel & Milelli (2008) and FBIS (2004) [98]; Zawahiri (2006). [73]

70 Zawahiri (unknown date). [35]

71 Zawahiri (2001) "Knights under the banner of the Prophet," initially published in *Al-Sharq al-Awsat* (December 2), available in translation from the Foreign Broadcast Information Service. [119]

72 Zawahiri (2007). [97]

73 Zawahiri (2011). [244]

74 Zawahiri (2008) "The open meeting with Sheikh Ayman al-Zawahiri, part one," answers published by *As-Sahab* (April 2), secured from Archive.org and Islamist Web forums, transcript also available in IntelCenter (2008-B). [105]

75 Zawahiri (2011). [235]

76 See, for example, Zawahiri (2008) "A message from Shaikh Ayman al-Zawahiri to Pakistan army and the people of Pakistan," in *As-Sahab* (August 10), transcript available from the NEFA Foundation; YouTube [41]; Zawahiri (2009) "The realities of jihad and fallacy of hypocrisy," in *As-Sahab* (August 4), secured via links from Islamist Web forums [140]; Zawahiri (2009) "The path of doom," in *As-Sahab* (August 26), secured via links from Islamist Web forums. [142]

77 Bin Ladin (2006) "Elegizing the ummah's martyr and emir of the martyrs, Abu Musab al-Zarqawi," in *As-Sahab* (June 29), transcript available in IntelCenter (2008-A). [92]

78 Bin Ladin (2003) "A message to our brothers in Iraq," distributed by Al Jazeera (February 11), transcript available from FBIS (2004); IntelCenter (2008-A); and Lawrence, B. (ed.) (2005) *Messages to the World: The Statements of Osama Bin Laden.* Verso Books, London. [79]; bin Ladin (2004) "People of Iraq," aired on Al Jazeera (May 6), IntelCenter (2008). [82]

79 Bin Ladin (2007). [27]

80 Bin Ladin (2004). [86]

81 Bin Ladin (2004). [86] See also: Bin Ladin (2003). [78]Zawahiri similarly talked of those who discouraged jihad and violence in Iraq as "traitors" in the eyes of God: Zawahiri (2006) "Four years since the Battle of Tora Bora—From Tora Bora to Iraq," published by *As-Sahab Media* (April 12), available in IntelCenter (2008-B). [238]

82 Zawahiri (1993). [99]

83 Zawahiri (2007) "Palestine is the concern of all Muslims," in *As-Sahab* (March 11), secured from Islamist Web forums, also available in IntelCenter (2008-B). [18]

84 Zawahiri (2007). [101]

85 Zawahiri (1991) *The Bitter Harvest: The Brotherhood in Sixty Years.* See in Ibrahim (2007); ed. Kepel & Milelli (2008). [46]

86 Zawahiri (2005) [49]. This representation of moderate Islam as an invention to please the West has been picked up by other extremist ideologues, such as Anwar Al-Awlaki in his audio lecture "The Battle of Hearts and Minds."

87 Fradkin, H. (2009) "The paradoxes of Shiism," in *Current Trends in Islamist Ideology* (vol. 8, pp. 5–26). Hudson Institute, Washington, DC: page 7.

88 Riedel, B. (2008) *The Search for Al Qaeda: Its Leadership, Ideology and Future* (2nd edition). Brookings Institution Press, Washington, DC: pages 13 and 104.

89 Zawahiri (2007). [13]

90 Kepel & Milelli (eds.) (2008): page 168.

91 Kepel (2008-B) *Beyond Terror and Martyrdom: The Future of the Middle East* (translated by Pascale Ghazaleh), Harvard University Press, Cambridge MA: pages 133–134.

92 Zawahiri (1995) "Our stance towards Iran: Response to the accusation of cooperation between the Salafi jihadi movement and renegade Iran," in *Nashrat al-Ansar* (April 1), excerpts published in McCants, W., Brachman, J., Felter, J. (2006) *Militant Ideology Atlas: Research Compendium.* Combating Terrorism Center, West Point, NY. [115]

93 Zawahiri (2007). [97]

94 Zawahiri (2007) "'A review of events'—As Sahab publishes fourth interview with Zawahiri," in *As-Sahab* (December 16), secured via links from Islamist Web forums, also available from IntelCenter (2008-B). [13]

95 Zawahiri (2010) "A victorious ummah, a broken Crusade," in *As-Sahab* (September 15), secured via links from Islamist Web forums. [226]

96 Referring to a great Persian Shia empire, but in this context the term is derogatory of Shia Muslims.

97 Zawahiri (2010) "Message to the people of Turkey," in *As-Sahab* (August 15), English version distributed by Ansarnet English Forum, secured via Islamist websites. [225]

98 Zawahiri (2013) "Unifying the word toward the word of monotheism (*tawhid*)," in *As-Sahab* (April 7), distributed by Al-Fajr Media Center via jihadi websites. English transcript from the Open Source Center [260]; Zawahiri (2013) "Sixty-five years since the establishment of the state of occupation: Israel," in *As-Sahab* (June 6), distributed by Al-Fajr Media Center via jihadi websites. English transcript from the Open Source Center. [259]

99 Zawahiri (2005) First in a series of interviews with Zawahiri, in *As-Sahab* (December 7), available in Ibrahim (2007). [49]

100 Zawahiri (2008) "The open meeting with Sheikh Ayman al-Zawahiri, part two," the second part of responses to the "Open Meeting" public appeal, in *As-Sahab* (April 21), available from IntelCenter (2008-B). [107]

101 See, for example, the section "Rafidah focus" in the fourth edition of the *Inspire* magazine (winter 2010).

102 Bin Ladin (2004). [86]

103 Zawahiri (2006). [238]

104 Bin Ladin (2006). [92] Emphasis added.

105 Zawahiri (2006). [94]

106 Zawahiri (2007) "The advice of one concerned," video statement published by *As-Sahab* on July 4, made available via Islamist websites. Transcript also available from IntelCenter (2008). [102]

107 Zawahiri (2007). [102]

108 Zawahiri (2011) "The noble knight dismounted," published by *As-Sahab* and the Global Islamic Media Front (June 8), secured via links from Islamist Web forums. [239]

109 Zawahiri (2008). [105]

110 Bin Ladin (1997) "Pakistan interviews Usama Bin Ladin," article/interview published in *Daily Pakistan* (March 18): See FBIS (2004). [154]

111 Zawahiri (2012), "Yemen: Between a fugitive puppet and his new replacement," in *As-Sahab* (May 15), distributed by jihadi websites. Transcript available from jihadi websites and Flashpoint Partners. [248] Note: The English transcript from Flashpoint Partners contains errors in comparison with the Arabic original in that words attributed to Zawahiri were actually Al-Awlaki's.

112 Bin Ladin (2008) "A way for the salvation of Palestine," in *As-Sahab* (March 20), secured via link from Islamist websites, transcript also available from the NEFA Foundation. [6]

113 Zawahiri (2001). [119]

114 Eleven statements, moreover, conveyed criticism of both elites and the general population together.

115 Zawahiri (2008) *Exoneration: A Letter Exonerating the Ummah of the Pen and the Sword from the Unjust Allegation of Feebleness and Weakness*, advertised by *As-Sahab* early in 2008, manuscript secured from the Open Source Center. [20]

116 Zawahiri (2008). [105]

117 See, for example, extensive criticism of the Brotherhood in Zawahiri (2008). [107]

118 Bin Ladin (1994). [40]

119 See, for example, Zawahiri (2012) "To the people of Tunisia: O' people of Tunisia, support your shariah," in *As-Sahab* (June 10), distributed by jihadist websites. English transcript available, for example, from globalterroralert. com [as of January 2013]. [249]

120 For example, Zawahiri (1993) [99]; bin Ladin (1994) [47]; bin Ladin (1994) "Open letter for Shaykh Bin Baz on the invalidity of his fatwa on peace with the Jews," open letter dated December 29, available from Harmony Database, document no. AFGP-2002-003345. Combating Terrorism Center, West Point, NY. [63]

121 Bin Ladin (1995) "Scholars are the Prophet's successors," open letter dated May 6, available from Harmony Database, document no. AFGP-2002-003345. Combating Terrorism Center, West Point, NY. [67]

122 Bin Ladin (2003). [78]

123 Bin Ladin (2004). [84]

124 Zawahiri (2005) "Wills of the knights of the London raid," in *As-Sahab* (November 15), transcript available in Ibrahim (2007). [53]

125 Zawahiri (1999), letter to Abu Yasir, published in Al-Shafey, M. "Al-Qaeda's secret emails," in *Al-Sharq al-Awsat* (June 12, 2005), letter dated April 19, 1999. Secured from the newspaper. [123]

126 Bin Ladin (1997) [154]; bin Ladin (1998) Statement published in Islamabad-based newspaper (January 19), available in FBIS (2004). [159]

127 Bin Ladin (2001) Letter from bin Ladin published in *The Dawn* (Karachi) (April 3) titled "Usama regrets curbs by Taliban," available in FBIS (2004). [195]

128 Zawahiri (2008). [105]

129 Zawahiri (2001). [119]

130 Also Filiu, J. P. (2009) "The Brotherhood vs. Al-Qaeda: A moment of truth?," in *Current Trends in Islamist Ideology* (vol. 9): page 23.

131 See, for example, Bin Ladin (2008) "A message to the Muslim nation," in *As-Sahab* (May 18), secured via link from Islamist Web forums [24]; Zawahiri (2009). [140]

132 Bin Ladin (2007). [27]

133 Bin Ladin (1999). [178]

134 Bin Ladin (1999). [184]

135 Bin Ladin & Zawahiri (2000) Statement regarding Muslim prisoners aired on Al Jazeera (September 21), available from FBIS (2004). [191]

136 Zawahiri (unknown date). [35]

137 Bin Ladin (2000) "Usama speaks on hijrah and the Islamic state?," statement published on ummah.net and elsewhere (May 22), made available in FBIS (2004). [189]

138 Bin Ladin (2001) Poem published in *Ausaf* (Islamabad) (March 3), available in FBIS (2004). [193]

139 Bin Ladin (2001) Speech published in *The News* (Islamabad) (May 7), available in FBIS (2004). [197]

140 Bin Ladin (2001) "Letter to the Pakistani people," aired on Al Jazeera (September 24), available from FBIS (2004). [201]

141 Bin Ladin (2001) Untitled statement aired on Al Jazeera (November 3), transcript available in Hegghammer (2003). [77]

142 Zawahiri (2008) [20]; bin Ladin (2002) Report of statement published in *Al-Sharq al-Awsat* (June 26), available in FBIS (2004). [210]

143 Bin Ladin (2002). [210]

144 Bin Ladin (2002) The "will" of bin Ladin published in *Al-Majallah* (London) (October 27), available in FBIS (2004). [213]

145 Bin Ladin (2004). [86]

146 Bin Ladin (2003). [78]

147 Bin Ladin (2011) "The speech by the Martyr of Islam" (*As-Sahab* title after bin Ladin's death), in *As-Sahab* (May 19). English version distributed by Global Islamic Media Front, secured from Islamist Web forums. [240]

148 Zawahiri (2002). [45]

149 Zawahiri (2005). [25]

150 Zawahiri (2006) "Support for Palestinians," in *As-Sahab* (June 9), transcript available in IntelCenter (2008). [85]

151 Zawahiri (2008) "A call to help our people in Gaza," in *As-Sahab* (March 23), transcripts available from IntelCenter (2008) and the NEFA Foundation. [17]

152 Zawahiri (2008). [107]

153 *As-Sahab* (2002). [108]

154 Zawahiri (2009) "Shaykh Dr. Ayman al-Zawahiri: Eulogy for the role model of the youth—The Commander and Shahid Baitullah [Mehsud]," in *As-Sahab* (September 28), secured via links from Islamist Web forums [147]; Zawahiri (2010) "Al-Quds will not be converted to Judaism," in *As-Sahab*, secured via links from Islamist Web forums (July 19). [223]

155 Zawahiri (2008) "On the anniversary of the Naksa ... Break the siege of Gaza," in *As-Sahab* (June 4), transcript secured from the Open Source Center [15]. This is in spite of the fact that a few months prior to Zawahiri's declaration, Al-Qaeda had been severely criticized in the "Open Meeting" initiative for failing to invest sufficient energy and resources in the

Palestinian campaign, a charge that put the leadership on the defensive in justifying the need to focus on Iraq.

156 Zawahiri (2011). [244]

157 See, for example, Bin Ladin (2004) [86]; bin Ladin (2006) [93]; Zawahiri (2006). [21]

158 Zawahiri (2004) Statement aired on Al Jazeera (March 25), transcript available from Hegghammer (2005). [59]

159 Bin Ladin (2007) "Come to jihad: A speech to the people of Pakistan," statement published by *As-Sahab* (September 20), transcripts available from the NEFA Foundation and IntelCenter (2008). [14]

160 Zawahiri (2007). [104]

161 Zawahiri (2009) "My Muslim brothers and sisters in Pakistan," in *As-Sahab* (July 15), secured via links from Islamist Web forums. [139]

162 Zawahiri (2009). [142]

163 Zawahiri (2010). [226]

164 Zawahiri (2007). [104]

165 Zawahiri (2010) "Who is going to support Aafia Sidique?," statement published by *As-Sahab* (November 4), translated and distributed by the Global Islamic Media Front, secured via link from Islamist Web forums. [229]

166 Zawahiri (2010). [226]

167 Zawahiri (2007). [13]

168 See, for example, Zawahiri (2007) "Shaykh Ayman Al-Zawahiri: On the fifth anniversary of the invasion and torture of Iraq," in *As-Sahab* (April 17), secured from Islamist Web forums, also available from IntelCenter (2008-B). [7]

169 Azzam is, for example, one of the most prominent and celebrated authors of books on the English-language Islamic media repository Kalamullah.com. See http://kalamullah.com/azzam.html [as of March 16, 2012].

Chapter 7

1 Zawahiri (2011) "The noble knight dismounted," in *As-Sahab* and the Global Islamic Media Front (June 8), secured via links from Islamist Web forums. [239]

2 Zawahiri (2012) "The lion of knowledge and jihaad: Martyrdom of Al-Sheikh Abu Yahya Al-Leebi (Rahimahullaah): Eulogy by Al-Ameer Al-Sheikh Ayman Al-Dhawaahiri," in *As-Sahab* and *Al-Fajr*, distributed on Islamist Web forums on September 11. [250]

3 Snow, D. & Benford, R. (1988) "Ideology, frame resonance, and participant mobilization," in *International Social Movement Research* (vol. 1, pp. 197–217): page 198.

4 See Harmony Archive (nd) Document no. AFGP-2002-600053. Combating Terrorism Center, West Point, NY.

5 Gerges, F. (2011) *The Rise and Fall of Al-Qaeda.* Oxford University Press, Oxford: page 113.

6 Pew Global Attitudes Project (2011-A) "Osama bin Laden largely discredited among Muslim publics in recent years" (May 2). http://www.pewglobal. org/2011/05/02/osama-bin-laden-largely-discredited-among-muslim-publics-in-recent-years/ [accessed August 2013].

7 Pew Global Attitudes Project (2003) *Views of A Changing World* (June). Pew Research Center, Washington, DC.

8 Pew Global Attitudes Project (2003).

9 Pew Global Attitudes Project (2011-B) "Common concerns over Islamic extremism: Muslim-Western tensions persist" (July 2011). http://www. pewglobal.org/2011/07/21/muslim-western-tensions-persist/ [accessed August 2013].

10 Al-Zayyat, M. (2004) *The Road to Al-Qaeda: The Story of Bin Laden's Right-Hand Man.* Pluto Press, London: page xiv.

11 BBC (2013) "Pakistani youth 'cool on democracy'" (published online on April 2). http://www.bbc.co.uk/news/world-22001263?print=true [as of April 2013].

12 Hegghammer, T. (2009) "The ideological hybridization of jihadi groups," in *Current Trends in Islamist Ideology* (vol. 9, pp. 26–46). Hudson Institute, Washington, DC: page 40.

13 See Snow & Benford (1988): pages 207–208.

14 Benford and Snow refer to this as questions concerning "empirical credibility." See Benford, R. D. & Snow, D. A. (2000) "Framing processes and social movements; an overview and assessment," in *Annual Review of Sociology* (vol. 26, pp. 611–639) and Snow & Benford (1988).

15 This is referred to as "experiential commensurability."

16 This is referred to as "narrative fidelity" in the literature on collective action frames.

17 See, for example, Kepel, G. (2008) *Beyond Terror and Martyrdom: The Future of the Middle East*, translated by Pascale Ghazaleh. Harvard University Press, Cambridge, MA: page 180.

18 Zawahiri (2007) "'A review of events'—As Sahab publishes fourth interview with Zawahiri," in *As-Sahab* (December 16), secured via links from Islamist Web forums (also available from IntelCenter (2008) *Words of Ayman al-Zawahiri Vol. 1.* Tempest Publishing, Alexandria, VA). [13]

19 Munson, H. (2006) "Lifting the veil: Understanding the roots of Islamic militancy," in *Harvard International Review* (May 6): page 2.

20 Randal, J. (2005) *Osama: Making of a Terrorist.* I.B. Tauris, London: page 290. See also on Israel focus in Zawahiri and bin Ladin communiqués in Blanchard, C. (2006) "Al-Qaeda: Statements and evolving ideology," in

CRS Report for Congress (January 26). Congressional Research Service, Washington, DC: page 11.

21 See Mendenhall, R. (2010) "Al-Qaeda: Who, what, why? Database applications for the Al-Qaeda Statements Index," senior thesis submitted to Haverford College (April 23). http://thesis.haverford.edu/dspace/handle/10066/5064 [as of December 5, 2012]: pages 142–143; Mendelsohn, B. (2009) "Al-Qaeda's Palestinian problem," in *Survival* (vol. 51, iss. 4, August–September, pp. 71–86): page 71; Blanchard, C. (2007) "Al-Qaeda: Statements and evolving ideology," in *CRS Report for Congress* (July 9). Congressional Research Service, Washington, DC: page 14.

22 Scheuer, M. (2011) *Osama bin Laden*. Oxford University Press, Oxford: pages 153–161.

23 Riedel, B. (2008) *The Search for Al Qaeda: Its Leadership, Ideology and Future* (2nd edition). Brookings Institution Press, Washington, DC: pages 11–12.

24 Hellmich, C. (2011) *Al-Qaeda: From Global Network to Local Franchise*. Zed Books, London: page 102.

25 Quoted in *The Economist* (2009) "The growing, and mysterious, irrelevance of al-Qaeda" (January 24).

26 Bin Ladin (1996) Interview with 'Abd al-Bari Atwan, in *Al-Quds Al-Arabi* (as "Bin Ladin interviewed on jihad against US," November 27), available from FBIS (2004) *FBIS: Compilation of Usama Bin Ladin Statements 1994–January 2004*. Foreign Broadcast Information Service, Reston, VA. [150]

27 Bergen, P. (2006) *The Osama Bin Laden I Know: An Oral History of Al-Qaeda's Leader*. Free Press, New York: page 15. In 1986, moreover, bin Ladin reportedly urged Muslims to boycott US goods since "the Americans take our money and give it to the Jews so they can kill our children with it in Palestine." See Bergen, P. (2011) *The Longest War: The Enduring Conflict between America and al-Qaeda. Free* Press, New York: location 48 (e-book).

28 Bin Ladin, Zawahiri et al. (1998) "Text of World Islamic Front's statement urging jihad against Jews and Crusaders," in *Al-Quds Al-Arabi* (London, February 23), translated in FBIS (2004). [161]

29 Zawahiri (2001) "Knights under the banner of the Prophet," initially published in *Al-Sharq al-Awsat* (December 2), available in translation from the Foreign Broadcast Information Service. [119]

30 Bin Ladin (2001) "Tayseer Allouni interviews bin Ladin in Afghanistan," interview with Al Jazeera (October 10): See transcripts in FBIS (2004) and Hegghammer, T. (2003) *FFI Rapport 1990–2002*. FFI, Oslo. [130]

31 Bin Ladin (2001) "The facts of the conflict between us and America," video statement aired on Al Jazeera (December 13), secured from Islamist Web forums. [129]

32 Bin Ladin (1998) Interview published in *Al-Akhbar* (Islamabad) (March 31), available in FBIS (2004). [163]

33 Bin Ladin (2008) "Reasons of the struggle on the occasion of the 60th anniversary of the founding of the occupying state of Israel," in *As-Sahab* (May 16), secured with help from ITSTIME, Catholic University of Milan. [8]

The centrality of the Palestinian cause for bin Ladin and its apparent role in inspiring the 9/11 attacks was reiterated on subsequent occasions, such as in bin Ladin (2009) [144] and in Zawahiri's (2011) [239] eulogy for bin Ladin.

34 Quoted in Burke, J. (2004) *Al-Qaeda: The True Story of Radical Islam* (2nd edition). Penguin Books, London: page 154.

35 Zawahiri (2006) "Elegizing the ummah's martyr and emir of the martyrs Abu Musab al-Zarqawi, may Allah have mercy on him," in *As-Sahab* (June 24), available in IntelCenter (2008). [32]

36 Zawahiri (2007) "Shaykh Ayman Al-Zawahiri: On the fifth anniversary of the invasion and torture of Iraq," in *As-Sahab* (April 17), secured from Islamist Web forums, also available from IntelCenter (2008). [7]

37 Zawahiri (2007) "Lessons, examples and great events in the year 1427," in *As-Sahab* (February 13), available from IntelCenter (2008). [97]

38 Steven Brooke discusses this element (although more as actual strategy rather than rhetoric) and the concept of, what he calls, the "cordon state" approach. See Brooke, S. (2010) "Chapter 3: Strategic fissures: The near and far enemy debate," in *Self-Inflicted Wounds: Debates and Divisions within Al-Qa'ida and Its Periphery*, ed. Moghadam, A. & Fishman, B., Harmony Project (December 16). Combating Terrorism Center, West Point, NY: pages 45–69.

39 Zawahiri (2012) "The rising sun of victory on the triumphant ummah over the vanquished crusaders," in *As-Sahab* (September 13), available from jihadist websites. Transcript from BBC Monitoring. [254]

40 Bin Ladin (1996). [150]

41 Bin Ladin (2001) "Interview with Hamid Mir," in *Dawn* (November 10). http://www.dawn.com/2001/11/10/top1.htm [accessed July 2013]; see also Hegghammer (2003). [125]

42 Zawahiri (2008) "The open meeting with Sheikh Ayman al-Zawahiri, part two," the second part of responses to the "open meeting" public appeal, in *As-Sahab* (April 21), available from IntelCenter (2008). [107]

43 See, for example, Zawahiri (2005) "Wills of the knights of the London raid," in *As-Sahab* (November 15), transcript available in Ibrahim, R. (2007) *The Al Qaeda Reader*. Broadway Books, New York. [53]

44 Surat Al-Mā'idah (5:51).

45 "You have two choices," Al-Awlaki warned Muslims in the West in his last statement: "either *hijra* [emigration] or jihad, you either leave or you fight." See Al-Awlaki, A. (2010) Statement released online by *Al-Malahem* in December 2010 and made available from Islamist Web forums. Prior to his flight to Yemen, Al-Awlaki repeatedly addressed numerous concerns of those living in the West, as have other radical preachers and ideologues such as Feiz Mohammed.

46 Hellmich (2011): page 17.

47 This is despite the fact that the two leaders condemned any form of nationalism and called for the, supposedly uninterrupted, application of Islamic norms regardless of geographic boundaries.

48 Hegghammer (2009), for instance, argued that traditionally rigid ranking of enemies according to prioritization in the discourse of Al-Qaeda and its affiliates during the 1990s to early 2000s became morphed into a fluid hybrid whereby group leaders sought to widen their support and recruitment base by covering more issues, mixing local and external belligerents. Others, most notably Gerges, have emphasized the hypotheses that Al-Qaeda saw an external, distant enemy in the United States and its Western allies and became convinced, and tried to convince others, of the merits of targeting this entity (Gerges, F. (2005) *The Far Enemy: Why Jihad Went Global*. Cambridge University Press, Cambridge).

49 For Scheuer (2011: pages 99–101), for example, bin Ladin always perceived and presented the United States both as a near and as a far enemy—providing external assistance to local tyrants and Israel while being physically present in the Arabian Peninsula, Iraq, and elsewhere. Bin Laden, according to this account, therefore, blurred the distinction between near and far enemies, but not necessarily in an incoherent way, as he traced the traditional set of local adversaries and tyrannical regimes to the core threat of the United States and its allies, wherever they could be found. In her study of Al-Qaeda statements, Mendenhall (2010: page 105) also cautioned against the use of crude dichotomies, including the separation of the "near *or* far enemy" in Al-Qaeda's discourse (emphasis in original).

50 Bin Ladin's nascent environmental agenda was, of course, cut short. In the long term, perhaps, this could have challenged empirical credibility as many strands of these messages were not specific to Muslims and included as victims those who suffered the consequences of Hurricane Katrina (i.e., US citizens), with implicit recognition of the humanitarian role of the United Nations. This might have been part of a more elaborate strategy designed to make sense of a growing range of global issues affecting the world. Zawahiri also had a brief spell seeking to appeal to the oppressed all over the world, regardless of creed, presenting Al-Qaeda as a fair, legitimate, and pertinent actor on the global stage.

51 Zawahiri (2008) "The open meeting with Sheikh Ayman al-Zawahiri, part one," answers published in *As-Sahab* (April 2), secured from Archive.org and Islamist Web forums, transcript also available in IntelCenter (2008). [105]

52 Zawahiri (2012) "Days with the Imam" (part 2), in *As-Sahab* (June 3), translated by the Global Islamic Media Front and posted on Islamist Web forums. [252]

53 Berntzen, L. and Sandberg, S. (2014) "The collective nature of lone wolf terrorism: Anders Behring Breivik and the anti-Islamic social movement," in *Terrorism and Political Violence* (published online, February 5, pp. 1–21): page 21.

54 *Economist* (2011) (May 7).

Chapter 8

1 Zawahiri (2012) "The rising sun of victory on the triumphant ummah over the vanquished crusaders," in *As-Sahab* (September 13), available from jihadist websites. Transcript from BBC Monitoring. [254]

2 Bergen, P. & Cruickshank, P. (2012) "Revisiting the early Al Qaeda: Updated account of its formative years," in *Studies in Conflict and Terrorism* (vol. 35, iss. 1, pp. 1–36): page 30.

3 Moghadam, A. & Fishman, B. (eds.) (2010) "Chapter 1: Debates and divisions within and around Al-Qa'ida," in *Self-Inflicted Wounds: Debates and Divisions within Al-Qa'ida and Its Periphery*, Harmony Project (December 16). Combating Terrorism Center, West Point, NY: page 10.

4 Mann, M. quoted in Lawrence, B. (ed.) (2005) *Messages to the World: The Statements of Osama bin Laden*. Verso Books, London: page xx. Originally published as Mann, Michael (2003) *Incoherent Empire*. Verso, London: page 169. Emphasis in original.

5 Hellmich, C. (2011) *Al-Qaeda: From Global Network to Local Franchise*. Zed Books, London: page 92.

6 Quoted in Lawrence (ed.) (2005): page xx.

7 Hellmich (2011): page 92.

8 See, for example, Zawahiri (2012). [254]

9 See bin Ladin (2006) "Oh people of Islam," in *As-Sahab* (April 23), secured via links from Islamist Web forums [90], and numerous other references to Darfur as part of Western imperialism in the Al-Qaeda leadership discourse.

10 Bin Ladin (2002) "Letter from Usama Bin Muhammad Bin Ladin to the American people," first published in *Waaqiah* (October 26), available in FBIS (2004) *FBIS: Compilation of Usama Bin Ladin Statements 1994–January 2004*. Foreign Broadcast Information Service, Reston, VA. [212]

11 Suspects in a recent thwarted terror plot in the UK for instance reportedly branded those living in the West as animals that "want to have sex like donkeys in the street." Sanderson, D. (2012) "Terror suspect: Britons 'have sex like donkeys' and deserve to be blown up," *Times* (October 25).

12 Cronin, A. (2011) "9/11: How and why do terrorist campaigns end?," British Academy and University of St. Andrews symposium "9/11: Ten years on," held at the British Academy, London (September 2).

13 Gerges, F. (2011) *The Rise and Fall of Al-Qaeda*. Oxford University Press, Oxford: page 116.

14 In this context, Ciovacco, for instance, argues that the targeting of Muslim innocents by Al-Qaeda affiliates has been so damaging for the leadership that its "moral case for war [has become] problematic, and many of its key ideological assertions are considerably weakened" (Brahimi, A. (2010) 'Crushed in the Shadows: Why Al Qaeda Will Lose the War of Ideas', *Studies in Conflict & Terrorism*, vol. 33, iss. 2, pp. 93–110).

15 Moghadam & Fishman (2010): page 8.

16 The resulting dispute prompted Zawahiri to issue a private rebuke of the leaders of both the an-Nusra front as well as the Al-Qaeda in Iraq. See, for example, BBC (2013) "Syria crisis: Al-Nusra pledges allegiance to al-Qaeda" (April 10). http://www.bbc.co.uk/news/world-middle-east-22095099 [as of April 2013]. See also transcript of Zawahiri's rebuke in Atassi, B. (2013)

"Qaeda chief annuls Syrian-Iraqi jihad merger," Al Jazeera. http://www. aljazeera.com/news/middleeast/2013/06/2013699425657882.html [as of August 2013].

17 See SomaliaReport.com (2012) "Somali Islamists reportedly disagree over Al-Qa'idah merger" (March 16), transcript from BBC Monitoring.

18 Gerges (2011): page 201.

19 Shahzad, Syed Saleem (2011) *Inside Al-Qaeda and the Taliban: Beyond bin Laden and 9/11*. Palgrave Macmillan, Melbourne: pages 5–6.

20 See, for example, Gardell, Mattias (2003) *Gods of the Blood: The Pagan Revival and White Separatism*. Duke University Press, Durham, NC.

Appendix

Details of statements analyzed

Date released	Distributor	AQ rep.	Description/title	[ID]
N/A	Minbar al-Tawhid wa'l-Jihad	AAZ	"Response to a Grave Uncertainty from Shaykh al-Albani Regarding Silence in the Face of Apostate Rulers"	[117]
N/A	Minbar al-Tawhid wa'l-Jihad	UBL	"Methodological Guidelines (1) According to the Guidelines of Bin Ladin: We Proceed in the Way of Manhattan in Order to Defy America and Put an End to Their Controlling Evil"; (2); (3)	[112]
N/A	unknown	AAZ	"The Forbidden Word"	[113]
N/A	N/A	UBL	"Letter from UBL to Mullah Omar"	[61]
N/A	Egyptian Islamic Jihad	AAZ	Introduction in new journal—"Characteristics of Jihad"	[35]
N/A	N/A	Purport. AAZ	"Jihad, Martyrdom, and the Killing of Innocents"	[48]

(*Continued*)

Date released	Distributor	AQ rep.	Description/title	[ID]
Jan 01, 91	N/A	AAZ	"The Bitter Harvest: The Brotherhood in Sixty Years"	[46]
Jan 01, 92	Minbar al-Tawhid wa'l-Jihad	AAZ	"The Black Book: An Account of the Torture of Muslims in the Time of Husni Mubarak"	[114]
Jan 01, 93	N/A	AAZ/Islamic Jihad	"Advice to the Community to Reject the Fatwa of Sheikh Bin Baz Authorizing Parliamentary Representation: Published under the Supervision of Ayman al-Zawahiri"	[99]
Mar 09, 94	Al-Quds Al-Arabi	UBL	"Usama Bin Ladin Denies 'Terrorism' Link London AL-QUDS AL-'ARABI in Arabic 9 Mar 94 p 4"	[1]
Apr 12, 94	N/A	UBL	"Our Invitation to Give Advice and Reform"	[36]
Jun 07, 94	N/A	UBL	"Saudi Arabi Supports the Communists in Yemen"	[37]
Jul 11, 94	N/A	UBL	"The Banishment of Communism from the Arabian Peninsula: The Episode and the Proof"	[38]
Jul 19, 94	N/A	UBL	"Quran Scholars in the Face of Despotism"	[39]

(Continued)

Date released	Distributor	AQ rep.	Description/title	[ID]
Aug 08, 94	Al-Quds Al-Arabi	UBL	"Saudi Islamic Opposition Opens London Office London AL-QUDS AL-'ARABI in Arabic 8 Aug 94 p 1"	[2]
Sep 12, 94	N/A	UBL	"Saudi Arabia Unveils Its War against Islam and Its Scholars"	[40]
Sep 16, 94	N/A	UBL	"Urgent Letter to Security Officials"	[42]
Oct 15, 94	N/A	UBL	"Higher Committee for Harm!!"	[47]
Dec 29, 94	N/A	UBL	"Open Letter for Shaykh Bin Baz on the Invalidity of His Fatwa on Peace with the Jews"	[63]
Jan 29, 95	N/A	UBL	"Second Letter to Shaykh Abd Al Aziz Bin Baz from the Reform and Advice Foundation"	[64]
Feb 12, 95	N/A	UBL	"Prince Salman and Ramadan Alms"	[65]
Mar 09, 95	N/A	UBL	"Saudi Arabia Continues Its War against Islam and Its Scholars"	[66]
Apr 01, 95	Nashrat al-Ansar	AAZ	"Our Stance towards Iran: Response to the Accusation of Cooperation between the Salafi Jihadi Movement and Renegade Iran"	[115]

(Continued)

Date released	Distributor	AQ rep.	Description/title	[ID]
May 06, 95	N/A	UBL	"Scholars Are the Prophet's Successors"	[67]
Jul 11, 95	N/A	UBL	"Prince Sultan and the Air Aviation Commissions"	[68]
Aug 03, 95	N/A	UBL	"An Open Letter to King Fahd On the Occasion of the Recent Cabinet Reshuffle"	[62]
Aug 11, 95	N/A	UBL	"The Bosnia Tragedy and the Deception of the Servant of the Two Mosques"	[69]
Jan 01, 96	Minbar al-Tawhid wa'l-Jihad	AAZ	"Healing the Hearts of Believers: On Some Concepts of Jihad in the Islamabad Operation"	[118]
Jun 17, 96	Rose Al-Yusuf + Fayizah Sa'd	UBL	"Usama Bin Ladin Reportedly Interviewed in London Cairo ROSE AL-YUSUF in Arabic on 17 June 1996 on pp 25–27"	[3]
Jul 10, 96	Robert Fisk, The Independent	UBL	"Interview with Saudi Dissident Bin Ladin London INDEPENDENT in English, 10 Jul 96 p 14"	[4]
Sep 02, 96	Al-Islah	UBL	"Bin Ladin Declares Jihad on Americans London AL-ISLAH in Arabic, 2 Sep 96. ['Message from Usama Bin- Muhammad Bin	[5]

(Continued)

Date released	Distributor	AQ rep.	Description/title	[ID]
			Ladin to His Muslim Brothers in the Whole World and Especially in the Arabian Peninsula: Declaration of Jihad against the Americans Occupying the Land of the Two Holy Mosques; Expel the Heretics from the Arabian Peninsula]"	
Nov 27, 96	Al-Quds al-Arabi—interview with 'Abd al-Bari 'Atwan	UBL	"Bin Ladin Interviewed on Jihad against US"	[150]
Feb 20, 97	Channel 4/Gwyn Robert	UBL	"Correspondent Meets with Opposition Leader Bin Ladin"	[151]
Mar 03, 97	Al-Islah (London)	UBL	"Bin Ladin Cited on Prince Sultan's US Visit"	[152]
Mar 15, 97	The Muslim (Islamabad)	UBL	"Bin Ladin Charges US Involvement in China Bombings"	[153]
Mar 18, 97	Pakistan (Islamabad) Hamid Mir	UBL	"Pakistan Interviews Usama Bin Ladin"	[154]
Mar 22, 97	The Independent	UBL	"Interview with Usama bin Ladin"	[155]
Apr 16, 97	N/A	UBL	"The Saudi Regime and the Reputed Tragedies of the Pilgrims"	[70]

(Continued)

Date released	Distributor	AQ rep.	Description/title	[ID]
Jun 06, 97	Daily Pakistan/ Hamid Mir	UBL	"Usama Bin Ladin Dares US Commandos to Come to Afghanistan"	[156]
Aug 07, 97	Daily Pakistan	UBL	"Usama Bin Ladin Urges 'Befitting Reply' to Horan"	[157]
Nov 27, 97	FBIS	UBL	"Daily Reports Usama Bin Ladin's Threat against Americans"	[158]
Jan 17, 98	Pakistan newspaper (Islamabad)	UBL	"Bin Ladin Claims Foiling of UN's Afghan 'Conspiracy'"	[159]
Feb 16, 98	Al-Quds al-Arabi	UBL	"Bin Ladin Condoles with Al-Bashir on Salih's Death"	[160]
Feb 23, 98	Al-Quds Al-Arabi	UBL, AAZ (as amir of the Jihad Group, Egypt) plus Abu Yasir Taha, Mir Hamzah, and Fazlul Rahman	"Text of Fatwa Urging Jihad against Americans" and "Text of World Islamic Front's Statement Urging Jihad against Jews and Crusaders"	[161]
Mar 23, 98	Al-Quds Al-Arabi	UBL	"Bin Ladin Urges Expulsion of 'Invaders'," statement titled "One of Them Bears Witness"	[162]
Mar 31, 98	FBIS	UBL	"Interview with Usama Bin Ladin Reported"	[163]

(Continued)

Date released	Distributor	AQ rep.	Description/title	[ID]
Apr 15, 98	Al-Quds Al-Arabi	UBL	"Bin Ladin Warns against Richardson Mission to Afghanistan"	[164]
May 07, 98	N/A	UBL	"Supporting the Fatwa of the Afghani Religious Scholars of Ejecting the American Forces from the Land of the Two Holy Mosques"	[71]
May 14, 98	Al-Quds Al-Arabi	UBL	"Clerics in Afghanistan Issue Fatwa on Necessity to Move US Forces Out of the Gulf; Saudi Oppositionist Usama Bin Ladin Supports It"	[165]
May 18, 98	Al-Quds Al-Arabi	UBL	"Bin Ladin: Afghanistan's Inclusion on US 'Terrorism List' Is 'Certificate of Good Conduct' for Taliban"	[166]
May 19, 98	Al-Hayah (London)	UBL	"World Islamic Front Backs 'Intifadah of Palestine's Sons'. Title of statement: 'Wounds of Al-Aqsa Mosque'"	[167]
May 28, 98	The Dawn (Islamabad)	UBL	"Bin Ladin Creates New Front against US, Israel"	[168]

(Continued)

Date released	Distributor	AQ rep.	Description/title	[ID]
May 29, 98	Al-Quds Al-Arabi	UBL	"United States Admits That Keeping Its Troops in the Gulf Is Causing Dissatisfaction; Bin Ladin Threatens to Launch Attack Soon"	[169]
Jun 01, 98	Al-Quds Al-Arabi	UBL	"Bin Ladin Congratulates Pakistan on Its Possession of Nuclear Weapons"	[170]
Jun 15, 98	The News (Islamabad)	UBL	"'In the Way of Allah'— Interview with UBL"	[171]
Aug 21, 98	AFP (Hong Kong Branch) + The News (Islamabad— Peshawar)	UBL	"Bin Ladin Calls for 'Jihad' against Jews, Americans"	[172]
Aug 23, 98	Al-Quds Al-Arabi/ Abd-al Bari Atwan	UBL	"The Battle Has Not Yet Started, We Will Reply to Clinton in Deeds"	[173]
Sep 02, 98	The Nation (Islamabad)	UBL	"Bin Ladin Praises Pakistanis for Love of Islam"	[174]
Sep 12, 98	Al-Akhbar, Pakistani newspaper in Urdu + Bodansky (1999)	UBL	"Letter to Anti-US Islamist Conference in Islamabad"	[126]
Nov 18, 98	Jang (Rawalpindi)	UBL	"Bin Ladin: Expel Jews, Christians from Holy Places"	[175]

(Continued)

Date released	Distributor	AQ rep.	Description/title	[ID]
Dec 24, 98	Afghan Islamic Press through AFP (Hong Kong)	UBL	"Bin Ladin Denies Role in Bombings of US Missions"	[176]
Jan 06, 99	The News (Islamabad)/ Rahimullah Yusufzai	UBL	"Taliban Let Bin Ladin Break His Silence"	[177]
Jan 11, 99	Time Magazine	UBL	"Wrath of God; Usama Bin Ladin Lashes Out against the West"	[178]
Jan 13, 99	CBS	UBL	"Accused Terrorist Leader Usama bin Ladin Declares War on All Americans"	[180]
Jan 14, 99	Minbar al-Tawhid wa'l-Jihad	AAZ	"Muslim Egypt between the Whips of the Torturers and the Administration of Traitors"	[116]
Feb 01, 99	Esquire Magazine/ John Miller + ABC News	UBL	"Esquire Interview with Bin Ladin"; see also "President Bush on Terrorist Attacks; Interview with Usama Bin Ladin from 1998" (ABC News, Sep 18, 2001)	[179]
Feb 20, 99	Pakistani newspaper (Islamabad, Urdu)	UBL	"May 1998 Interview with Bin Ladin Reported"	[182]
Apr 19, 99	Al-Sharq al-Awsat	AAZ	"Letter to Abu Yasir"	[123]

(*Continued*)

Date released	Distributor	AQ rep.	Description/title	[ID]
Jun 08, 99	Wahdat (Peshawar)	UBL	"Usama Bin Ladin Pens Letter in Support of Kashmir Jihad"	[183]
Jun 10, 99	Al Jazeera	UBL	"Usama Bin Ladin, the Destruction of the Base"	[184]
Jul 25, 99	Jang (Rawalpindi)	UBL	"Bin Ladin Calls on Muslims to Declare Jihad against US"	[185]
Sep 12, 99	Khabrain (Islamabad)	UBL	"UBL Orders Mujahidin to Shoot US Commandos 'on Sight'"	[186]
Jan 09, 00	Daily Pakistan (Islamabad)	UBL	"Usama Bin Ladin Denounces US-Sponsored 'World Order'"	[187]
May 02, 00	Daily Pakistan (Islamabad)	UBL	"UBL Sees Holy War in 'Every Street' of US"	[188]
May 22, 00	Ummah.net + Al-Jihaad newsletter of Supporters of Shari'ah	UBL	"Usama Speaks on Hijrah and the Islamic State?"	[189]
Jun 26, 00	Pakistan Observer (Islamabad)	UBL	"Usama Bin Ladin Renews Call For Jihad"	[190]
Sep 21, 00	Al Jazeera	UBL & AAZ	"Bin Ladin, Others Pledge 'Jihad' to Release Prisoners in US, Saudi Jails"	[191]
Nov 13, 00	al-Ra'i al-'Amm, Kuwaiti newspaper	UBL	"Short Telephone Interview with Kuwaiti Newspaper"	[124]

(Continued)

Date released	Distributor	AQ rep.	Description/title	[ID]
Jan 07, 01	Nawa-i-Waqt (Rawalpindi)	UBL	"Daily Prints Usama Bin Ladin 'Letter' Calling for Global Islamic State" (FBIS title)	[192]
Mar 03, 01	Ausaf (Islamabad)	UBL	"Ausaf Receives Bin Ladin's Poem on Resolve to Continue Jihad"	[193]
Mar 07, 01	Al Jazeera	UBL	"Bin Laden Poem on USS Cole Attack"	[194]
Apr 01, 01	N/A	UBL	"Letter from Usama Bin Laden to the Scholars of Deyubende in Peshawar in Pakistan"	[120]
Apr 03, 01	The Dawn (Karachi)	UBL	"Usama Regrets Curbs by Taliban"	[195]
Apr 10, 01	The Nation (Lahore Edition)	UBL	"Usama Urges Muslims to help Afghans, Wage Jihad"	[196]
May 07, 01	The News (Islamabad)	UBL	"Usama Urges Ummah to Continue Jihad"	[197]
May 17, 01	Islamabad	UBL	"If Taleban Allow, I Can Make US Life Miserable: Usama"	[198]
May 27, 01	Al-Arab Al-Alamiyah (London)	UBL	"Bin Ladin Sends Voice Message to Palestinian People: 'We Will Not Let You Down!'"	[199]
Sep 16, 01	Afghan Islamic Press Agency	UBL	"Afghanistan: Bin Ladin Denies Involvement in Terrorist Attacks in US" (FBIS title)	[200]

(Continued)

Date released	Distributor	AQ rep.	Description/title	[ID]
Sep 21, 01	Daily News—New York	UBL	"BIN LADIN: FROM RICH KID TO TERRORIST RINGLEADER Sheds His Fancy Clothes to Hide in Afghani Hills"	[181]
Sep 24, 01	Al Jazeera	UBL	"Text of Bin Ladin's Letter to the Pakistani People 24 Sep"	[201]
Sep 28, 01	Ummat (Karachi)	UBL	"'The US Should Search Attackers within Itself'—Exclusive Interview with Usama bin Ladin"	[202]
Oct 10, 01	Al Jazeera & Jihad Online News Network (and others)	UBL	"Tayseer Allouni Interviews bin Ladin in Afghanistan"	[130]
Nov 03, 01	Al Jazeera	UBL	"Bin Laden Condemns the UN"	[77]
Nov 07, 01	Al Jazeera	UBL	"Al-Jazirah Carries Bin Ladin's Address on US Strikes" (FBIS title)	[203]
Nov 10, 01	The Dawn, Pakistani newspaper	UBL	"Osama Claims He Has Nukes: If US Uses N-arms It Will Get Same Response"—Interview with Hamid Mir	[125]
Dec 02, 01	Al-Sharq al-Awsat	AAZ	"Knights under the Prophet's Banner: Mediations on the Jihadist Movement"	[119]

(Continued)

Date released	Distributor	AQ rep.	Description/title	[ID]
Dec 13, 01	Al Jazeera	UBL	"The Facts of the Conflict between Us and America"	[129]
Feb 01, 02	CNN (and Al Jazeera)	UBL	"Al-Jazirah TV Website Reports on 'Row' with CNN over Bin Ladin's Tape" (FBIS title)	[204]
Mar 28, 02	Al-Quds Al-Arabi + See also www.jihad.net	UBL	"Usama Bin Ladin: Prince Abdallah's Initiative Is High Treason"	[205]
Apr 17, 02	MBC Television (London)	UBL [and other AQ]	"MBC TV Carries Video of Bin Ladin, Aides Supporting 911 Attacks" (FBIS title)	[206]
Apr 18, 02	Al Jazeera + As-Sahab	UBL + AAZ	"The Wills of the Martyrs of the New York and Washington Battles: The Will of the Martyr Ibn ul Jarah Al-Ghamidee Ahmed al-Haznawi"	[207]
Apr 19, 02	As-Sahab	UBL, others	"'The Wills of the Martyrs of the New York and Washington Battles: The Will of the Martyr Abdulaziz Alomari' (Abu al-Abbas al-Janoobi) a.k.a. 19 Martyrs (part 1)"	[108]
May 19, 02	The Times (London) + AFP Paris	UBL	"Bin Ladin Film Vows Revenge on the UK" + "British-Based Islamic News Agency Receives Encrypted Bin Ladin Video"	[209]

(Continued)

Date released	Distributor	AQ rep.	Description/title	[ID]
Jun 01, 02	N/A	UBL [purported, or close affiliation]	"Al-Qaeda's Declaration in Response to the Saudi Ulema: It's Best You Prostrate Yourselves in Secret"	[43]
Jun 26, 02	Al-Sharq al-Awsat	UBL	"A Site Close to Al-Qaedah Posts a Poem by Bin Ladin in Which He Responds to His Son Hamzah, Who Inquires about the Future"	[210]
Sep 01, 02	As-Sahab	AAZ	"The Interview of Dr Ayman al-Zawahiri"	[22]
Oct 06, 02	Al Jazeera	UBL	"A Message Addressed to the American People"	[75]
Oct 14, 02	Al-Qal'ah	UBL	"Statement from Shaykh Usama Bin Ladin, May God Protect Him, and Al-Qaeda Organization"	[211]
Oct 26, 02	Waaqiah	UBL	"Letter from Usama Bin Muhammad Bin Ladin to the American People"	[212]
Oct 27, 02	Al-Majallah (London)	UBL	"Al-Majallah Obtains Bin Ladin's Will: It Bears His Signature in His Own Hand and Is Dated Ramadan 1422 Hegira, Corresponding to December 14, 2001 ..."	[213]

(*Continued*)

Date released	Distributor	AQ rep.	Description/title	[ID]
Nov 12, 02	Al Jazeera	UBL	"Osama bin Laden Hails Recent Operations in Bali, Moscow, Jordan"	[76]
Nov 21, 02	Alneda (Internet)	UBL	"Statement from Abdallah Usama Bin Ladin to the Peoples of Countries Allied to Tyrannical US Government"	[214]
Nov 28, 02	Al-Quds Al-Arabi	UBL	"Bin Ladin in a Special Message to the 'People of the Peninsula': Take Up Arms to Defend Your Honor. Warned of 'Critical Days and All-out War'"	[215]
Dec 30, 02	N/A	AAZ	"Al Walaa wa al Baraa" '(Loyalty and Enmity: An Inherited Doctrine and a Lost Reality' (Ibrahim's translation), "Loyalty and Separation: Changing an Article of Faith and Losing Sight of Reality" (Kepel & Milelli)	[45]
Jan 19, 03	Al-Sharq al-Awsat	UBL	"Islamic Action between Causes of Consensus and Advocates of Disagreement"	[216]

(*Continued*)

Date released	Distributor	AQ rep.	Description/title	[ID]
Feb 01, 03	unknown	UBL	On the obligation of jihad for everyone, the weak foundations of America, the plot to annex Saudi Arabia and establish a Jewish superstate	[78]
Feb 11, 03	Al Jazeera	UBL	"A Message to Our Brothers in Iraq"	[79]
Apr 09, 03	Ausaf (Islamabad)	UBL	"Usama Bin Ladin Urges Muslims to Launch Suicide Attacks against US"	[217]
May 18, 03	Le Matin (Algiers) + Khilafa News (Algeria)	UBL	"Riyadh, Casablanca Attacks" (FBIS title)	[218]
May 21, 03	Al Jazeera + BBC	AAZ	Attack on Arab support for US war in Iraq	[54]
May 29, 03	Movement for Islamic Reform website (London)	UBL	"Very Urgent: Shaykh Bin Ladin and the Mujahidin Threaten Terrible Response to Two Shaykhs' Death"	[219]
Jul 11, 03	Ilaf news	UBL	"'Ilaf' Learns from Its Own Sources in Jeddah: Usama Bin Ladin to His Mother through an Intermediary: I Did Not Carry Out Terrorist Actions against Saudi Arabia"	[220]
Aug 03, 03	Al-Arabiya	AAZ	Audiotape about Guantanamo prisoners	[55]

(Continued)

Date released	Distributor	AQ rep.	Description/title	[ID]
Sep 10, 03	Al Jazeera	UBL & AAZ	"Al-Jazirah Airs Bin Ladin, Al-Zawahiri Tape on Anniversary of 11 Sep Attacks"	[110]
Sep 28, 03	Al Jazeera + Al-Arabiya + BBC	AAZ	"Message to Muslims in Pakistan and Afghanistan"	[56]
Oct 18, 03	Al Jazeera	UBL	"Second Letter to the Muslims of Iraq"	[98]
Nov 16, 03	Al-Quds Al-Arabi + Al Jazeera	UBL	"Al-Jazirah TV: Al-Qaeda Claims Responsibility for Istanbul Bombings"	[221]
Dec 19, 03	Al Jazeera + BBC	AAZ	"Audiotape Recognizing the Two Year Anniversary of the Battle of Tora Bora"	[57]
Jan 04, 04	Al Jazeera, Observer	UBL	"Bin Ladin Warns of 'Grand Plots' against Arabs, Criticizes Gulf Rulers … 'Resist the New Rome'"	[111]
Feb 24, 04	Al Jazeera + Al-Arabiya	AAZ	Zawahiri on the state of the union speech and the French headscarf ban	[58]
Mar 25, 04	Al Jazeera	AAZ	Audiotape calling for Musharraf overthrow	[59]
Apr 14, 04	Audiotape delivered to media	UBL	Offer of peace treaty to Europeans	[52]
Apr 15, 04	Al Jazeera + Al-Arabiya	UBL	Peace offering to Europeans	[80]
May 06, 04	Al Jazeera	UBL	"People of Iraq"	[82]

(Continued)

Date released	Distributor	AQ rep.	Description/title	[ID]
Oct 29, 04	As-Sahab	UBL	Threat to the United States	[31]
Oct 30, 04	As-Sahab	UBL	"Message to Americans. On 9/11, How the Idea (Allegedly) Was Formed, and the Policies of the Two Presidents Bush"	[83]
Dec 16, 04	unknown	UBL	Message concerning Saudi Arabia	[84]
Dec 27, 04	As-Sahab	UBL	To the people of Iraq Muslims. On the Allawi regime, elections	[86]
Feb 11, 05	Jihadunspun. com	AAZ	"The Freeing of Humanity and Homelands under the Banner of the Quran"	[109]
May 25, 05	As-Sahab	AAZ	"In Condolence of the Two Martyred Leaders of the Islamic State of Iraq"	[222]
Jun 17, 05	As-Sahab	AAZ	On the need to rid the Muslim world of Crusaders and their supporters, implement shariah. Need to unite Iraqis	[[72]
Aug 04, 05	Al Jazeera	AAZ	Interview with Ayman al-Zawahiri aired on Al Jazeera	128]
Nov 15, 05	As-Sahab	AAZ	"Wills of the Knights of the London Raid"	[53]

(Continued)

Date released	Distributor	AQ rep.	Description/title	[ID]
Dec 06, 05	As-Sahab	AAZ	"The Victory of the Islamic Religion in Iraq"	[26]
Dec 07, 05	As-Sahab	AAZ	First interview with Ayman al-Zawahiri	[49]
Dec 10, 05	As-Sahab	AAZ	"Obstacles to Jihad"	[25]
Jan 19, 06	Al Jazeera	UBL	Bin Laden truce offer to the Americans	[50]
Jan 20, 06	As-Sahab	AAZ	Zawahiri presents a poem from Maulawi Muhibbullah al-Kandahari	[29]
Jan 21, 06	As-Sahab	AAZ	"Bajawr Massacre and the Lies of the Crusaders"—Response to attempted attack on Zawahiri's location in the FATA (the village of Damdula, in Bajuar), which killed 18 people	[51]
Mar 04, 06	As-Sahab	AAZ	"The Alternative Is Da'wa and Jihad"	[73]
Apr 12, 06	As-Sahab	AAZ	"Four Years since the Battle of Tora Bora—From Tora Bora to Iraq"	[238]
Apr 23, 06	As-Sahab	UBL	"Oh People of Islam"	[90]
Apr 28, 06	As-Sahab	AAZ	"Letter to the People of Pakistan"	[81]
May 23, 06	As Sahab	UBL	"A Testimony to the Truth"	[91]
Jun 09, 06	As-Sahab	AAZ	"Support for Palestinians"	[85]

(Continued)

Date released	Distributor	AQ rep.	Description/title	[ID]
Jun 21, 06	As-Sahab	AAZ	"American Crimes in Kabul"	[87]
Jun 24, 06	As-Sahab	AAZ	Lamentation of Abu Musab Al-Zarqawi— "Elegizing the Ummah's Martyr and Emir of the Martyrs Abu Musab al-Zarqawi, May Allah Have Mercy on Him"	[32]
Jun 27, 06	As-Sahab	AAZ	"The Zionist Crusader's Aggression on Gaza and Lebanon"	[88]
Jun 29, 06	As-Sahab	UBL	"Elegizing the Ummah's Martyr and Emir of the Martyrs, Abu Musab al-Zarqawi"	[92]
Jul 01, 06	As-Sahab	UBL	"To the Ummah in General and to the Mujahideen in Iraq and Somalia in Particular"	[93]
Sep 02, 06	As-Sahab	AAZ + Gadahn/ Amriki	"An Invitation to Islam"	[33]
Sep 11, 06	As-Sahab	AAZ	"Hot Issues with Shaykh Ayman Al-Zawahiri"	[21]
Sep 29, 06	As-Sahab	AAZ	"Bush, the Vatican's Pope, Darfur and the Crusaders"	[89]
Dec 22, 06	As-Sahab	AAZ	"Realities of the Conflict between Islam and Unbelief"	[94]

(Continued)

Date released	Distributor	AQ rep.	Description/title	[ID]
Dec 30, 06	As-Sahab	AAZ	"Congratulations on the Eid to the Ummah of Tawhid"	[95]
Jan 05, 07	As-Sahab	AAZ	"Rise and Support Our Brothers in Somalia"	[96]
Jan 22, 07	As-Sahab	AAZ	"The Correct Equation"	[28]
Feb 13, 07	As-Sahab	AAZ	"Lessons, Examples and Great Events in the Year 1427"	[97]
Mar 11, 07	As-Sahab	AAZ	"Palestine Is the Concern of All Muslims"	[18]
May 05, 07	As-Sahab	AAZ	"The Empire of Evil Is About to End, and a New Dawn Is About to Break over Mankind"	[23]
May 23, 07	As-Sahab	AAZ	Announces the death of Taliban leader Mullah Dadullah Akhund	[30]
Jun 25, 07	As-Sahab	AAZ	"Forty Years since the Fall of Jerusalem"	[101]
Jul 04, 07	As-Sahab	AAZ	"The Advice of One Concerned"	[102]
Jul 10, 07	As-Sahab	AAZ	"Malicious Britain and Its Indian Slaves"	[103]
Jul 11, 07	As-Sahab	AAZ	"The Aggression against Lal Masjid"	[104]
Sep 07, 07	As-Sahab	UBL	"The Solution: A Message from Shaykh Osama bin Laden to the American People"	[10]

(Continued)

Date released	Distributor	AQ rep.	Description/title	[ID]
Sep 20, 07	As-Sahab	UBL	"Come to Jihad: a Speech to the People of Pakistan"	[14]
Oct 22, 07	As-Sahab	UBL	"Message to the People of Iraq"	[16]
Nov 30, 07	As-Sahab	UBL	"Message to the People of Europe"	[9]
Dec 14, 07	As-Sahab	AAZ	"Annapolis—The Betrayal"	[12]
Dec 16, 07	As-Sahab	AAZ	"A Review of Events"—As Sahab publishes fourth interview with Zawahiri	[13]
Dec 29, 07	As-Sahab	UBL	"The Way to Frustrate the Conspiracies"	[27]
Jan 01, 08	Advertised by As-Sahab	AAZ	"Exoneration: A Letter Exonerating the Ummah of the Pen and the Sword from the Unjust Allegation of Feebleness and Weakness" or "Exoneration: A Treatise on the Exoneration of the Nation of the Pen and Sword of the Denigrating Charge of Being Irresolute"	[20]
Feb 27, 08	As-Sahab	AAZ	"An Elegy to the Martyred Commander Abu al-Layth al-Libi"	[19]
Mar 06, 08	N/A	AAZ	Letter to Abu Umar al-Baghdadi of the Islamic State of Iraq	[44]

(Continued)

Date released	Distributor	AQ rep.	Description/title	[ID]
Mar 19, 08	As-Sahab	UBL	"May Our Mothers Be Bereaved of Us if We Fail to Help Our Prophet. (Peace Be upon Him)"	[11]
Mar 20, 08	As-Sahab	UBL	"A Way for the Salvation of Palestine"	[6]
Mar 23, 08	As-Sahab	AAZ	"A Call to Help Our People in Gaza"	[17]
Apr 02, 08	As-Sahab	AAZ	"The Open Meeting with Sheikh Ayman al-Zawahiri, Part One"	[105]
Apr 17, 08	As-Sahab	AAZ	"Shaykh Ayman Al-Zawahiri—On the Fifth Anniversary of the Invasion and Torture of Iraq"	[7]
Apr 21, 08	As-Sahab	AAZ	"The Open Meeting with Sheikh Ayman al-Zawahiri, Part Two"	[107]
May 16, 08	As-Sahab	UBL	"Reasons of the Struggle on the Occasion of the 60th Anniversary of the Founding of the Occupying State of Israel"	[8]
May 18, 08	As-Sahab	UBL	"A Message to the Muslim Nation"	[24]
Jun 04, 08	As-Sahab	AAZ	"On the Anniversary of the Naksa … Break the Siege of Gaza"	[15]

(Continued)

Date released	Distributor	AQ rep.	Description/title	[ID]
Aug 10, 08	As-Sahab	AAZ	"A Message from Shaikh Ayman al-Zawahiri to Pakistan Army and the People of Pakistan"	[41]
Aug 24, 08	As-Sahab	AAZ	"In Lamentation of a Group of Heroes"	[74]
Nov 19, 08	As-Sahab	AAZ	"The Exit of Bush and Arrival of Obama"	[100]
Nov 21, 08	As-Sahab	AAZ	"Al-Azhar: The Lion's Den: Interview with Shaykh Ayman al-Zawahiri"	[237]
Dec 01, 08	As-Sahab	AAZ	"The Death of Our Heroes and Betrayal of Our Rulers"	[106]
Jan 06, 09	Global Islamic Media Front—As-Sahab	AAZ	"The Massacre of Gaza and the Siege of the Traitors"	[121]
Jan 14, 09	As-Sahab, Jihad Media Battalion (translation)	UBL	"Call for Jihad to Stop the Gaza Assault"	[122]
Feb 03, 09	As-Sahab/GIMF	AAZ	"The Sacrifices of Gaza ... and Conspiracies"	[131]
Feb 22, 09	As-Sahab	AAZ	"From Kabul to Mogadishu"	[132]
Mar 14, 09	As-Sahab	UBL	"Practical Steps to Liberate Palestine"	[133]
Mar 19, 09	As-Sahab	UBL	"Fight On, O' Champions of Somalia"	[134]
Mar 24, 09	As-Sahab	AAZ	"The Crusade Sets Its Sights on the Sudan"	[135]

(*Continued*)

Date released	Distributor	AQ rep.	Description/title	[ID]
Apr 20, 09	As-Sahab + Global Islamic Media Front	AAZ	"Six Years since the Invasion of Iraq and Thirty Years since the Signing of the Israeli Peace Accords"	[136]
Jun 02, 09	As-Sahab	AAZ	"'The Executioner', Egypt and the American Puppets Welcome Obama"	[137]
Jul 12, 09	As-Sahab	UBL	"And Fight with Them Until There Is No More Persecution and Religion Should Be Only for Allah: A Message to the People of Pakistan"	[138]
Jul 15, 09	As-Sahab	AAZ	"My Muslim Brothers and Sisters in Pakistan"	[139]
Aug 04, 09	As-Sahab	AAZ	"The Realities of Jihad and Fallacy of Hypocrisy"	[140]
Aug 26, 09	As-Sahab	AAZ	"The Path of Doom"	[142]
Sep 13, 09	As-Sahab + Global Islamic Media Front	UBL	"A Statement to the American People"	[144]
Sep 25, 09	As-Sahab	UBL	"A Message to the European People"	[143]
Sep 28, 09	As-Sahab	AAZ	"Shaykh Dr. Ayman al-Zawahiri: Eulogy for the Role Model of the Youth—The Commander and Shahid Baitullah [Mehsud]"	[147]

(Continued)

Date released	Distributor	AQ rep.	Description/title	[ID]
Oct 04, 09	As-Sahab	AAZ	"Eulogy for Ibn Sheikh Al Libi by Sheikh Ayman Al Zawahiri"	[145]
Dec 14, 09	As-Sahab	AAZ	"The (Palestinian) National Unity: A Worshipped Idol"	[146]
Dec 16, 09	As-Sahab— translated by Abu Musa Abdussalam	AAZ	"The Morning and the Lamp to Be Extinguished: An Analysis of the Claim That the Constitution of Pakistan Is Islamic"	[141]
Feb 16, 10	Al Jazeera	UBL	"From Osama to Obama"	[148]
Feb 19, 10	As-Sahab	UBL	"The Way to Save the Earth"	[149]
Jul 19, 10	As-Sahab	AAZ	"Al-Quds Will Not Be Converted to Judaism"	[223]
Jul 27, 10	As-Sahab	AAZ	"In Condolence of Sheikh Mustafa Abu al-Yazid R.A"	[224]
Aug 15, 10	As-Sahab/ Ansarnet English	AAZ	"Message to the People of Turkey"	[225]
Sep 15, 10	As-Sahab	AAZ	"A Victorious Ummah, A Broken Crusade"	[226]
Oct 01, 10	As-Sahab	UBL	"Some Points regarding the Method of Relief Work"	[227]
Oct 13, 10	As-Sahab	UBL	"Help Your Brothers in Pakistan"	[228]

(Continued)

Date released	Distributor	AQ rep.	Description/title	[ID]
Nov 04, 10	As-Sahab/Global Islamic Media Front	AAZ	"Who Is Going to Support Aafia Sidique?"	[229]
Nov 07, 10	As-Sahab/ Ansar Al-Mujahideen English Forum (Ansarnet)	UBL	"Message from Shaykh Usama bin Ladin to the People of France"	[230]
Jan 22, 11	As-Sahab	UBL	"From al-Sheikh Osama bin Mohammed bin laden To ... the French People"	[231]
Feb 19, 11	As-Sahab/Global Islamic Media Front	AAZ	"A Message of Hope and Glad Tidings to Our People in Egypt (1) 'By Sheikh Ayman Al-Zawahri H.A.'"	[232]
Feb 24, 11	As-Sahab/Global Islamic Media Front	AAZ	"A Message of Hope and Glad Tidings to Our People in Egypt (2) 'By Sheikh Ayman Al-Zawahri H.A.'"	[233]
Feb 27, 11	As-Sahab/Global Islamic Media Front	AAZ	"A Message of Hope and Glad Tidings to Our People in Egypt (3) 'By Sheikh Ayman Al-Zawahri H.A.'"	[234]
Mar 04, 11	As-Sahab/Global Islamic Media Front	AAZ	"A Message of Hope and Glad Tidings to Our People in Egypt (4) 'By Sheikh Ayman Al-Zawahri H.A.'"	[235]

(Continued)

Date released	Distributor	AQ rep.	Description/title	[ID]
Apr 14, 11	As-Sahab/Global Islamic Media Front	AAZ	"A Message of Hope and Glad Tidings to Our Fellow Muslims in Egypt (5) 'By Sheikh Ayman Al Zawahiri (H.A.)'"	[236]
May 19, 11	Global Islamic Media Front (GIMF)	UBL	"The Speech by the Martyr of Islam (as We Consider Him) the Mujahid Sheikh Usama Bin Laden— May Allah Have Mercy on Him— To His Muslim Ummah"	[240]
May 21, 11	As-Sahab	AAZ	"Message of Hope and Glad Tidings to Our People in Egypt, Episode 6"	[267]
Jun 08, 11	As-Sahab + GIMF	AAZ	"The Noble Knight Dismounted"	[239]
Jul 28, 11	As-Sahab + GIMF	AAZ	"Glory of the East...the First Being Damascus— Sheikh Mujaahid Ayman Al-Zawahiri (Hafidhahullaah)"	[241]
Aug 09, 11	As-Sahab	AAZ	"A Message of Hope and Glad tidings to our people in Egypt (7) (The Victory of Allah Support You) 'By Sheikh Ayman Al-Zawahri H.A.'"	[242]
Aug 15, 11	As-Sahab	AAZ	"Do Not Become Weak Nor Grieve" or "Be Neither Weakened or Saddened"	[243]

(Continued)

Date released	Distributor	AQ rep.	Description/title	[ID]
Dec 01, 11	As-Sahab + Al-Masadh Media	AAZ	"Message of Hope and Glad Tidings to Our People in Egypt Part 8: And What about the American Hostage Warren Weinstein"	[244]
Feb 09, 12	As-Sahab— GIMF	AAZ	"Glad Tidings by the Two Sheikhs Abu al-Zubayr and Ayman al-Zawahiri/Bay'ah— Shaykh Abu al Zubayr [Ameer of Harakat Shabaab al Mujahideen] and Ameer Shaykh Ayman Al Zawahiri (May Allah Protect Them)"	[258]
Feb 12, 12	As-Sahab, Al-Fajr, GIMF	AAZ	"Move Forward, O Lions of Sham"	[247]
Feb 29, 12	As-Sahab, GIMF	AAZ	"A Message of Hope and Glad Tidings to Our People in Egypt Part 9: Why Did We Rebel against Him?"	[245]
May 05, 12	As-Sahab, Al-Fajr, GIMF	AAZ	"The Burning of the Qur'an in Kabul"	[253]
May 15, 12	As-Sahab	AAZ	"Yemen: Between a Fugitive Puppet and His New Replacement"	[248]
May 18, 12	As-Sahab, Fursan Al-Balagh Media	AAZ	"To Our People in the Place of the Revelation and the Cradle of Islam"	[246]
June 03, 12	As-Sahab, GIMF	AAZ	"Days with the Imam" (1)	[252]

(Continued)

Date released	Distributor	AQ rep.	Description/title	[ID]
June 10, 12	As-Sahab	AAZ	"To the People of Tunisia: O' People of Tunisia, Support Your Shariah"	[249]
Jul 17, 12	As-Sahab	AAZ	"A Message of Hope and Glad Tidings to Our Fellow Muslims in Egypt (10) 'By Sheikh Ayman Al Zawahiri H.A.'"	[263]
Sep 11, 12	As-Sahab, Al-Fajr	AAZ	"The Lion of Knowledge and Jihaad: Martyrdom of Al-Sheikh Abu Yahya Al-Leebi (Rahimahullaah): Eulogy by Al-Ameer Al-Sheikh Ayman Al-Zawahiri"	[250]
Sep 13, 12	As-Sahab, Al-Fajr	AAZ	"The Rising Sun of Victory on the Triumphant Ummah over the Vanquished Crusaders"	[254]
Sep 26, 12	As-Sahab, Al-Fajr	AAZ	"Days with the Imam" (2)	[255]
Oct 12, 12	As-Sahab, Al-Fajr	AAZ	"In Support of the Messenger, May the Peace and Blessings of God Be upon Him"	[256]
Nov 06, 12	As-Sahab, Al-Fajr	AAZ	"The Crusader Invasion of Somalia: a New Battle from the Battles of Jihad against the Crusaders"	[262]
Nov 13, 12	As-Sahab	AAZ	"Document of the Support of Islam"	[257]

(Continued)

Date released	Distributor	AQ rep.	Description/title	[ID]
Nov 15, 12	As-Sahab, Al-Fajr	AAZ	"Days with the Imam" (3)	[251]
Nov 29, 12	As-Sahab, Al-Fajr	AAZ	"Eulogy of the Leader Shaykh Hisham al-Sa'idni (Abu Walid al-Maqdisi)"	[261]
Apr 07, 13	As-Sahab, Al-Fajr	AAZ	"Unifying the Word toward the Word of Monotheism"	[260]
Jun 06, 13	As-Sahab, Al-Fajr	AAZ	"Sixty-Five Years since the Establishment of the State of Occupation: Israel"	[259]
Jul 31, 13	As-Sahab/Al-Fajr	AAZ	"Forty-Six Years since the Year of al-Naksah"	[264]
Aug 03, 13	As-Sahab/Al-Fajr	AAZ	"The Idol of the Democratic State"	[265]
Sep 14, 13	As-Sahab	AAZ	"General Guidelines for Jihad"	[266]

Bibliography

Secondary sources

Aaron, D. (2008) *In Their Own Words: Voices of Jihad.* RAND Corporation, Santa Monica, CA.

Aldis, A. and G. P. Herd (eds) (2007) *The Ideological War on Terror: Worldwide Strategies for Counter-Terrorism.* Routledge, London.

Al-Rasheed, M. (2009) "The Local and the Global in Salafism," in Meijer, R. (ed.), pp. 301–321, *Global Salafism: Islam's New Religious Movement.* Hurst, London.

Al-Zayyat, M. (2004) *The Road to Al-Qaeda: The Story of Bin Laden's Right-Hand Man.* Pluto Press, London, UK.

Anonymous (Scheuer, M.) (2002) *Through Our Enemies' Eyes: Osama bin Laden, Radical Islam, and the Future of America.* Brassey's Inc, Washington, DC.

Arab, S., E. Reid, and H. Chen (2009) "Multimedia Content Coding and Analysis: Unraveling the Content of Jihadi Extremist Groups' Videos," in *Studies in Conflict and Terrorism* (vol. 31, iss. 7, pp. 605–626).

Arquilla, J., D. Ronfeldt, and M. Zanini (2002) "Networks, Netwar, and Information-Age Terrorism," in Howard, R. and Sawyer, R. (eds.), *Terrorism and Counter-Terrorism – Understanding the New Security Environment*, McGraw-Hill, New York.

Atassi, B. (2013) "Qaeda Chief Annuls Syrian-Iraqi Jihad Merger," in *Al-Jazeera*, available at http://www.aljazeera.com/news/middleeast/2013/06/2013699425657882.html (accessed August 2013).

Baker, R. W. (1997) "Invidious Comparisons: Realism, Postmodern Globalism, and Centrist Islamic Movements in Egypt," in Esposito, J. L. (ed.), pp. 115–135, *Political Islam: Revolution, Radicalism, or Reform?* Lynne Rienner Publishers, Boulder, CO.

Bakier, A. H. (2008) "Jihadi Website Advises Recruits on How to Join al-Qaeda," in *Jamestown Terrorism Focus* (vol. v, iss. 18, May 6).

Bale, J. M. (2009) "Jihadist Ideology and Strategy and the Possible Employment of WMD," in Ackerman, G. and Tamsett, J. (eds.), pp. 3–59, *Jihadists and Weapons of Mass Destruction*, CRC Press, Boca Raton, FL.

BBC (2013) "Syria Crisis: Al-Nusra Pledges Allegiance to Al-Qaeda" (April 10), available at http://www.bbc.co.uk/news/world-middle-east-22095099 (accessed April 2013).

Benford, R. D. (1997) "An Insider's Critique of the Social Movement Framing Perspective," in *Sociological Inquiry* (vol. 67, iss. 4, pp. 409–430, November).

———. and D. A. Snow (2000) "Framing Processes and Social Movements; An Overview and Assessment," in *Annual Review of Sociology* (vol. 26, pp. 611–639).

Bergen, P. (2006) *The Osama Bin Laden I Know: An Oral History of Al-Qaeda's Leader*. Free Press, New York.

———. (2007a) "Where You Bin? The Return of al Qaeda," in *New Republic* (vol. 236, iss. 5, January 29, pp. 16–16).

———. (2007b) "Afghanistan 2007: Problems, Opportunities and Possible Solutions", in *The House Committee on Foreign Affairs* (February 15), available at http://foreignaffairs.house.gov/110/ber021507.htm (accessed January 19, 2011).

———. (2011) *The Longest War: The Enduring Conflict between America and al-Qaeda*. Free Press, New York.

———. and P. Cruickshank (2008) "The Unraveling: The Jihadist Revolt against Bin Laden," in *New Republic* (Wednesday, June 11, pp. 16–21).

———. and P. Cruickshank (2012) "Revisiting the Early Al Qaeda: Updated Account of its Formative Years," in *Studies in Conflict and Terrorism* (vol. 35, iss. 1, pp. 1–36).

Berntzen, L. and S. Sandberg. "The Collective Nature of Lone Wolf Terrorism: Anders Behring Breivik and the Anti-Islamic Social Movement," in *Terrorism and Political Violence* (forthcoming, published online 05 February 2014 (pp. 1–21)).

Blanchard, C. (2006) "Al-Qaeda: Statements and Evolving Ideology," in *CRS Report for Congress* (January 26). Congressional Research Service, Washington, DC.

Borhek, J. T. and R. F. Curtis (1975) *A Sociology of Belief*. Wiley, New York.

Bowie, N. G. and A. P. Schmid (2011) "Databases on Terrorism," in Schmid, A. P. (ed.), pp. 294–341, *The Routledge Handbook of Terrorism Research*. Routledge, Abingdon.

Brachman, J. (2008) *Global Jihadism: Theory and Practice*. Routledge, London.

———., B. Fishman, and J. Felter (2008) *The Power of Truth: Questions for Ayman Al-Zawahiri* (April 21). Combating Terrorism Center, West Point, NY.

Brahimi, A. (2010) "Crushed in the Shadows: Why Al Qaeda Will Lose the War of Ideas," *Studies in Conflict & Terrorism* (vol. 33, iss. 2, pp. 93–110).

Brooke, S. (2010) "Strategic Fissures: The Near and Far Enemy Debate," in Moghadam, A. and Fishman, B. (eds), *Self-Inflicted Wounds: Debates and Divisions within Al-Qa'ida and Its Periphery*, Harmony Project (December 16). Combating Terrorism Center, West Point, NY.

Buechler, S. (1990) *Women's Movements in the United States*. Rutgers University Press, New Brunswick, NJ.

Burke, J. (2004a) *Al-Qaeda: The True Story of Radical Islam* (2nd edition). Penguin Books, London.

———. (2004b) "Think Again: Al Qaeda," in *Foreign Policy* (iss. 142, pp.18–26, May/June).

———. (2011) *The 9/11 Wars*. Allen Lane/Penguin Books, London.

———. (2013) "Why Al-Qaida Is a Spent Force," in *Guardian Weekly* (vol. 188, iss. 8, February 1–7).

Campbell, J. (1988) *The Power of Myth*. Doubleday, New York.

Carpenter, J. S., M. Levitt, S. Simon, and J. Zarate (2010) *Fighting the Ideological Battle: The Missing Link in U.S. Strategy to Counter Violent Extremism*. The Washington Institute for Near East Policy, Washington, DC.

Cetina, L. (2005) "Complex Global Microstructures: The New Terrorist Societies," in *Theory, Culture and Society* (vol. 22, iss. 5, pp. 213–234).

Cigar, N. (2008) *Al-Qaeda's Doctrine for Insurgency: Abd al-Aziz al-Muqrin's "A Practical Course for Guerrilla War."* Potomac Books, Dulles, VA.

Ciovacco, C. J. (2009) "The Contours of Al Qaeda's Media Strategy," in *Studies in Conflict and Terrorism* (vol. 32, iss. 10, pp. 853–875).

Combating Terrorism Center (2007) *Cracks in the Foundation: Leadership Schisms in Al-Qaeda from 1989–2006*, Harmony Project. Combating Terrorism Center, West Point, NY.

Converse, P. E. (1964) "The Nature of Belief Systems in Mass Publics," in Apter, D. (ed.), pp. 206–261, *Ideology and Discontent*, Free Press, New York.

Corman, S. R. and J. S. Schiefelbein (2006) "Communication and Media Strategy in the Jihadi War of Ideas," in Consortium for Strategic Communication, Arizona State University (eds.) *Report #0601 Consortium for Strategic Communication* (April 20). Arizona State University, Phoenix.

Cozzens, J. B. (2007) "Approaching al-Qaeda's Warfare: Function, Culture and Grand Strategy," in Ranstorp, M. (ed.), *Mapping Terrorism Research: State of the Art, Gaps and Future Direction.* Routledge, Abingdon.

Cragin, K. (2009) "Al Qaeda Confronts Hamas: Divisions in the Sunni Jihadist Movement and Its Implications for U.S. Policy," *Studies in Conflict and Terrorism* (vol. 32, iss. 7, pp. 576–590).

Crenshaw, M. (2000) "The Psychology of Terrorism: An Agenda for the 21st Century," in *Political Psychology* (vol. 21, iss. 2, pp. 405–420).

Cruickshank, P. (ed.) (2012) *Al Qaeda*. London, Routledge.

———. and M. A. Hage (2007) "Abu Musab Al Suri: Architect of the New Al Qaeda," in *Studies in Conflict and Terrorism* (vol. 30, iss. 1, pp. 1–14).

Cullison, A. (2004) "Inside Al Qaeda's Hard Drive," in *Atlantic Monthly* (vol. 294, iss. 2, September, pp. 63–65).

Danmarks Radio (2006) "Billede fra grisefestival i imamers mappe" (February 7), available at http://www.dr.dk/Nyheder/Indland/2006/02/07/234208.htm (accessed April 19, 2011).

Della Porta, D. (1995) *Social Movements, Political Violence, and the State: A Comparative Analysis of Italy and Germany.* Cambridge University Press, Cambridge.

———. (2001) "Left-Wing Terrorism in Italy," in Crenshaw, M. (ed.), *Terrorism in Context.* Pennsylvania State University Press, State College, PA.

The Economist (2008) "Special Report" (July 17), secured from.online archive.

———. (2009a) "Now, Kill His Dream" (May 7).

———. (2009b) "The Growing, and Mysterious, Irrelevance of al-Qaeda" (January 24), secured from.online archive.

Egner, M. (2009) "Social-Science Foundations for Strategic Communications," in Davis, P. and Cragin, K. (eds.), pp. 323–355, *Social-Science Foundations for Strategic Communications in the Global War on Terrorism.* RAND Corporation, Santa Monica, CA.

Eickelman, D. F. and J. Piscatori (1996) *Muslim Politics.* Princeton University Press, Princeton, NJ.

Elad-Altman, I. (2007) "The Sunni-Shi'a Conversion Controversy," in *Current Trends in Islamist Ideology* (vol. 5, pp. 1–11).

Esposito, J. L. (1984) *Islam and Politics*. Syracuse University Press, Syracuse, NY.
———. (2002) *Unholy War: Terror in the Name of Islam.*Oxford University Press, Oxford, UK.
Filiu, J. P. (2009) "The Brotherhood vs. Al-Qaeda: A Moment of Truth?," in *Current Trends in Islamist Ideology* (vol. 9, pp. 18–26).
Fisher, W. R. (1984) "Narration as a Human Communication Paradigm: The Case of Public Moral Argument," *Communication Monographs* (vol. 51, pp. 1–23).
Fradkin, H. (2008) "The History and Unwritten Future of Salafism," in *Current Trends in Islamist Ideology* (vol. 6, pp. 5–20).
———. (2009) "The Paradoxes of Shiism," in *Current Trends in Islamist Ideology* (vol. 8, pp. 5–26).
Gamson, W. A. (1992) "The Social Psychology of Collective Action," in Morris, A. D. and Mueller, C. M. (eds.), pp. 53–77. *Frontiers in Social Movement Theory.* Yale University Press, New Haven, CT.
———. (1995) "Constructing Social Protest," in Johnston, H. and Klandermans, B. (eds.), pp. 85–107, *Social Movements and Culture.* UCL Press, London.
———., B. Fireman, and S. Rytina (1982) *Encounters with Unjust Authority.* Dorsey Press, Homewood, IL.
Gardell, Mattias (2003) *Gods of the Blood: The Pagan Revival and White Separatism.* Duke University Press, Durham, NC.
Gerges, F. (2005) *The Far Enemy: Why Jihad Went Global.* Cambridge University Press, Cambridge.
———. (2011) *The Rise and Fall of Al-Qaeda.* Oxford University Press, Oxford.
Gerhards, J. and D. Rucht (1992) "Mesomobilization: Organizing and Framing in Two Protest Campaigns in West Germany," in *American Journal of Sociology* (vol. 98, iss. 3, pp. 555–595).
Goffman, E. (1974) *Frame Analysis: An Essay on the Organization of the Experience.* Harper Colophon, New York.
Gouldner, A. W. (1970) *The Coming Crisis in Western Sociology.* Basic Books, New York.
Greenberg, K. (ed.) (2005) *Al-Qaeda Now: Understanding Today's Terrorists.* Cambridge University Press, Cambridge.
Gregg, H. (2010) "Fighting the Jihad of the Pen: Countering Revolutionary Islam's Ideology," in *Terrorism and Political Violence* (vol. 22, iss. 2, pp. 292–314).
Gregory, S. (2007) "Al-Qaeda in Pakistan," *Brief Number* (vol. 5, March 1, pp. 1–7).
Gul, P. (2006) "Waziristan Accord Signed," *Dawn* (September 6), available at http://archives.dawn.com/2006/09/06/index.htm (accessed March 5, 2012).
Gusfield, J. (1981) "Social Movements and Social Change: Perspectives of Linearity and Fluidity," in Kriesberg, L. (ed.), pp. 317–339, *Research in Social Movements, Conflict and Change* (vol. 4). JAI Press, Greenwich, CT.
Hafez, M. (2010) "Tactics, *Takfir*, and Anti-Muslim Violence," in Moghadam, A. and Fishman, B. (eds.), pp. 19–45, *Self-Inflicted Wounds: Debates and Divisions within Al-Qa'ida and Its Periphery*, Harmony Project (December 16). Combating Terrorism Center, West Point, NY.
Hegghammer, T. (2006) "Global Jihadism after the Iraq War," in *Middle East Journal* (vol. 60, iss. 1, pp. 11–32, Winter).
———. (2009a) "The Ideological Hybridization of Jihadi Groups," in *Current Trends in Islamist Ideology* (vol. 9, pp. 26–46).

———. (2009b) "Jihadi-Salafis or Revolutionaries? On Religion and Politics in the Study of Militant Islamism," in Meijer, R. (ed.), pp.244–267, *Global Salafism: Islam's New Religious Movement*. Hurst, London.

———. (2010) "The Rise of Muslim Foreign Fighters: Islam and the Globalization of Jihad," in *International Security* (vol. 35, iss. 3, pp. 53–94, Winter 2010/2011).

Hellmich, C. (2008) "Creating the Ideology of Al Qaeda: From Hypocrites to Salafi-Jihadists," in *Studies in Conflict and Terrorism* (vol. 31, iss. 2, pp. 111–124).

———. (2011) *Al-Qaeda: From Global Network to Local Franchise*.Zed Books, London, UK.

Hoffman, B. (2006) *Inside Terrorism* (revised edition). Columbia University Press, New York.

———. (2007) "Challenges for the U.S. Special Operations Command Posed by the Global Terrorist Threat: Al Qaeda on the Run or on the March?," Written testimony submitted to The House Armed Services Subcommittee on Terrorism, Unconventional Threats and Capabilities, Washington, DC.

———. (2008) "The Myth of Grass-Roots Terrorism: Why Osama bin Laden Still Matters," in *Foreign Affairs* (vol. 87, pp. 133–138, May/June).

———. (2013) "Al-Qaeda's Uncertain Future," in *Studies in Conflict and Terrorism* (vol. 36, iss. 8, pp. 635–653).

———. and G. McCormick (2004) "Terrorism, Signaling, and Suicide Attack," in *Studies in Conflict and Terrorism* (vol. 27, iss. 4, pp. 243–281).

Holbrook, D. (2012) "Al-Qaeda's Response to the Arab Spring," in *Perspectives on Terrorism* (vol. 6, iss. 6, pp. 4–21).

Hopkins, N. (2012) "MI5 Warns Al-Qaeda Regaining UK Toehold after Arab Spring," in *Guardian* (June 25).

Horgan, J. (2004) "The Case for Firsthand Research," in Silke, A (ed.), pp. 30–57, *Research on Terrorism: Trends, Achievements and Failures*. Frank Cass, London.

———. (2005) *The Psychology of Terrorism*. Routledge, London.

———. (2009) *Walking Away from Terrorism: Accounts of Disengagement from Radical and Extremist Movements*. Routledge, London: page xx.

Hovland, C. I. and W. Weiss (1951) "The Influence of Source Credibility on Communication Effectiveness," *Public Opinion Quarterly* (vol. 50, pp. 635–650).

Ibrahim, R. (2007) *The Al Qaeda Reader*. Broadway Books, New York.

Jurgensmeyer, M. (2003) *Terror in the Mind of God: The Global Rise of Religious Violence* (3rd edition). University of California Press, Berkeley.

Kane, A. E. (1997) "Theorizing Meaning Construction in Social Movements: Symbolic Structures and Interpretations during the Irish Land War, 1879–1882," in *Sociological Theory* (vol. 15, iss. 3, pp. 249–276, November).

Kepel, G. (1984) *Muslim Extremism in Egypt: The Prophet and Pharaoh*. University of California Press, Berkeley.

———. (2004) *The War for Muslim Minds: Islam and the West*, translated by Pascale Ghazaleh. The Belknap Press of Harvard University Press, Cambridge, MA.

———. (2008a) "The Brotherhood in the Salafist Universe," *Current Trends in Islamist Ideology* (vol. 6, pp. 20–29).

———. (2008b) *Beyond Terror and Martyrdom: The Future of the Middle East*, translated by Pascale Ghazaleh. Harvard University Press, Cambridge, MA.

————. and J. P. Milelli, (eds) (2008) *Al Qaeda in Its Own Words*. Harvard University Press, Cambridge, MA.

Khan, I. (2005) "Waziristan Draft Accord Approved," in *Dawn* (February 2), available at http://archives.dawn.com/2005/02/02/top3.htm (accessed March 5, 2012).

Kimmage, D. (2008) "The Al-Qaeda Media Nexus: The Virtual Network behind the Global Message," in *RFE/RL Special Report* (March), Radio Free Europe.

Klandermans, B. (1984) "Mobilization and Participation: Social-Psychological Expansions of Resource Mobilization Theory," in *American Sociological Review* (vol. 49, pp. 583–600).

Lacroix, S. (2008) "Notes to Part III: Ayman Al-Zawahiri," in Kepel, G. and Milelli, J. P. (eds.), pp. 316–341, *Al Qaeda in Its Own Words*. Harvard University Press, Cambridge, MA.

Lahoud, N. (2005) *Political Thought in Islam: A Study in Intellectual Boundaries*. Routledge, Abingdon.

Lawrence, B. (ed.) (2005) *Messages to the World: The Statements of Osama bin Laden*. Verso Books, London.

Lia, B. (2007) *Architect of Global Jihad: The Life of Al-Qaeda Strategist Abu Mus'ab al-Suri*. Hurst, London.

————. (2008) "Dissidents in Al-Qaeda: Abu Mus'ab al-Suri's Critique of Bin Ladin and the Salafi-Jihadi Current," Lecture at Princeton University (December 3, 2007). Norwegian Defence Research Establishment (FFI), Oslo.

————. (2009) " 'Destructive Doctrinarians': Abu Mus'ab al-Suri's Critique of the Salafis in the Jihadi Current," in Meijer, R. (ed.), pp. 281–301, *Global Salafism: Islam's New Religious Movement*. Hurst, London.

Mann, M. (2005) *Incoherent Empire*. Verso Books, London, UK.

Mansfield, P. (2003) *A History of the Modern Middle East* (2nd edition). Penguin Books, London.

Mayntz, R. (2004) "Organizational Focus of Terrorism. Hierarchy, Network, or a Type Sui Generis," in *MPIfG Discussion Paper* (04/4). Max-Planck-Institut für Gesellschaftsforschung, Cologne.

McAllister, Bradley and Alex P. Schmid (2011) "Theories of Terrorism," in Schmid, Alex P. (ed.), pp. 201–272, *The Routledge Handbook of Terrorism Research*. Routledge, Abingdon.

McCants, W., J. Brachman, and J. Felter (2006) *Militant Ideology Atlas: Executive Report* (November). Combating Terrorism Center, West Point, NY.

Meijer, R. (ed.) (2009) "Introduction," in *To Global Salafism: Islam's New Religious Movement*. Hurst, London, pp. 1–33.

Mendenhall, R. (2010) "Al-Qaeda: Who, What, Why? Database Applications for the Al-Qaeda Statements Index," Senior thesis submitted to Haverford College (April 23), available at http://thesis.haverford.edu/dspace/handle/10066/5064 (accessed December 5, 2012).

Michot, Y. (2006) *Muslims under Non-Muslim Rule: Ibn Taymiyya on Fleeing from Sin; Kinds of Emigration; the Status of Mardin; Domain of Peace/War, Domain Composite; the Conditions for Challenging Power*. Interface Publications, Oxford.

Milward, H. B. and J. Raab (2003) "Dark Networks as Problems," in *Journal of Public Administrations and Theory* (vol. 13, iss. 4, pp. 413–439).

———. (2005) "Dark Networks as Problems Revisited: Adaptation and Transformation of Islamic Terror Organizations since 9/11," Paper presented at the 8th Public Management Research Conference at the School of Policy, Planning and Development at the University of Southern California (September 29–October 1, 2005), available at www.usc.edu/schools/sppd/private/documents/.../dark_networks.pdf (accessed January 30, 2011).

Mir, H., et al. (2005) "The Real Twin Towers: Al-Qaeda's Influence on Saudi Arabia and Pakistan," in Greenberg, K. (ed.), pp. 135–151, *Al-Qaeda Now: Understanding Today's Terrorists*. Cambridge University Press, Cambridge.

Mishal, S. and M. Rosenthal (2005) "Al Qaeda as a Dune Organization: Toward a Typology of Islamic Terrorist Organizations," in *Studies in Conflict and Terrorism* (vol. 28, iss. 4, pp. 275–293, July).

Moghadam, A. and B. Fishman (2010) "Chapter 1: Debates and Divisions within and around Al-Qa'ida," in Moghadam, A. and Fishman, B. (eds.), pp. 1–19, *Self-Inflicted Wounds: Debates and Divisions within Al-Qa'ida and Its Periphery*, Harmony Project (December 16). Combating Terrorism Center, West Point, NY.

Mohamedau, M. (2007) *Understanding Al-Qaeda: The Transformation of War*. Pluto Press, London, UK.

Munson, H. (2004) "Lifting the Veil: Understanding the Roots of Islamic Militancy," in *Harvard International Review* (Winter, vol. 25, iss. 4, pp. 20–23).

Neidhardt, F. and D. Rucht (1991) "The Analysis of Social Movements: The State of the Art and Some Perspectives for further Research," in Rucht, D. (ed.), pp. 421–464, *Research on Social Movements: The State of the Art in Western Europe and the USA*. Campus, Frankfurt.

Page, M., L. Challita, and A. Harris (2011) "Al Qaeda in the Arabian Peninsula: Framing Narratives and Prescriptions," in *Terrorism and Political Violence* (vol. 23, iss. 2, pp. 150–172).

Paz, R. (2009) "Debates within the Family: Jihadi-Salafi Debates on Strategy, *Takfir*, Extremism, Suicide Bombings and the Sense of the Apocalypse," in Meijer, R. (ed.), pp. 267–281, *Global Salafism: Islam's New Religious Movement*. Hurst, London.

Pennebaker, J. and C. Chung (2007) "Computerized Text Analysis of Al-Qaeda Transcripts," in Krippendorff, K. and Bock, M. (eds.), pp. 453–467, *A Content Analysis Reader*. Sage, Thousand Oaks, CA.

Pew Global Attitudes Project (2003) *Views of a Changing World* (June). Pew Research Center, Washington, DC.

———. (2011a) "Osama bin Laden Largely Discredited among Muslim Publics in Recent Years" (May 2), available at http://pewglobal.org/2011/05/02/osama-bin-laden-largely-discredited-among-muslim-publics-in-recent-years/ (accessed August 12, 2011).

———. (2011b) "Common Concerns over Islamic Extremism: Muslim-Western Tensions Persist" (July 2011). Pew Research Center.

Powell, W. (1990) "Neither Market Nor Hierarchy: Network Forms of Organization," in *Research in Organizational Behavior* (vol. 12, pp. 295–336).

Quiggin, T. (2009) "Understanding al-Qaeda's Ideology for Counter-Narrative Work," in *Perspectives on Terrorism* (vol. 3, iss. 2, pp. 18–24, August).

Rabasa, A., P. Chalk, K. Cragin, S. A. Daly, H. S. Gregg, T. W. Karasik, et al. (2006) *Beyond al-Qaeda: The Global Jihadist Movement* (Part 1). RAND Corporation, Santa Monica, CA.

Randal, J. (2005) *Osama: Making of a Terrorist*. I.B. Tauris, New York, NY.

Ranstorp, M. (ed.) (2007) "Introduction to," in *Mapping Terrorism Research: State of the Art, Gaps and Future Direction*. Routledge, Abingdon, pp. 1–29.

———. (2009) "Mapping Terrorism Studies after 9/11: An Academic Field of Old Problems and New Problems," in Jackson, R., Smyth, M. B. and Gunning, J. (eds.), pp. 13–34, *Critical Terrorism Studies: A New Research Agenda*, Routledge, Abingdon.

———. and G. Herd (2007) "Approaches to Countering Terrorism and CIST," in Aldis, A. and Herd, G. P. (eds.), pp. 3–21, *The Ideological War on Terror: Worldwide Strategies for Counter-Terrorism*. Routledge, London.

Real, M.'s (2005) "Introduction," in Greenberg, K. (ed.), pp. xv–xxi, *Al-Qaeda Now: Understanding Today's Terrorists*. Cambridge University Press, Cambridge.

Riedel, B. (2007) "Al Qaeda Strikes Back," in *Foreign Affairs* (vol. 86, iss. 3, May–June, pp. 24–40).

———. (2008) *The Search for Al Qaeda: Its Leadership, Ideology and Future* (2nd edition). Brookings Institution Press, Washington, DC.

Ronfeldt, D. (2003) "Foreword: Netwar Observations," in Bunker, R. J. (ed.), pp. xv–xix, *Non-State Threats and Future Wars*. Frank Cass, London.

———. (2007) *Al-Qaeda and Its Affiliates: A Global Tribe Waging Segmental Warfare*, RAND Corporation, Santa Monica, CA, available at www.rand.org/pubs/reprints/2008/RAND_RP1371.pdf (accessed January 20, 2011) (originally published in: *Information Strategy and Warfare: A Guide to Theory and Practice*, chapter 2, pp. 34–55).

Rothman, A. J. and P. Salovey (1997) "Shaping Perceptions to Motivate Healthy Behaviour: The Role of Message Framing," in *Psychological Bulletin* (vol. 121, iss. 1, pp. 3–19, January).

Roy, O. (2004) *The Rise of Globalised Islam: The Search for a New Ummah*. Columbia University Press, New York.

———. (2008) "Al-Qaeda: A True Global Movement," in Coolsaet, R. (ed.), pp. 19–27, *Jihadi Terrorism and the Radicalisation Challenge: European and American Experiences*. Ashgate, Aldershot.

Rude, G. (1980) *Ideology and Popular Protest*. Knopf, New York.

Sageman, M. (2004) *Understanding Terror Networks*. University of Pennsylvania Press, Philadelphia.

———. (2008) *Leaderless Jihad: Terror Networks in the Twenty-first Century*. University of Pennsylvania Press, Philadelphia.

Sanderson, D. (2012) "Terror Suspect: Britons 'Have Sex like Donkeys' and Deserve to Be Blown Up," *Times* (October 25).

Scheuer, M. (2006) "The Western Media's Misreading of Al-Qaeda's Latest Videotape," in *Terrorism Focus* (vol. 3, iss. 34).

———. (2011) *Osama bin Laden*. Oxford University Press, Oxford.

Schmid, A. (1989) "Terrorism and the Media: The Ethics of Publicity," in *Terrorism and Political Violence* (vol. 1, iss. 4, pp. 539–565).

———. (2005) "Terrorism as Psychological Warfare," in *Democracy and Security* (vol. 1, iss. 2, pp. 137–146).

———. and A. Jongman (2006) *Political Terrorism: A New Guide to Actors, Authors, Concepts, Data Bases, Theories, & Literature* (2nd edition). With the collaboration of Michael Stohl, Jan Brand, Peter A. Flemming, Angela van der Poel, and Rob Thijsse. Transaction Publishers, New Brunswick, NJ.

Seliger, M. (1976) *Ideology and Politics.* Allen and Unwin, London.

Shahzad, S. S. (2011) *Inside Al-Qaeda and the Taliban: Beyond bin Laden and 9/11.* Pluto Press, London.

Shapiro, J. (2013) *The Terrorist's Dilemma: Managing Violent Covert Organizations.* Princeton University Press, Princeton, NJ.

Shepard, W. (1992) "The Development of the Thought of Sayyid Qutb as Reflected in Earlier and Later Editions of Social Justice in Islam," in *Die Welt des Islams, New Series* (vol. 32, iss. 2, pp. 196–236).

Silke, A. (ed.) (2004a) "An Introduction to Terrorism Research," in *Research on Terrorism: Trends, Achievements and Failures.* Frank Cass, London.

———. (ed.) (2004b) "The Road Less Travelled: Recent Trends in Terrorism Research," in *Research on Terrorism: Trends, Achievements and Failures.* Frank Cass, London.

Sindawi, K. (2007) "The Shiite Turn in Syria," in *Current Trends in Islamist Ideology* (vol. 8, pp. 82–108).

Snow, D. and R. Benford (1988) "Ideology, Frame Resonance, and Participant Mobilization," in *International Social Movement Research* (vol. 1, pp. 197–217).

———. and R. D. Benford (1992) "Master Frames and Cycles of Protest," in Moms, A. D. and Mueller, C. M. (eds.), pp. 133–156, *Frontiers in Social Movement Theory.* Yale University Press, New Haven, CT.

———. and S. Byrd (2007) "Ideology, Framing Processes, and Islamic Terrorist Movements," in *Mobilization* (vol. 12, iss. 2, June, pp.119–136).

———. and S. Marshall (1984) "Cultural Imperialism, Social Movements, and the Islamic Revival," in Kriesberg, L. (ed.), pp. 131–152, *Research in Social Movements, Conflict, and Change,* vol. 7. JAI Press, Greenwich, CT.

Snow, D. A., E. B. Rochford, S. K. Worden, and R. D. Benford (1986) "Frame Alignment Processes, Micromobilization, and Movement Participation," in *American Sociological Review* (vol. 51, no. 4, August, pp. 464–481).

Solomon, J. (2008) "The Funding Methods of FATA's Terrorists and Insurgents," in *Combating Terrorism Sentinel* (vol. 1, iss. 6, May, pp. 4–7).

SomaliaReport.com (2012) "Somali Islamists Reportedly Disagree over Al-Qa'idah Merger" (March 16), transcript from BBC Monitoring.

Soriano, M. R. T. (2009) "Spain as an Object of Jihadist Propaganda," in *Studies in Conflict and Terrorism* (vol. 32, iss. 11, pp. 933–952).

Stepanova, E. (2008) *SIPRI Research Report No. 23 Terrorism in Asymmetrical Conflict: Ideological and Structural Aspects.* Stockholm International Peace Research Institute, Stockholm.

Stout, M. (2009) "In Search of Salafi *Jihadist* Strategic Thought: Mining the Words of the Terrorists," in *Studies in Conflict and Terrorism* (vol. 32, iss. 10, pp. 876–892).

Stout, M. E., J. M. Huckabey, J. R. Schindler, and W. Lacey (2008) *The Terrorist Perspectives Project: Strategic and Operational views of Al Qaeda and Associated Movements.* Naval Institute Press, Annapolis, MD.

Taylor, M. and M. Elbushra (2006) "Hassan al-Turabi, Osama bin Laden and al Qaeda in Sudan," *Terrorism and Political Violence* (vol. 18, pp. 449–464).

Tibi, B. (2008) "Religious Extremism or Religionization of Politics? The Ideological Foundations of Political Islam," in Frisch, H. and Inbar, E. (eds.), pp. 11–37, *Radical Islam and International Security.* Routledge, New York

Tololyan, K. (2006) "Cultural Narrative and the Motivation of the Terrorist," in Rapoport, D. (ed.), *Critical Concepts in Political Science: Terrorism Volume IV: The Fourth or Religious Wave*. Routledge, London.

Totten, M. J. (2012) "Arab Spring or Islamist Winter," in *World Affairs* (January/February), available at http://www.worldaffairsjournal.org/article/arab-spring-or-islamist-winter (accessed December 2012).

Tversky, A. and D. Kahneman (1981) "The Framing of Decisions and the Psychology of Choice," in *Science* (vol. 211, iss. 4481, January, pp. 453–458).

Vergés, M. (1997) "Genesis of a Mobilization: The Young Activists of Algeria's Islamic Salvation Front," in Beinin, J. and Stork, J. (eds.), pp. 292–309, *Political Islam: Essays from Middle East Report*. I.B. Tauris, London.

Wagemakers, J. (2012) *A Quietist Jihadi: The Ideology and Influence of Abu Muhammad al-Maqdisi*. Cambridge University Press, Cambridge.

Weinberg, L. (2008) "Two Neglected Areas of Terrorism Research: Careers after Terrorism and How Terrorists Innovate," in *Perspectives on Terrorism* (vol. 2, iss. 9, June, pp. 11–18).

Wiktorowicz, Q. (ed.) (2004) "Introduction," in *Islamic Activism: A Social Movement Theory Approach*. Indiana University Press, Bloomington, Ind., pp. 1–37.

———. (2006) "Anatomy of the Salafi Movement," in *Studies in Conflict and Terrorism* (vol. 29, iss. 3, pp. 207–239).

Wilkinson, P. (1971) *Social Movement*. Pall Mall Press, London.

———. (2005) "International Terrorism: The Changing Threat and the EU's Response," in *Chaillot Paper*, no. 84, October. Institute of Security Studies, European Union, Paris.

———. (2006) *Terrorism versus Democracy: The Liberal State Response* (2nd edition). Routledge, Abingdon.

Williams, R. H. (1995) "Constructing the Public Good: Social Movements and Cultural Resources," in *Social Problems* (vol. 42, iss. 1, pp. 124–144, February).

Wilson, J. (1973) *Introduction to Social Movements*. Basic Books, New York.

Wright, L. (2006a) *The Looming Tower: Al-Qaeda's Road to 9/11*. Penguin Books, London.

———. (2006b) "The Master Plan: For the New Theorists of Jihad, Al Qaeda Is Just the Beginning," in *New Yorker* (September 11).

Zahab, M. and O. Roy (2002) *Islamist Networks: The Afghan-Pakistan Connection*. Hurst, London.

Lectures

Cronin, A. (2011) "9/11: How and Why Do Terrorist Campaigns End?," Lecture delivered at British Academy and University of St. Andrews symposium "9/11: Ten Years On," held at the British Academy, London (September 2).

Ramsay, G. and D. Holbrook. (2013) "The Violent Part of Violent Extremism," Paper delivered at the Society for Terrorism Research, University of East London (June 27–28).

Primary sources: Official/Government reports and legal texts

HM Government (2011) *Prevent Strategy*. Presented to Parliament by the Secretary of State for the Home Department by Command of Her Majesty (June). Cm 8092.

Intelligence and Security Committee (2006) "Report into the London Terrorist Attacks in London on 7 July 2005" (May), available at http://www.official-documents.gov.uk/document/cm67/6785/6785.asp (accessed February 24, 2012).

ODNI (Office of the Director of National Intelligence) (2007) *National Intelligence Estimate: The Terrorist Threat to the US Homeland* (July). ODNI, Washington, DC.

Security Council Committee established pursuant to resolution 1267 (2008) *Report of the Analytical Support and Sanctions Monitoring Team Pursuant to Resolution 1735 (2006) concerning Al-Qaeda and the Taliban and Associated Individuals and Entities* (2008/324).

Senate Select Committee on Intelligence (2008) *Annual Worldwide Threat Assessment* (February 5), Washington, DC, available at www.dni.gov/testimonies/20080205_transcript.pdf (accessed January 21, 2011).

UK Racial and Religious Hatred Act 2006 and the Public Order Act 1986. Available at http://www.legislation.gov.uk (accessed May 2012).

UK Terrorism Act 2000. Available at http://www.legislation.gov.uk (accessed May 2012).

———. (2006). Available at http://www.legislation.gov.uk (accessed May 2012).

Zelikow, P., et al. (2004) *Final Report of the National Commission on Terrorist Attacks upon the United States ("The 9/11 Commission Report")*. US Congress, Washington, DC.

Primary sources: Al-Qaeda and other militant Islamist/Jihadi statements

Al-Awlaki, A. (2010) Statement released online by Al-Malahem in December 2010 and made available from Islamist Web forums.

Al-Zawahiri, A. (2013) "General Guidelines for Jihad," published by *As-Sahab* (September 14) and distributed via Islamist Web forums and Archive.org, available at http://ia801006.us.archive.org/8/items/tawakkalo-00/en.pdf (accessed September 18, 2013) [266].

As-Sahab (2002a) "The Wills of the Martyrs of the New York and Washington Battles: The Will of the Martyr Ibn ul Jarah Al-Ghamidee Ahmed al-Haznawi," published April 18, secured via link from Islamist Web forums [207].

———. (2002b) "The Wills of the Martyrs of the New York and Washington Battles: The Will of the Martyr Abdulaziz Alomari," published April 19, secured via link from Islamist Web forums [108].

Azhar, M. M. (1996) *The Virtues of Jihad, The Virtues of Jihad*. Ahle Sunnah Wal Jama'at Publications (unknown location).

Azzam, A. (2001) *Join the Caravan* (initially published in 1988). Published and translated by Azzam Publications.

———. (2003) *The Lofty Mountain*. Published and translated by Azzam Publications [first published in 1989].

Bin Ladin, U. (1994) "Our Invitation to Give Advice and Reform," open letter dated April 12, available from Harmony Database (document no. AFGP-2002-003345). CTC, West Point, NY [36].

———. (1994) "Saudi Arabi Supports the Communists in Yemen," open letter dated June 7, available from Harmony Database (document no. AFGP-2002-003345). CTC, West Point, NY [37].

———. (1994) "The Banishment of Communism from the Arabian Peninsula: The Episode and the Proof," open letter dated July 7, available from Harmony Database (document no. AFGP-2002-003345) [38].

———. (1994) "Saudi Arabia Unveils Its War against Islam and Its Scholars," open letter dated September 12, available from Harmony Database (document no. AFGP-2002-003345). CTC, West Point, NY [40].

———. (1994) "Higher Committee for Harm!!," open letter dated October 15, available from Harmony Database (document no. AFGP-2002-003345). CTC, West Point, NY [47].

———. (1994) "Open Letter for Shaykh Bin Baz on the Invalidity of His Fatwa on Peace with the Jews," open letter dated December 29, available from Harmony Database (document no. AFGP-2002-003345). CTC, West Point, NY [63].

———. (1995) "Saudi Arabia Continues Its War against Islam and Its Scholars," open letter dated March 9, available from Harmony Database (document no. AFGP-2002-003345). CTC, West Point, NY [66].

———. (1995) "Scholars Are the Prophet's Successors," open letter dated May 6, available from Harmony Database (document no. AFGP-2002-003345). CTC, West Point, NY [67].

———. (1995) "An Open Letter to King Fahd on the Occasion of the Recent Cabinet Reshuffle" (July 11), available from Harmony Database (document no. AFGP-2002-000103-HT-NVTC), available at http://www.ctc.usma.edu/wp-content/uploads/2010/08/AFGP-2002-000103-Trans.pdf. CTC, West Point, NY [62].

———. (1995) "Prince Sultan and the Air Aviation Commissions," Committee for Advice and Reform (July 11), London, UK, Harmony Database (document no. AFGP-2002-003345). Department of Defense [68].

———. (1995) "The Bosnia Tragedy and the Deception of the Servant of the Two Mosques," open letter dated August 11, from Harmony Database (document no. AFGP-2002-003345). CTC, West Point, NY [69].

———. (1996) Interview with Robert Fisk published in *The Independent* (June 10, 14), available from FBIS (2004) *FBIS: Compilation of Usama Bin Ladin Statements 1994–January 2004*. Foreign Broadcast Information Service, Reston, Virginia [4].

———. (1996) "Message from Usama Bin-Muhammad Bin Ladin to His Muslim Brothers in the Whole World and Especially in the Arabian Peninsula: Declaration of Jihad against the Americans Occupying the Land of the Two Holy Mosques; Expel the Heretics from the Arabian Peninsula," *Al-Islah* (September 2, pp. 1–12), published in FBIS (2004) *FBIS: Compilation of Usama Bin Ladin Statements 1994–January 2004*. Foreign Broadcast Information Service, Reston, Virginia [5].

———. (1996) Interview with 'Abd al-Bari Atwan, published in *Al-Quds Al-Arabi* (as "Bin Ladin Interviewed on Jihad against US," November 27), available from FBIS (2004) *FBIS: Compilation of Usama Bin Ladin Statements 1994–January 2004.* Foreign Broadcast Information Service, Reston, Virginia [150].

———. (1997) Interview with "Dispatches" aired on *Channel Four Television* (February 20), transcript in FBIS (2004) *FBIS: Compilation of Usama Bin Ladin Statements 1994 – January 2004,* titled "Correspondent Meets with Opposition Leader Bin Ladin". Foreign Broadcast Information Service, Reston, Virginia [151].

———. (1997) "Pakistan Interviews Usama Bin Ladin," article/interview published in *Daily Pakistan* (March 18): See FBIS (2004) *FBIS: Compilation of Usama Bin Ladin Statements 1994–January 2004.* Foreign Broadcast Information Service, Reston, Virginia [154].

———. (1997) Report of interview published in *The Independent* (as "Interview with Usama bin Ladin," March 22), available from FBIS (2004) *FBIS: Compilation of Usama Bin Ladin Statements 1994 – January 2004.* Foreign Broadcast Information Service, Reston, Virginia. See full transcript: "Transcript of Osama Bin Laden Interview" by Peter Arnett (CNN, March 22) (accessed March 3, 2009) [155].

———. (1997) "The Saudi Regime and the Reputed Tragedies of the Pilgrims," open letter dated April 16, from Harmony Database (document no. AFGP-2002-003345). CTC, West Point, NY [70].

———. (1997) "Usama Bin Ladin Urges 'Befitting Reply' to Horan," article with comments from bin Ladin, first published in *Daily Pakistan* (August 7), available in FBIS (2004) *FBIS: Compilation of Usama Bin Ladin Statements 1994–January 2004.* Foreign Broadcast Information Service, Reston, Virginia [157].

———. (1997) Statement published in *Nawa-i-Waqt* (Rawalpindi) (November 27), available from FBIS (2004) *FBIS: Compilation of Usama Bin Ladin Statements 1994–January 2004.* Foreign Broadcast Information Service, Reston, Virginia [158].

———. (1998) Statement published in Islamabad-based newspaper (January 17), available in FBIS (2004) *FBIS: Compilation of Usama Bin Ladin Statements 1994–January 2004.* Foreign Broadcast Information Service, Reston, Virginia [159].

———. (1998) "Bin Ladin Condoles with Al-Bashir on Salih's Death," statement embedded within article published in *Al-Quds al-Arabi* (February 16): See FBIS (2004) *FBIS: Compilation of Usama Bin Ladin Statements 1994–January 2004.* Foreign Broadcast Information Service, Reston, Virginia [160].

———. et al. (1998) "Text of World Islamic Front's Statement Urging Jihad against Jews and Crusaders," published in *Al-Quds Al-Arabi* (London, February 23, 3) and translated in FBIS (2004) *FBIS: Compilation of Usama Bin Ladin Statements 1994–January 2004.* Foreign Broadcast Information Service, Reston, Virginia [161].

———. (1998) "One of Them Bears Witness," statement embedded within article published in *Al-Quds Al-Arabi* (March 23), available from FBIS (2004) *FBIS: Compilation of Usama Bin Ladin Statements 1994–January 2004.* Foreign Broadcast Information Service, Reston, Virginia [162].

———. (1998) Interview published in *Al-Akhbar* (Islamabad) (March 31), available in FBIS (2004) *FBIS: Compilation of Usama Bin Ladin Statements 1994–January 2004*. Foreign Broadcast Information Service, Reston, Virginia [163].

———. (1998) "Bin Ladin Congratulates Pakistan on Its Possession of Nuclear Weapons," article in *Al-Quds Al-Arabi* (June 1) featuring a statement from bin Ladin: See FBIS (2004) *FBIS: Compilation of Usama Bin Ladin Statements 1994–January 2004*. Foreign Broadcast Information Service, Reston, Virginia [170].

———. (1998) "In the Way of Allah," statement in article published in *The News* (June 15) (Islamabad), available in FBIS (2004) *FBIS: Compilation of Usama Bin Ladin Statements 1994–January 2004*. Foreign Broadcast Information Service, Reston, Virginia [171].

———. (1998) Interview with *The News* (Islamabad/Peshawar) reported in AFP (August 21) as "Bin Ladin Calls for 'Jihad' against Jews, Americans," available in FBIS (2004) *FBIS: Compilation of Usama Bin Ladin Statements 1994–January 2004*. Foreign Broadcast Information Service, Reston, Virginia [172].

———. (1998) Statement published in *Al-Quds Al-Arabi* (August 23), available in FBIS (2004) *FBIS: Compilation of Usama Bin Ladin Statements 1994–January 2004*. Foreign Broadcast Information Service, Reston, Virginia [173].

———. (1998) interview published in *Jang* (Rawalpindi) (November 18), available from FBIS (2004) *FBIS: Compilation of Usama Bin Ladin Statements 1994–January 2004*. Foreign Broadcast Information Service, Reston, Virginia [175].

———. (1998) Statement distributed by Afghan Islamic Press, reported in AFP (December 24) titled "Bin Ladin Denies Role in Bombings of US Missions," available in FBIS (2004) *FBIS: Compilation of Usama Bin Ladin Statements 1994– January 2004*. Foreign Broadcast Information Service, Reston, Virginia [176].

———. (1998) "United States Admits That Keeping Its Troops in the Gulf Is Causing Dissatisfaction; Bin Ladin Threatens to Launch Attack Soon," article in *Al-Quds Al-Arabi* featuring a statement from bin Ladin: See FBIS (2004) *FBIS: Compilation of Usama Bin Ladin Statements 1994–January 2004*. Foreign Broadcast Information Service, Reston, Virginia [169].

———. (1999) Interview with Rahimullah Yusufzai, published in *The News* (Islamabad) (January 6), available in FBIS (2004) *FBIS: Compilation of Usama Bin Ladin Statements 1994–January 2004*. Foreign Broadcast Information Service, Reston, Virginia [177].

———. (1999) "Wrath of God: Osama Bin Laden Lashes Out against the West," *Time Magazine* (January 11, vol. 153, iss. 1, p. 178).

———. (1999) War declaration distributed by CBS (January 13), published in FBIS (2004) *FBIS: Compilation of Usama Bin Ladin Statements 1994–January 2004*. Foreign Broadcast Information Service, Reston, Virginia [180].

———. (1999) Interview published in Pakistani newspaper (February 20), available in FBIS (2004) *FBIS: Compilation of Usama Bin Ladin Statements 1994–January 2004*. Foreign Broadcast Information Service, Reston, Virginia [182].

———. (1999) "Usama Bin Ladin Pens Letter in Support of Kashmir Jihad," report giving text of letter published in *Wahdat* (Peshawar) (June 8), available in FBIS (2004) *FBIS: Compilation of Usama Bin Ladin Statements 1994–January 2004*. Foreign Broadcast Information Service, Reston, Virginia [183].

———. (1999) Interview with bin Ladin titled "Usama Bin Ladin, the Destruction of the Base" aired on Al Jazeera (June 10), full-length version aired on Al Jazeera (September 20, 2001), transcript available from FBIS (2004) *FBIS: Compilation of Usama Bin Ladin Statements 1994–January 2004*. Foreign Broadcast Information Service, Reston, Virginia [184].

———. (1999) "UBL Orders Mujahidin to Shoot US Commandos 'on Sight'," published in *Khabrain* (September 12): See FBIS (2004) *FBIS: Compilation of Usama Bin Ladin Statements 1994–January 2004*. Foreign Broadcast Information Service, Reston, Virginia [186].

———. (1999) Interview with John Miller and *Esquire Magazine* (February), interview conducted in 1998, later aired on *ABC News* (September 18), available from *Esquire Magazine* and FBIS (2004) *FBIS: Compilation of Usama Bin Ladin Statements 1994–January 2004*. Foreign Broadcast Information Service, Reston, Virginia [179].

———. (2000) Statement published in Pakistani daily (May 2), available in FBIS (2004) *FBIS: Compilation of Usama Bin Ladin Statements 1994–January 2004*. Foreign Broadcast Information Service, Reston, Virginia [188].

———. (2000) "Usama Speaks on Hijrah and the Islamic State?," statement published on ummah.net and elsewhere (May 22), made available in FBIS (2004) *FBIS: Compilation of Usama Bin Ladin Statements 1994–January 2004*. Foreign Broadcast Information Service, Reston, Virginia [189].

———. (2001) Untitled open letter published in *Nawa-i-Waqt* (Rawalpindi) (January 7), available in FBIS (2004) *FBIS: Compilation of Usama Bin Ladin Statements 1994–January 2004*. Foreign Broadcast Information Service, Reston, Virginia [192].

———. (2001) Poem published in *Ausaf* (Islamabad) (March 3), available in FBIS (2004) *FBIS: Compilation of Usama Bin Ladin Statements 1994–January 2004*. Foreign Broadcast Information Service, Reston, Virginia [193].

———. (2001) Letter from Bin Ladin published in *The Dawn* (Karachi) (April 3) titled "Usama Regrets Curbs by Taliban," available in FBIS (2004) *FBIS: Compilation of Usama Bin Ladin Statements 1994–January 2004*. Foreign Broadcast Information Service, Reston, Virginia [195].

———. (2001) Speech published in *The News* (Islamabad) (May 7), available in *FBIS: Compilation of Usama Bin Ladin Statements 1994–January 2004*. Foreign Broadcast Information Service, Reston, Virginia [197].

———. (2001) Statement published in *Pakistani Newspaper* (May 17) in article titled "If Taleban Allow, I Can Make US Life Miserable: Usama," available in FBIS (2004) *FBIS: Compilation of Usama Bin Ladin Statements 1994–January 2004*. Foreign Broadcast Information Service, Reston, Virginia [198].

———. (2001) Statement reported by the Afghan Press Agency (September 16), available in *FBIS: Compilation of Usama Bin Ladin Statements 1994–January 2004*. Foreign Broadcast Information Service, Reston, Virginia [200].

———. (2001) "Letter to the Pakistani People," aired on *Al Jazeera* (September 24), available from *FBIS: Compilation of Usama Bin Ladin Statements 1994–January 2004*, Foreign Broadcast Information Service, Reston, Virginia [201].

———. (2001) "The US Should Search Attackers within Itself," interview with *Ummat* (Karachi) (September 30), available from FBIS (2004) *FBIS:*

Compilation of Usama Bin Ladin Statements 1994–January 2004. Foreign
Broadcast Information Service, Reston, Virginia [202].

———. (2001) "Tayseer Allouni Interviews Bin Ladin in Afghanistan," interview
with *Al-Jazeera* (October 10), see transcripts in FBIS (2004) *FBIS: Compilation
of Usama Bin Ladin Statements 1994–January 2004* and Hegghammer, T.
(2003) *FFI Rapport 1990–2002.* FFI, Oslo [130].

———. (2001) untitled statement aired on *Al Jazeera* (November 3), transcript
available in Hegghammer, T. (2003) *FFI Rapport 1990–2002.* FFI, Oslo [77].

———. (2001) statement aired on *Al Jazeera* (November 7), transcript available
from FBIS (2004) *FBIS: Compilation of Usama Bin Ladin Statements
1994–January 2004.* Foreign Broadcast Information Service, Reston,
Virginia [203].

———. (2001) Interview with Hamid Mir published in *The Dawn* (November 10),
available at http://www.dawn.com/2001/11/10/top1.htm (accessed July 2013);
see also Hegghammer, T. (2003) *FFI Rapport 1990–2002.* FFI, Oslo [125].

———. (2001) "The Facts of the Conflict between Us and America," video
statement aired on Al Jazeera (December 13), secured from Islamist Web
forums [129].

———. (2002) Statement published in *Al-Quds Al-Arabi* (March 28) also
distributed through www.jihad.net, available from FBIS (2004) *FBIS:
Compilation of Usama Bin Ladin Statements 1994–January 2004.* Foreign
Broadcast Information Service, Reston, Virginia [205].

———. (2002) Statement aired on MBC Television (London) (April 17), transcript
available in FBIS (2004) *FBIS: Compilation of Usama Bin Ladin Statements
1994–January 2004.* Foreign Broadcast Information Service, Reston, Virginia
[206].

———. (2002) "The Wills of the Martyrs of the New York and Washington
Battles: The Will of the Martyr Abdulaziz Alomari," in *As-Sahab* (April 19),
secured from Islamist Web forums. (See under *As-Sahab.*)

———. (2002) Untitled video release reported and quoted in *The Times* ("Bin
Ladin Film Vows Revenge on the UK," May 19), available from FBIS (2004)
FBIS: Compilation of Usama Bin Ladin Statements 1994–January 2004.
Foreign Broadcast Information Service, Reston, Virginia [209].

———. (2002) (purported), "Al-Qaeda's Declaration in Response to the Saudi
Ulema: It's Best You Prostrate Yourselves in Secret" (dated June 2002). See in
Ibrahim (2007) [43].

———. (2002) "Report of Statement," published in *Al-Sharq al-Awsat* (June 26),
available in FBIS (2004) *FBIS: Compilation of Usama Bin Ladin Statements
1994–January 2004.* Foreign Broadcast Information Service, Reston, Virginia
[210].

———. (2002) "A Message Addressed to the American People," message aired
on Al Jazeera (October 6), available in IntelCenter (2008) *Words of Osama bin
Laden Vol. 1.* Tempest Publishing, Alexandria, VA [75].

———. (2002) Untitled statement distributed by Al-Qal'ah (October 14),
available from FBIS (2004) *FBIS: Compilation of Usama Bin Ladin
Statements 1994–January 2004.* Foreign Broadcast Information Service,
Reston, Virginia [211].

———. (2002) "Letter from Usama Bin Muhammad Bin Ladin to the American People," first published in *Waaqiah* (October 26), available in FBIS (2004) *FBIS: Compilation of Usama Bin Ladin Statements 1994–January 2004*. Foreign Broadcast Information Service, Reston, Virginia [212].

———. (2002) The "will" of Bin Ladin published in *Al-Majallah* (London) (October 27), available in FBIS (2004) *FBIS: Compilation of Usama Bin Ladin Statements 1994–January 2004*. Foreign Broadcast Information Service, Reston, Virginia [213].

———. (2002) Untitled statement aired on Al Jazeera (November 12), available from IntelCenter (2008) *Words of Osama Bin Laden Vol. 1*. Tempest Publishing, Alexandria, VA, and FBIS (2004) *FBIS: Compilation of Usama Bin Ladin Statements 1994–January 2004*. Foreign Broadcast Information Service, Reston, Virginia [76].

———. (2002) "Statement from Abdallah Usama Bin Ladin to the Peoples of Countries Allied to Tyrannical US Government," distributed by *Alneda* (November 21), available in FBIS (2004) *FBIS: Compilation of Usama Bin Ladin Statements 1994–January 2004*. Foreign Broadcast Information Service, Reston, Virginia [214].

———. (2003) "Statement Reported," published in *Al-Sharq al-Awsat* (January 19), available in FBIS (2004) *FBIS: Compilation of Usama Bin Ladin Statements 1994–January 2004*. Foreign Broadcast Information Service, Reston, Virginia [216].

———. (2003) "Untitled Audio Statement," unknown distributor (February), available from IntelCenter (2008) *Words of Osama bin Laden Vol. 1*. Tempest Publishing, Alexandria, VA [78].

———. (2003) "A Message to Our Brothers in Iraq," distributed by *Al-Jazeera* (February 11), transcript available from FBIS (2004) *FBIS: Compilation of Usama Bin Ladin Statements 1994–January 2004*. Foreign Broadcast Information Service, Reston, Virginia; IntelCenter (2008) *Words of Osama bin Laden Vol. 1*. Tempest Publishing, Alexandria, VA; and Lawrence, B. (ed.) (2005) *Messages to the World: The Statements of Osama Bin Laden*. Verso Books, London [79].

———. (2003) "Usama Bin Ladin Urges Muslims to Launch Suicide Attacks against US," statement embedded within article published in *Ausaf* (Islamabad) (April 9), available from FBIS (2004) *FBIS: Compilation of Usama Bin Ladin Statements 1994–January 2004*. Foreign Broadcast Information Service, Reston, Virginia [217].

———. (2003) Statement distributed by Movement for Islamic Reform (London) (May 29), available from FBIS (2004) *FBIS: Compilation of Usama Bin Ladin Statements 1994–January 2004*. Foreign Broadcast Information Service, Reston, Virginia [219].

———. (2003) "Second Letter to the Muslims of Iraq," Statement released October 18. Available in Kepel and Milelli (eds.) (2008) and FBIS (2004) *FBIS: Compilation of Usama Bin Ladin Statements 1994–January 2004*. Foreign Broadcast Information Service, Reston, Virginia [98].

———. (2004) "Resist the New Rome," audio statement aired on Al Jazeera (January 4), transcript also published in *The Observer*, available from *The Observer* (January 4) and FBIS (2004) *FBIS: Compilation of Usama Bin Ladin*

Statements 1994–January 2004. Foreign Broadcast Information Service, Reston, Virginia [111].

———. (2004) Statement offering peace treaty to Europeans, audiotape distributed to media networks (April 14), transcript available in Ibrahim (2007) [52].

———. (2004) Untitled audio statement aired on Al Jazeera and Al-Arabiya (April 15), transcript available in IntelCenter (2008) *Words of Osama bin Laden Vol. 1.* Tempest Publishing, Alexandria, VA [80].

———. (2004) "People of Iraq," aired on Al Jazeera (May 6), transcript available in IntelCenter (2008) *Words of Osama bin Laden Vol. 1.* Tempest Publishing, Alexandria, VA [82].

———. (2004) Untitled statement published by *As-Sahab* (October 29), secured via link from Islamist Web forums [31].

———. (2004) Untitled statement distributed by *As-Sahab* (October 30), transcript available in IntelCenter (2008) *Words of Osama bin Laden Vol. 1.* Tempest Publishing, Alexandria, VA [83].

———. (2004) Untitled audio statement (December 16), secured from Archive. org (January 12, 2009) via link from Islamist Web forums [84].

———. (2004) Audio statement (no title) published by *As-Sahab* (December 27), available in IntelCenter (2008) *Words of Osama bin Laden Vol. 1.* Tempest Publishing, Alexandria, VA [86].

———. (2006) "Oh People of Islam," published by *As-Sahab* (April 23), secured via links from Islamist Web forums [90].

———. (2006) "A Testimony to the Truth," published by *As-Sahab* (May 23), secured via links from Islamist Web forums [91].

———. (2006) "Elegizing the Ummah's Martyr and Emir of the Martyrs, Abu Musab al-Zarqawi," published by *As-Sahab* (June 29), transcript available in IntelCenter (2008) *Words of Osama bin Laden Vol. 1.* Tempest Publishing, Alexandria, VA [92].

———. (2006) "To the Ummah in General and to the Mujahideen in Iraq and Somalia in Particular," statement published by *As-Sahab* in July. Transcript available, for example, from IntelCenter (2008) *Words of Osama bin Laden Vol. 1.* Tempest Publishing, Alexandria, VA [93].

———. (2008) "May Our Mothers Be Bereaved of Us If We Fail to Help Our Prophet. Peace Be upon Him," published by *As-Sahab* (March 19), transcript available in IntelCenter (2008) *Words of Osama bin Laden Vol. 1.* Tempest Publishing, Alexandria, VA [11].

———. (2008) "A Way for the Salvation of Palestine," published by *As-Sahab* (March 20), secured via link from Islamist websites, transcript also available from the NEFA foundation [6].

———. (2008) "Reasons of the Struggle on the Occasion of the 60th Anniversary of the Founding of the Occupying State of Israel," published by *As-Sahab* (May 16), secured with help from ITSTIME, Catholic University of Milan [8].

———. (2008) "A Message to the Muslim Nation," published by *As-Sahab* (May 18), secured via link from Islamist Web forums [24].

———. (2007) "The Solution: A Message from Shaykh Osama Bin Laden to the American People," *As-Sahab* (September). Secured via links from Islamist Web forums [10].

———. (2007) "Come to Jihad: A Speech to the People of Pakistan," statement published by *As-Sahab* (September 20), transcript available from the NEFA Foundation and IntelCenter (2008) *Words of Osama bin Laden Vol. 1.* Tempest Publishing, Alexandria, VA [14].

———. (2007) "The Way to Frustrate the Conspiracies," published by *As-Sahab Media* (December 29), transcript available in IntelCenter (2008) *Words of Osama bin Laden Vol. 1.* Tempest Publishing, Alexandria, VA [27].

———. (2009) "Call for Jihad to Stop the Gaza Assault," published by *As-Sahab* (January 14), translated by Jihad Media Battalion, secured via link from Islamist Web forums [122].

———. (2009) "Fight On, O' Champions of Somalia," published by *As-Sahab* (March 19), secured via link from Islamist Web forums [134].

———. (2009) "A Statement to the American People," published by *As-Sahab* (September 13), translated and distributed by the Global Islamic Media Front, secured via link from Islamist Web forums [144].

———. (2010) "The Way to Save the Earth," published by *As-Sahab* (February 19), secured via link from Islamist Web forums [149].

———. (2010) "Help Your Brothers in Pakistan," published by *As-Sahab* (October 13), secured via link from Islamist Web forums [228].

———. (2010) "Some Points Regarding the Method of Relief Work," published by *As-Sahab* (October), secured via link from Islamist Web forums [227].

———. (2010) "Message from Shaykh Usama bin Ladin to the People of France," published by *As-Sahab* (November 7), translated and distributed by "Ansar Al Mujahideen English Forum," secured via link from Islamist Web forums [230].

———. (2011) "From al-Sheikh Osama bin Mohammed bin laden to … the French people," published/translated by *As-Sahab* (January 22), secured via link from Islamist Web forums [231].

———. (2011) "The Speech by the Martyr of Islam" (*As-Sahab* title after bin Ladin's death), published by *As-Sahab* (May 19). English version distributed by Global Islamic Media Front, secured via link from Islamist Web forums [240].

———. (unknown date) Letter from bin Ladin to "*Amir al-Mu'ineen*" Mullah Omar, made available by Department of Defense (translated June 5, 2002), available from the Harmony Database (document number AFGP-2002-600321) [61].

———. (unknown date) "Methodological Guidelines: According to the Guidelines of Bin Ladin: We Proceed in the Way of Manhattan in Order to Defy America and Put an End to Their Controlling Evil," published online on "Minbar al-Tawhid wa'l-Jihad." See McCants, et al. (2006) [112].

Bin Ladin & Zawahiri (2000) Statement regarding Muslim prisoners aired on Al Jazeera (September 21), available from FBIS (2004) *FBIS: Compilation of Usama Bin Ladin Statements 1994–January 2004.* Foreign Broadcast Information Service, Reston, Virginia [191].

———. (2003) Audio statement aired on *Al Jazeera* (September 10), available from FBIS (2004) *FBIS: Compilation of Usama Bin Ladin Statements 1994–January 2004.* Foreign Broadcast Information Service, Reston, Virginia [110].

Faraj, M. S. (2000) *Jihaad: Absent Obligation.* Maktabah al-Ansaar, Birmingham. This version is still available at Muhammad al-Maqdisi's website tawhed.net (www.tawhed.net/dl.php?i=AbsntObl, accessed January 18, 2011).

Hamza, Abu (2000) *Khawarij and Jihad*, distributed online and available, for example, at http://www.4shared.com/office/3GhaaPJf/khawarij-and-jihaad-abu-hamza.html (accessed March 16, 2012).

Harmony Archives (unknown date), document no. AFGP-2002-600086, available at http://www.ctc.usma.edu/programs-resources/harmony-program. Department of Defense/Combating Terrorism Center, West Point, NY.

———. (unknown date), document no. AFGP-2002-003345, available at http://www.ctc.usma.edu/programs-resources/harmony-program. Department of Defense/Combating Terrorism Center, West Point, NY.

———. (unknown date), document no. AFGP-2002-000026, available at http://www.ctc.usma.edu/programs-resources/harmony-program. Department of Defense/Combating Terrorism Center, West Point, NY.

———. (unknown date), document no. AFGP-2002-600053, available at http://www.ctc.usma.edu/programs-resources/harmony-program. Department of Defense/Combating Terrorism Center, West Point, NY.

Qutb, S. (2006) *Milestones*, translation by publisher. Islamic Book Service, New Delhi, India. [First published in Arabic in 1965.]

Zawahiri (1991) *The Bitter Harvest: The Brotherhood in Sixty Years*. See in Ibrahim (2007); Kepel and Milelli (eds.) (2008) [46].

———. (1993) "Advice to the Community to Reject the Fatwa of Sheikh Bin Baz Authorizing Parliamentary Representation: Published under the Supervision of Ayman al-Zawahiri," in Kepel and Milelli (eds.) (2008) [99].

———. (1995) "Our Stance towards Iran: Response to the Accusation of Cooperation between the Salafi Jihadi Movement and Renegade Iran," in *Nashrat al-Ansar* (April 1), excerpts published in McCants et al. (2006) [115].

———. (1996) "Healing the Hearts of Believers: On Some Concepts of Jihad in the Islamabad Operation," distributed online through "Minbar al-Tawhid wa'l-Jihad," excerpts published in McCants et al. (2006) [118].

———. (1999) "Muslim Egypt between the Whips of the Torturers and the Administration of Traitors" posted in "Minbar al-Tawhid wa'l-Jihad" (January 14): See McCants et al. (2006) [116].

———. (1999) Letter to Abu Yasir, published in Al-Shafey, M. "Al-Qaeda's Secret Emails," in *Al-Sharq al-Awsat* (June 12, 2005), letter dated April 19, 1999. Secured from the newspaper [123].

———. (2001) *Knights under the Banner of the Prophet*, initially published in *Al-Sharq al-Awsat* (December 2), available in translation from the Foreign Broadcast Information Service, Reston, Virginia [119].

———. (2002) *Al Walaa wa al Baraa—Loyalty and Separation: Changing an Article of Faith and Losing Sight of Reality*, available in Kepel and Milelli (eds.) (2008) [45].

———. (2002) "The Interview of Dr Ayman al-Zawahiri," available from IntelCenter (2008) *Words of Ayman al-Zawahiri Vol. 1*. Tempest Publishing, Alexandria, VA [22].

———. (2003) Untitled statement aired on Al-Arabiya (August 3), available in IntelCenter (2008) *Words of Ayman al-Zawahiri Vol. 1*. Tempest Publishing, Alexandria, VA, and Hegghammer, T. (2005) "Al-Qaida Statements 2003–2004: A Compilation of Translated Texts by Usama bin Ladin and Ayman Al-Zawahiri" in *FFI Rapport* (2005/01428). Forsvarets Forskningsinstitutt (Norwegian Defence Research Establishment), Kjeller, Norway [55].

———. (2004) Untitled statement aired on Al-Arabiya and Al Jazeera (February 24): See Hegghammer, T. (2005) "Al-Qaida Statements 2003–2004: A Compilation of Translated Texts by Usama bin Ladin and Ayman Al-Zawahiri," in *FFI Rapport*. FFI, Kjeller [58].

———. (2004) Statement aired on Al Jazeera (March 25), transcript available from Hegghammer, T. (2005) "Al-Qaida Statements 2003–2004." FFI, Oslo [59].

———. (2005) "The Freeing of Humanity and Homelands under the Banner of the Quran," posted February 11, available from Jihadunspun.com (accessed May 4, 2009) [109].

———. (2005) Unknown title, video statement published by *As-Sahab* (June 17), available from IntelCenter (2008) *Words of Ayman al-Zawahiri Vol. 1*. Tempest Publishing, Alexandria, VA [72].

———. (2005) Interview with Al-Zawahiri aired on *Al-Jazeera* (August 4): See MEMRI clips nos. 799 and 791 [128].

———. (2005) "Wills of the Knights of the London Raid," published by *As-Sahab* (November 15), transcript available in Ibrahim (2007) [53].

———. (2005) "The Victory of the Islamic Religion in Iraq," published by *As-Sahab* (December 6), available from IntelCenter (2008) *Words of Ayman al-Zawahiri Vol. 1*. Tempest Publishing, Alexandria, VA [26].

———. (2005) First in a series of interviews with Zawahiri, published by *As-Sahab* (December 7), available in Ibrahim (2007) [49].

———. (2005), "Obstacles to Jihad," published by *As-Sahab* (December 10), available in IntelCenter (2008) *Words of Ayman al-Zawahiri Vol. 1*. Tempest Publishing, Alexandria, VA [25].

———. (2006) "Bajawr Massacre and the Lies of the Crusaders," published by *As-Sahab* (January 21), available in Ibrahim (2007) and IntelCenter (2008) *Words of Ayman al-Zawahiri Vol. 1*. Tempest Publishing, Alexandria, VA [51].

———. (2006) "The Alternative Is Da'wa and Jihad," published by *As-Sahab* (March 4), available from IntelCenter (2008) *Words of Ayman al-Zawahiri Vol. 1*. Tempest Publishing, Alexandria, VA [73].

———. (2006) "Four Years since the Battle of Tora Bora—From Tora Bora to Iraq," published by *As-Sahab Media* (April 12), available in IntelCenter (2008) *Words of Ayman al-Zawahiri Vol. 1*. Tempest Publishing, Alexandria, VA [238].

———. (2006) "Letter to the People of Pakistan," published by *As-Sahab* (April 28), available from IntelCenter (2008) *Words of Ayman al-Zawahiri Vol. 1*. Tempest Publishing, Alexandria, VA [81].

———. (2006) "Support for Palestinians," published by *As-Sahab* (June 9), transcript available in IntelCenter (2008) *Words of Ayman al-Zawahiri Vol. 1*. Tempest Publishing, Alexandria, VA [85].

———. (2006) "American Crimes in Kabul," published by *As-Sahab* (June 21), available from IntelCenter (2008) *Words of Ayman al-Zawahiri Vol. 1*. Tempest Publishing, Alexandria, VA [87].

———. (2006) "Elegizing the Ummah's Martyr and Emir of the Martyrs Abu Musab al-Zarqawi, May Allah Have Mercy on Him," published by *As-Sahab* (June 24), available in IntelCenter (2008) *Words of Ayman al-Zawahiri Vol. 1*. Tempest Publishing, Alexandria, VA [32].

———. (2006) "The Zionist Crusader's Aggression on Gaza and Lebanon," published by *As-Sahab* (June 27), available from IntelCenter (2008) *Words of Ayman al-Zawahiri Vol. 1*. Tempest Publishing, Alexandria, VA [88].

———. (2006) "Hot Issues with Shaykh Ayman Al-Zawahiri," published by *As-Sahab* (September 11), secured from Islamist Web forums, also available from IntelCenter (2008) *Words of Ayman al-Zawahiri Vol. 1*. Tempest Publishing, Alexandria, VA [21].

———. (2006) "Bush, the Vatican's Pope, Darfur and the Crusaders," published by *As-Sahab* (September 29), available in IntelCenter (2008) *Words of Ayman al-Zawahiri Vol. 1*. Tempest Publishing, Alexandria, VA [89].

———. (2006) "Realities of the Conflict between Islam and Unbelief," published by *As-Sahab* (December 22), available from IntelCenter (2008) *Words of Ayman al-Zawahiri Vol. 1*. Tempest Publishing, Alexandria, VA [94].

———. (2006) "Congratulations on the Eid to the Ummah of Tawhid," published by *As-Sahab* (December 30), available in IntelCenter (2008) *Words of Ayman al-Zawahiri Vol. 1*. Tempest Publishing, Alexandria, VA [95].

———. (2007) "Lessons, Examples and Great Events in the Year 1427," published by *As-Sahab* (February 13), available from IntelCenter (2008) *Words of Ayman al-Zawahiri Vol. 1*. Tempest Publishing, Alexandria, VA [97].

———. (2007) "Palestine Is the Concern of All Muslims," published by *As-Sahab* (March 11), secured from Islamist Web forums (also available in IntelCenter (2008) *Words of Ayman al-Zawahiri Vol. 1*. Tempest Publishing, Alexandria, VA) [18].

———. (2007) "Shaykh Ayman Al-Zawahiri: On the Fifth Anniversary of the Invasion and Torture of Iraq," published by *As-Sahab* (April 17), secured from Islamist Web forums, also available from IntelCenter (2008) *Words of Ayman al-Zawahiri Vol. 1*. Tempest Publishing, Alexandria, VA [7].

———. (2007) "Rise and Support Our Brothers in Somalia," statement published by *As-Sahab* (May), available in IntelCenter (2008) *Words of Ayman al-Zawahiri Vol. 1*. Tempest Publishing, Alexandria, VA [96].

———. (2007) "The Empire of Evil Is About to End, and a New Dawn Is About to Break over Mankind," published by *As-Sahab* (May 5), available from IntelCenter (2008) *Words of Ayman al-Zawahiri Vol. 1*. Tempest Publishing, Alexandria, VA [23].

———. (2007) "Forty Years since the Fall of Jerusalem," audio statement published by *As-Sahab* on June 25, transcript available from IntelCenter (2008) *Words of Ayman al-Zawahiri Vol. 1*. Tempest Publishing, Alexandria, VA [101].

———. (2007) "The Advice of One Concerned," video statement published by *As-Sahab* on July 4, made available via Islamist websites. Transcript also available from IntelCenter (2008) *Words of Ayman al-Zawahiri Vol. 1*. Tempest Publishing, Alexandria, VA [102].

———. (2007) "Malicious Britain and Its Indian Slaves," published by *As-Sahab* (July 10), available in IntelCenter (2008) *Words of Ayman al-Zawahiri Vol. 1*. Tempest Publishing, Alexandria, VA [103].

———. (2007) "The Aggression against Lal Masjid," published by *As-Sahab Media* (July 11), available in IntelCenter (2008) *Words of Ayman al-Zawahiri Vol. 1*. Tempest Publishing, Alexandria, VA [104].

———. (2007) "Annapolis: The Betrayal," published by *As-Sahab* (December 14), available in IntelCenter (2008) *Words of Ayman al-Zawahiri Vol. 1.* Tempest Publishing, Alexandria, VA [12].

———. (2007) " 'A Review of Events'—As Sahab publishes fourth interview with Zawahiri," published by *As-Sahab* (December 16), secured via links from Islamist Web forums (also available from IntelCenter (2008) *Words of Ayman al-Zawahiri Vol. 1.* Tempest Publishing, Alexandria, VA) [13].

———. (2008) *Exoneration: A Letter Exonerating the Ummah of the Pen and the Sword from the Unjust Allegation of Feebleness and Weakness,* advertised by *As-Sahab* early in 2008, manuscript secured from the Open Source Center [20].

———. (2008) "The Correct Equation," published by *As-Sahab* (January 22), available from IntelCenter (2008) *Words of Ayman al-Zawahiri Vol. 1.* Tempest Publishing, Alexandria, VA, also available as a collection of clips posted on YouTube [28].

———. (2008) "A Call to Help Our People in Gaza," published by *As-Sahab* (March 23), transcripts available from IntelCenter (2008) *Words of Ayman al-Zawahiri Vol. 1.* Tempest Publishing, Alexandria, VA, and the NEFA Foundation [17].

———. (2008) "The Open Meeting with Sheikh Ayman al-Zawahiri, Part One," answers published by *As-Sahab* (April 2), secured from Archive.org and Islamist Web forums, transcript also available in IntelCenter (2008) *Words of Ayman al-Zawahiri Vol. 1.* Tempest Publishing, Alexandria, VA [105].

———. (2008) "The Open Meeting with Sheikh Ayman al-Zawahiri, Part Two," the second part of responses to the "open meeting" public appeal, published by *As-Sahab* (April 21), available from IntelCenter (2008) *Words of Ayman al-Zawahiri Vol. 1.* Tempest Publishing, Alexandria, VA [107].

———. (2008) "On the Anniversary of the Naksa … Break the Siege of Gaza," published by *As-Sahab* (June 4), transcript secured from the Open Source Center [15].

———. (2008) "A Message from Shaikh Ayman al-Zawahiri to Pakistan Army and the People of Pakistan," published by *As-Sahab* (August 10), transcript available from the NEFA foundation, video distributed via YouTube [41].

———. (2008) "Al-Azhar: The Lion's Den: Interview with Shaykh Ayman al-Zawahiri," published by *As-Sahab* (November 21), secured from Archive.org via link from Islamist Web forums [237].

———. (2009) "The Massacre of Gaza and the Siege of the Traitors," published by *As-Sahab* (January 6), translated and distributed by the Global Islamic Media Front, secured from Archive.org via link from Islamist Web forums [121].

———. (2009) "From Kabul to Mogadishu," published by *As-Sahab* (February 22), secured from Islamist Web forums [132].

———. (2009) "Six Years Since the Invasion of Iraq and Thirty Years since the Signing of the Israeli Peace Accords," published by *As-Sahab* (April 20), translated by the Global Islamic Media Front, secured from Islamist Web forums [136].

———. (2009) "My Muslim Brothers and Sisters in Pakistan," published by *As-Sahab* (July 15), secured via links from Islamist Web forums [139].

———. (2009) "The Realities of Jihad and Fallacy of Hypocrisy," published by *As-Sahab* (August 4), secured via links from Islamist Web forums [140].

———. (2009) "The Path of Doom," published by *As-Sahab* (August 26), secured via links from Islamist Web forums [142].

———. (2009) "Shaykh Dr. Ayman al-Zawahiri: Eulogy for the Role Model of the Youth—The Commander and Shahid Baitullah [Mehsud]," published by *As-Sahab* (September 28), secured via links from Islamist Web forums [147].

———. (2009) *The Morning and the Lamp to Be Extinguished: An Analysis of the Claim That the Constitution of Pakistan Is Islamic*, translated by Abu Musa Abdussalam, published by *As-Sahab* (December 16), secured from Archive.org via link from Islamist Web forums [141].

———. (2010) "Al-Quds Will Not Be Converted to Judaism," published by *As-Sahab*, secured via links from Islamist Web forums (July 19) [223].

———. (2010) "Message to the People of Turkey," published by *As-Sahab* (August 15), English version distributed by "Ansarnet English Forum," secured via links from Islamist Web forums [225].

———. (2010) "A Victorious Ummah, A Broken Crusade," published by *As-Sahab* (September 15), secured via links from Islamist Web forums [226].

———. (2010) "Who Is Going to Support Aafia Sidique?," statement published by *As-Sahab* (November 4), translated and distributed by the Global Islamic Media Front, secured via link from Islamist Web forums [229].

———. (2011) "A Message of Hope and Glad Tidings to Our People in Egypt (1)," published by *As-Sahab* (February 19), secured via links from Islamist Web forums [232].

———. (2011) "A Message of Hope and Glad Tidings to Our People in Egypt (2)," published by *As-Sahab* (February 24), secured via links from Islamist Web forums [233].

———. (2011) "A Message of Hope and Glad Tidings to Our People in Egypt (3) 'By Sheikh Ayman Al-Zawahiri H.A'," published by *As-Sahab* (February 27), translated by Global Islamic Media Front, secured via links from Islamist Web forums [234].

———. (2011) "A Message of Hope and Glad Tidings to Our People in Egypt (4)," published by *As-Sahab* (March 4), secured via links from Islamist Web forums [235].

———. (2011) "A Message of Hope and Glad Tidings to Our Fellow Muslims in Egypt (5)," published by *As-Sahab* (April 14), secured via links from Islamist Web forums [236].

———. (2011) "The Noble Knight Dismounted," published by *As-Sahab* and the Global Islamic Media Front (June 8), secured via links from Islamist Web forums [239].

———. (2011) "Message of Hope and Glad Tidings to Our People in Egypt Part 8: And What about the American Hostage Warren Weinstein?," published by *As-Sahab* and *Al-Masadh Media* in December, English transcript by *As-Sahab*. Distributed by Islamist Web forums, such as Ansar1.info [244].

———. (2012) "Glad Tidings by the Two Sheikhs Abu al-Zubayr and Ayman al-Zawahiri," video statement published by *As-Sahab* (February 9), translated by the Global Islamic Media Front and distributed on jihadist forums [258].

———. (2012) "Yemen: Between a Fugitive Puppet and His New Replacement," published by *As-Sahab* (May 15), distributed by jihadi websites. Transcript available from jihadi websites and Flashpoint Partners [248].

———. (2012) "Days with the Imam" (part 2), published by *As-Sahab* (June 3), translated by the Global Islamic Media Front and posted on Islamist Web forums [252].

———. (2012) "To the People of Tunisia: O' People of Tunisia, Support Your Shariah," published by *As-Sahab* (June 10), distributed by jihadist websites. English transcript available, for example, from globalterroalert.com (accessed January 2013) [249].

———. (2012) "The Lion of Knowledge and Jihaad: Martyrdom of Al-Sheikh Abu Yahya Al-Leebi (Rahimahullaah): Eulogy by Al-Ameer Al-Sheikh Ayman Al-Dhawaahiri," published by *As-Sahab* and *Al-Fajr*, distributed on Islamist Web forums on September 11 [250].

———. (2012) "The Rising Sun of Victory on the Triumphant Ummah over the Vanquished Crusaders," published by *As-Sahab* (September 13), available from jihadist websites. Transcript from BBC Monitoring [254].

———. (2012) "In Support of the Messenger, May the Peace and Blessings of God Be upon Him," produced by *As-Sahab* and distributed on jihadi websites on October 12. BBC Monitoring transcript [256].

———. (2012) "Document of the Support of Islam," produced by *As-Sahab* and made available on jihadist forums on November 13, transcripts from the SITE Institute [257].

———. (2013) "Unifying the Word toward the Word of Monotheism (*Tawhid*)," published by *As-Sahab* (April 7), distributed by Al-Fajr Media Center via jihadi websites. English transcript from the Open Source Center [260].

Zawahiri (unknown date) "The Forbidden Word," excerpts published in McCants et al. (2006) [113].

Zawahiri (unknown date) "Response to a Grave Uncertainty from Shaykh al-Albani regarding Silence in the Face of Apostate Rulers," distributed online through "Minbar al-Tawhid wa'l-Jihad": See excerpts in McCants et al. (2006) [117].

Zawahiri (purported) (unknown date) "Jihad, Martyrdom, and the Killing of Innocents," available in Ibrahim (2007) [48].

Zawahiri (unknown date) Introduction to *Characteristics of Jihad*, a magazine of Egyptian militant Islamist activists, available in Harmony Database (document no. AFGP-2002-600321). Combating Terrorism Center, West Point, NY [35].

Zawahiri & Gadahn (2006) "An Invitation to Islam," video message published by *As-Sahab* (September 2), distributed on Al-Boraq.com [33].

Index

Made in the USA
Middletown, DE
19 June 2018